Onshape Exercises

Published by
CADin360
cadin360.com

Copyright © 2019 by CADin360, ALL Rights Reserved

This book is copyrighted and the CADin360 reserves all rights.
No part of this publication may be reproduced, stored in a retrieval system or transmitted, transcribed, stored in retrieval system or translated into any language, in any form or by any means, electronic, mechanical, photocopying, recording, scanning or otherwise, without the prior written permission of the publisher & Author.

Limit of Liability/Disclaimer of Warranty:

The publisher and the author make no representations or warranties with respect to the accuracy or completeness of the contents of this work and specifically disclaim all warranties, including without limitation warranties of fitness for a particular purpose. No warranty may be created or extended by sales or promotional materials. The advice and strategies contained herein may not be suitable for every situation. This work is sold with the understanding that the publisher is not engaged in rendering legal, accounting, or other professional services. If professional assistance is required, the services of a competent professional person should be sought. Neither the publisher nor the author shall be liable for damages arising herefrom. The fact that an organization or Web site is referred to in this work as a citation and/or a potential source of further information does not mean that the author or the publisher endorses the information the organization or Web site may provide or recommendations it may make. Further, readers should be aware that Internet Web sites listed in this work may have changed or disappeared between when this work was written and when it is read.

Examination Copies

Books received as examination copies in any form such as paperback and eBook are for review only and may not be made available for the use of the student. These files may not be transferred to any other party. Resale of examination copies is prohibited

Electronic Files

The electronic file/eBook in any form of this book is licensed to the original user only and may not be transferred to any other party.

Disclaimer:

All trademarks and registered trademarks appearing in this book are the property of their respective owners.

Preface

Onshape Exercises

- ❖ This book contain 200 3D CAD practice exercises and drawings.
- ❖ This book does not provide step by step tutorial to design 3D models.
- ❖ S.I Units is used.
- ❖ Predominantly used Third Angle Projection.
- ❖ This book is for **Onshape** and Other Feature-Based Modeling Software such as Inventor, Catia, SolidWorks, NX, Solid Edge, AutoCAD, PTC Creo etc.
- ❖ It is intended to provide Drafters, Designers and Engineers with enough CAD exercises for practice on **Onshape**.
- ❖ It includes almost all types of exercises that are necessary to provide, clear, concise and systematic information required on industrial machine part drawings.
- ❖ Third Angle Projection is intentionally used to familiarize Drafters, Designers and Engineers in Third Angle Projection to meet the expectation of world wide Engineering drawing print.
- ❖ Clear and well drafted drawing help easy understanding of the design.
- ❖ This book is for Beginner, Intermediate and Advance CAD users.
- ❖ These exercises are from Basics to Advance level.
- ❖ Each exercises can be assigned and designed separately.
- ❖ No Exercise is a prerequisite for another. All dimensions are in mm.
- ❖ Note: Assume any missing dimensions.

EXERCISE-01

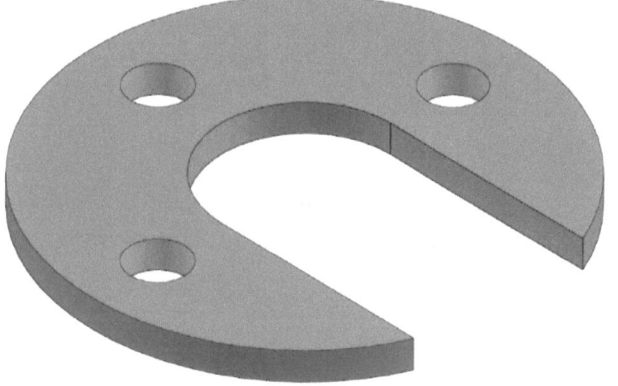

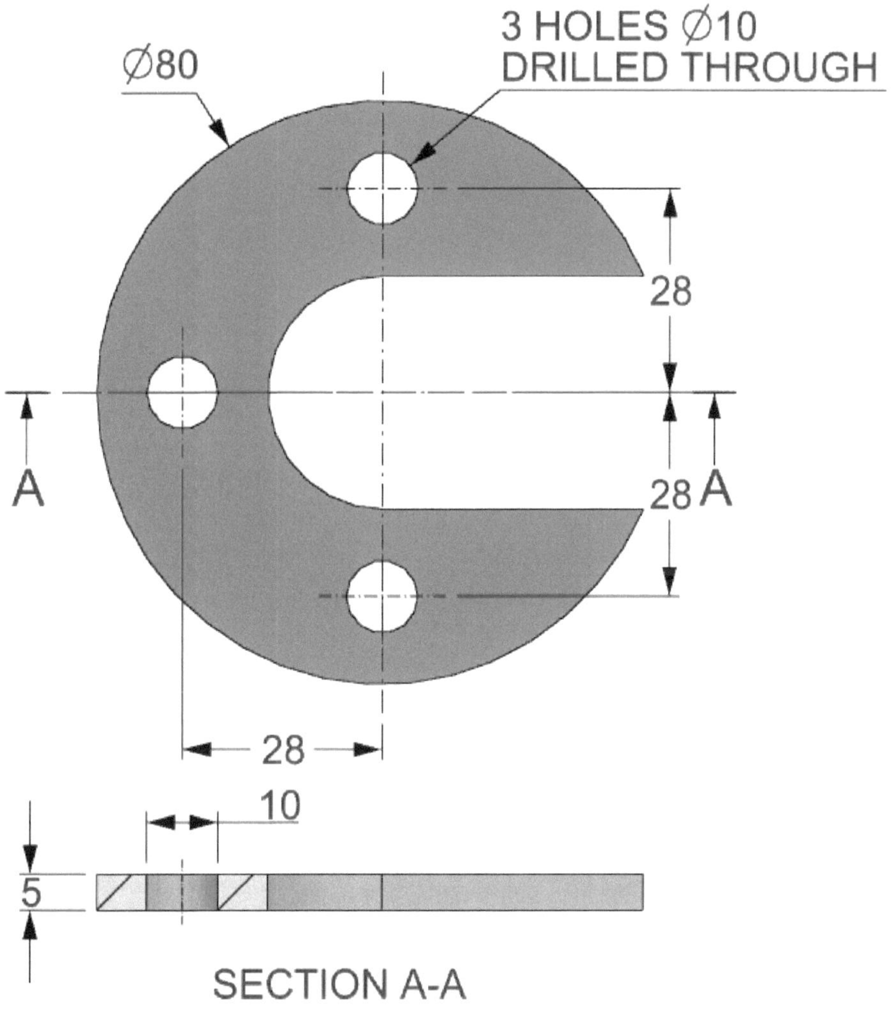

Ø80
3 HOLES Ø10 DRILLED THROUGH
28
28
28
10
5

SECTION A-A

EXERCISE-02

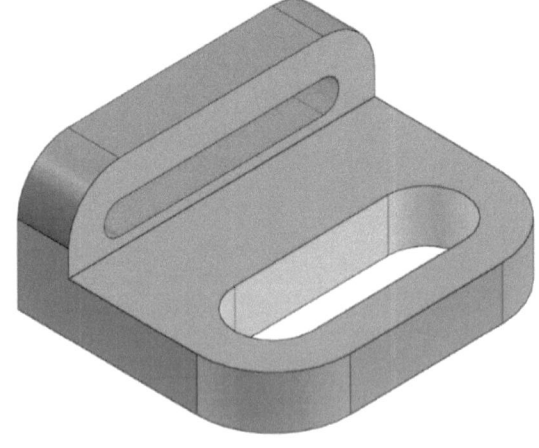

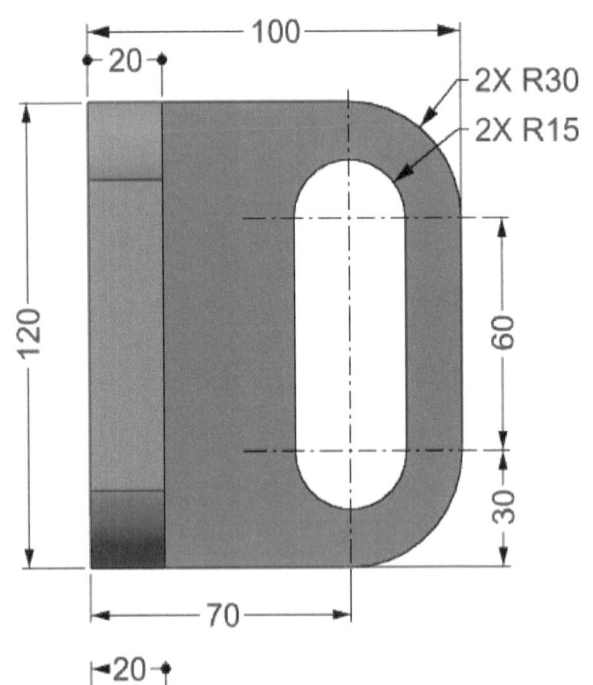

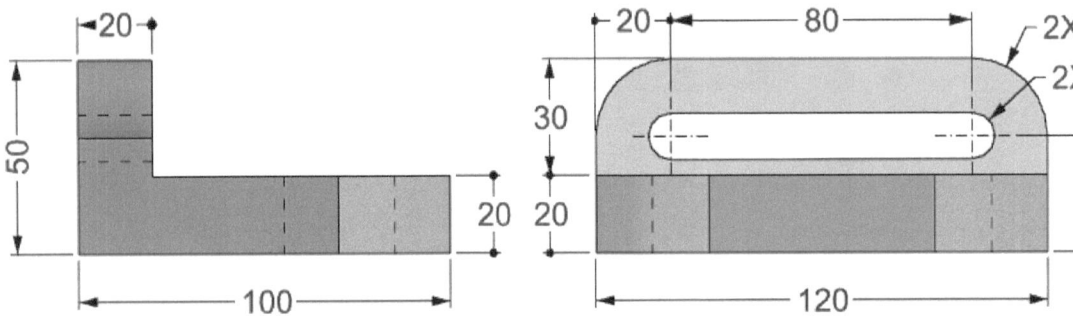

©Copyright 2019 CADin360, ALL Rights Reserved

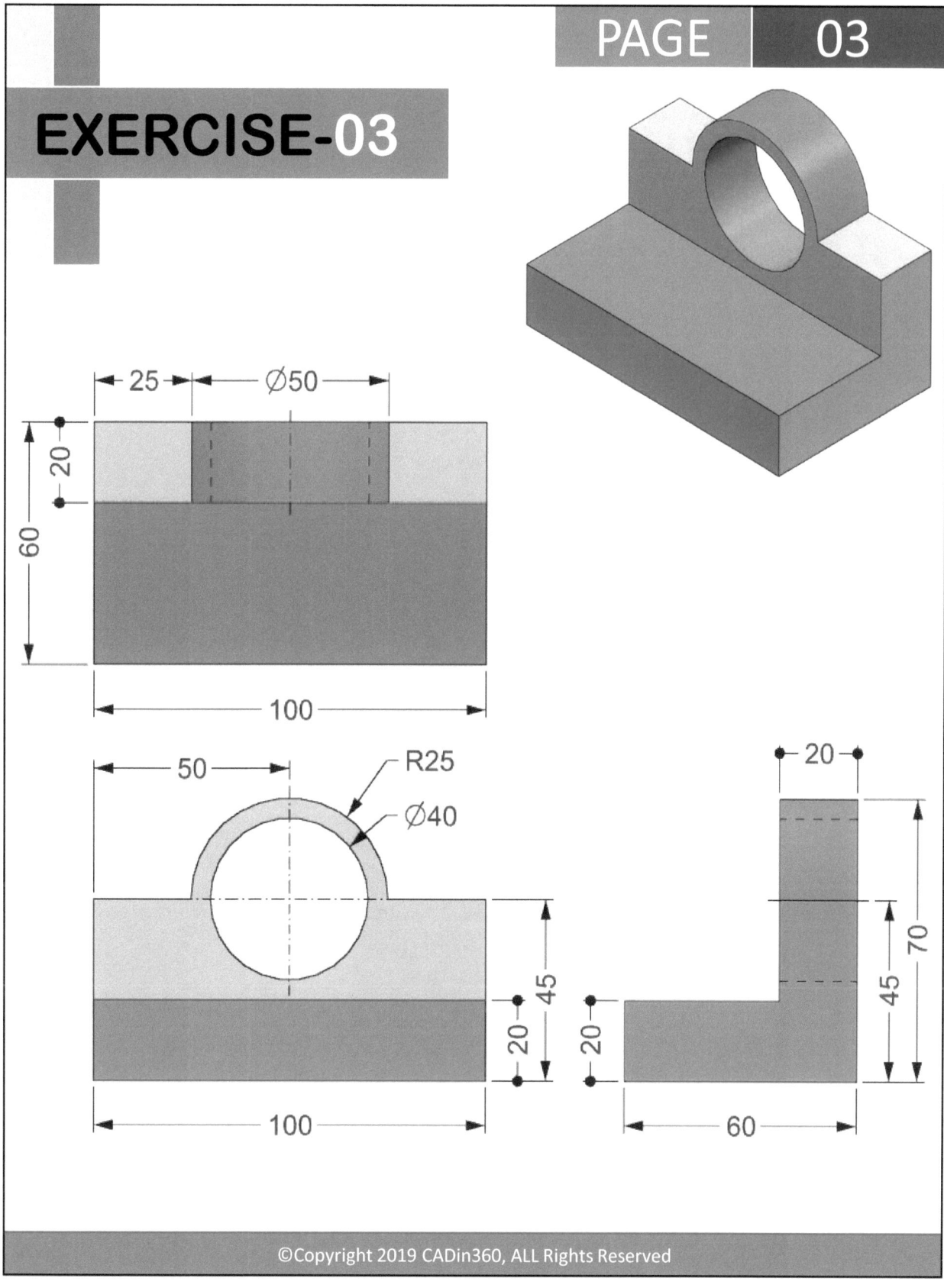

EXERCISE-04

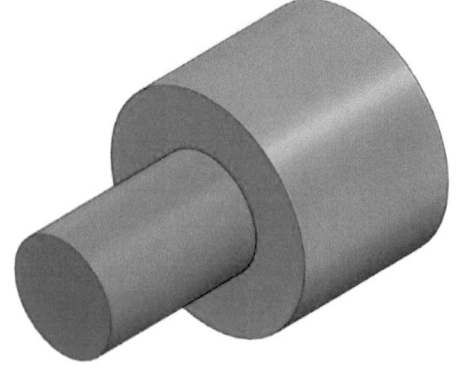

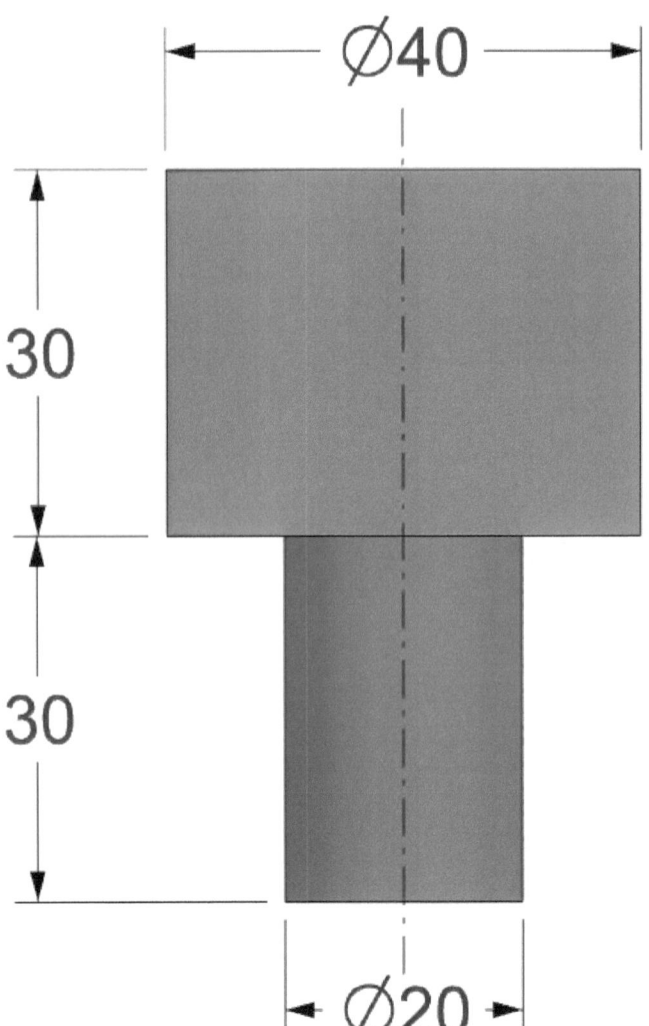

EXERCISE-05

130
40
65
R20
R10
10
20
40
25
∅50
∅50
∅30
30
40
10
130
10
20
10
10
40
20
40

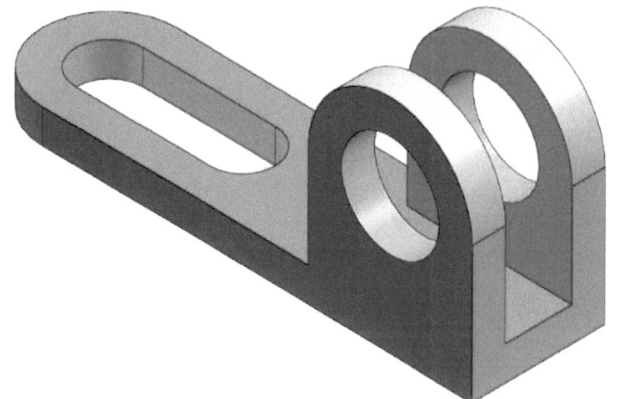

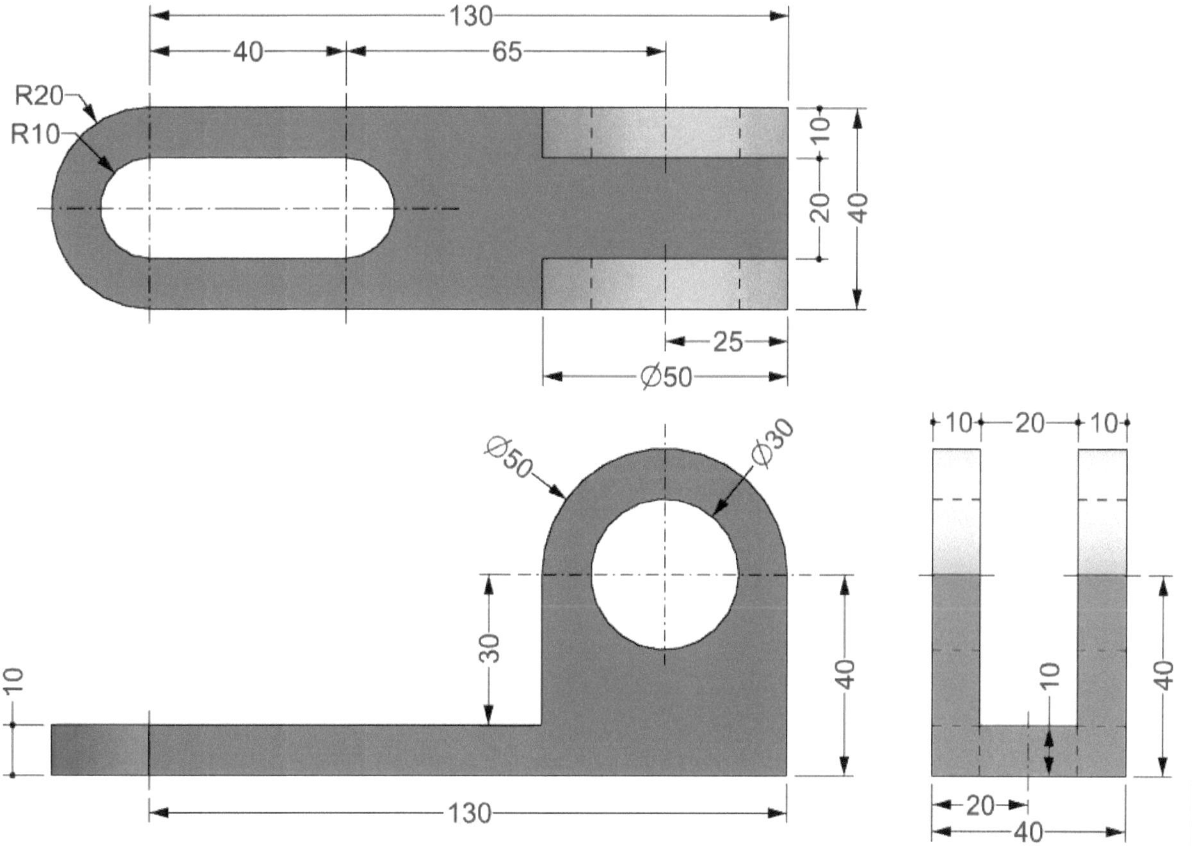

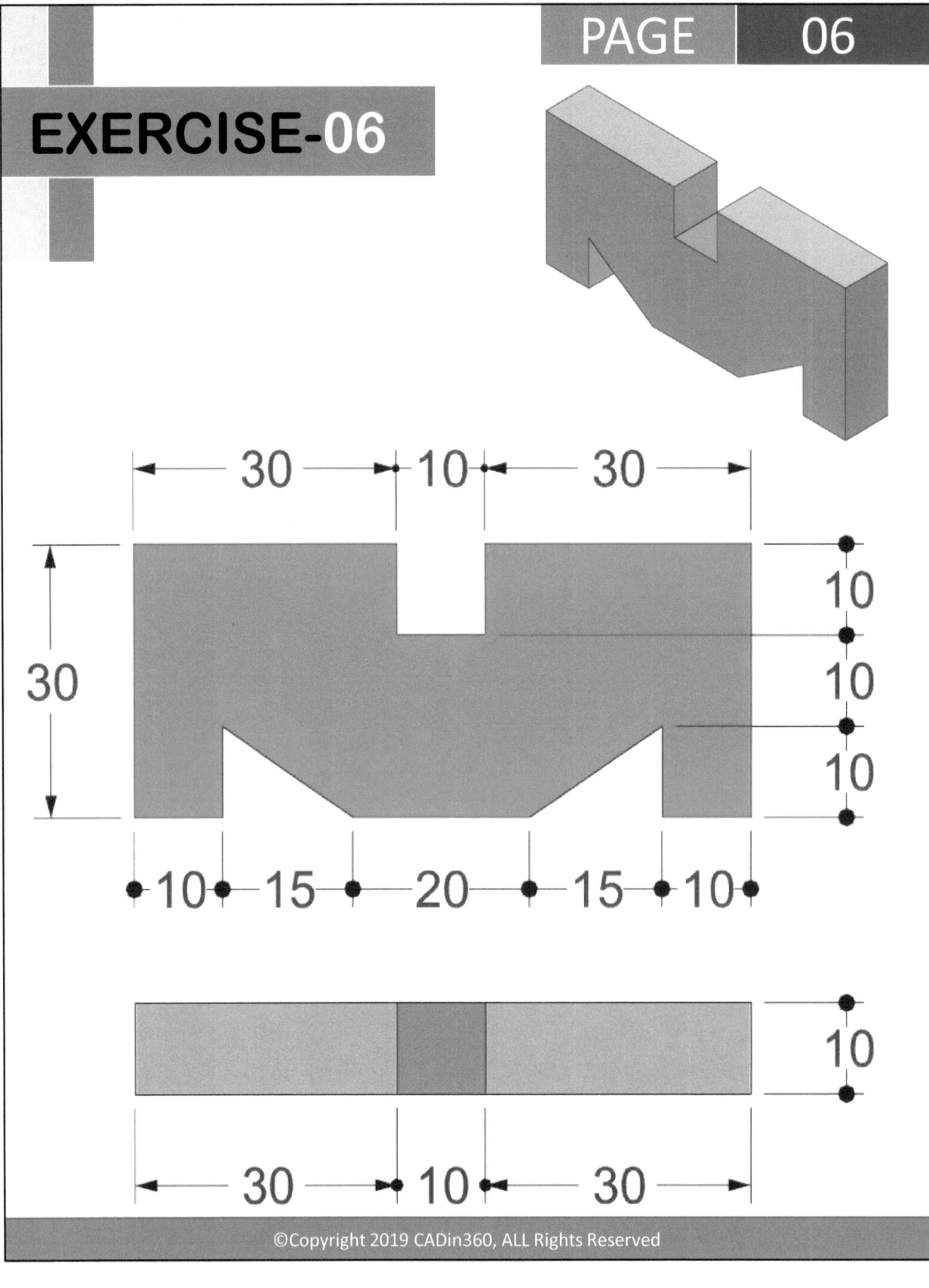

EXERCISE-07

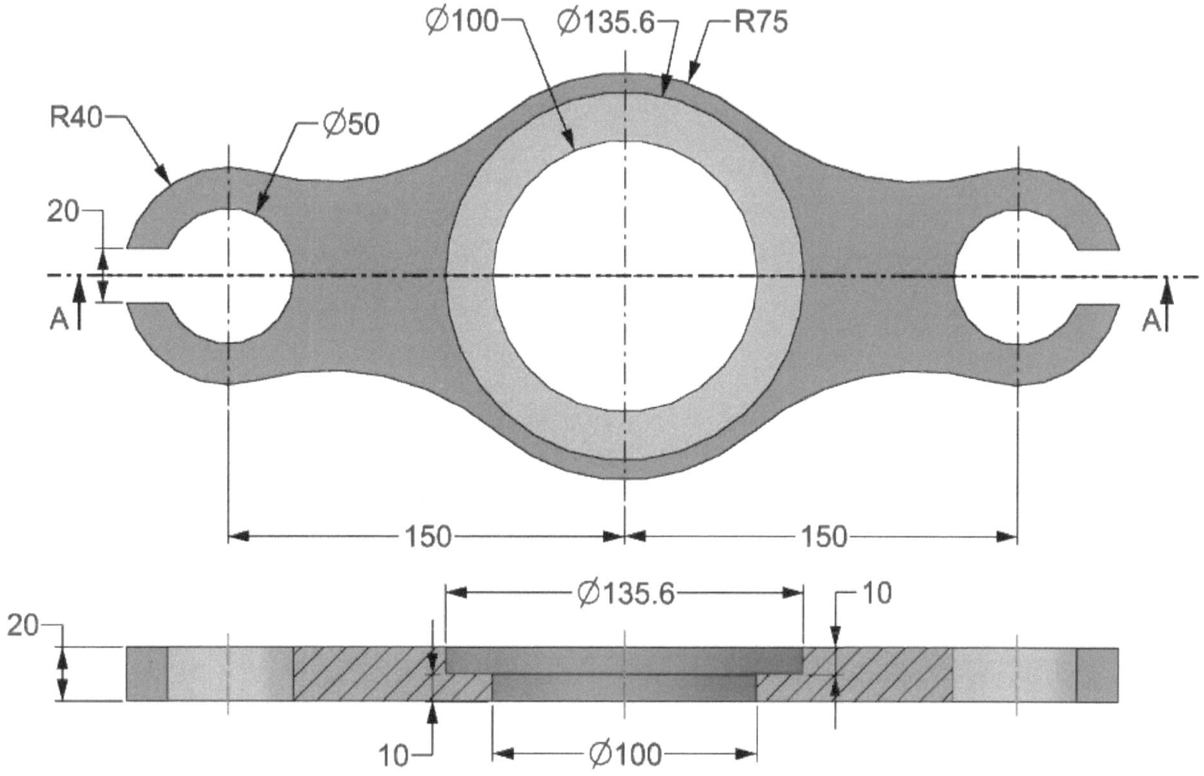

- Ø100
- Ø135.6
- R75
- R40
- Ø50
- 20
- 150
- 150
- Ø135.6
- 10
- 20
- 10
- Ø100

SECTION A-A
(SCALE 1:1)

©Copyright 2019 CADin360, ALL Rights Reserved

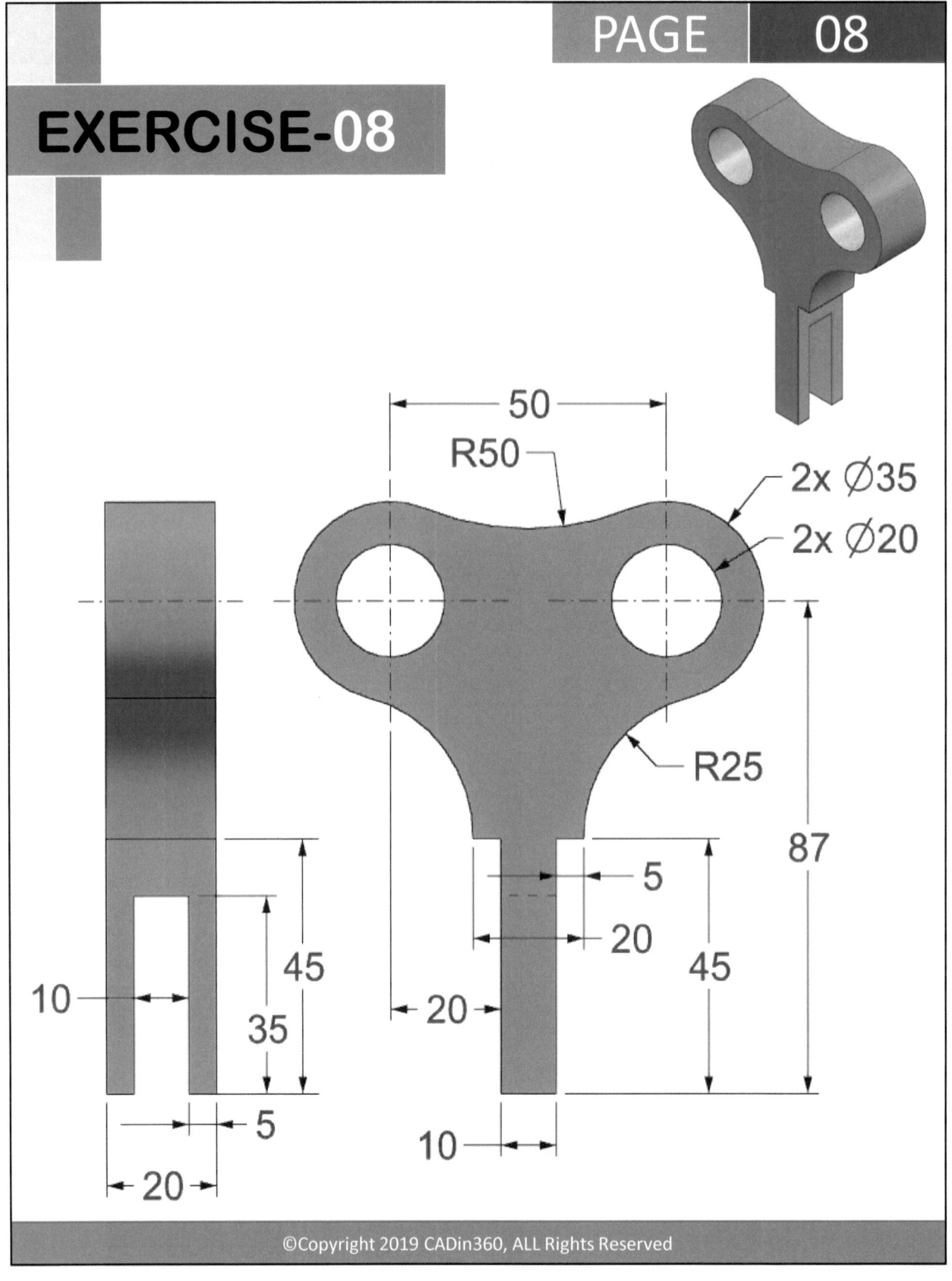

EXERCISE-09

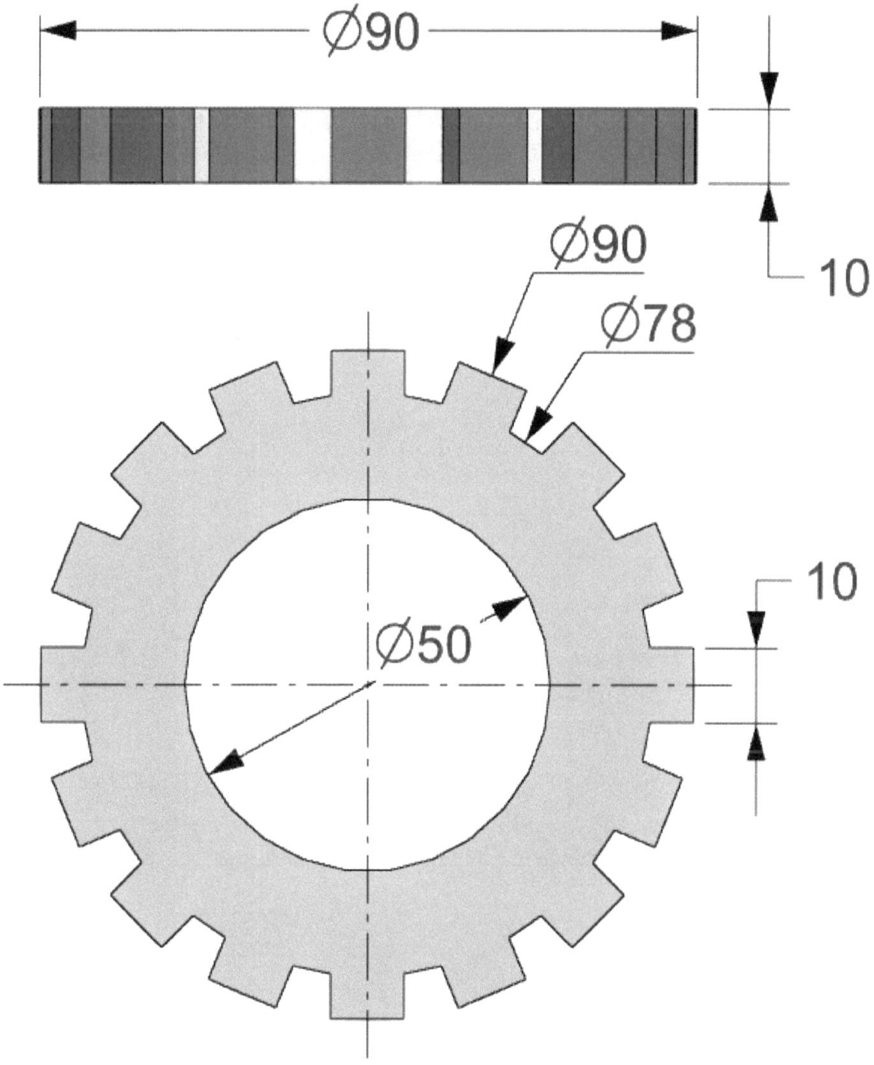

Ø90

10

Ø90
Ø78
Ø50
10

EXERCISE-10

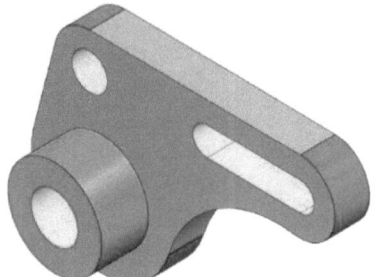

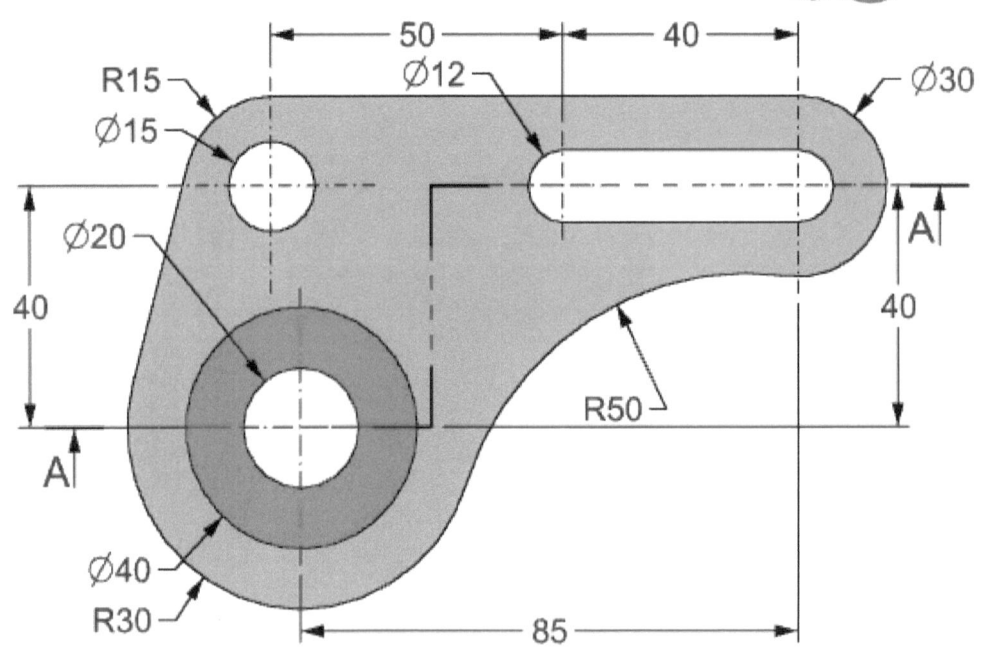

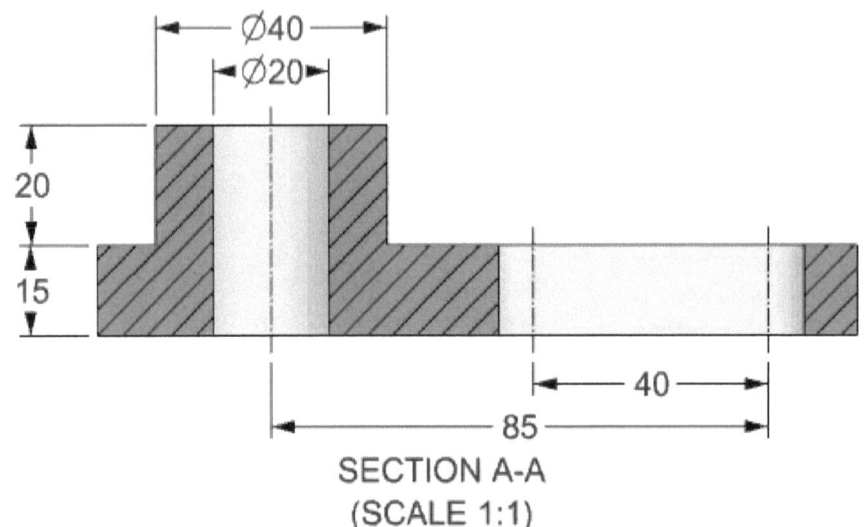

SECTION A-A
(SCALE 1:1)

©Copyright 2019 CADin360, ALL Rights Reserved

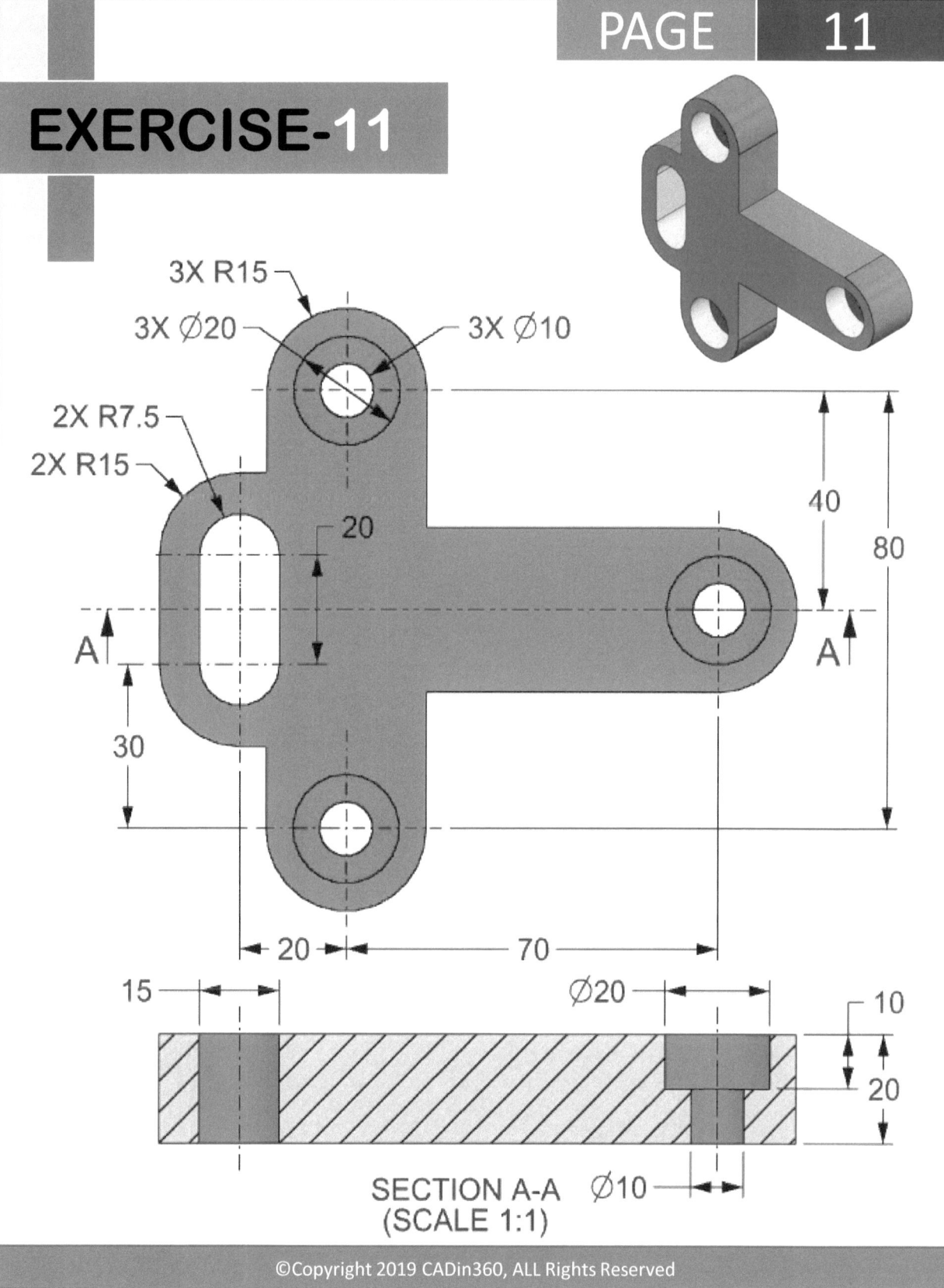

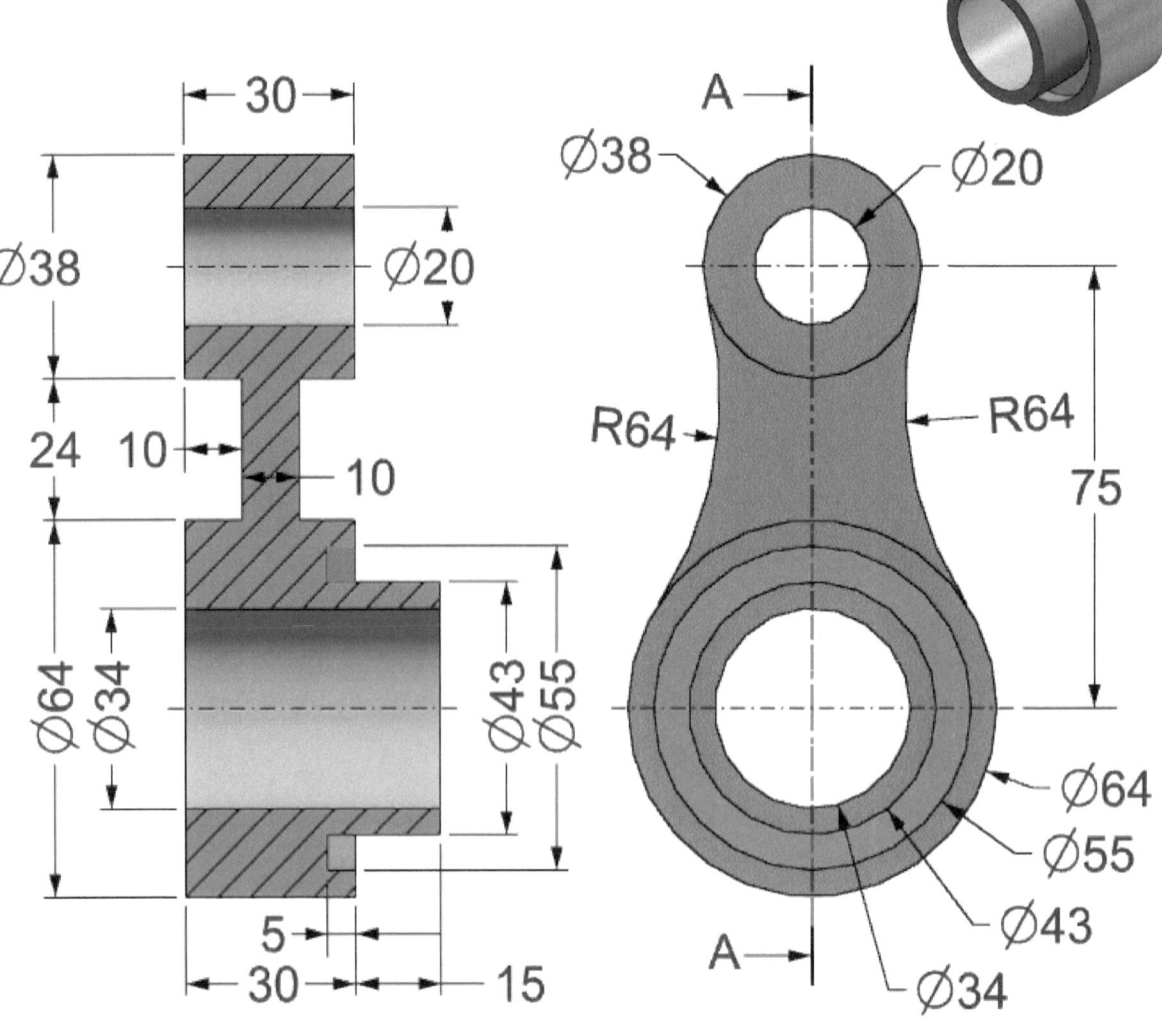

EXERCISE-13

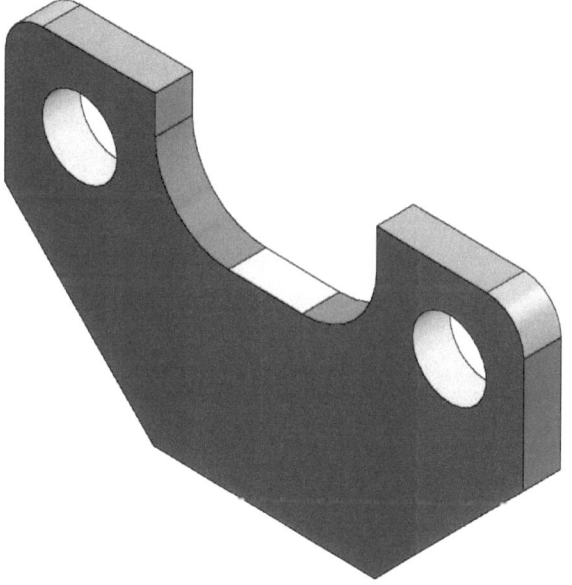

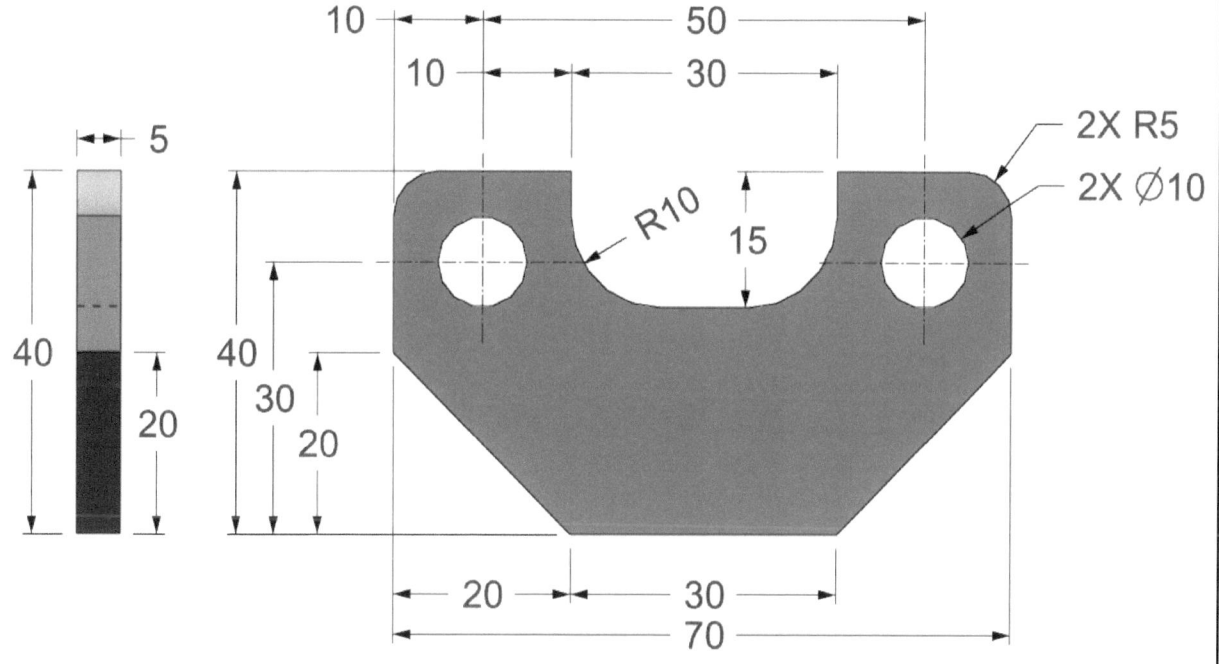

EXERCISE-14

30
30
30
30
30
4.5
30
45
A
A
30
4.5
150
4.5
15
10.5
4.5
SECTION A-A
(SCALE 1:1)

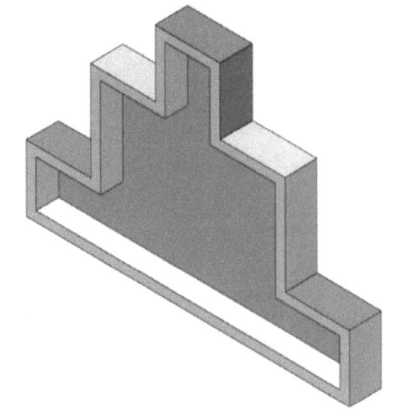

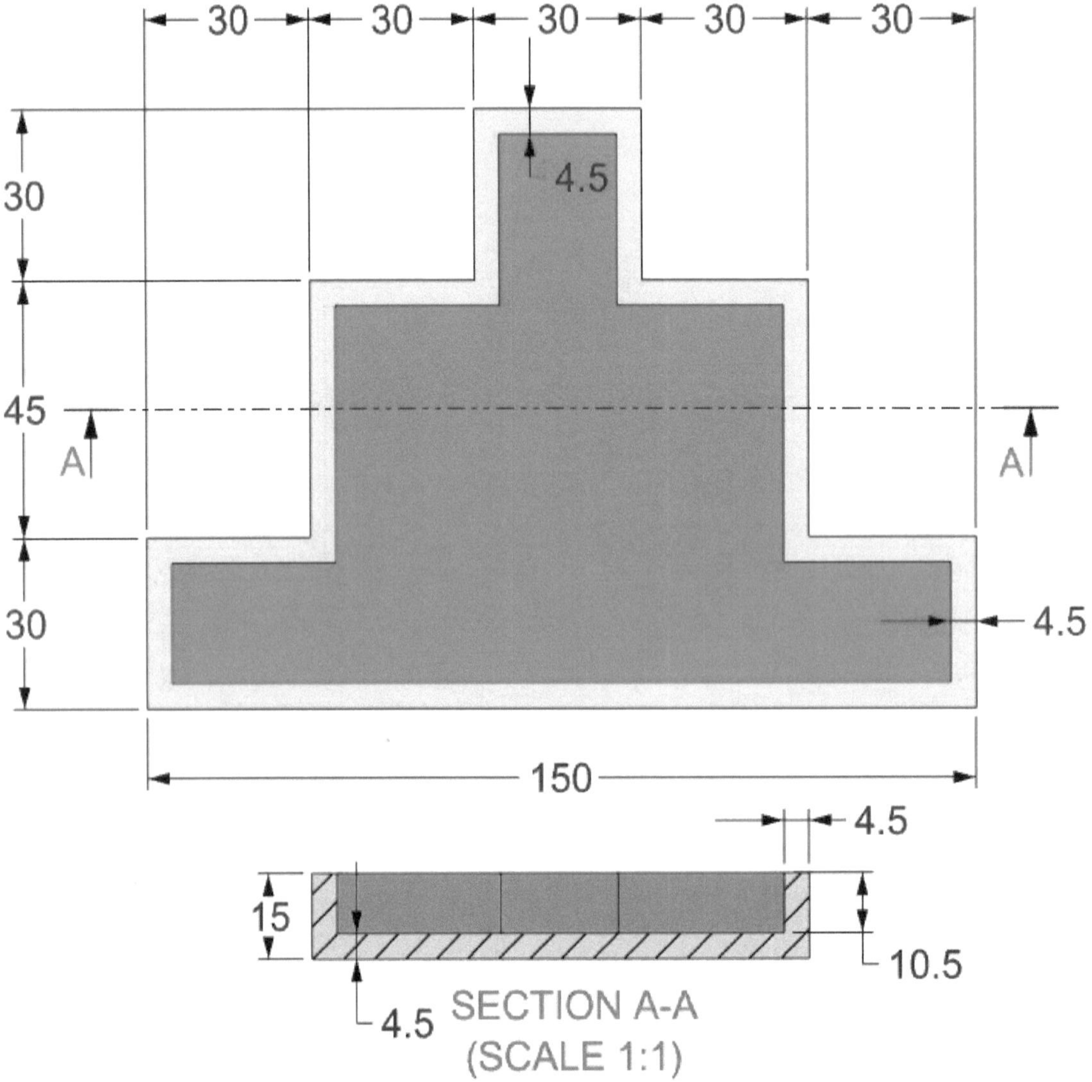

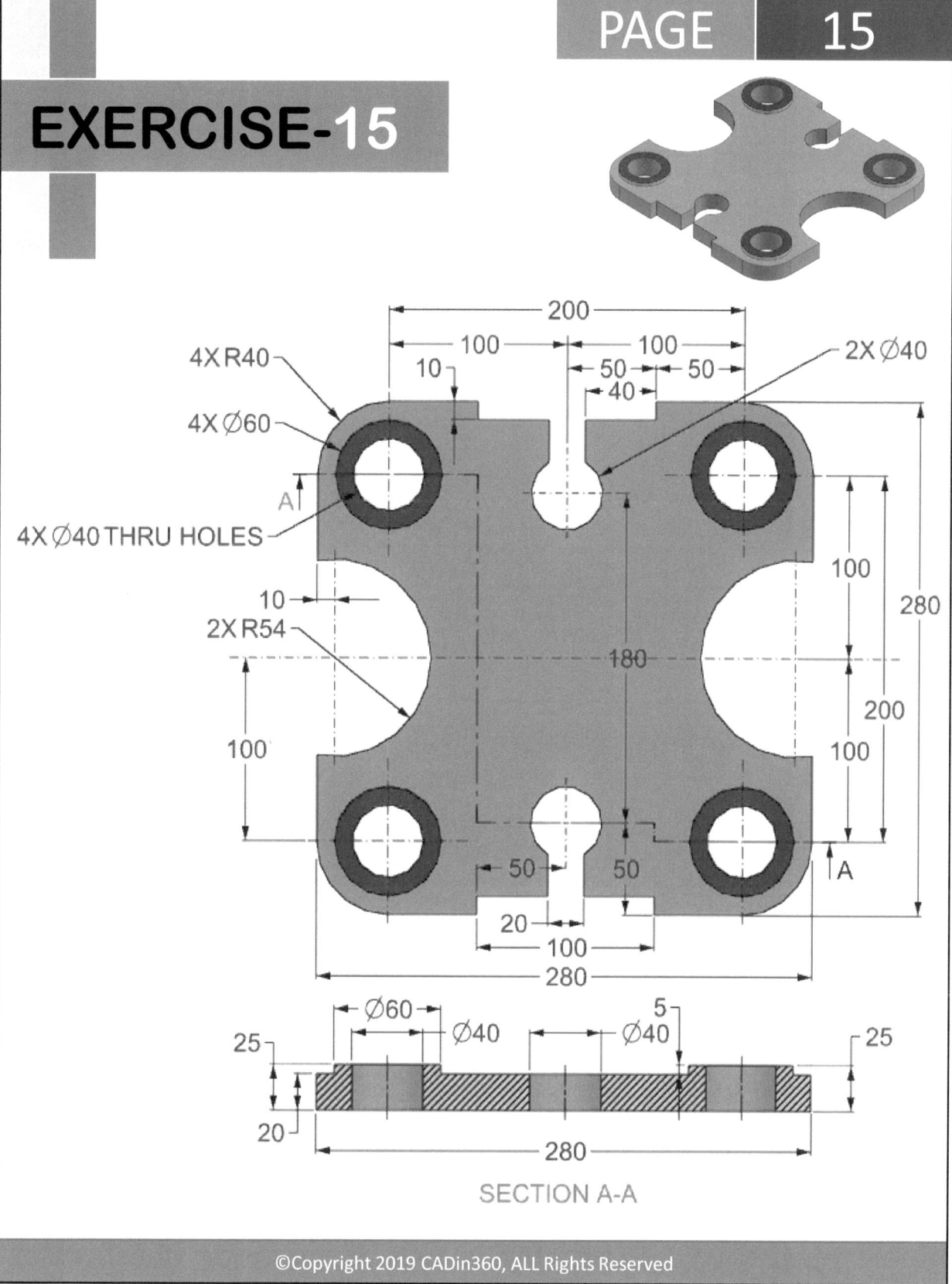

EXERCISE-16

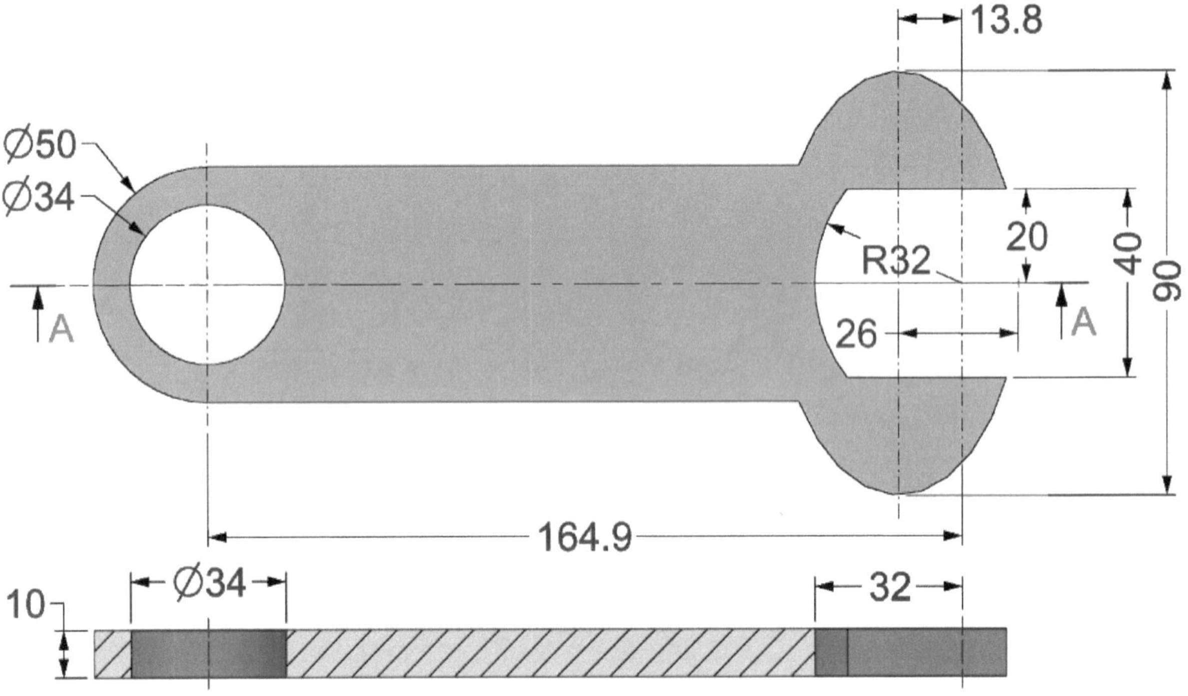

(SCALE 1:1) SECTION A-A

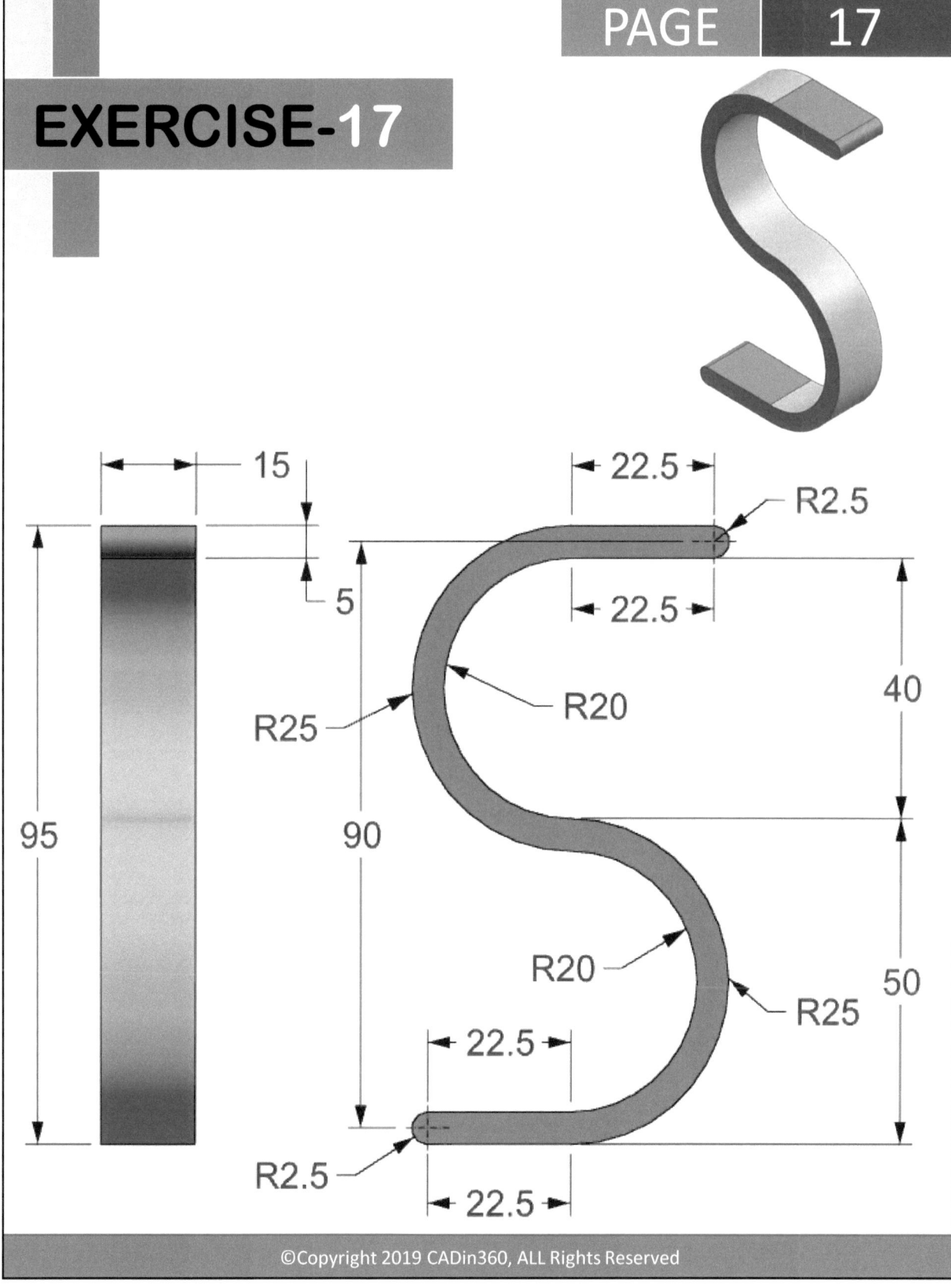

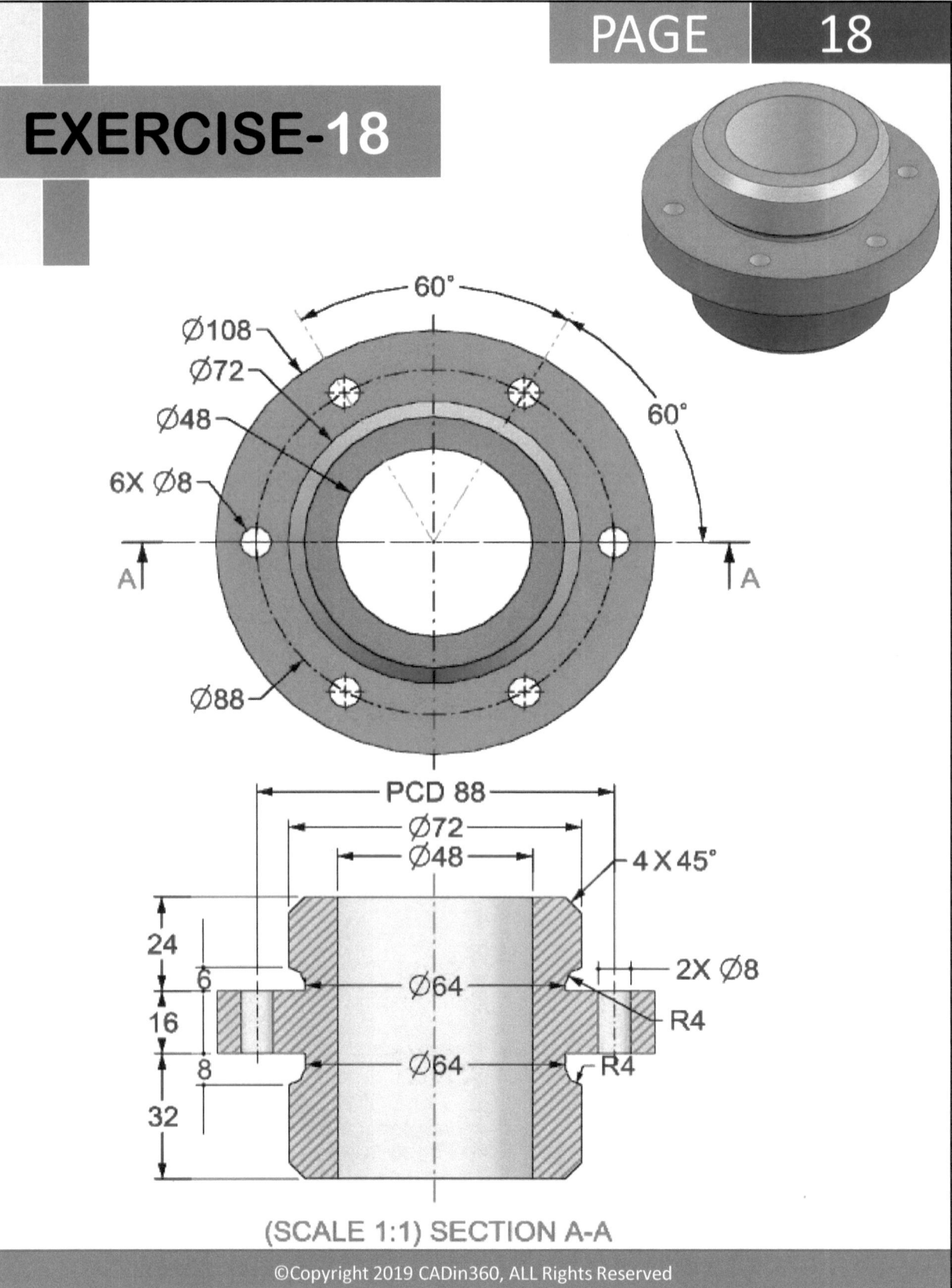

EXERCISE-19

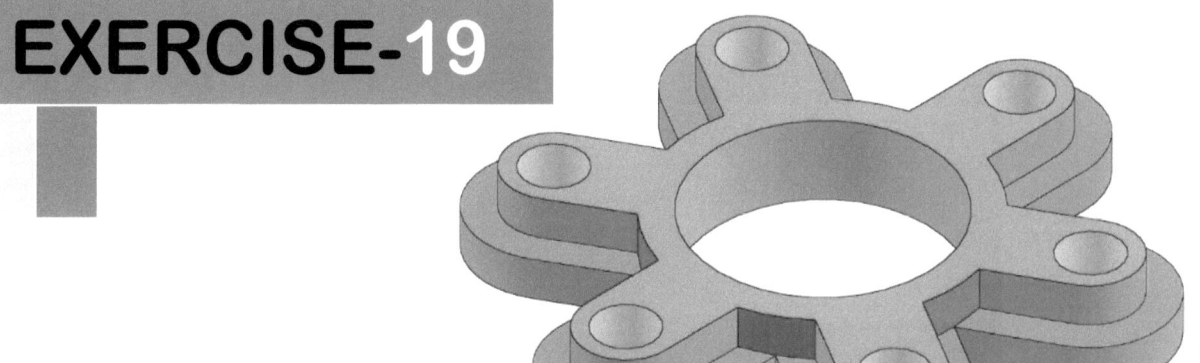

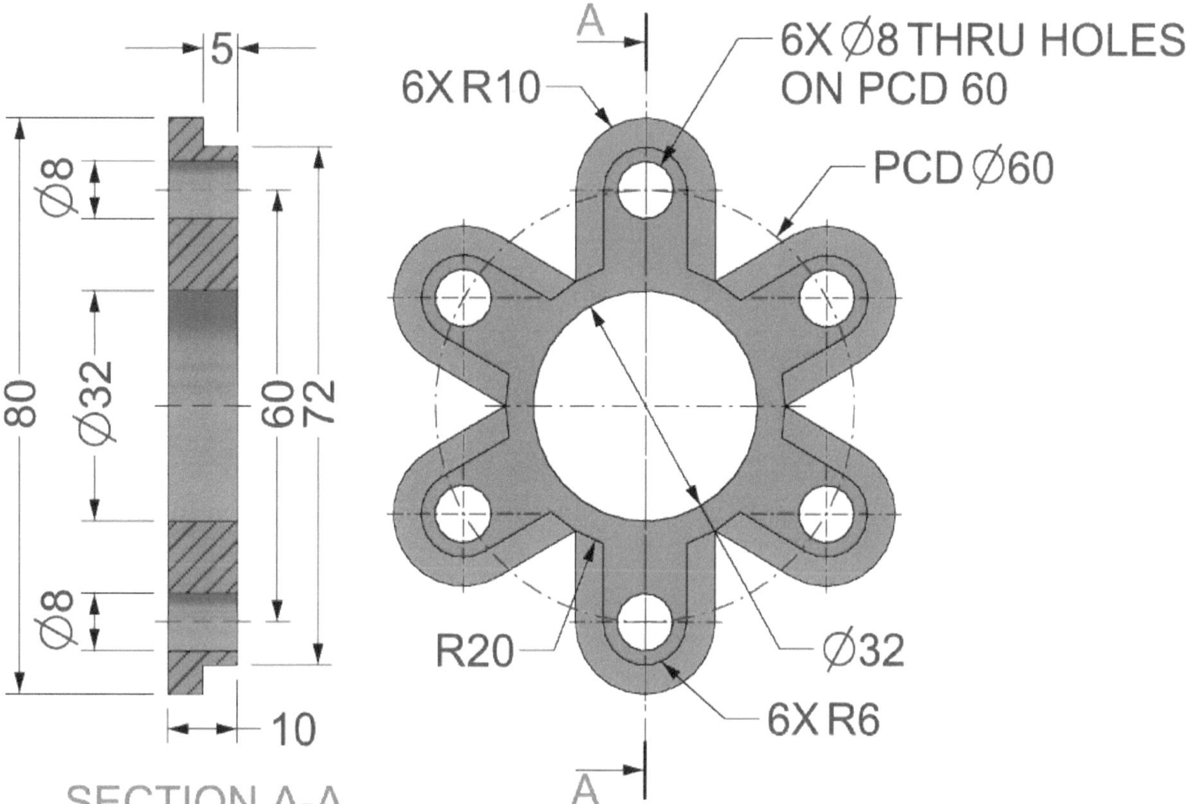
5
Ø8
80
Ø32
60
72
Ø8
10
A
6X Ø8 THRU HOLES
ON PCD 60
6X R10
PCD Ø60
R20
Ø32
6X R6
A

SECTION A-A

EXERCISE-20

216
12.3
126
12.7
R41
Ø60
63
214
126
63
4X R44.8
4X R32.5
A
A
146
4X R12
Ø60
25
146
SECTION A-A

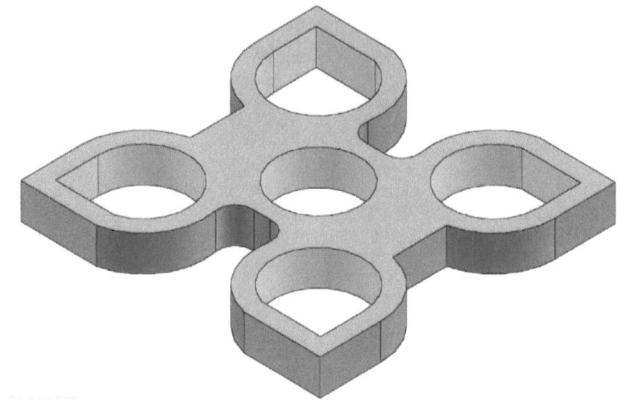

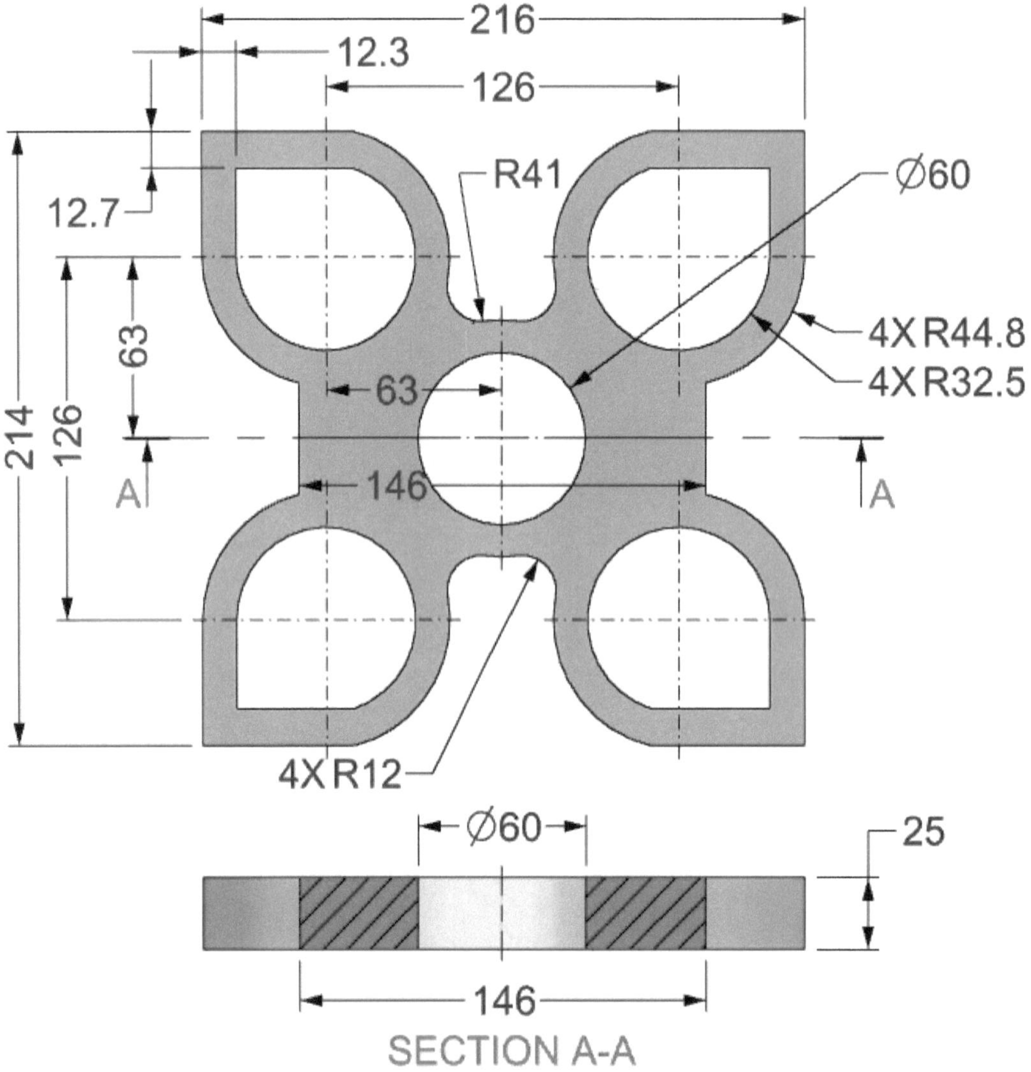

EXERCISE-21

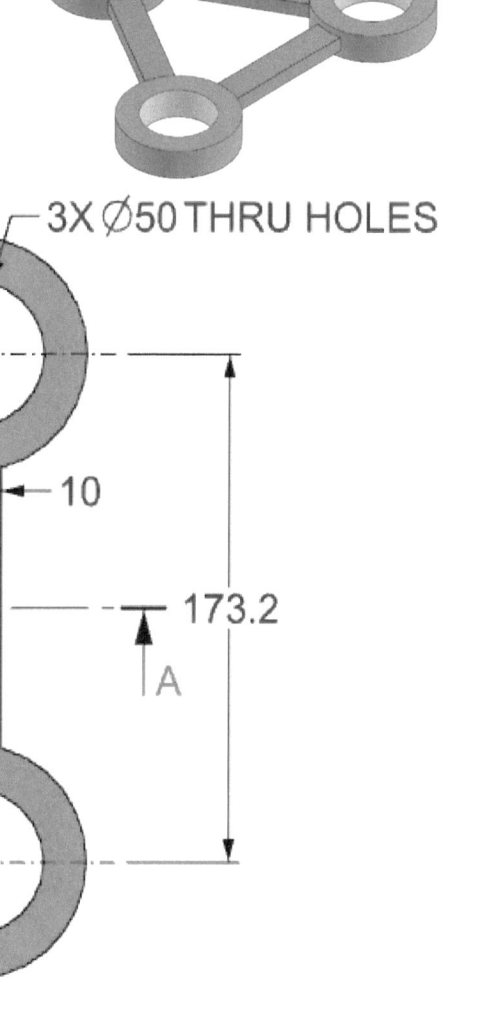

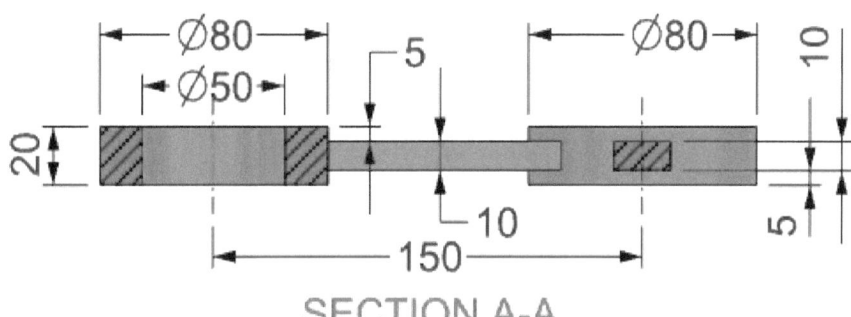

SECTION A-A

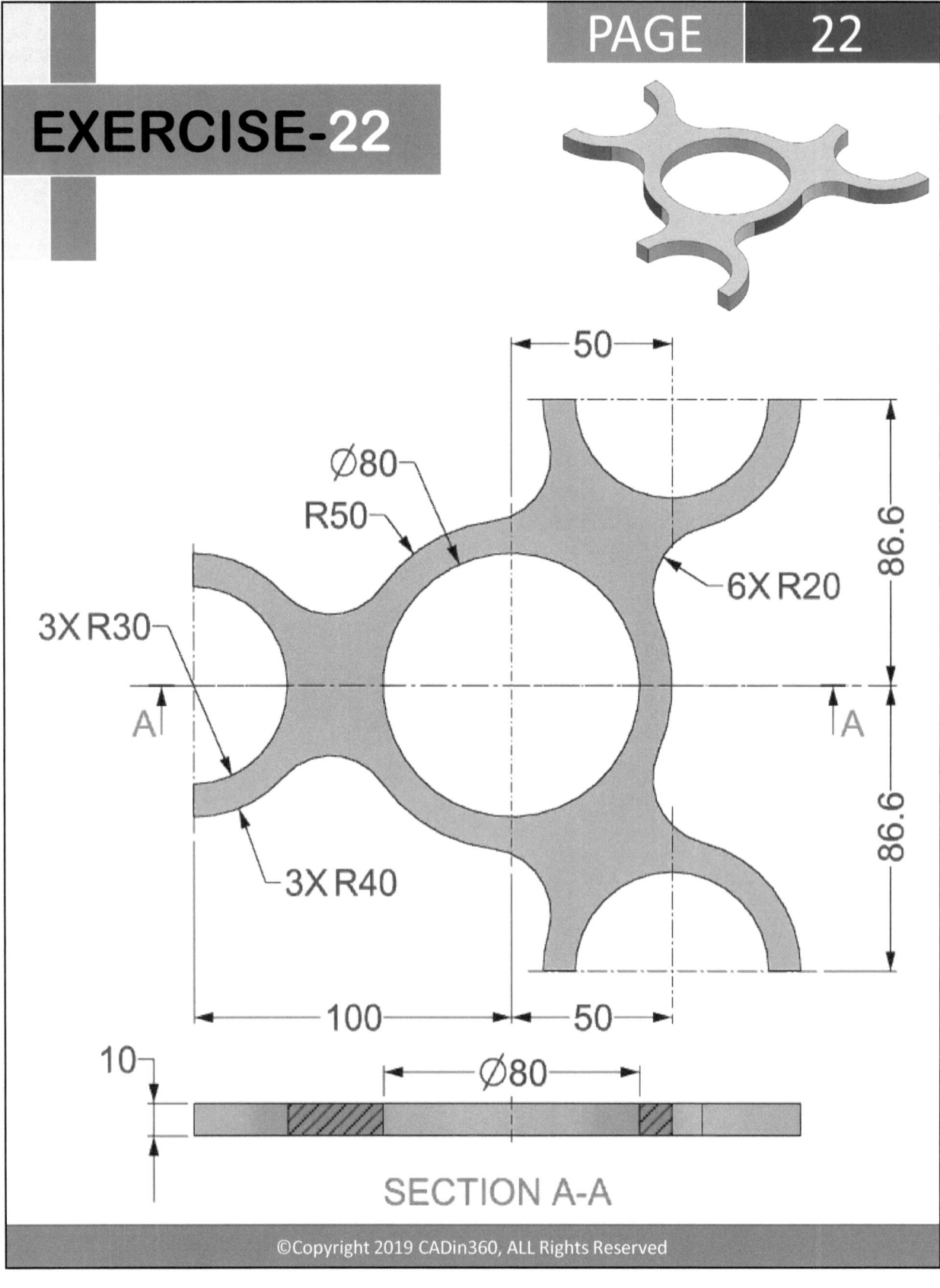

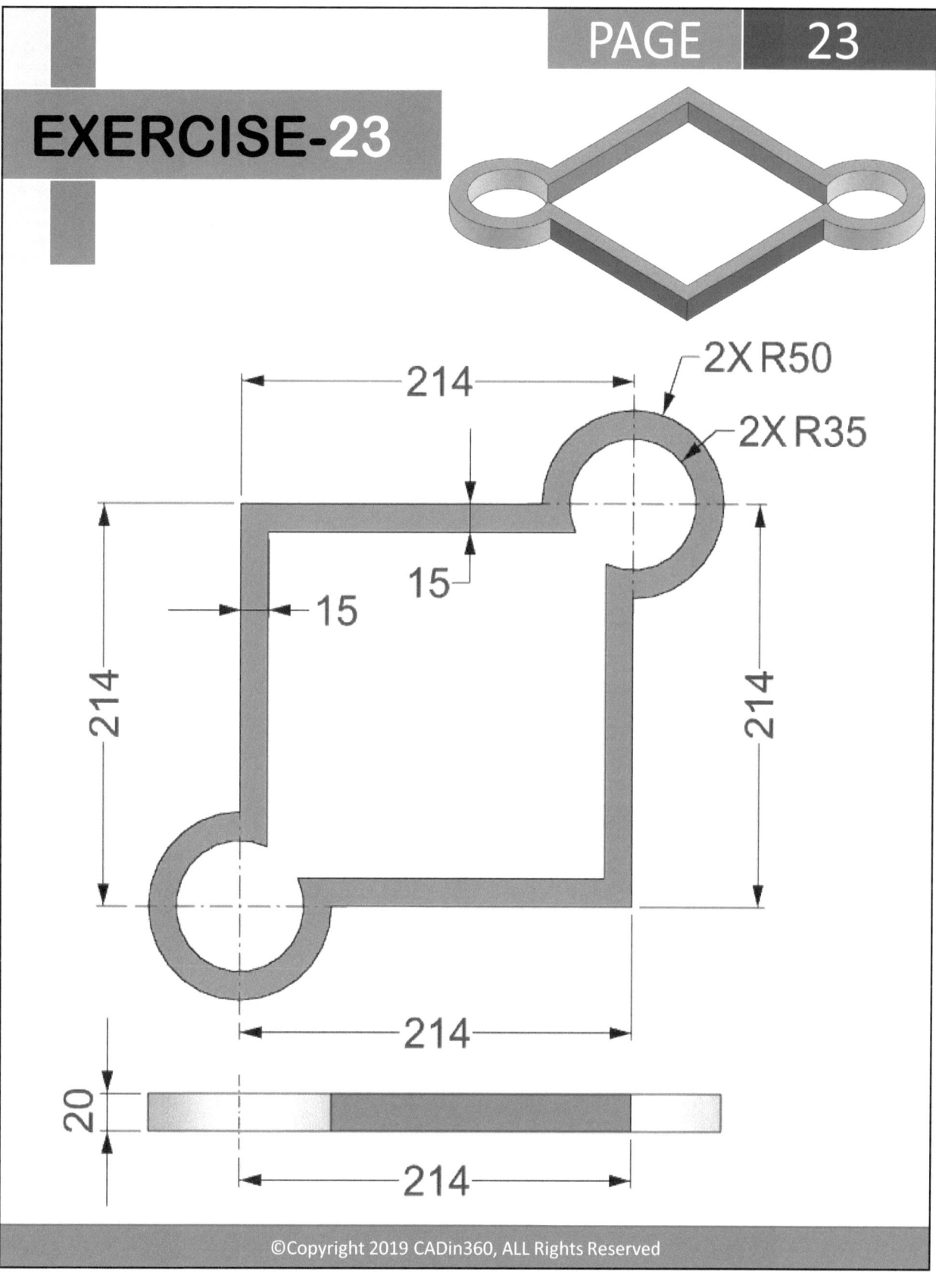

EXERCISE-24

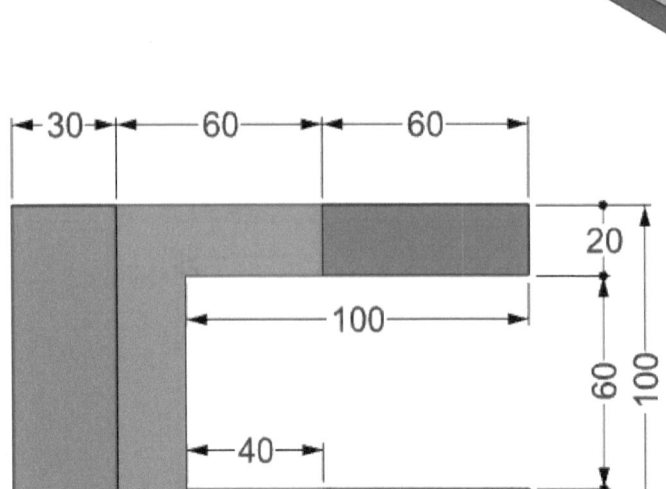
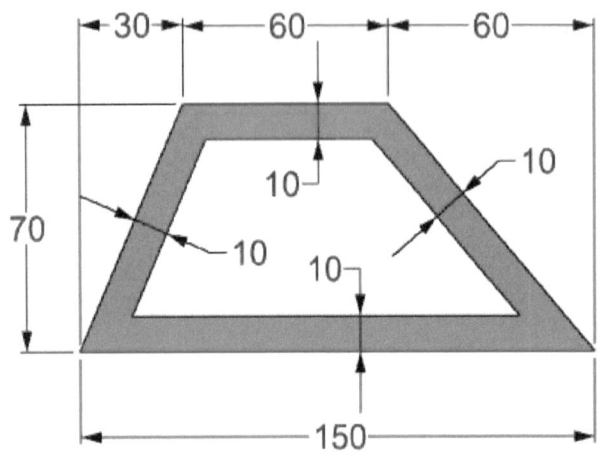
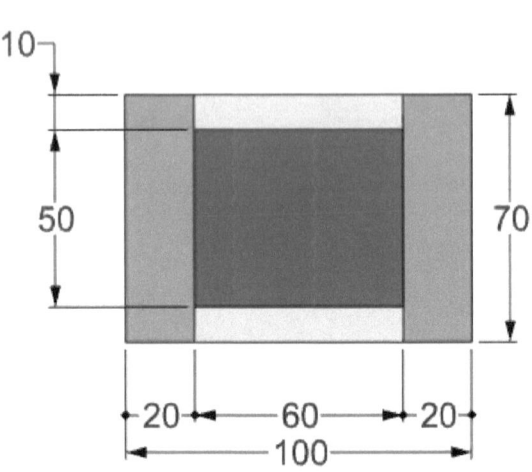

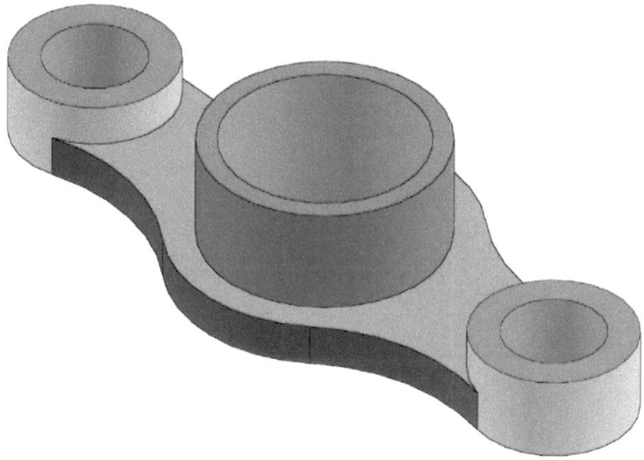

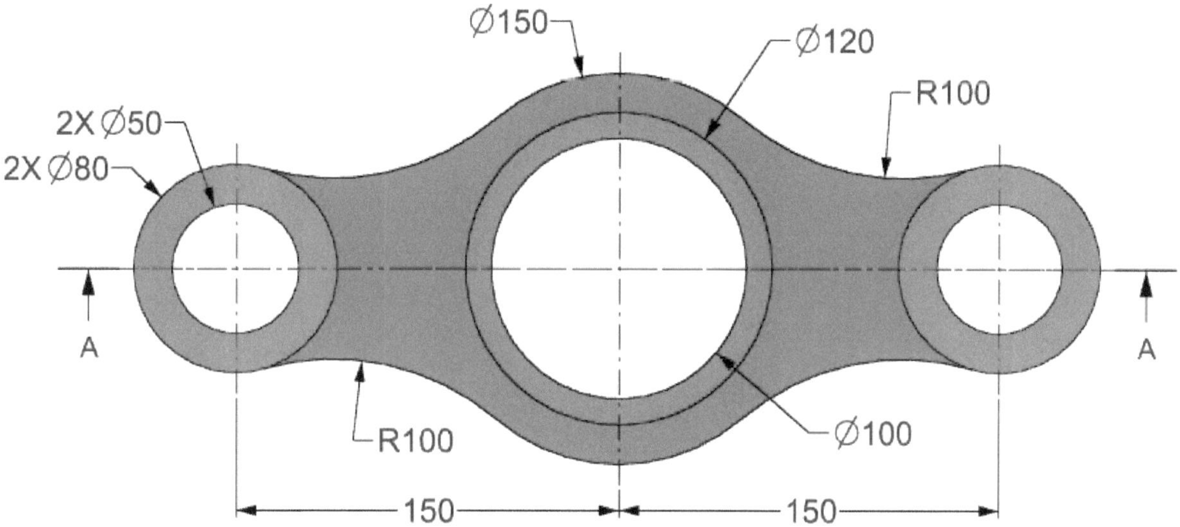

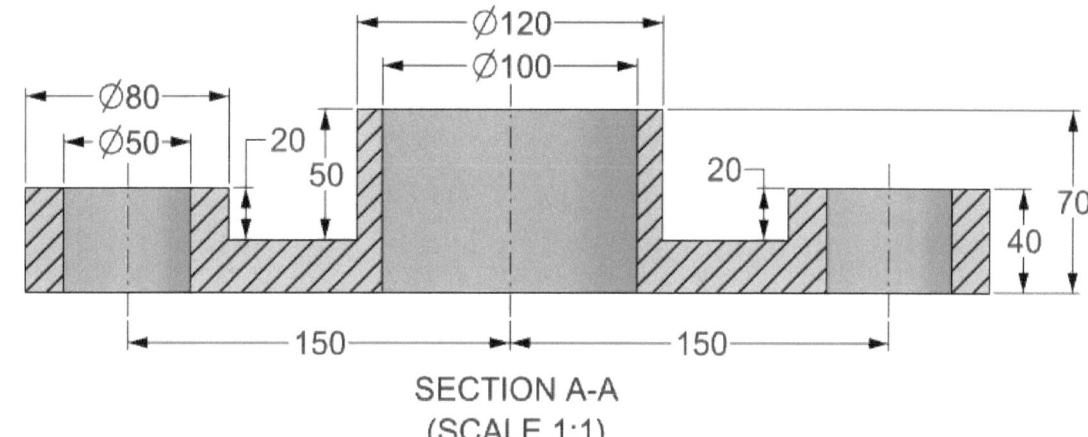

EXERCISE-26

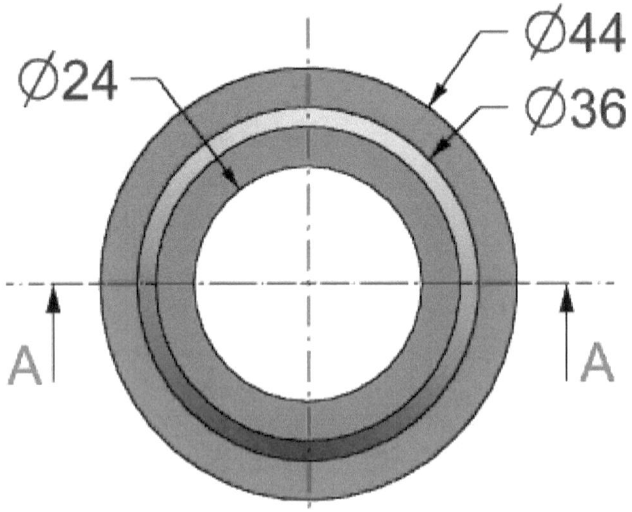

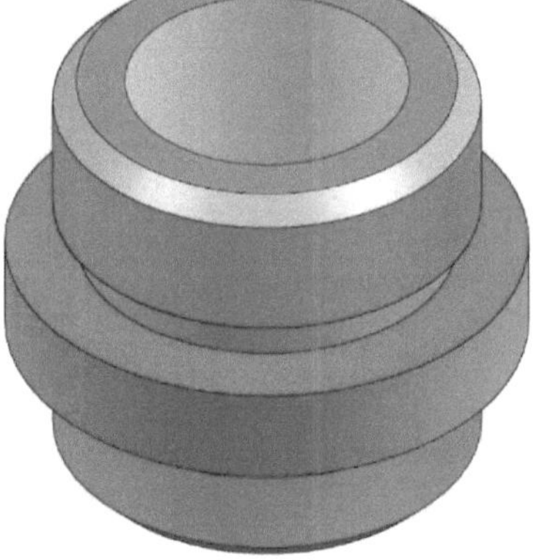

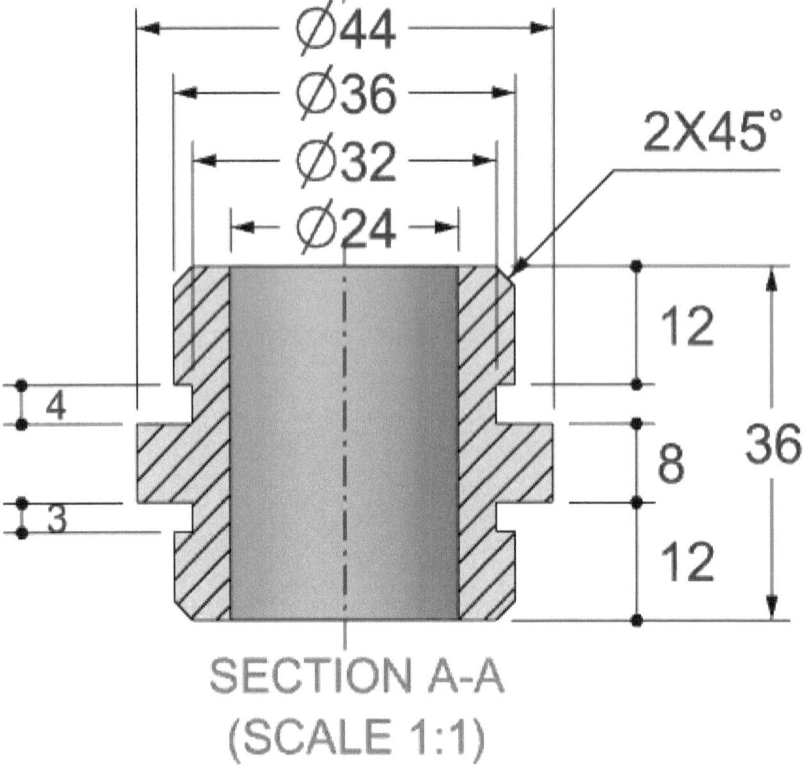

SECTION A-A
(SCALE 1:1)

Ø44
Ø36
Ø32
Ø24
Ø24 (top view)
2X45°
12
8
12
36
4
3

EXERCISE-27

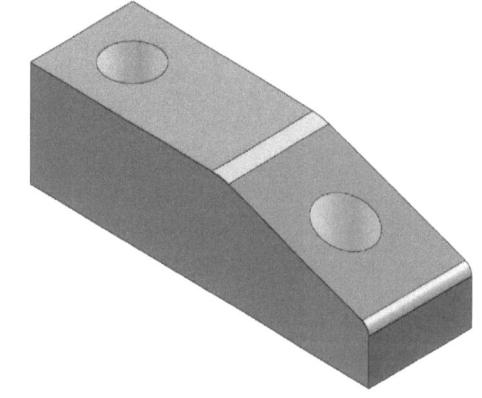

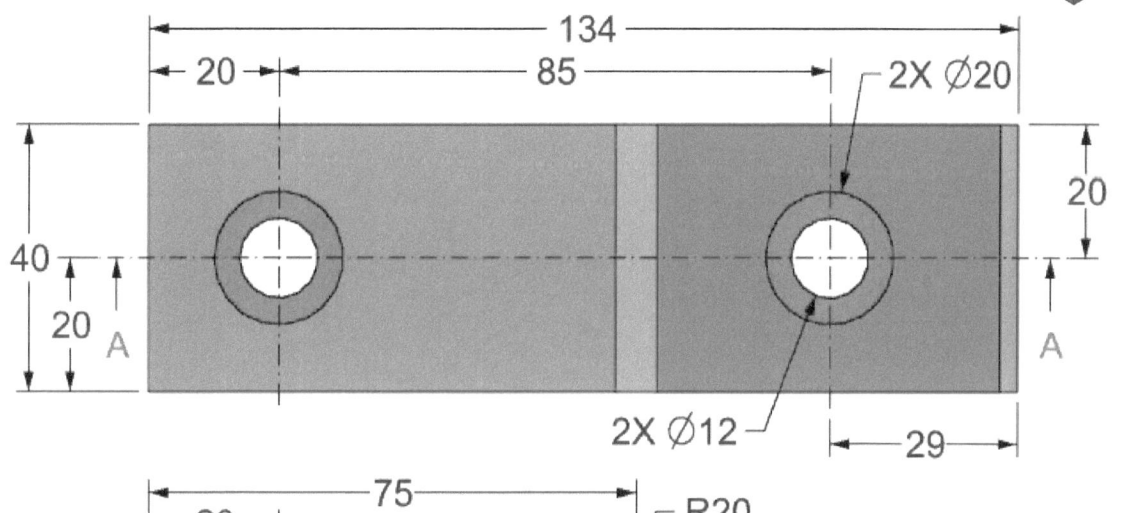

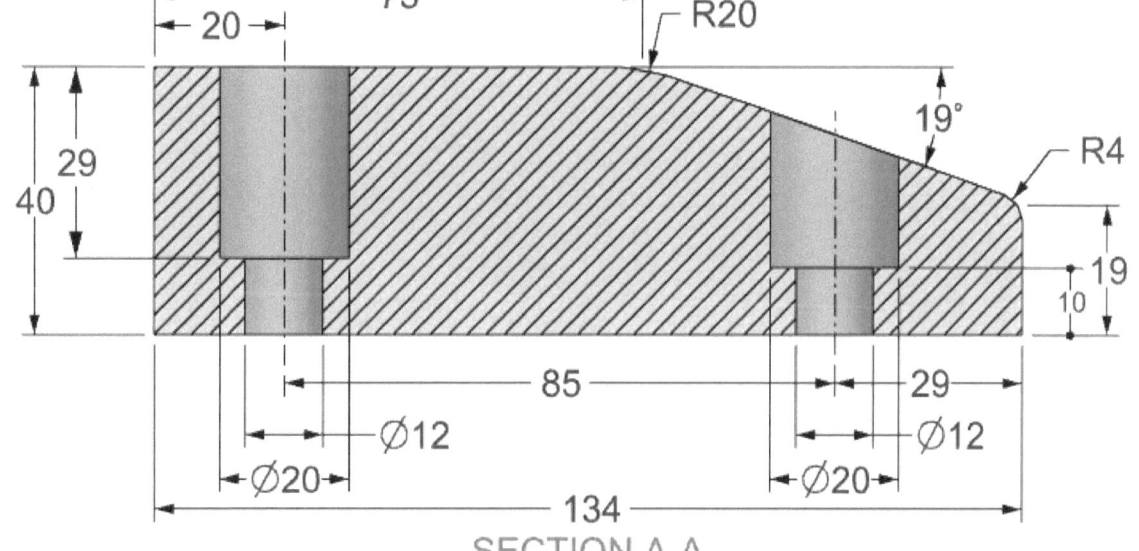

SECTION A-A
(SCALE 1:1)

EXERCISE-28

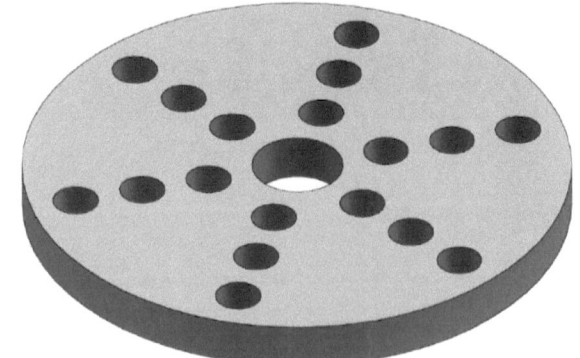

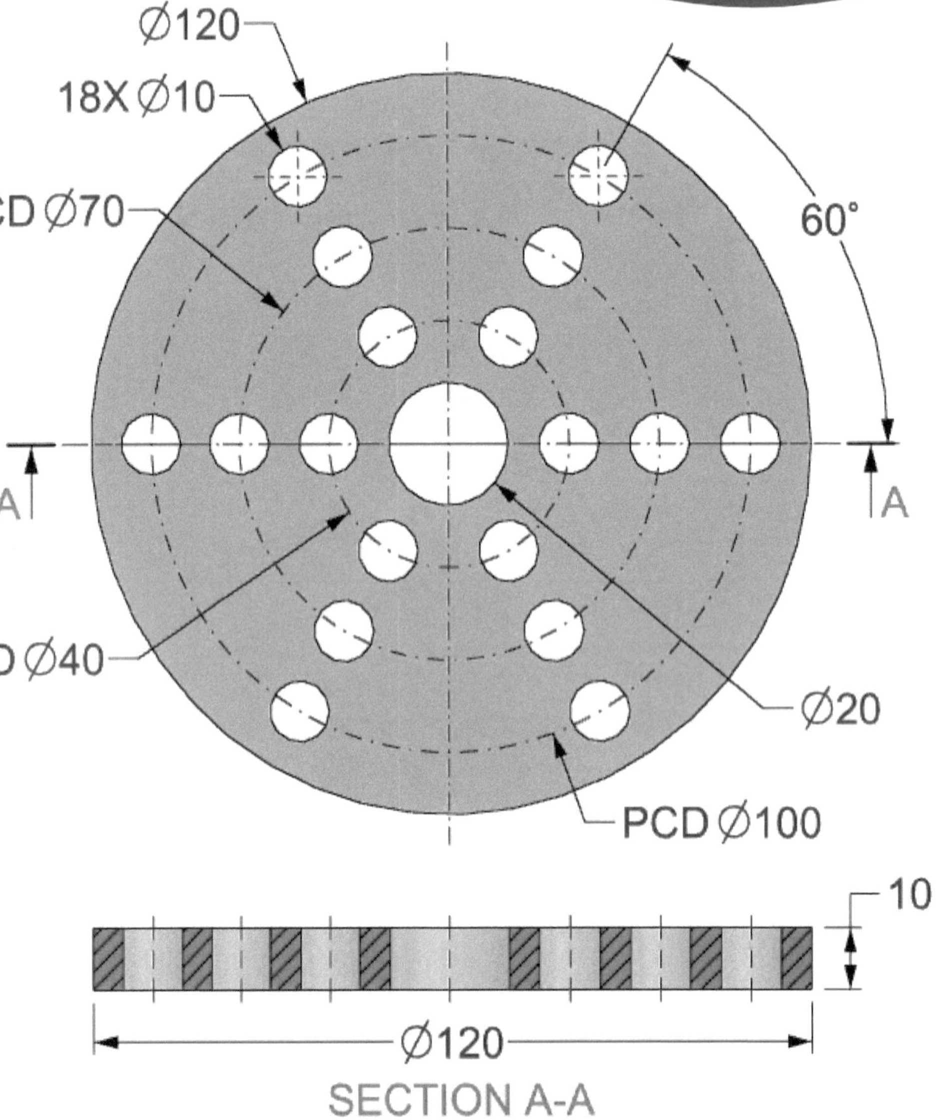

- Ø120
- 18X Ø10
- PCD Ø70
- 60°
- PCD Ø40
- Ø20
- PCD Ø100

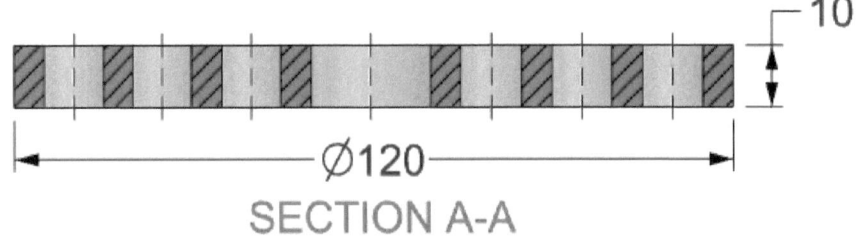

- 10
- Ø120

SECTION A-A

©Copyright 2019 CADin360, ALL Rights Reserved

EXERCISE-29

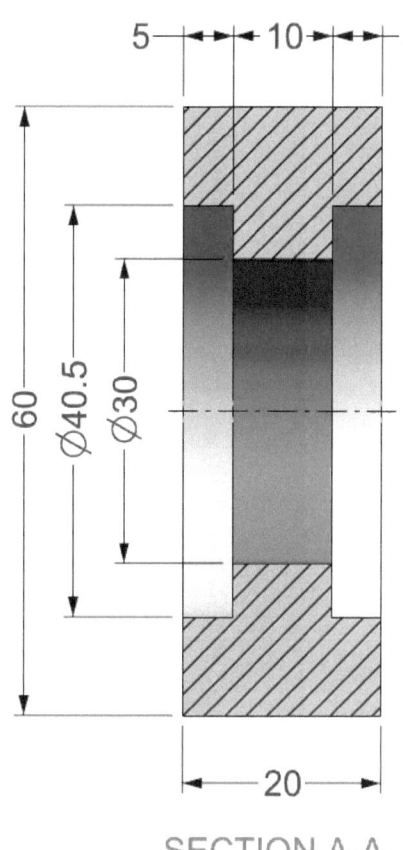

SECTION A-A

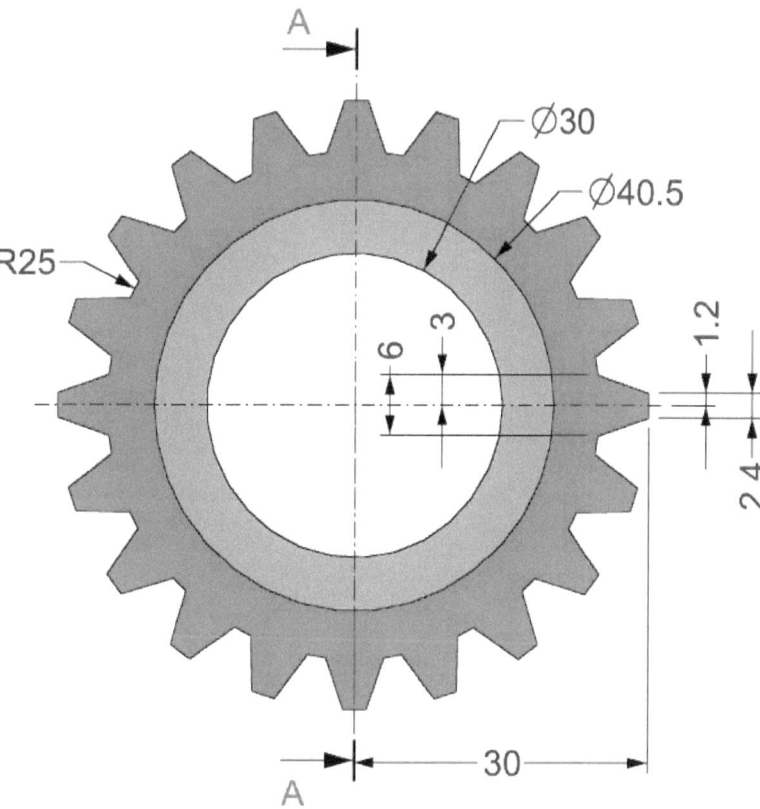

EXERCISE-30

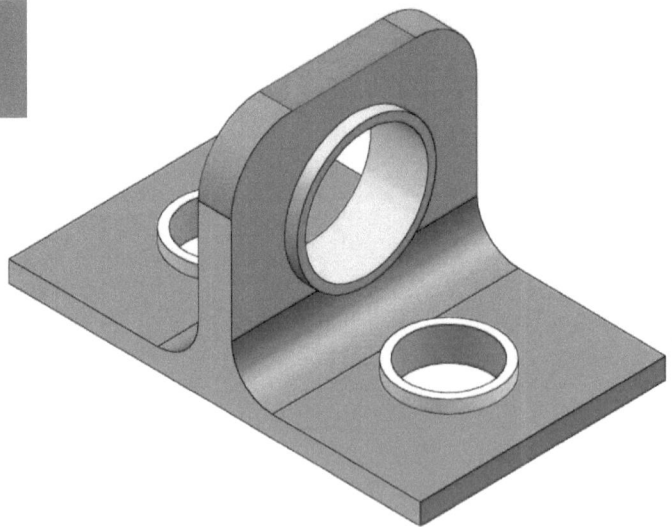

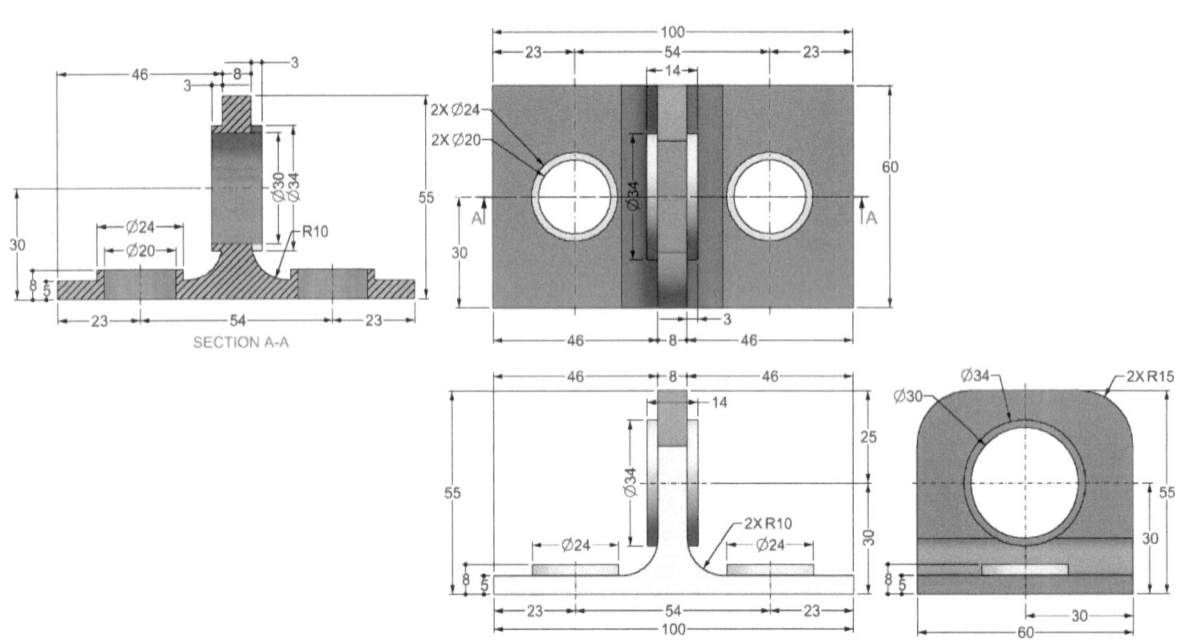

EXERCISE-31

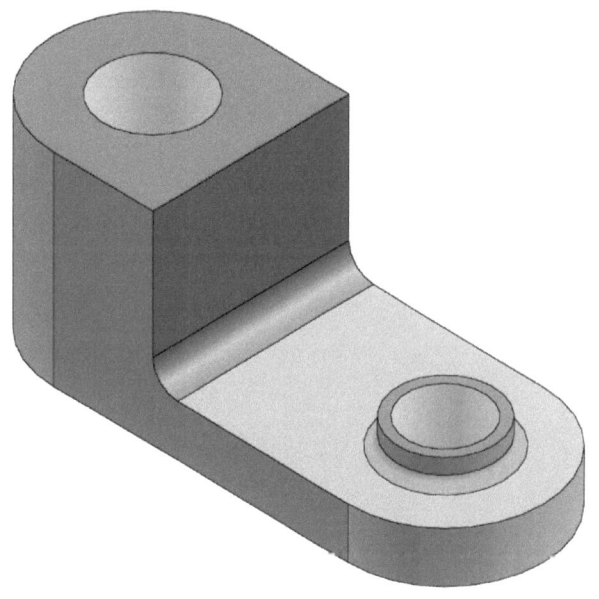

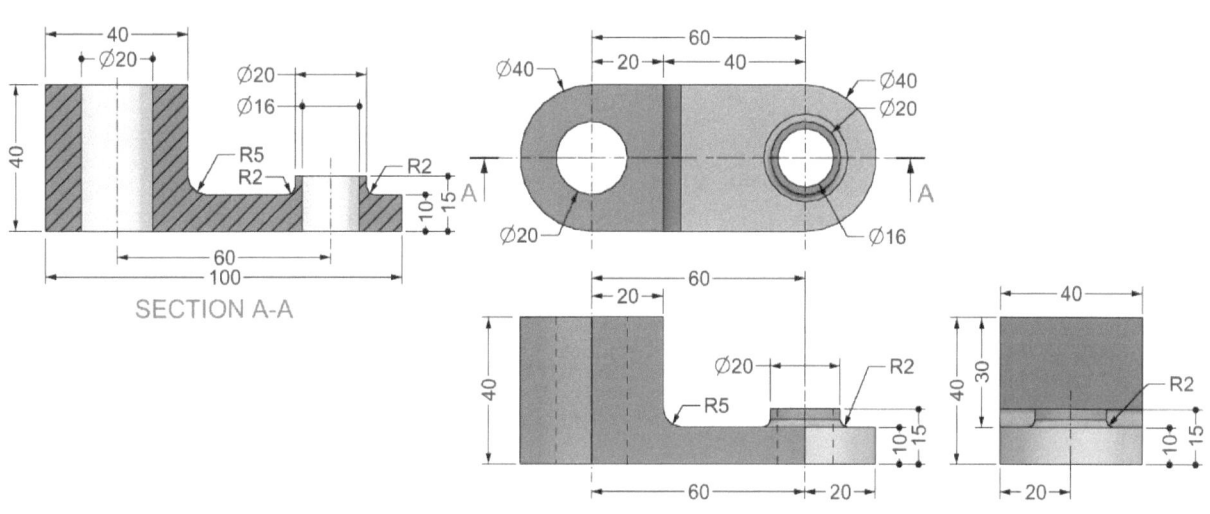

EXERCISE-32

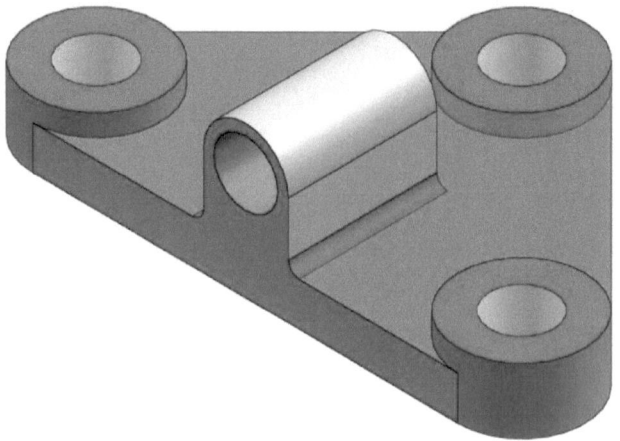

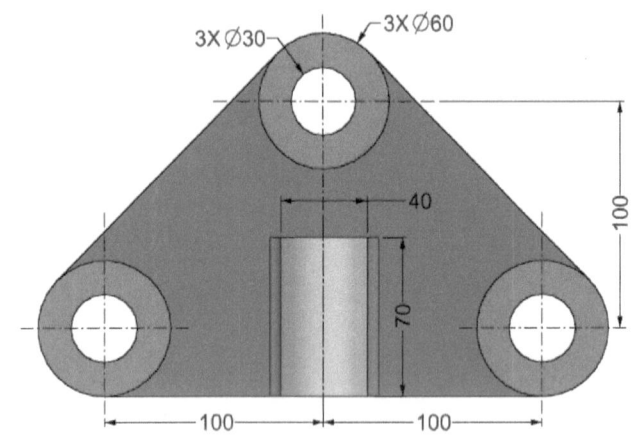

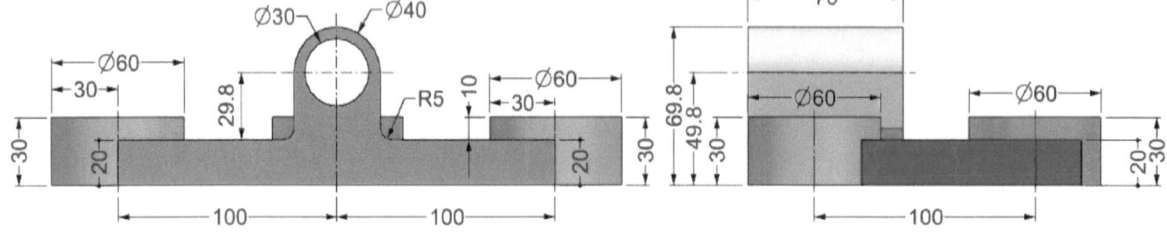

EXERCISE-33

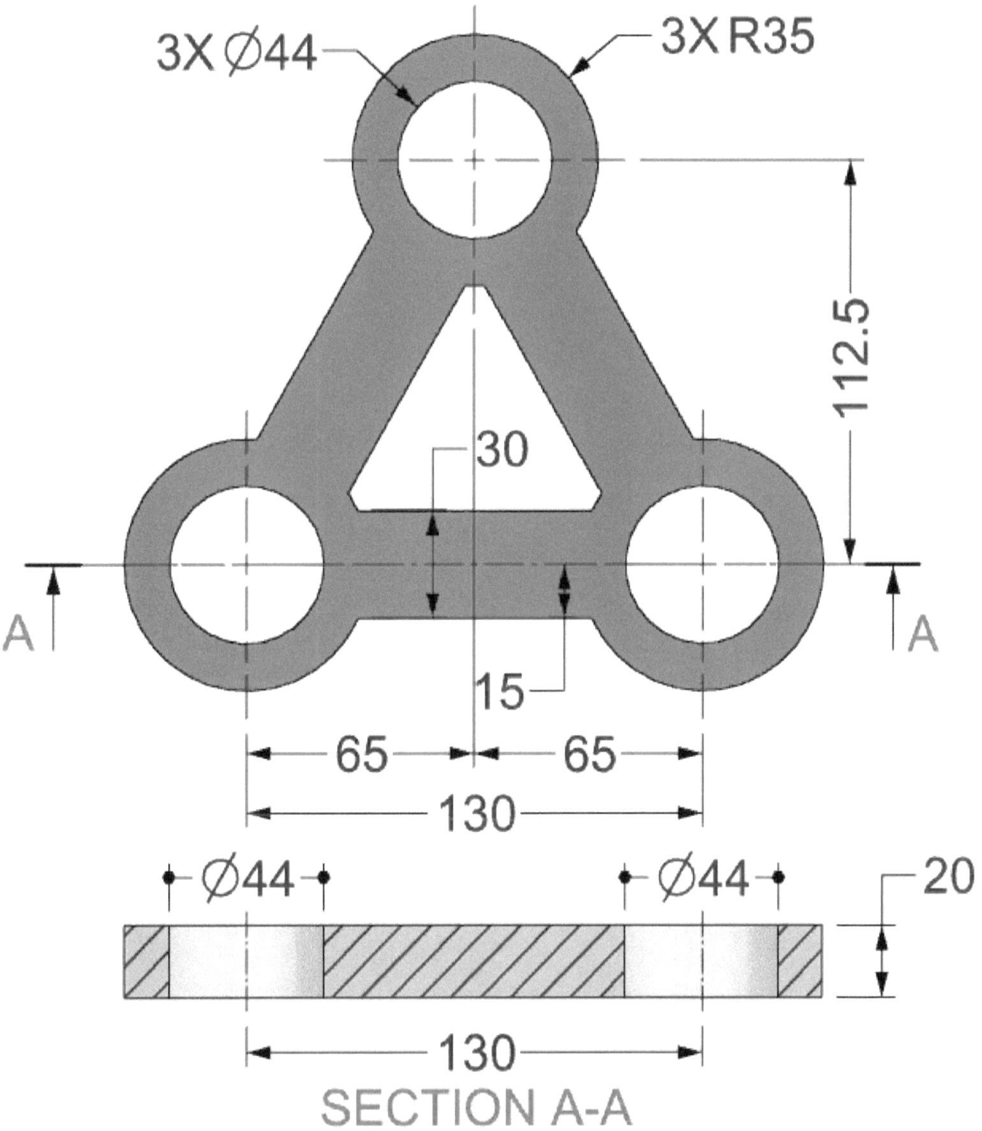

EXERCISE-34

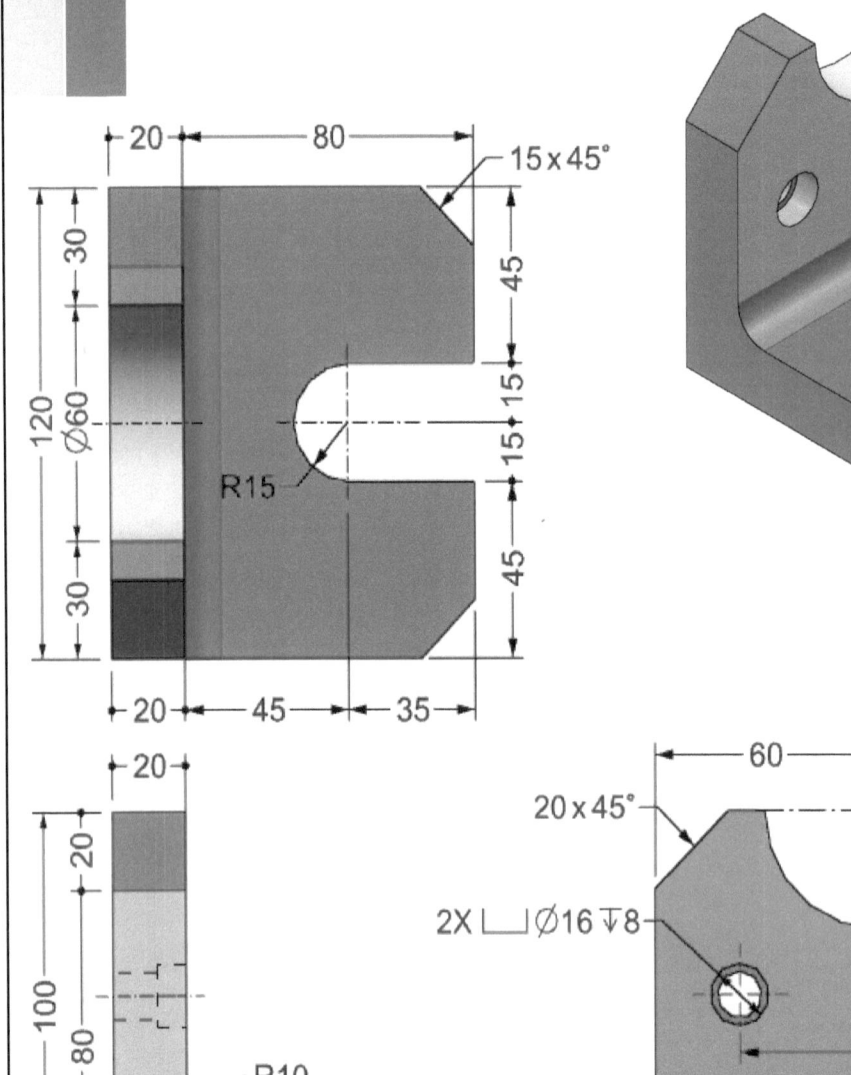

EXERCISE-35

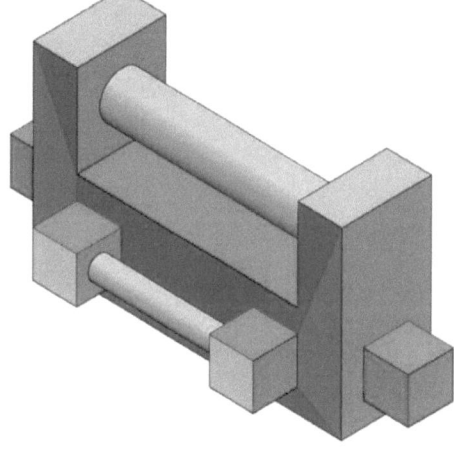

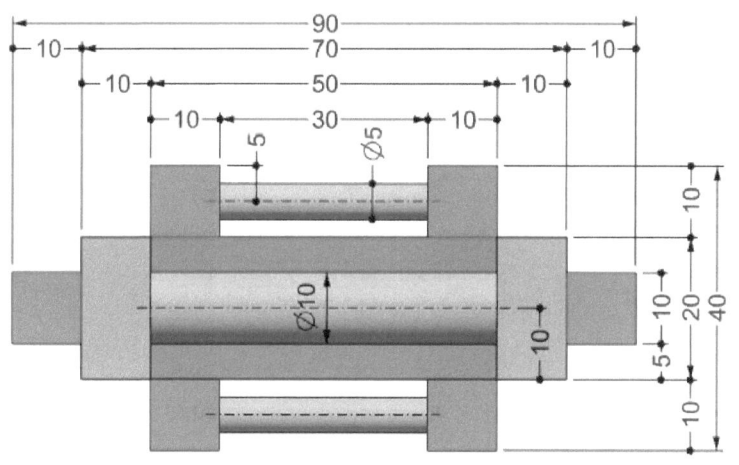

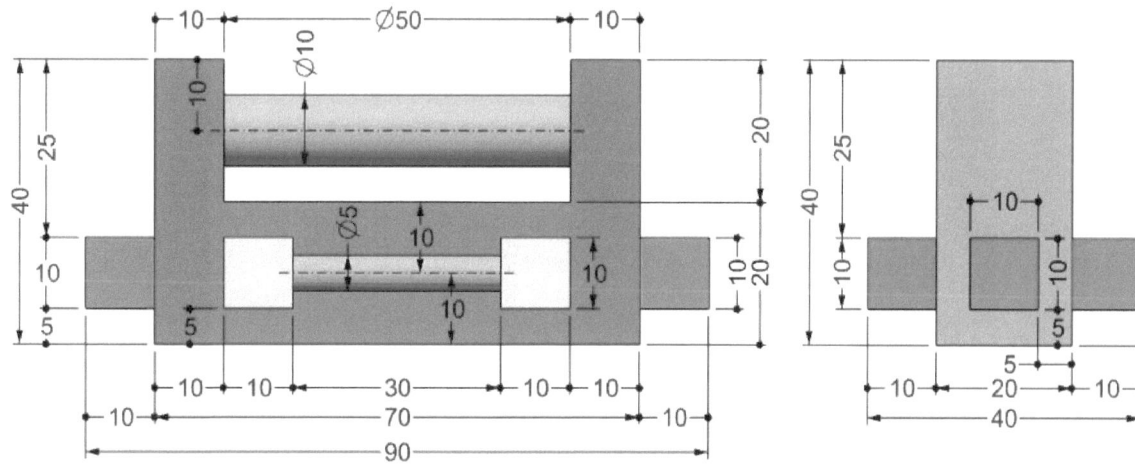

EXERCISE-36

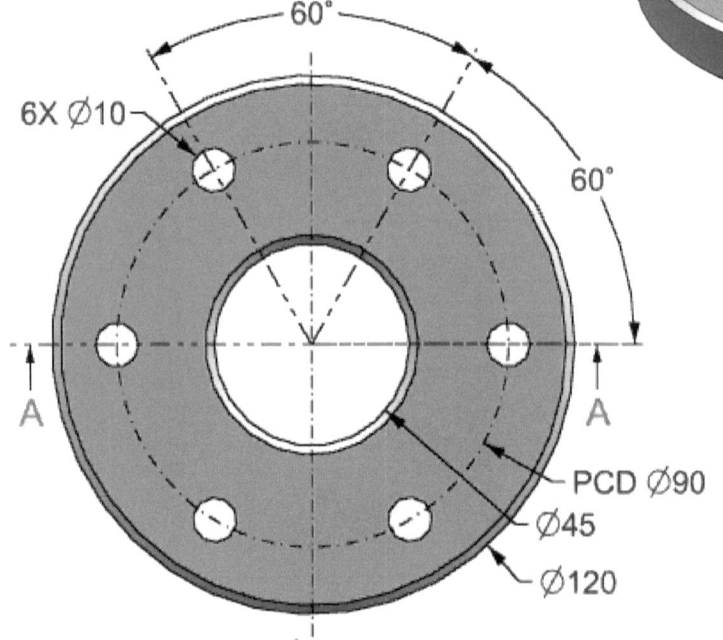

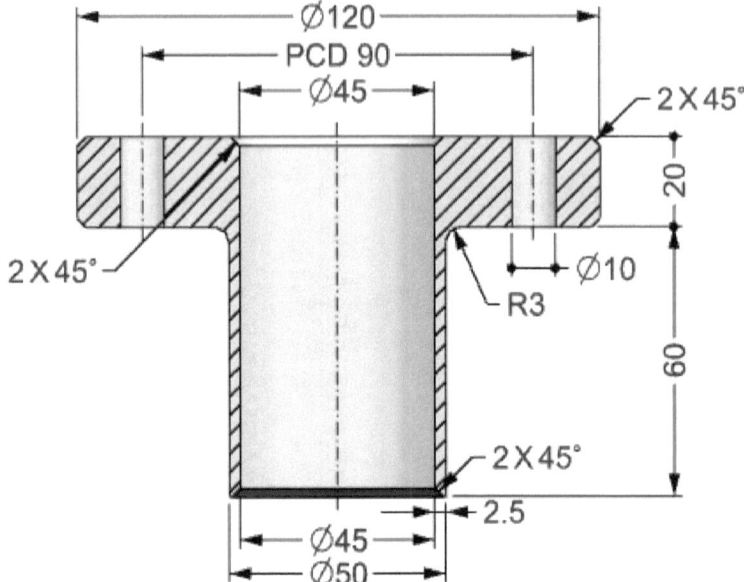

(SCALE 1:1) SECTION A-A

EXERCISE-37

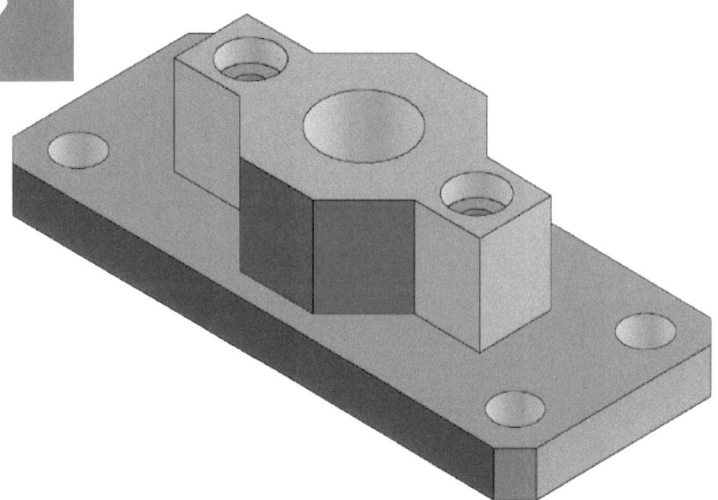

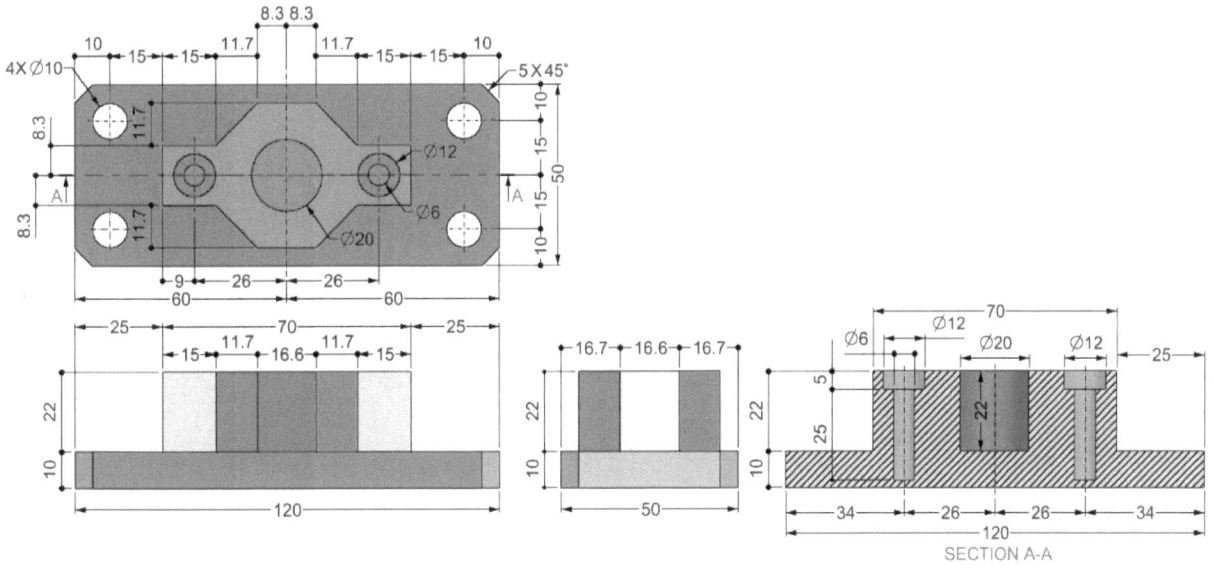

EXERCISE-38

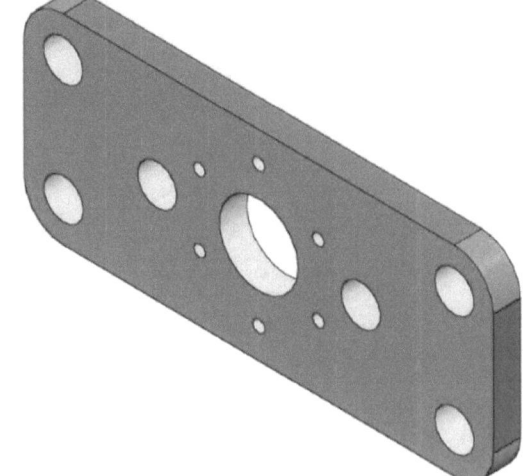

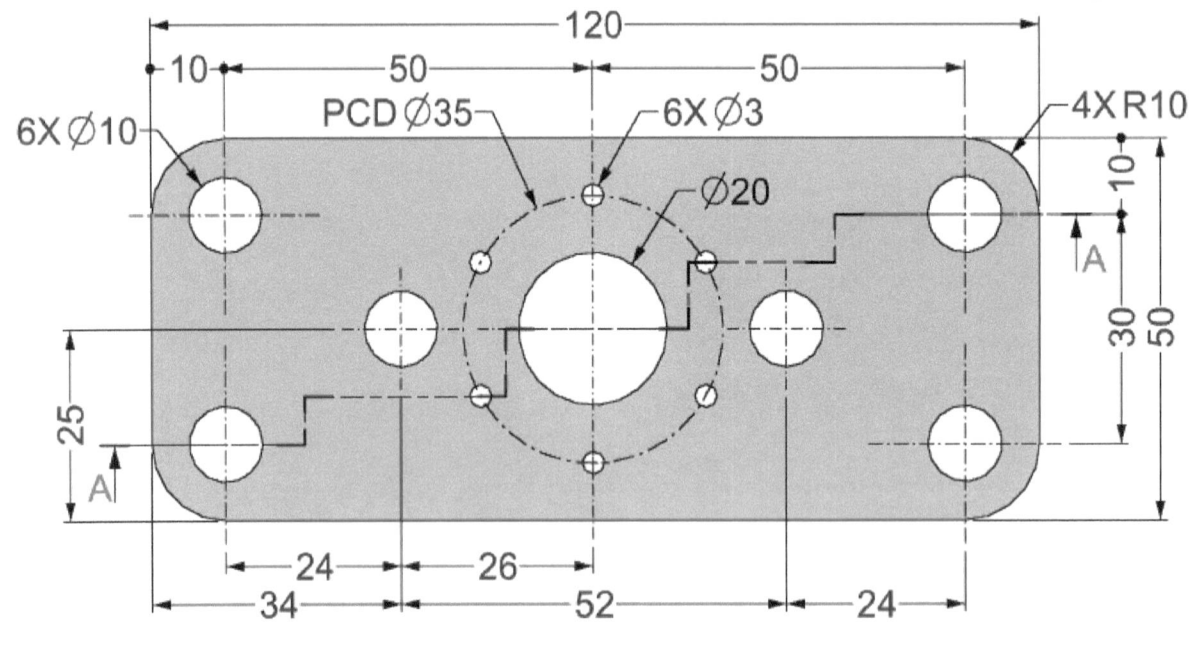

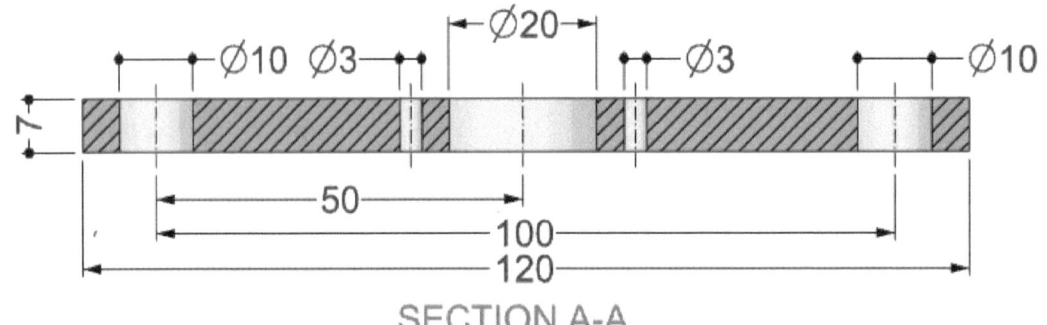

SECTION A-A

EXERCISE-39

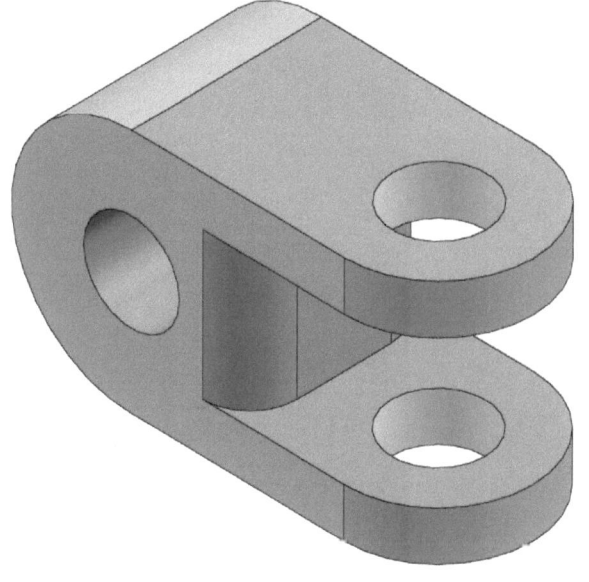

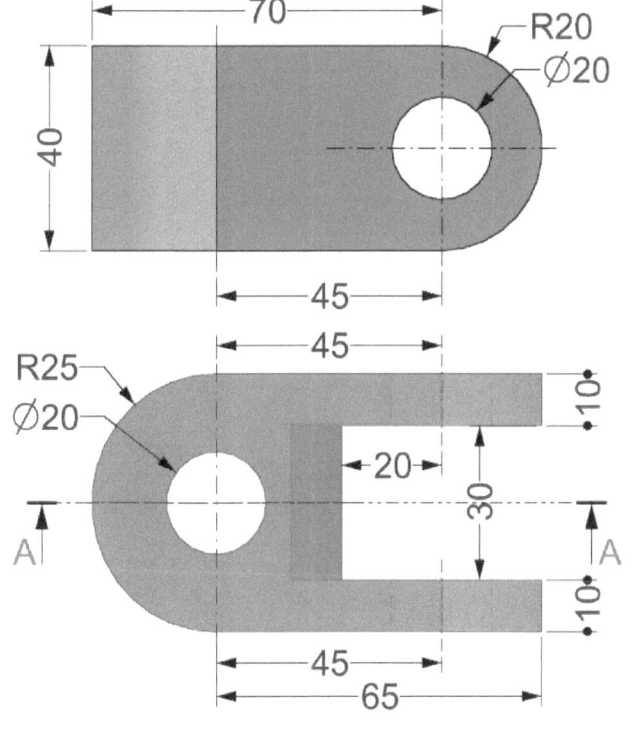

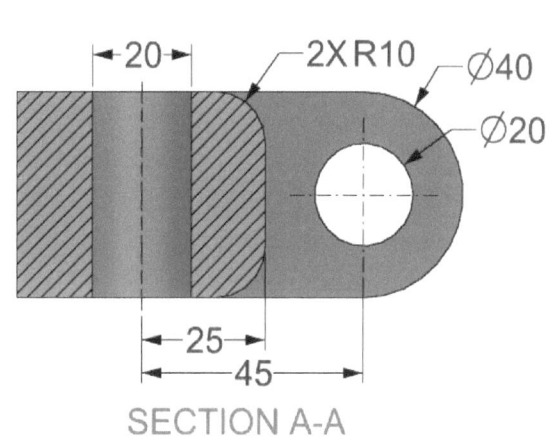

SECTION A-A

EXERCISE-40

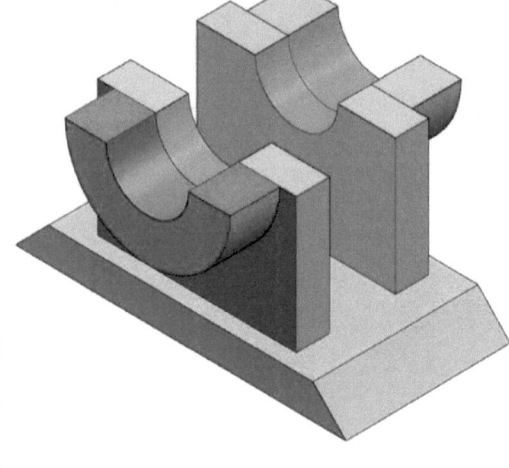

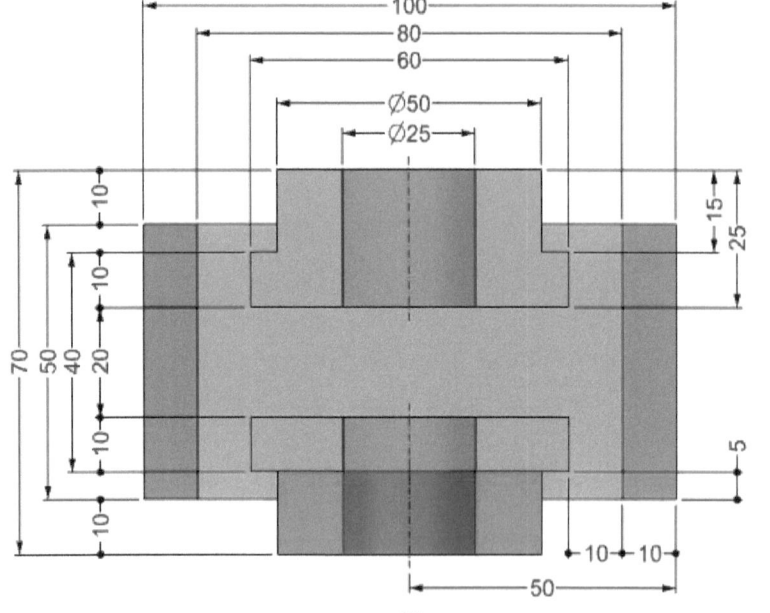

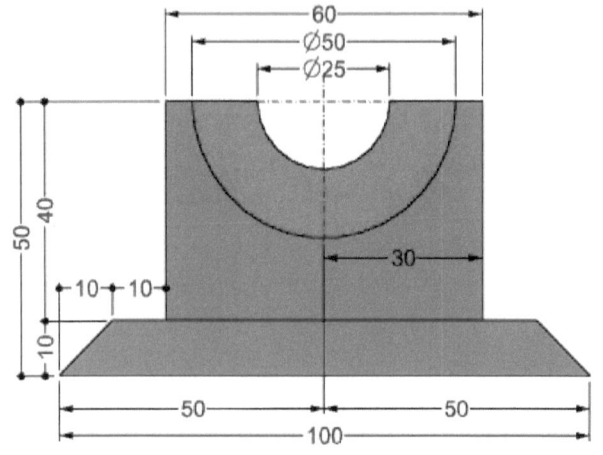
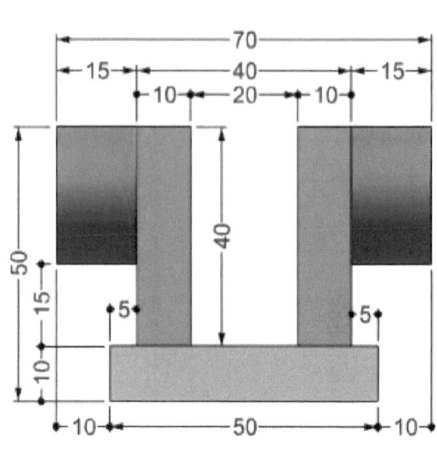

EXERCISE-41

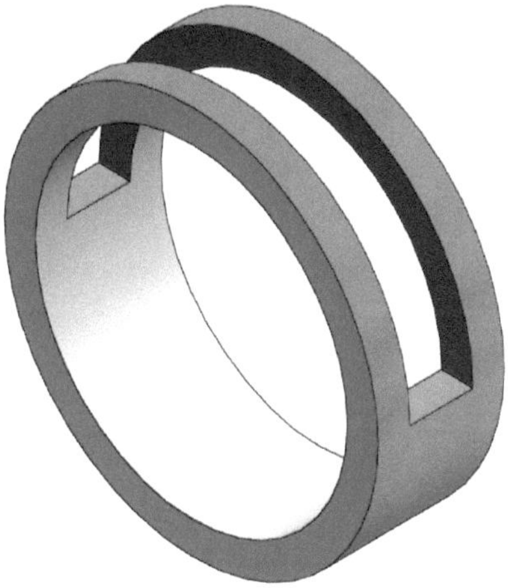

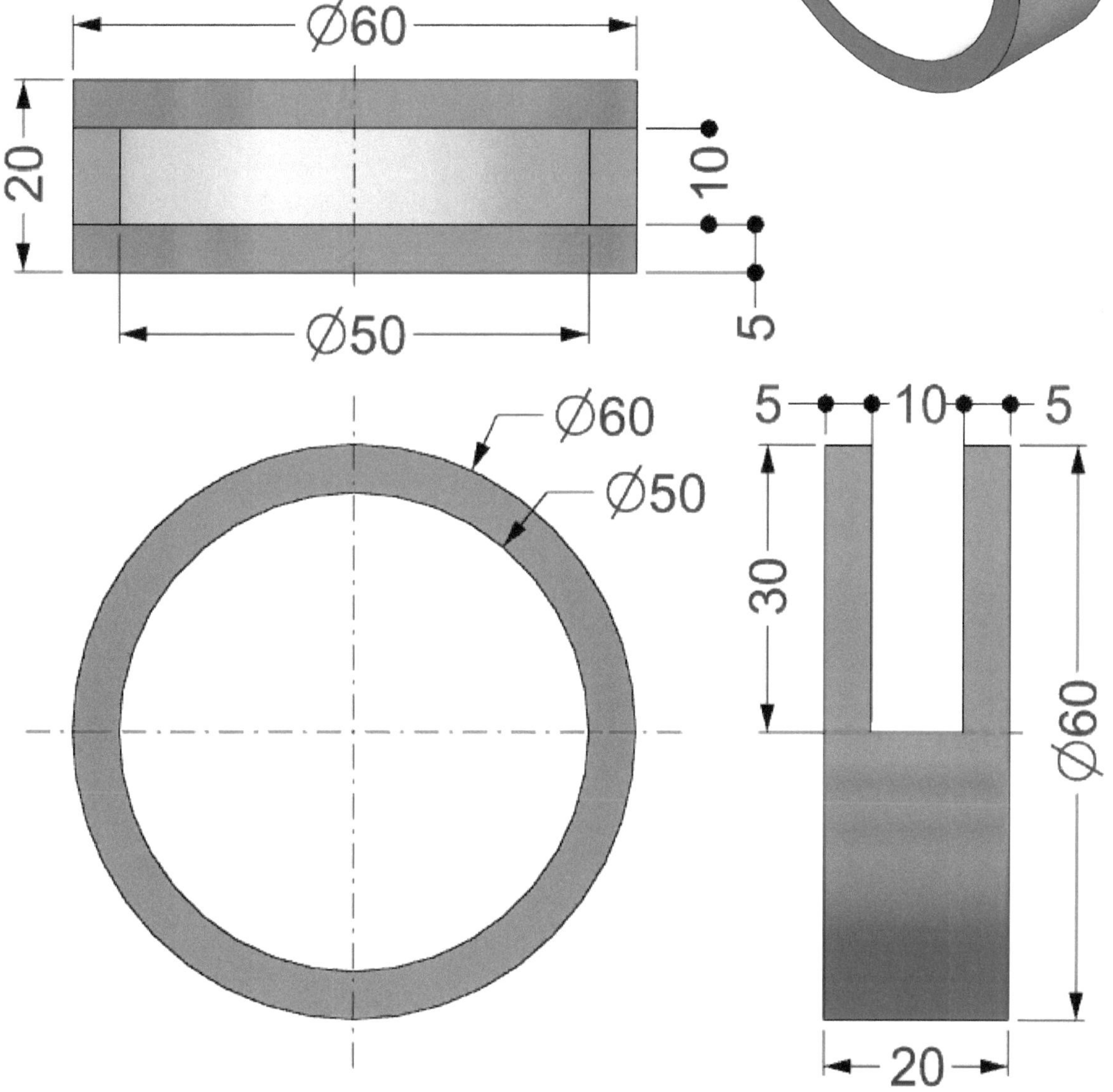

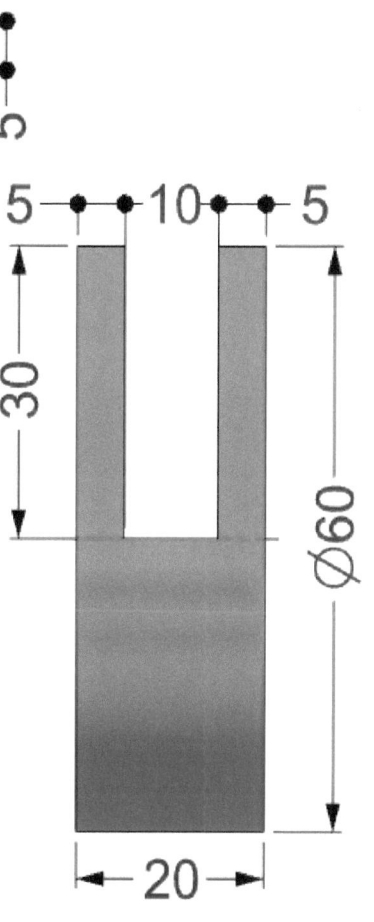

EXERCISE-42

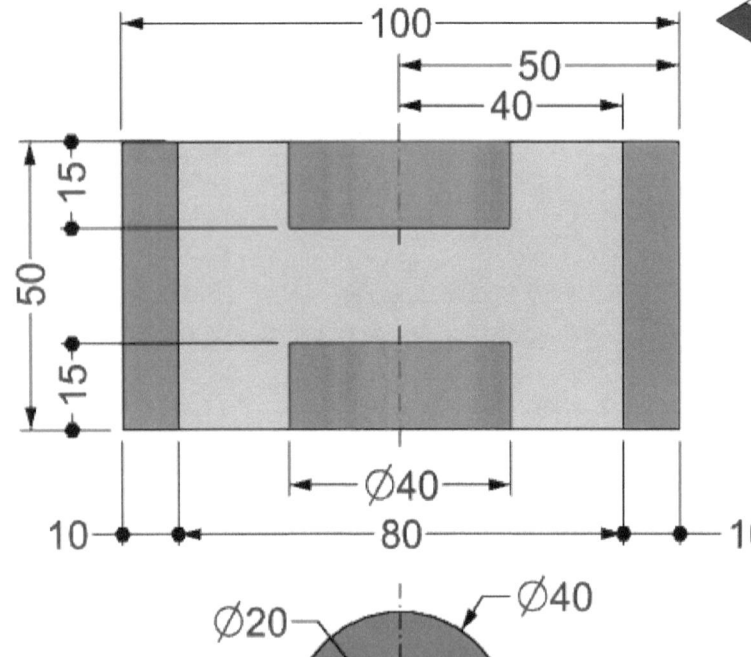

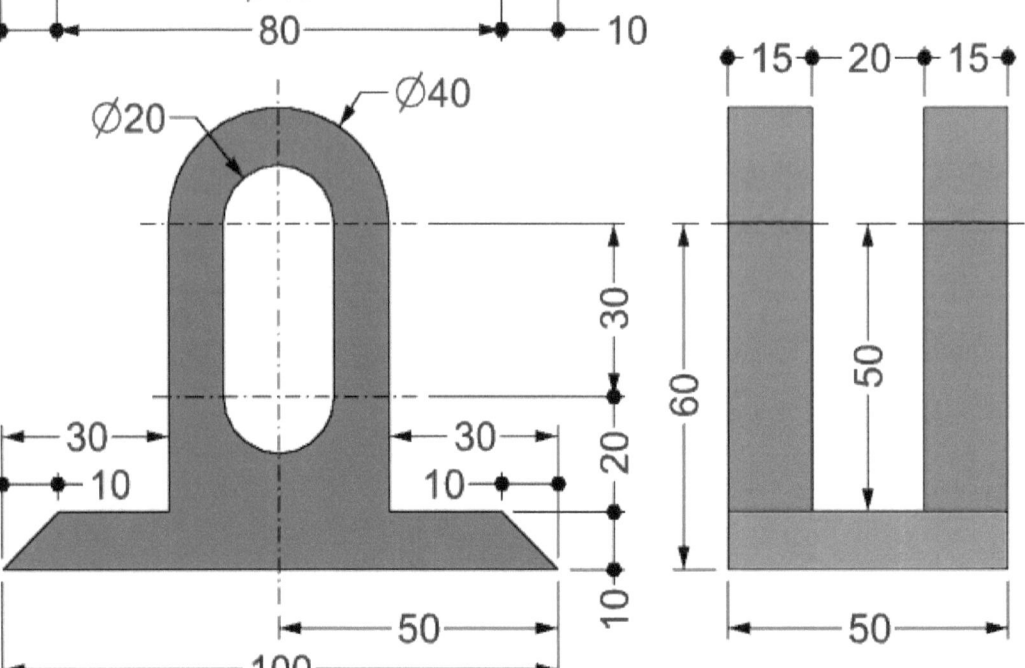

EXERCISE-43

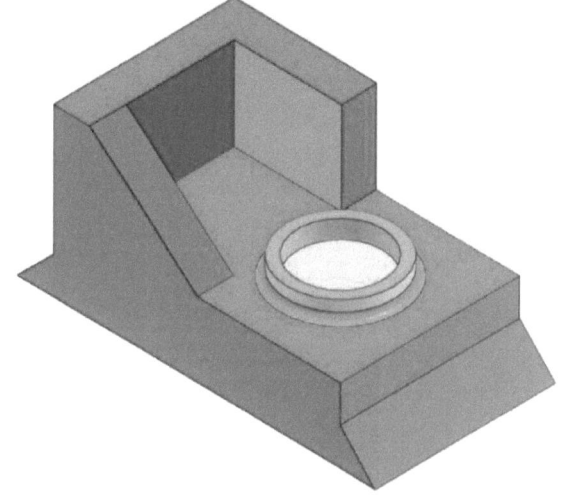
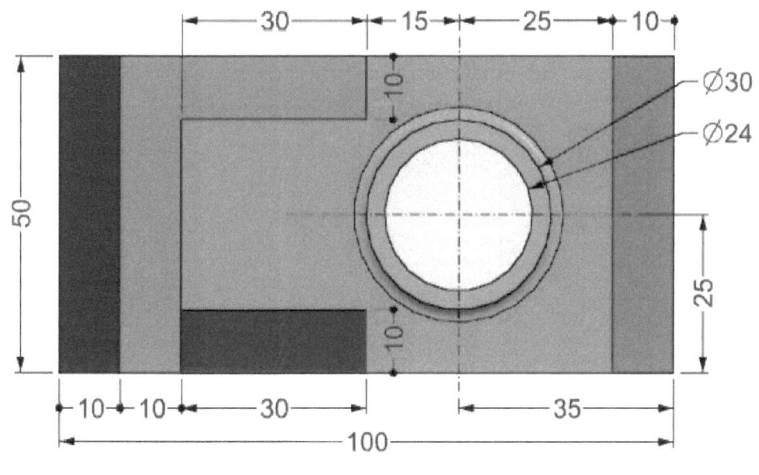
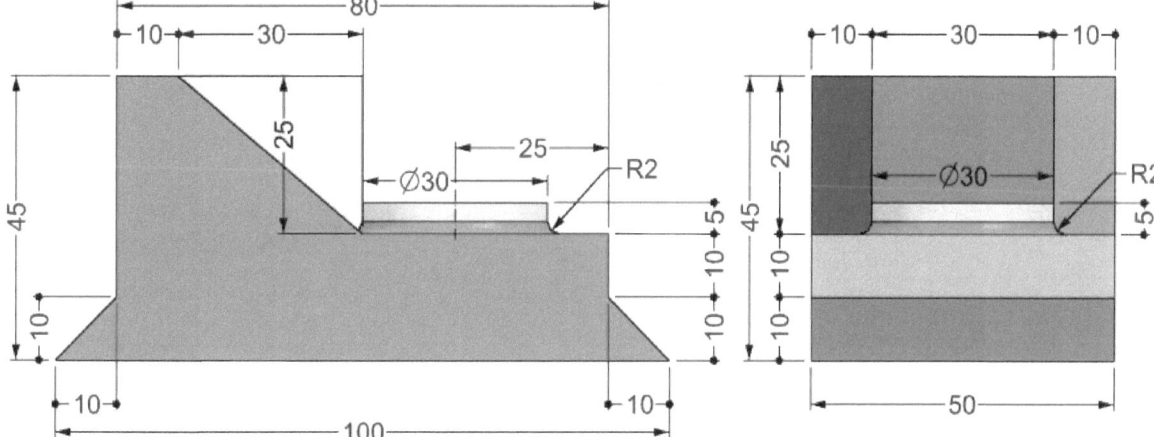

EXERCISE-44

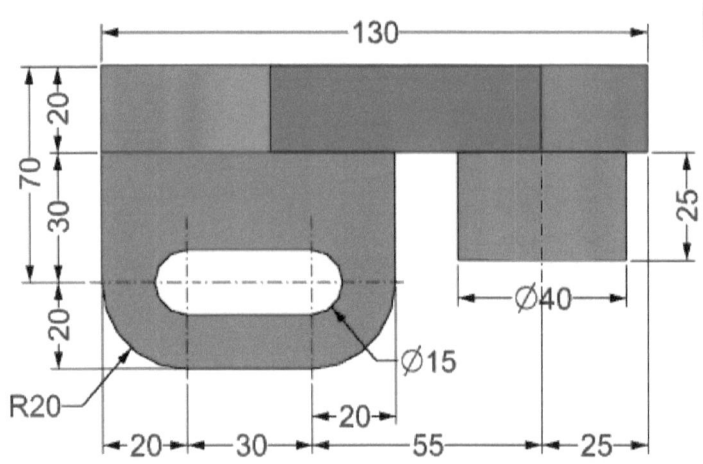

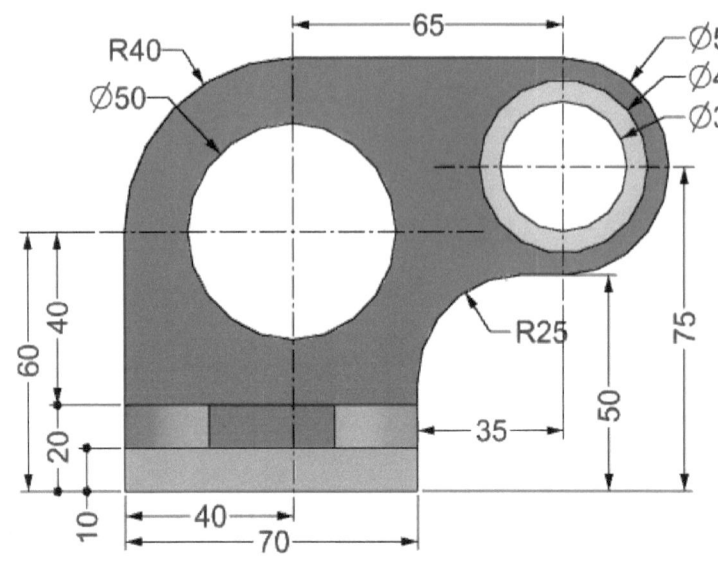

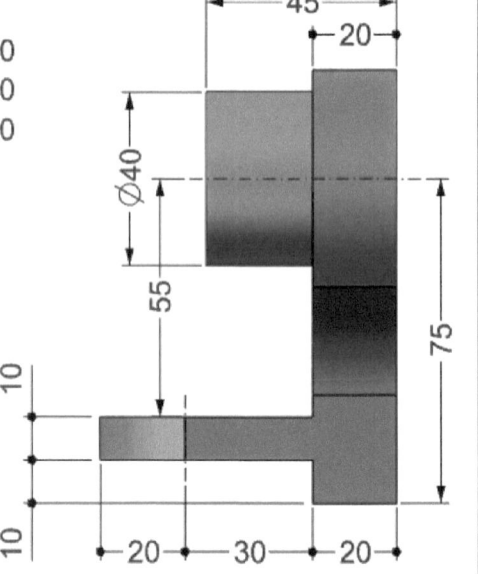

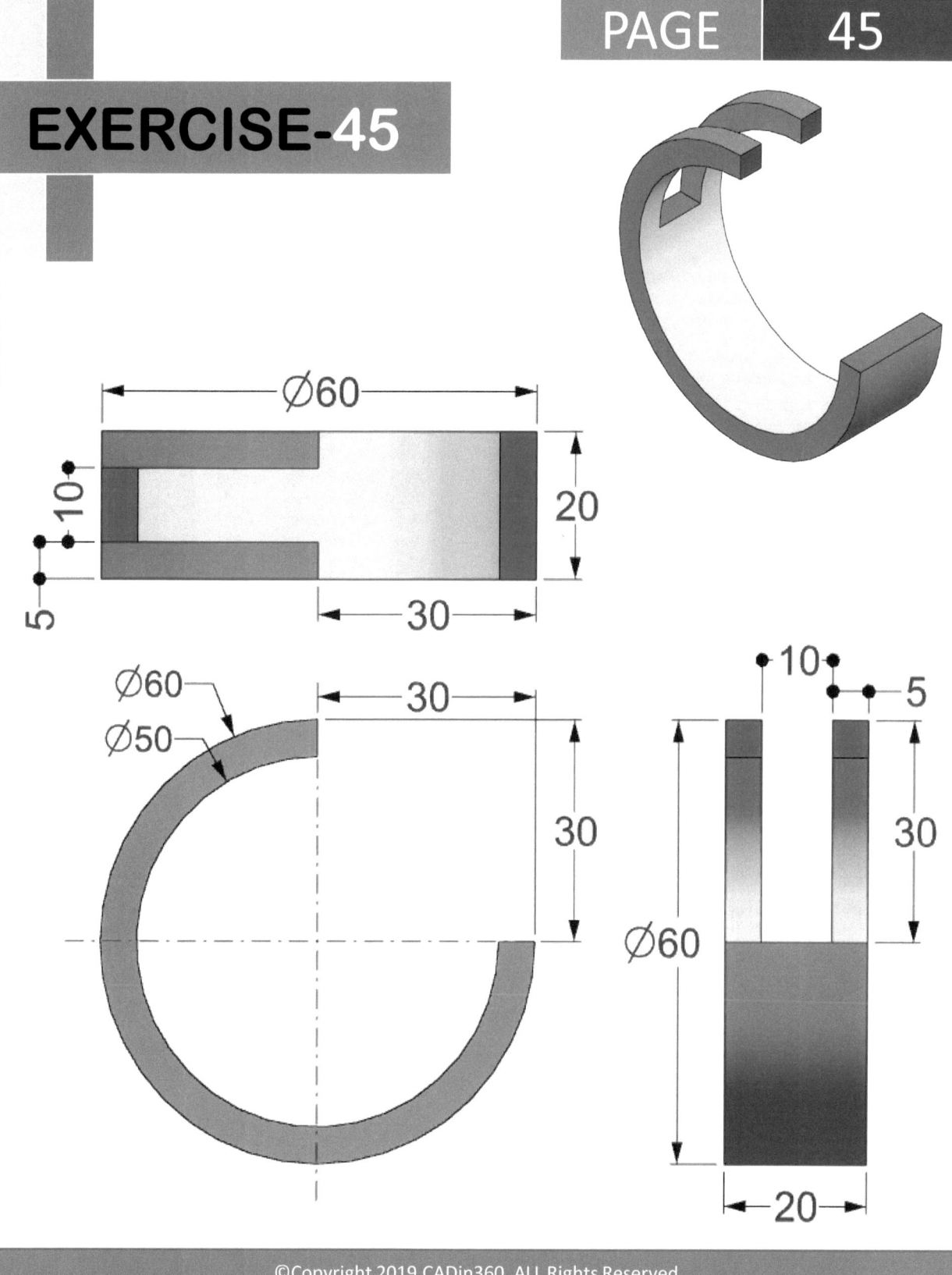

EXERCISE-46

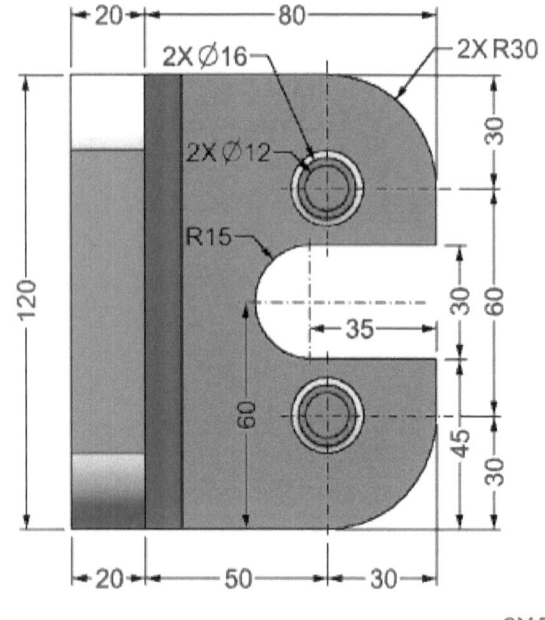
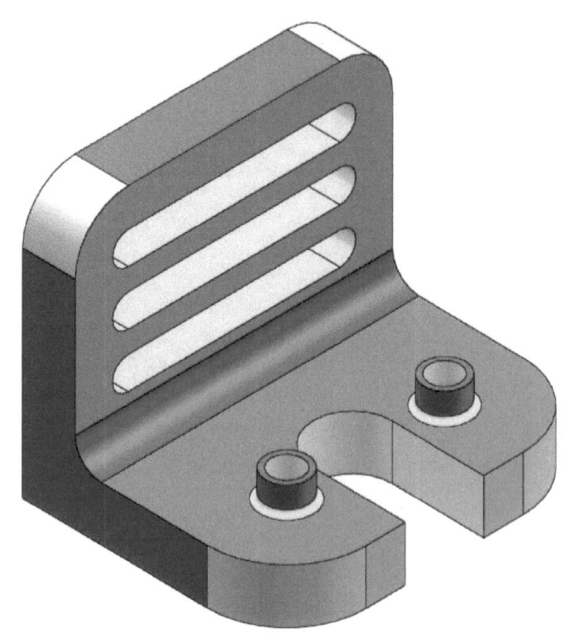
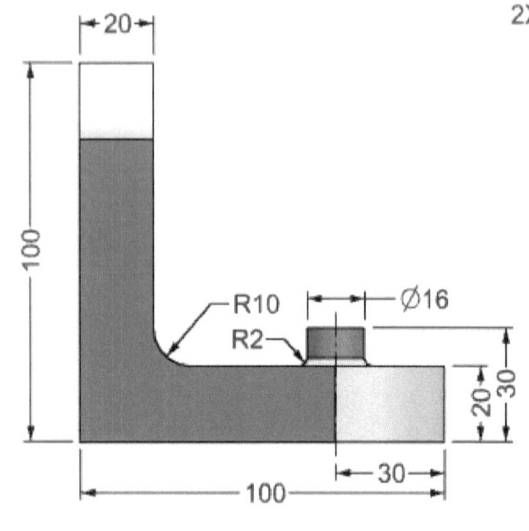
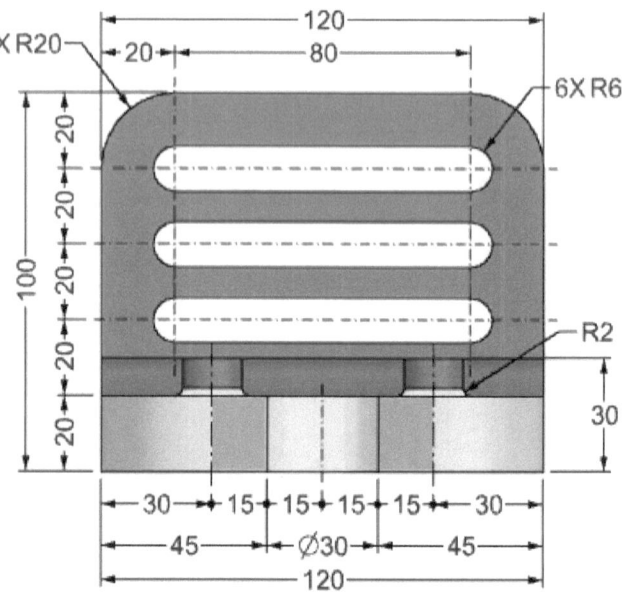

EXERCISE-47

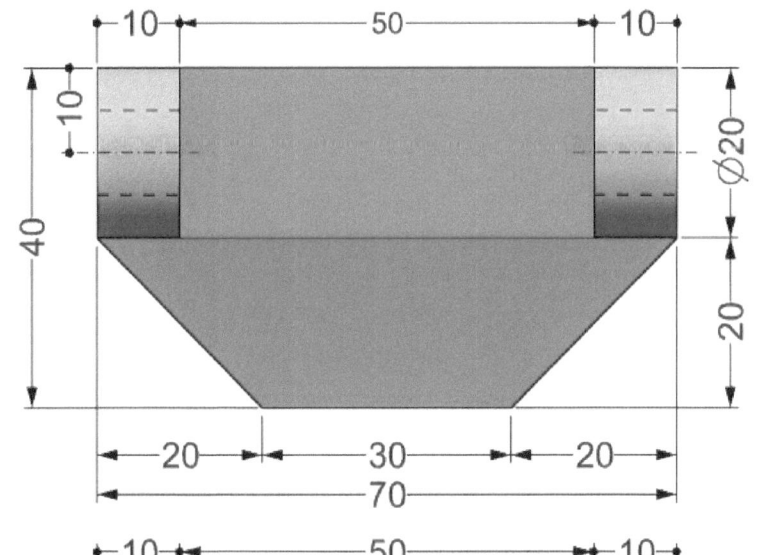
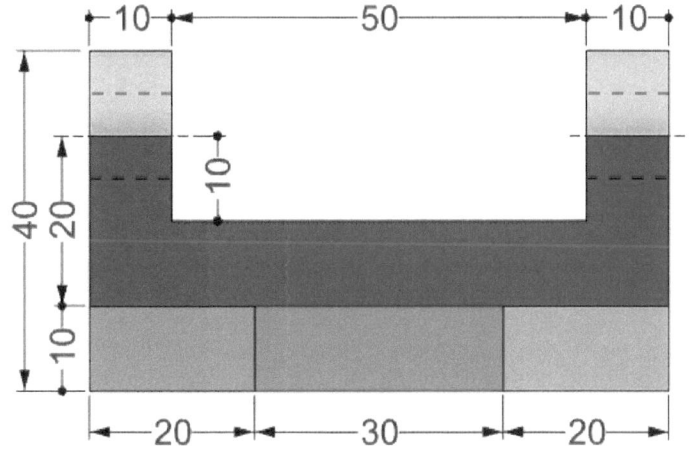
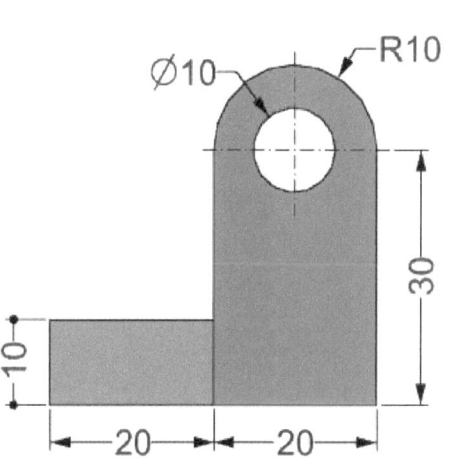

EXERCISE-48

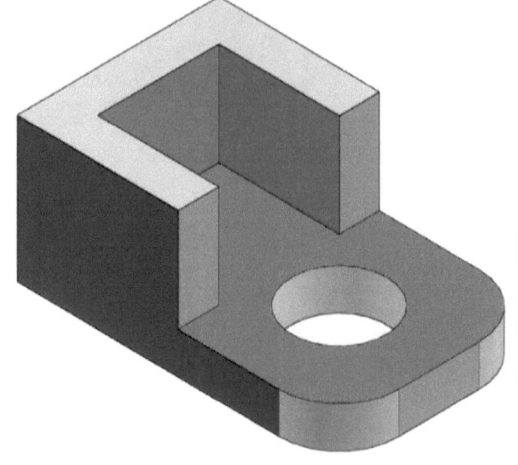

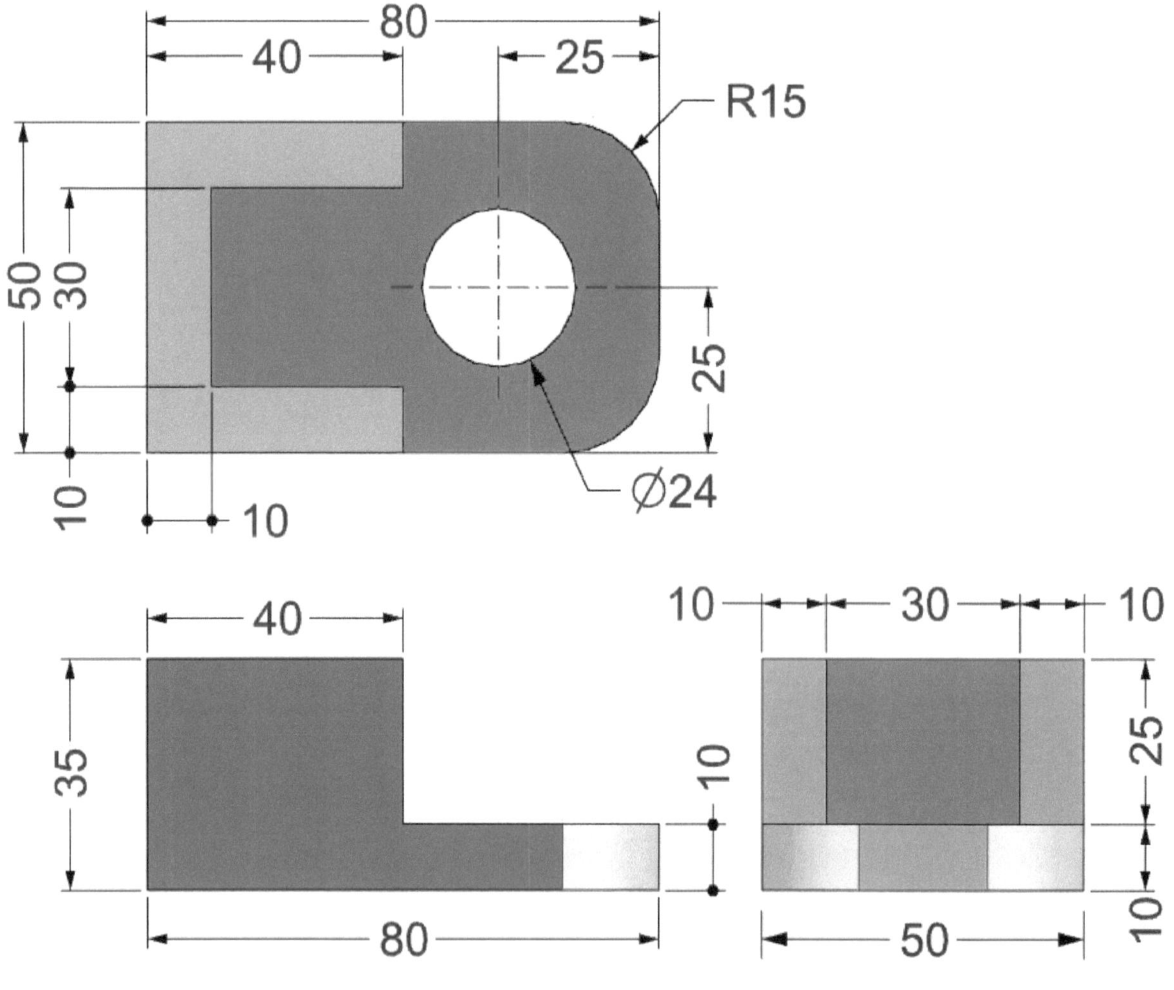

EXERCISE-49

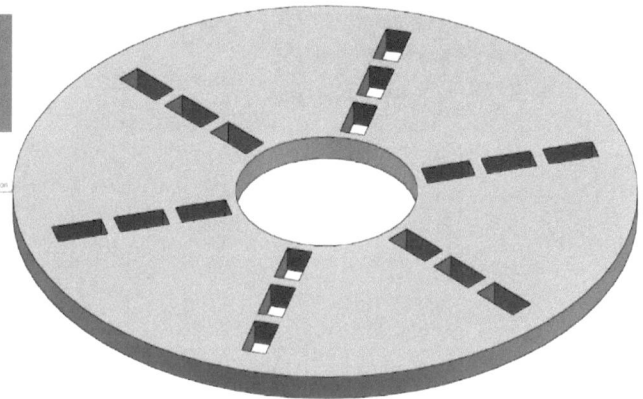

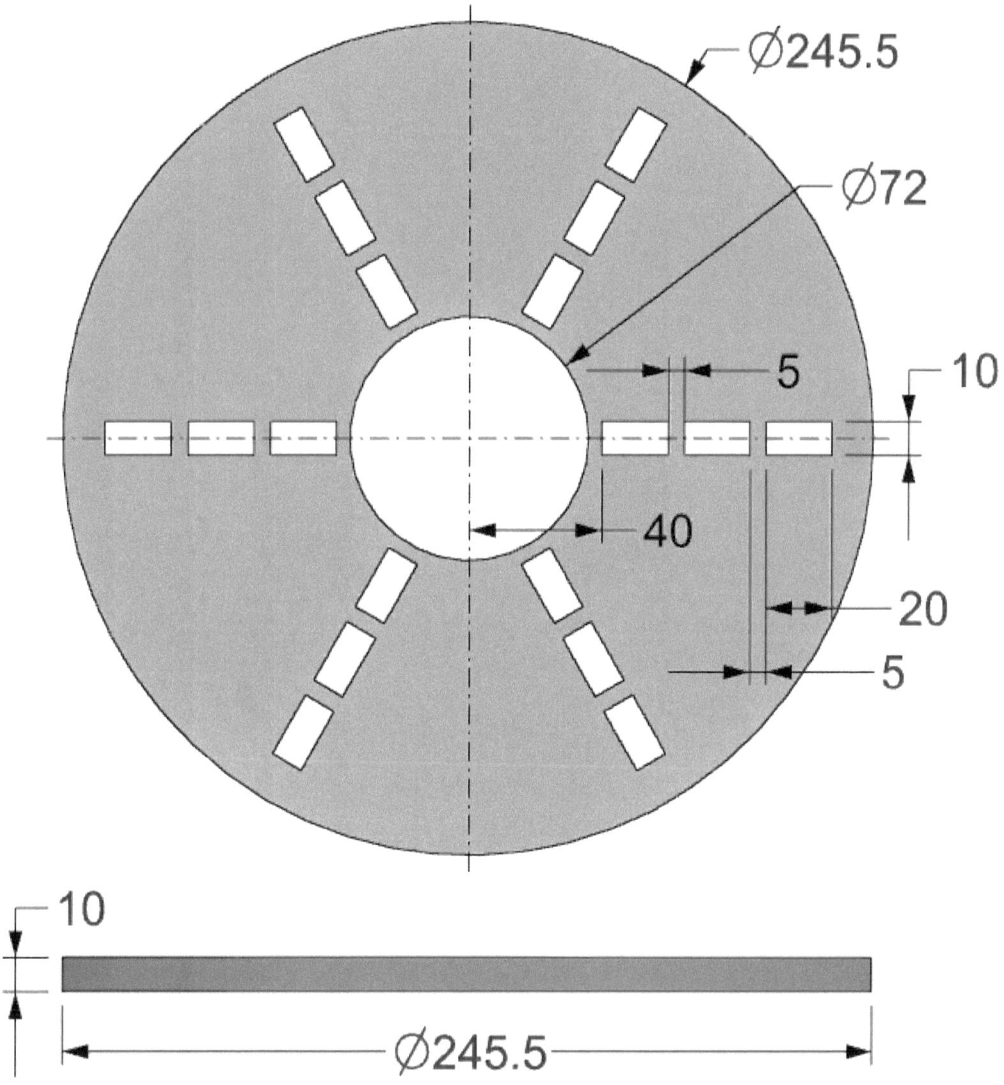

Ø245.5
Ø72
5
10
40
20
5

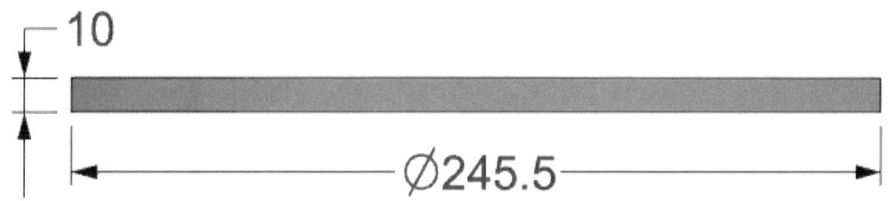

EXERCISE-50

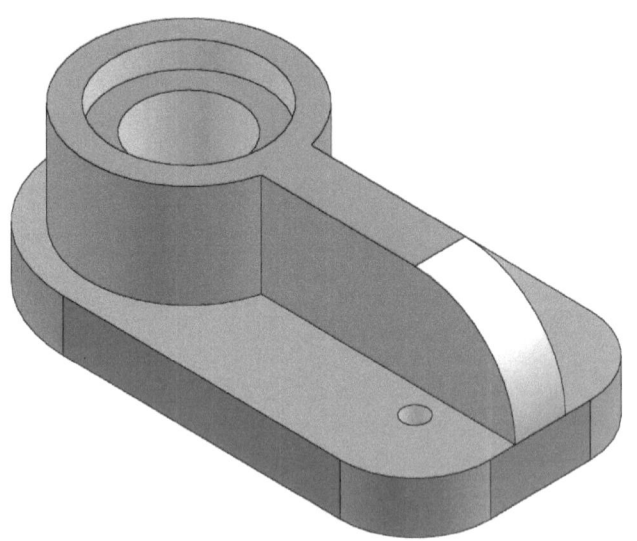

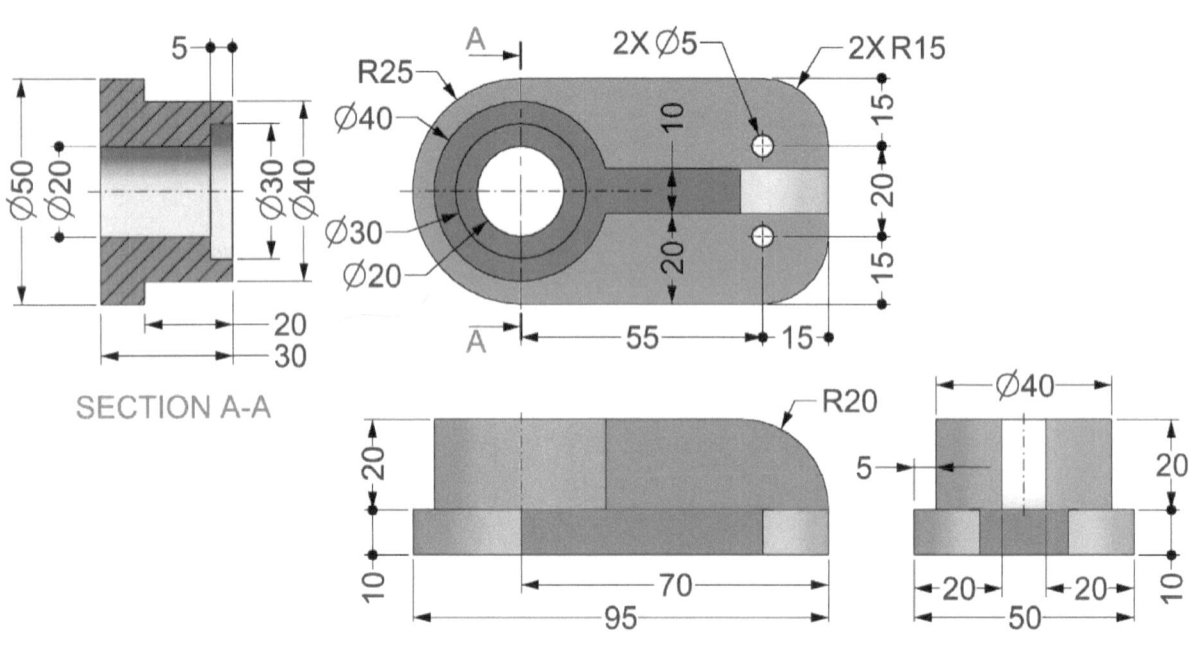

SECTION A-A

EXERCISE-51

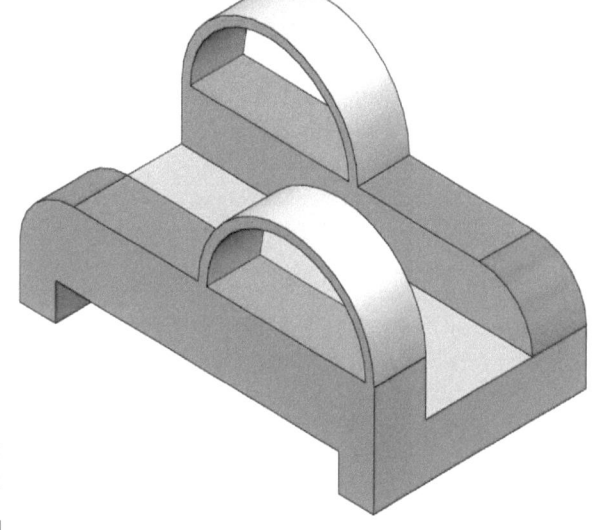

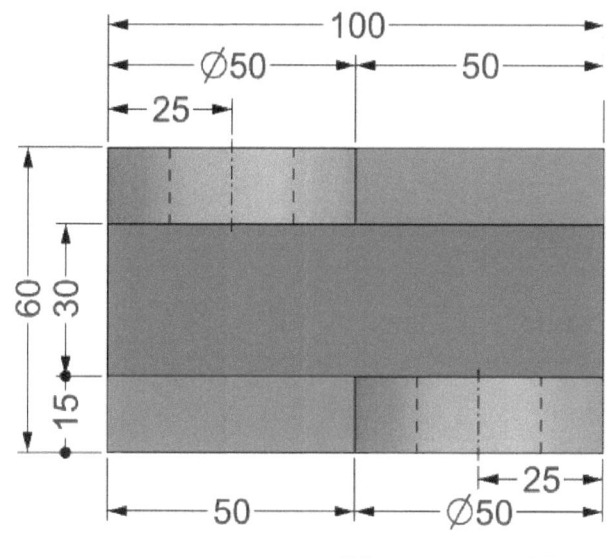

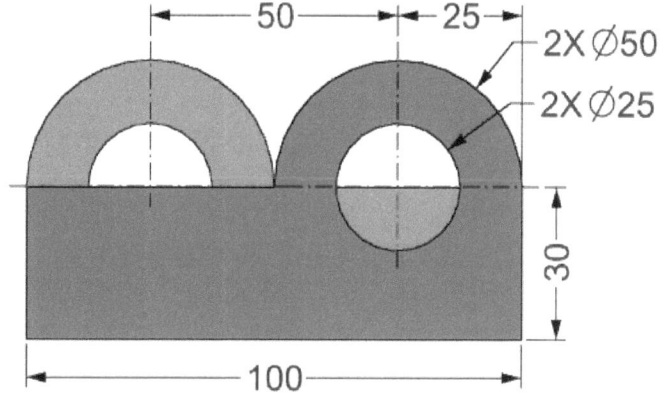

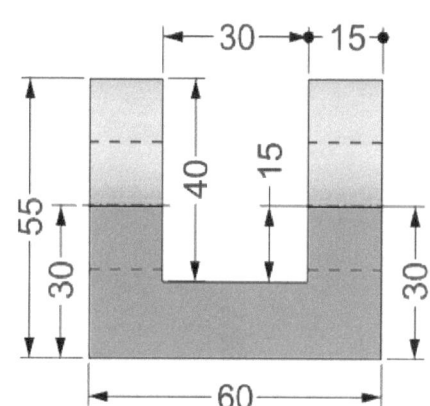

EXERCISE-52

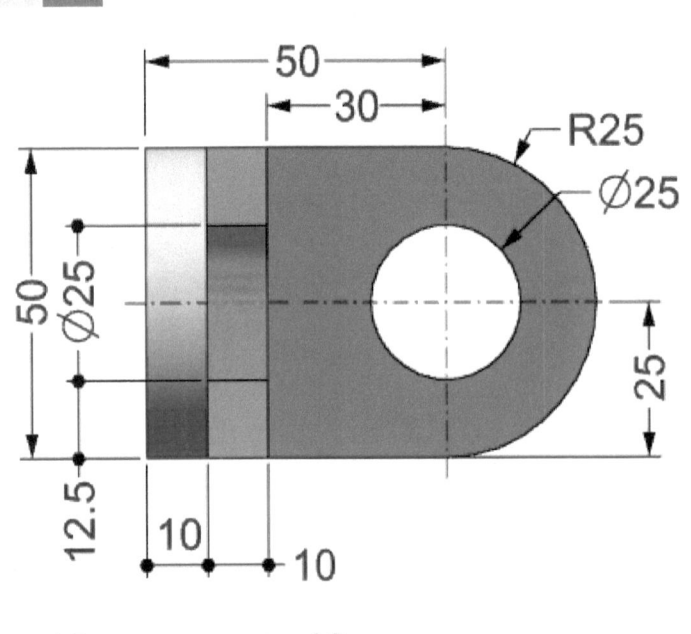
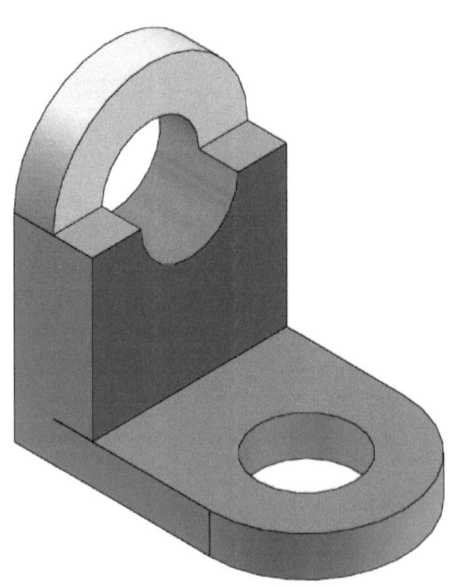
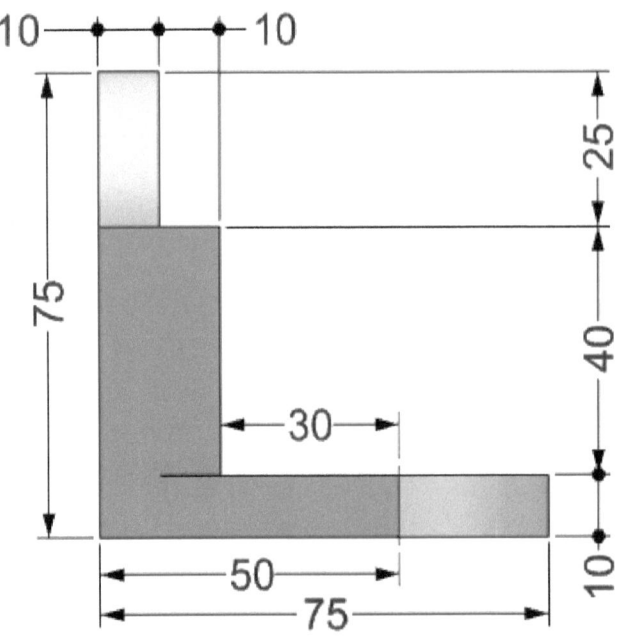
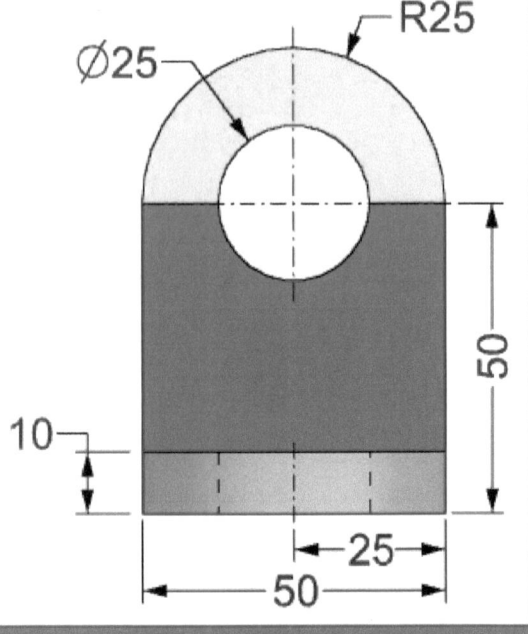

EXERCISE-53

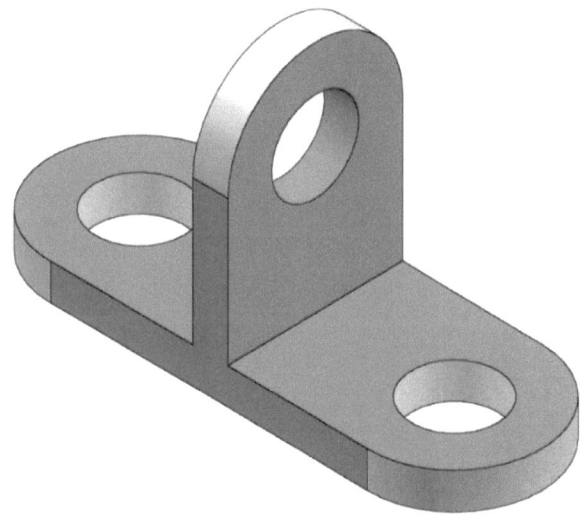

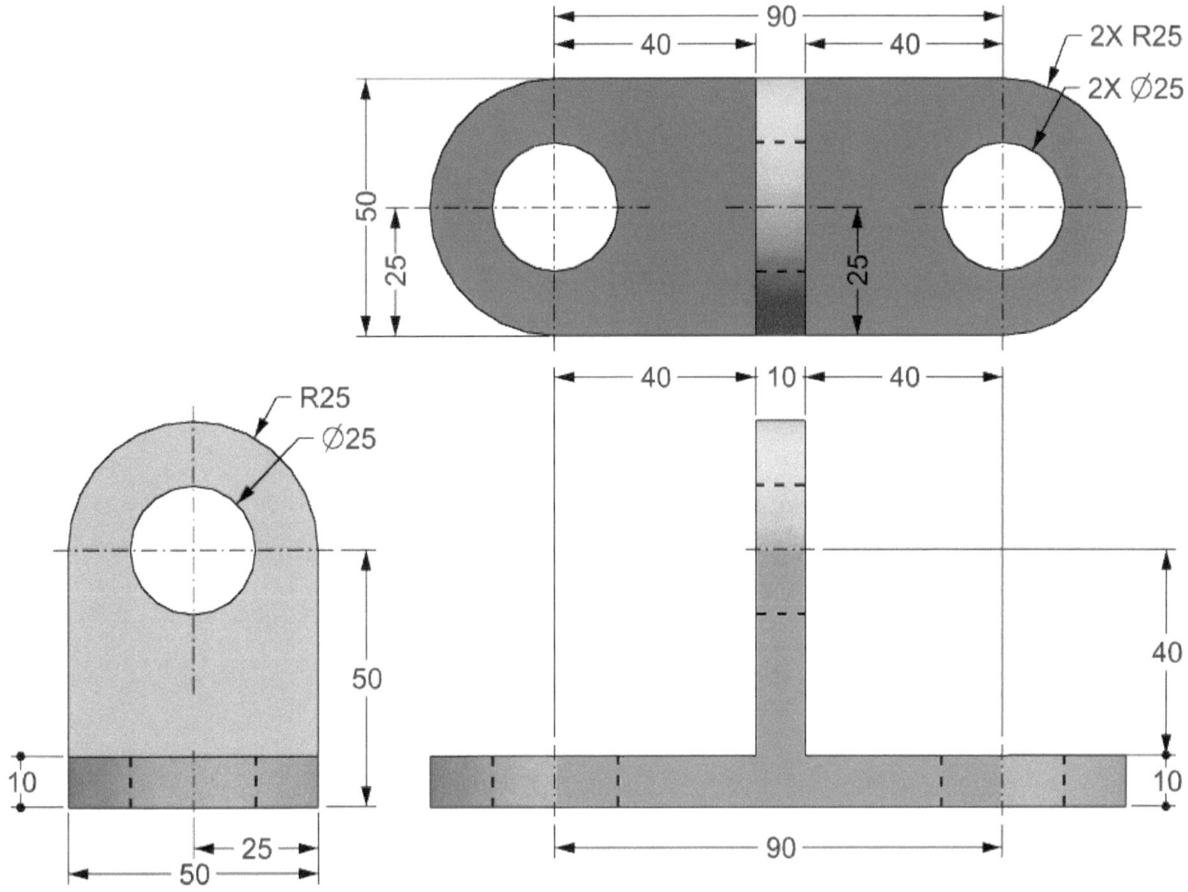

EXERCISE-54

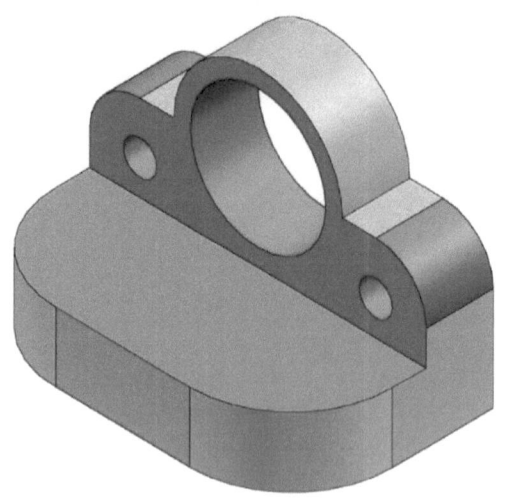
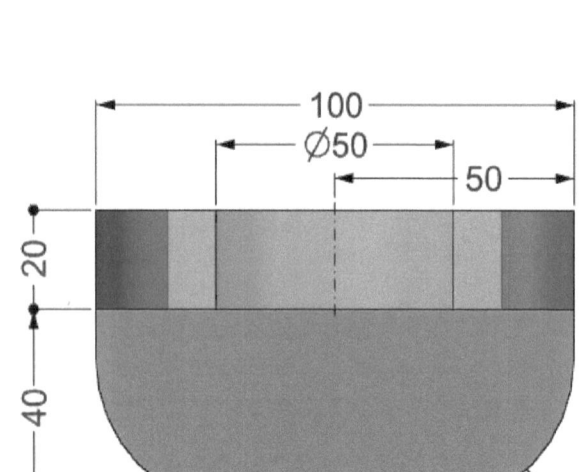
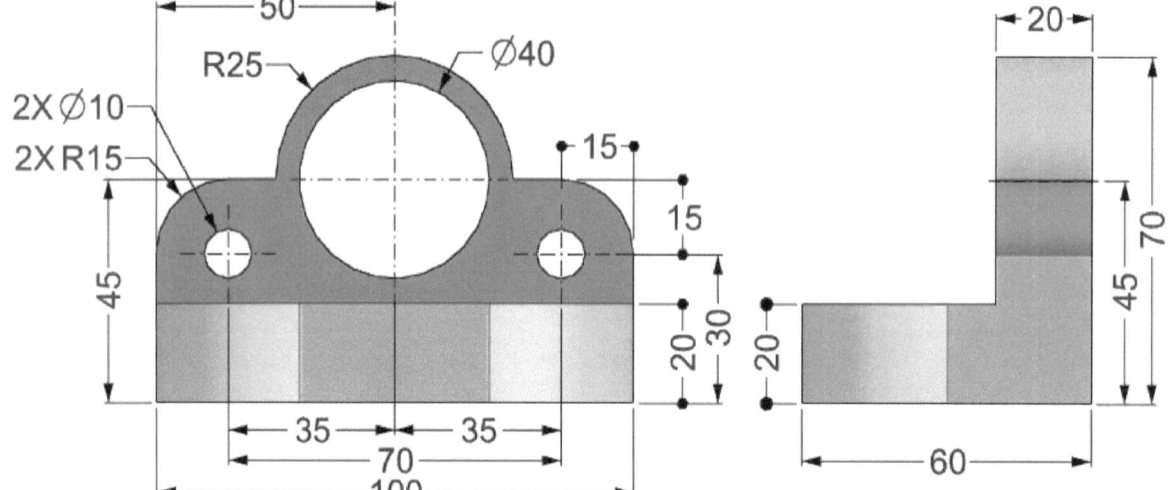

EXERCISE-55

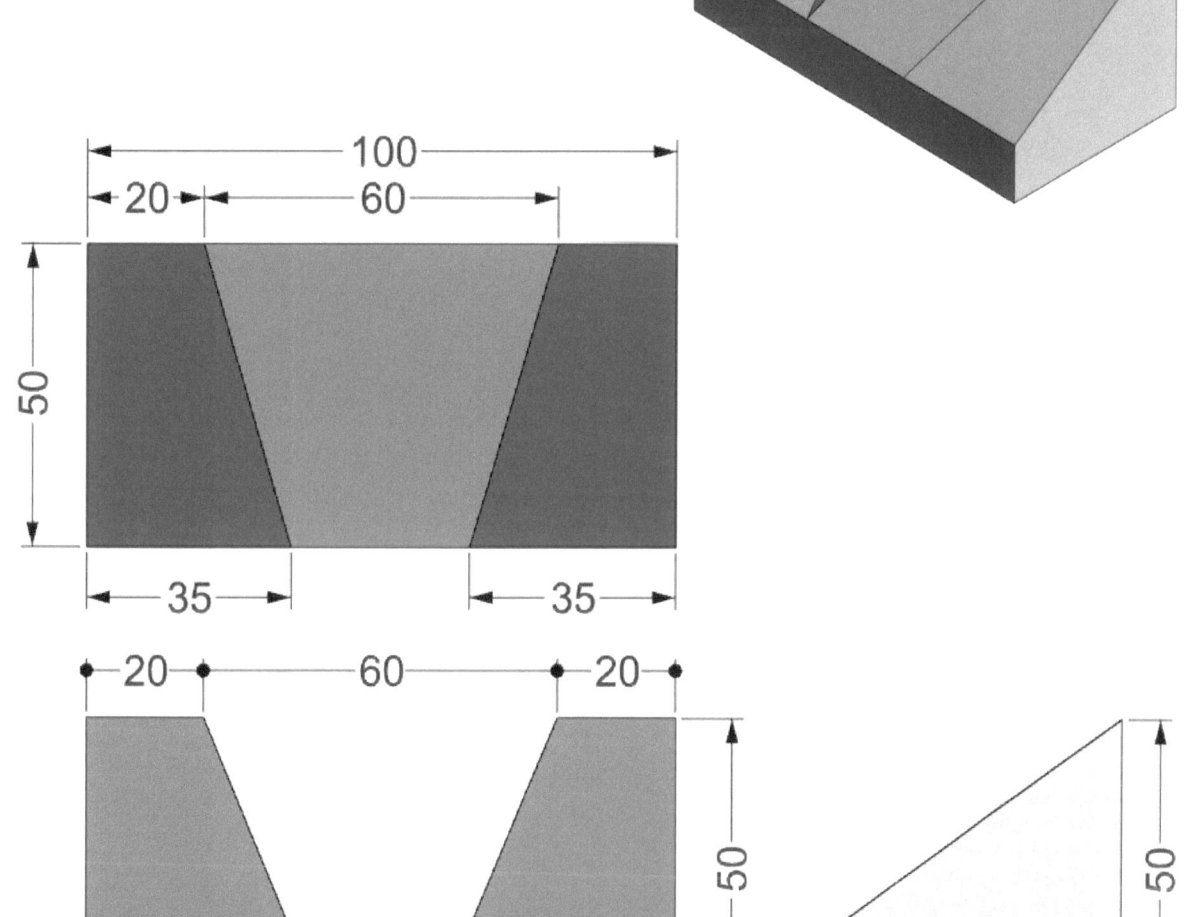

EXERCISE-56

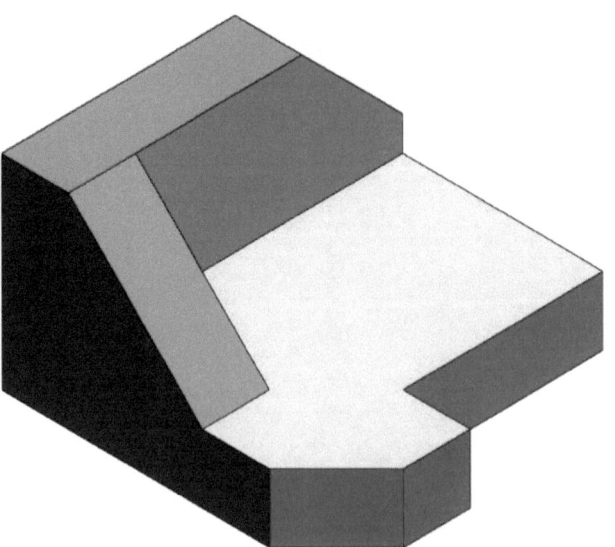
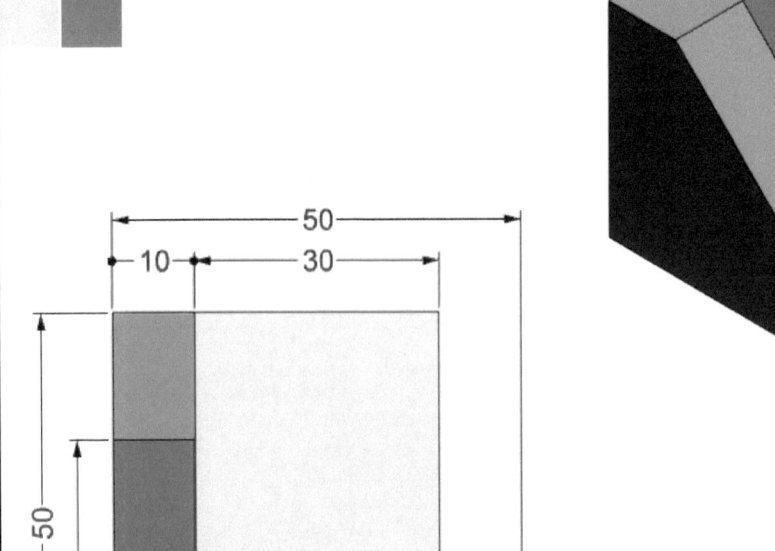
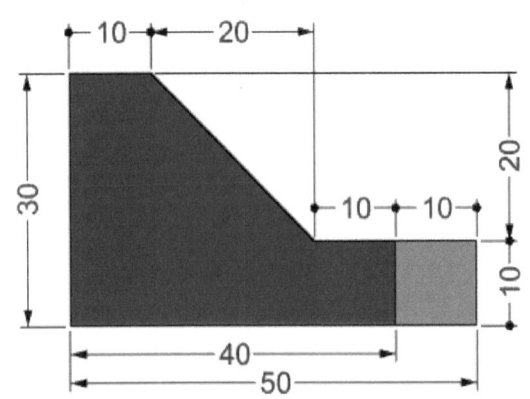
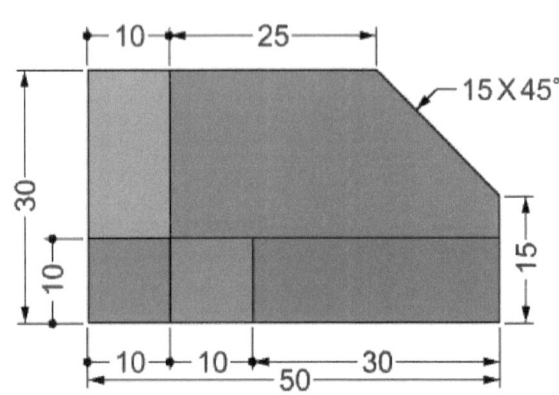

EXERCISE-57

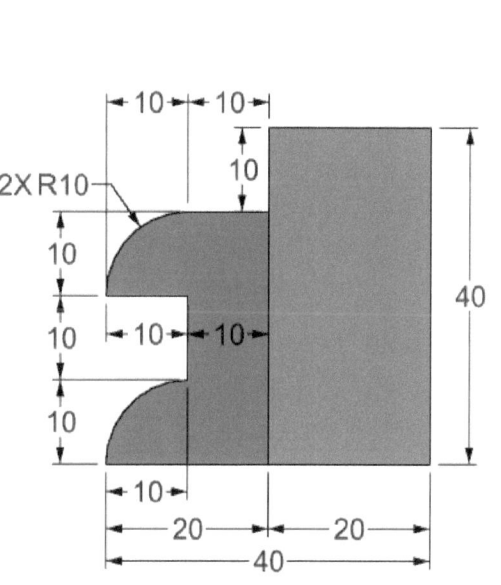

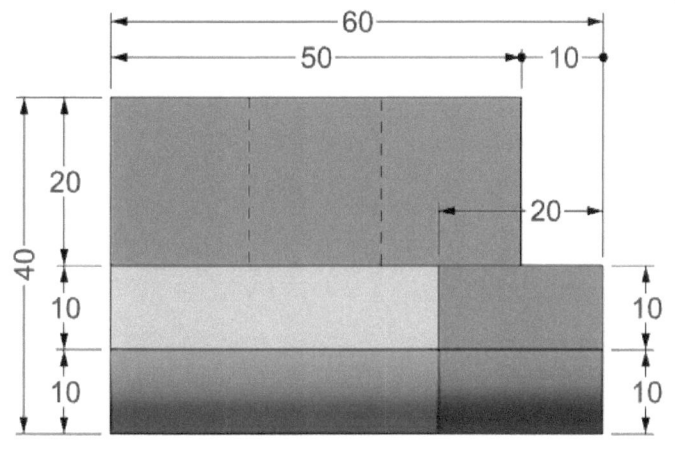

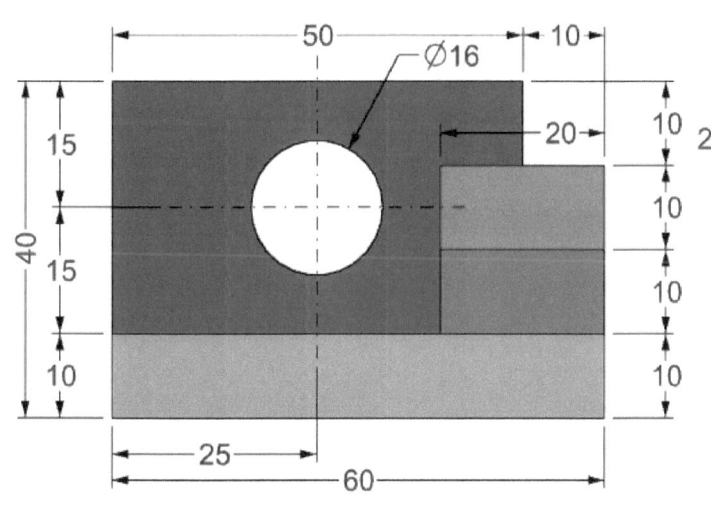

EXERCISE-58

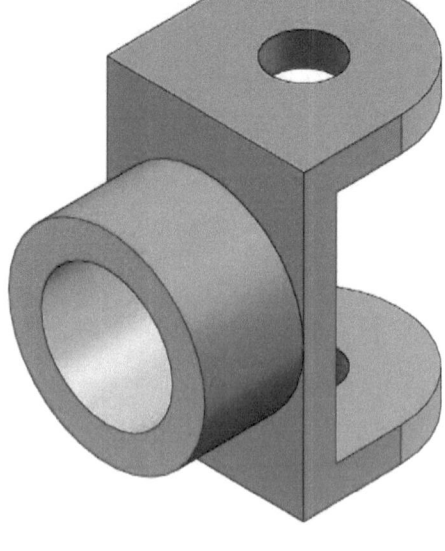
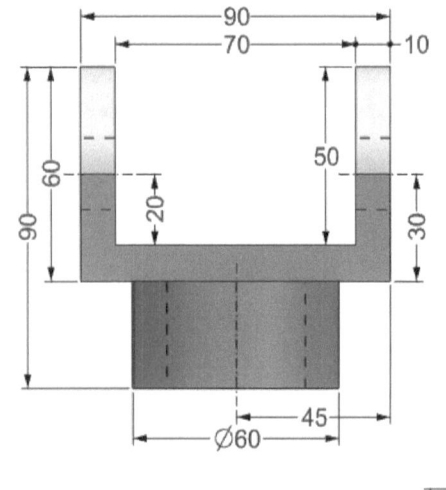
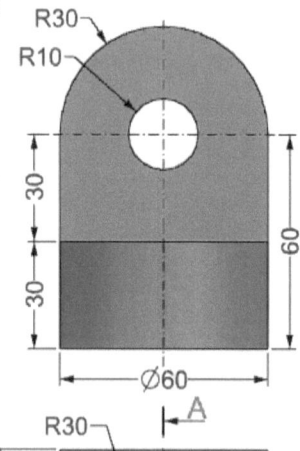
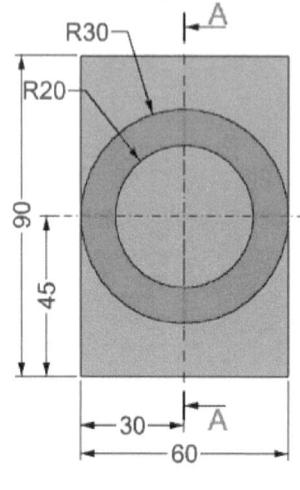
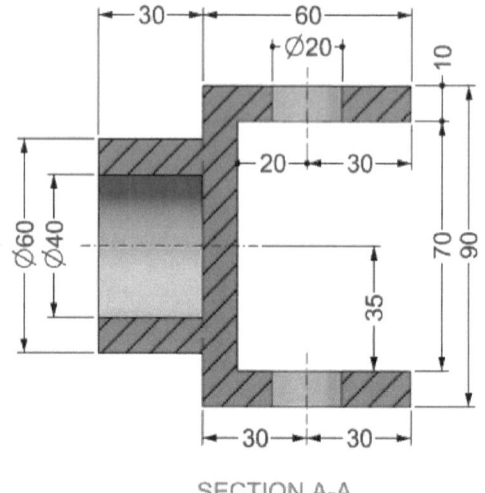

SECTION A-A

EXERCISE-59

EXERCISE-60

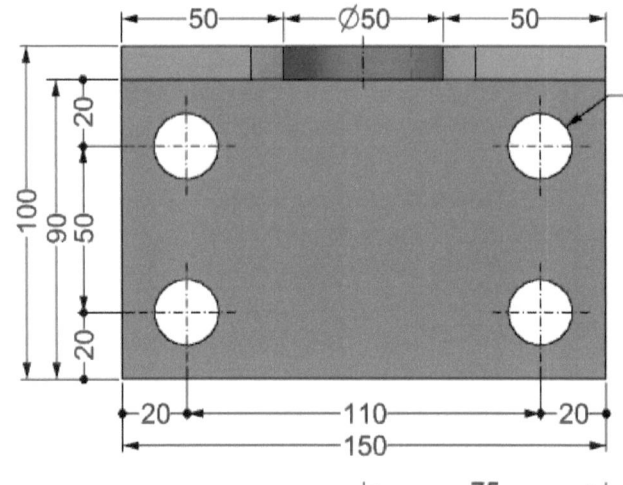
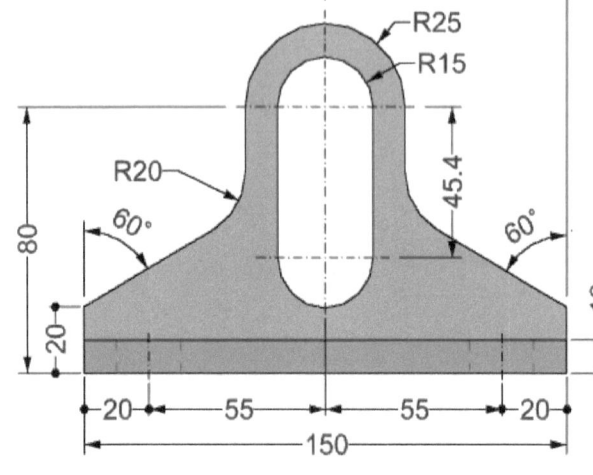
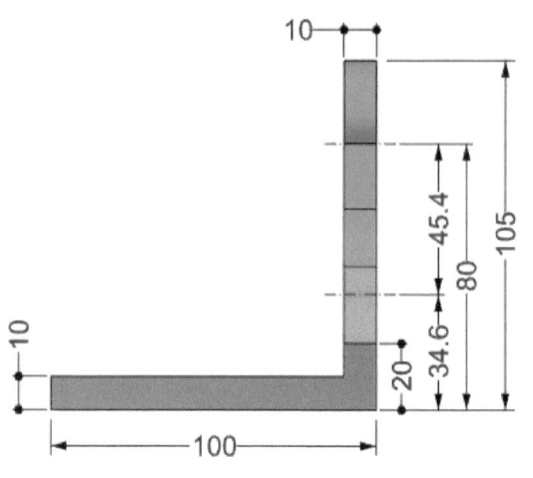

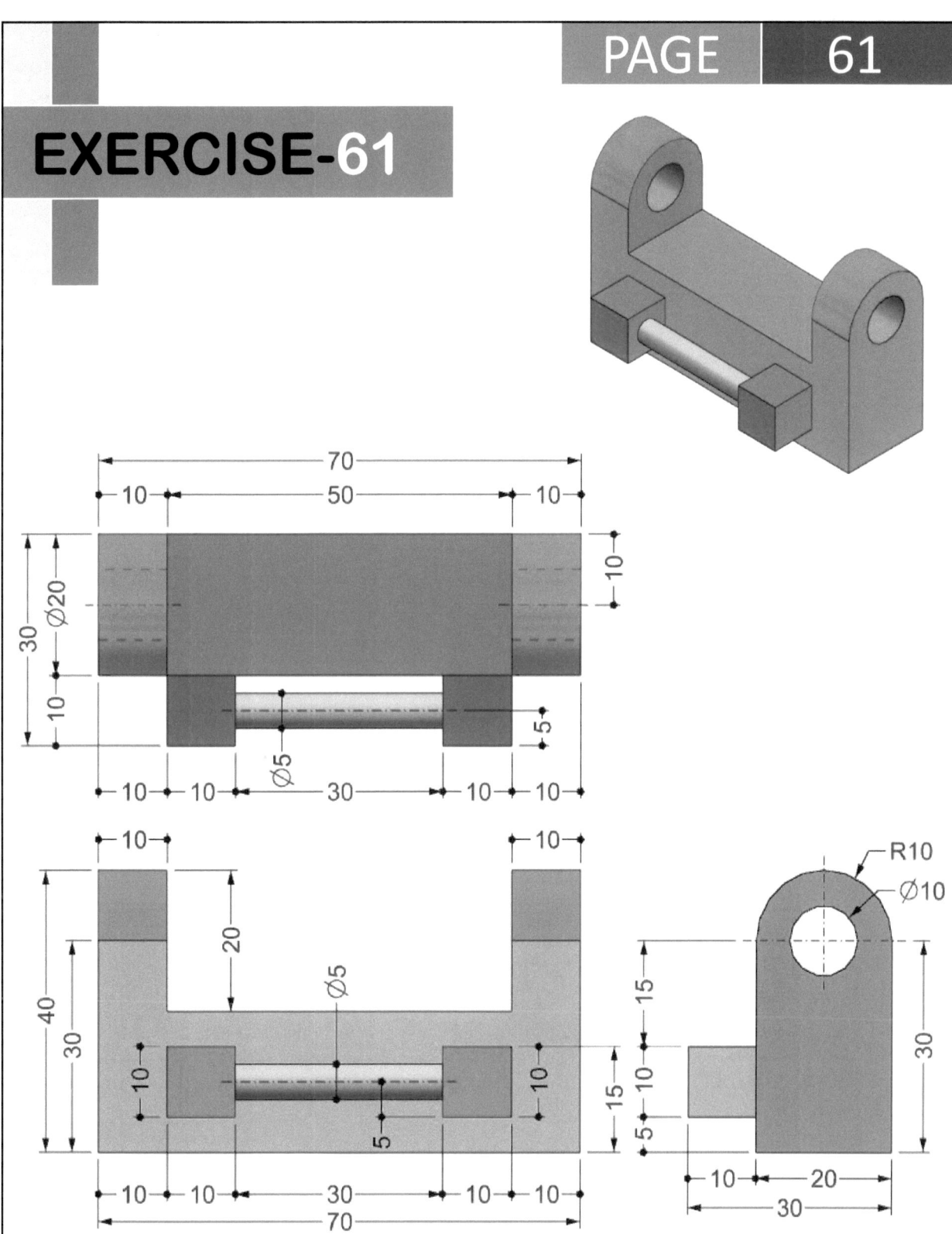

EXERCISE-62

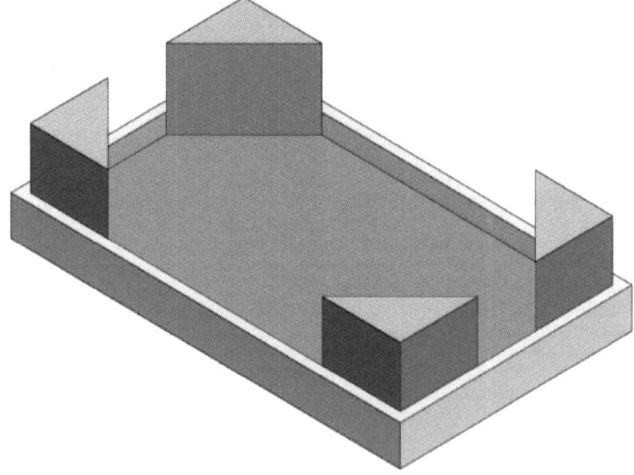

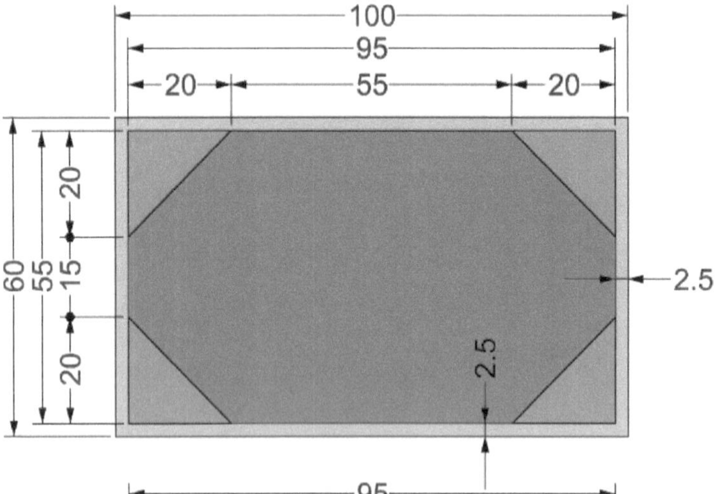
100
95
20
55
20
60
55
20
15
20
2.5
2.5

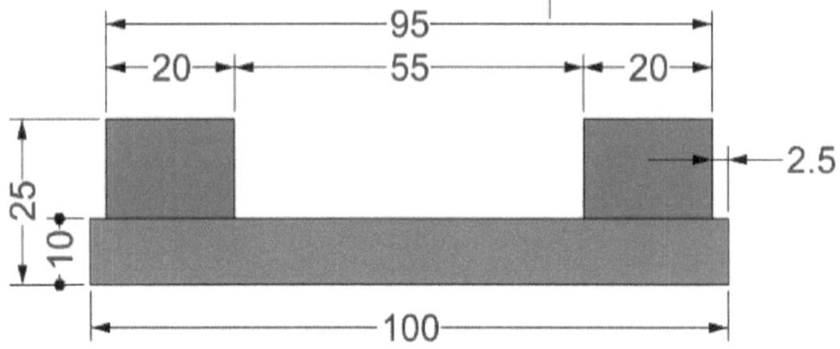
95
20
55
20
2.5
25
10
100

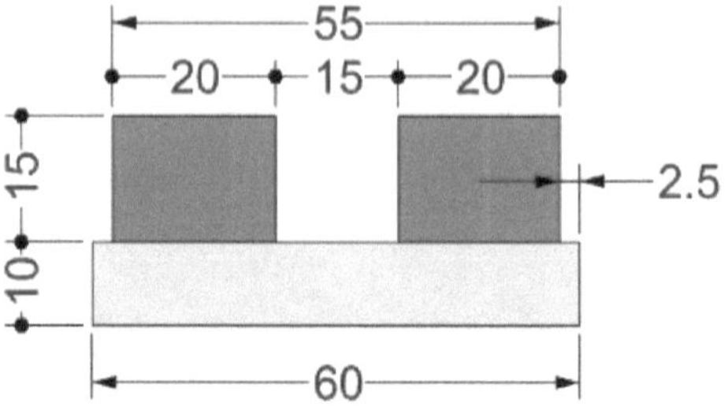
55
20
15
20
15
10
2.5
60

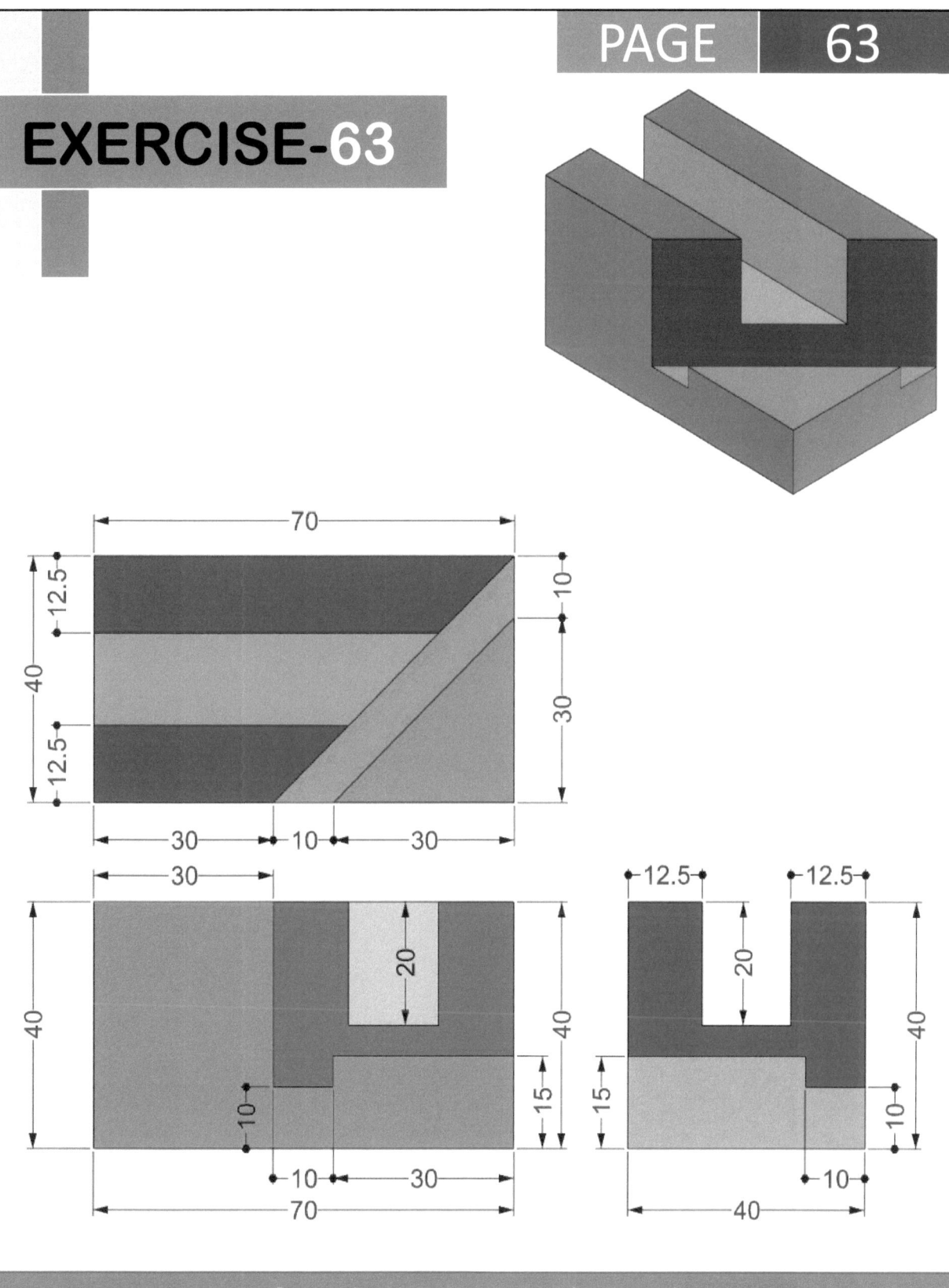

EXERCISE-64

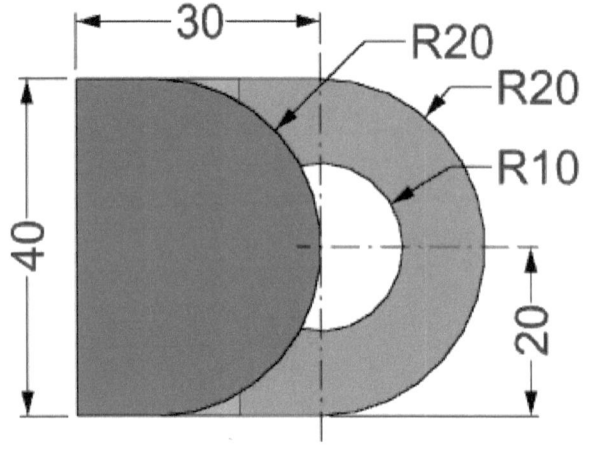
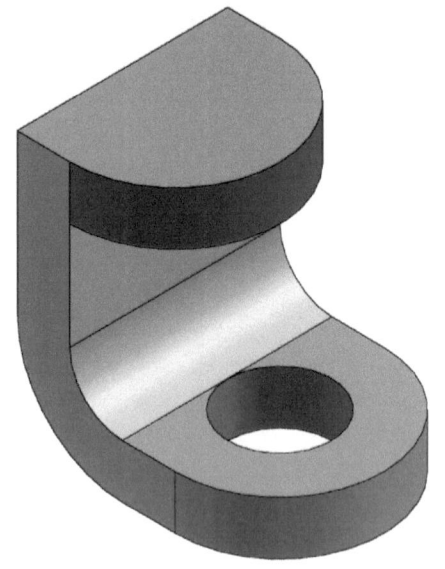
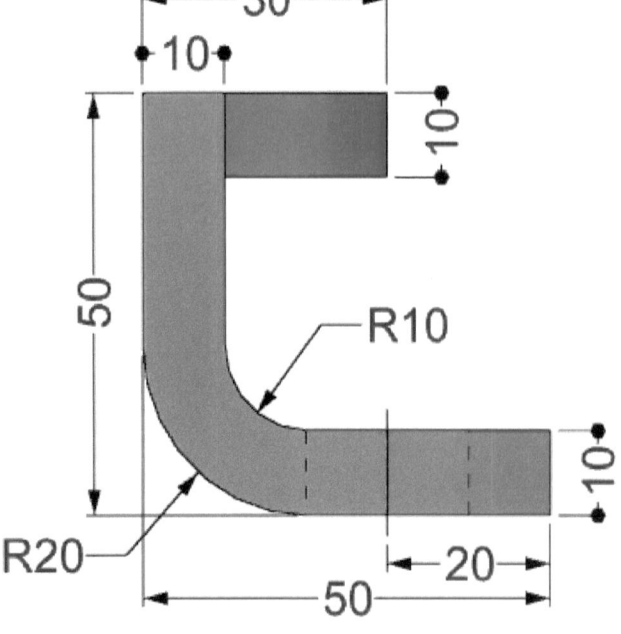
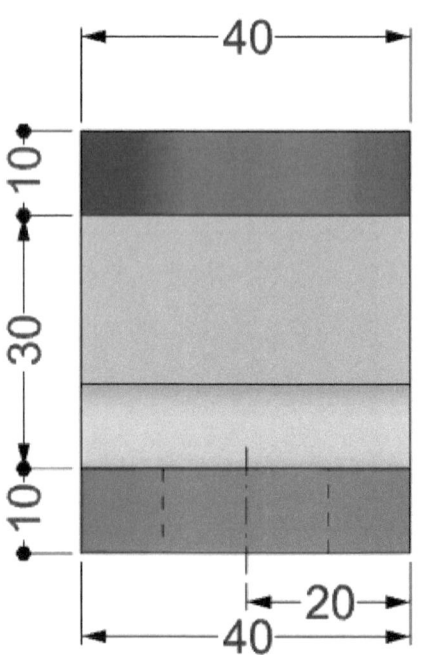

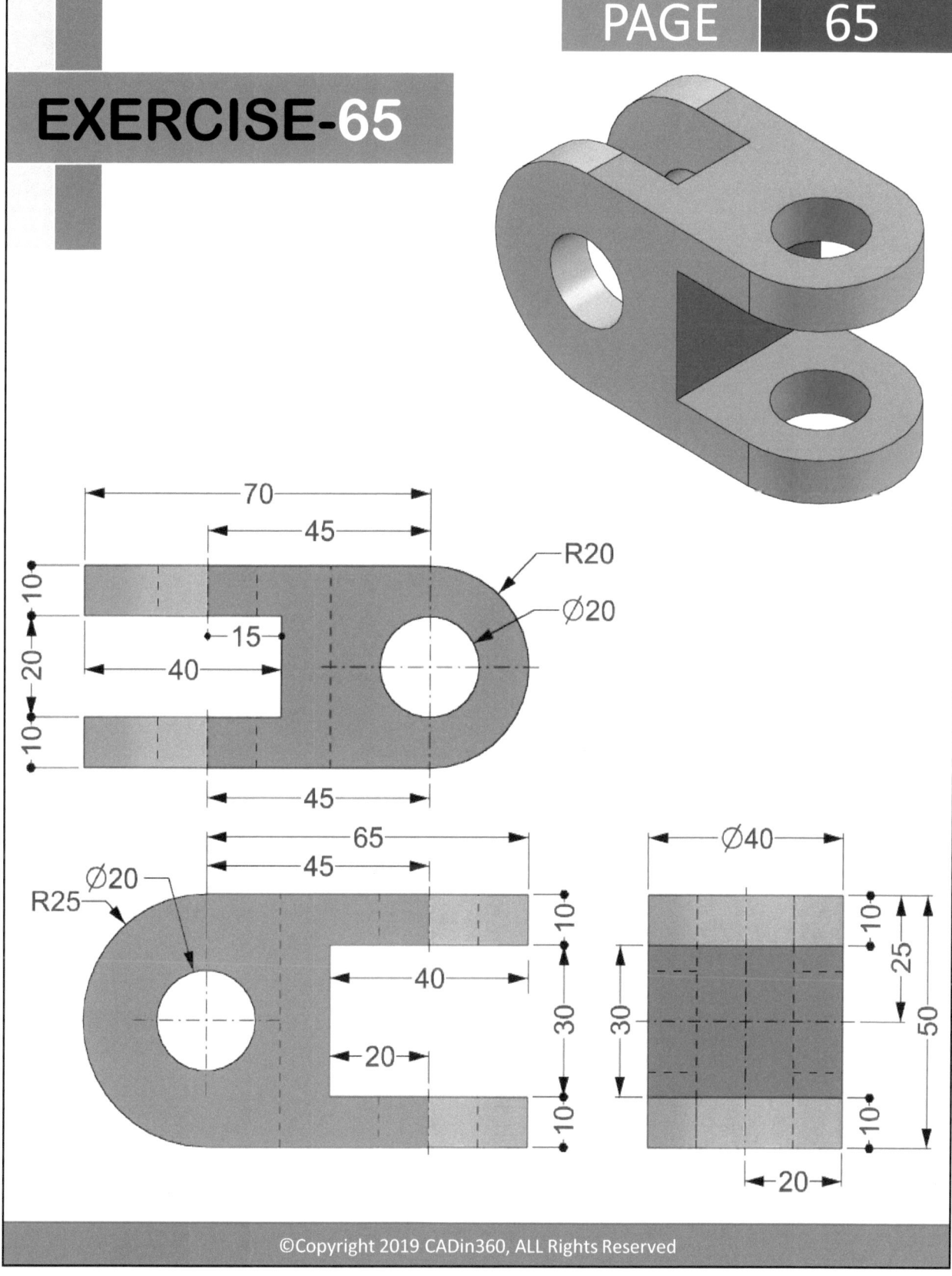

EXERCISE-66

EXERCISE-67

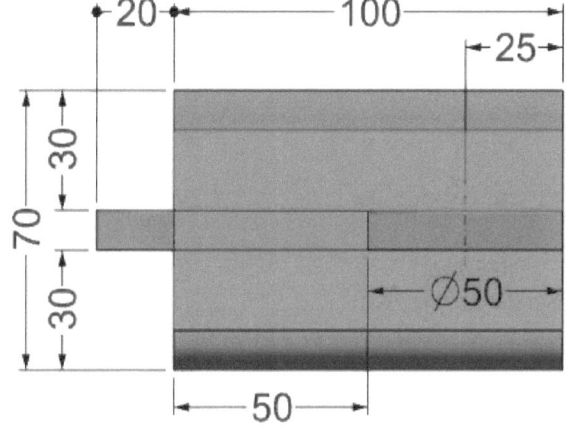
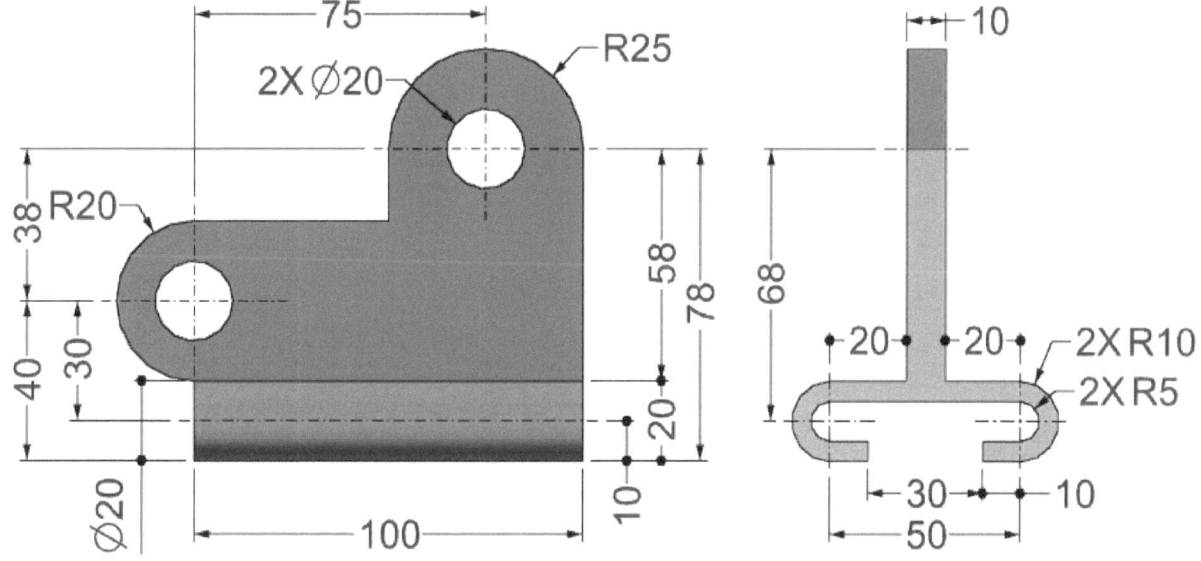

EXERCISE-68

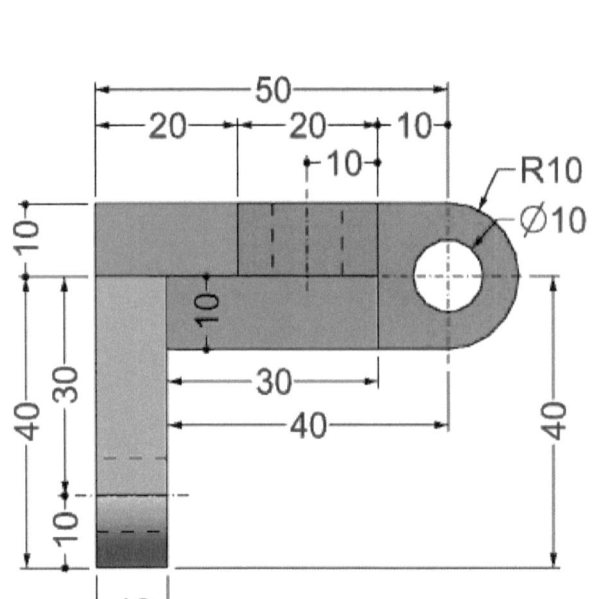
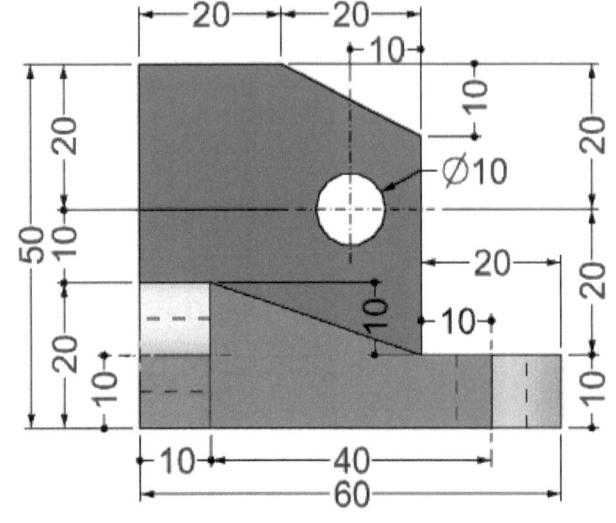
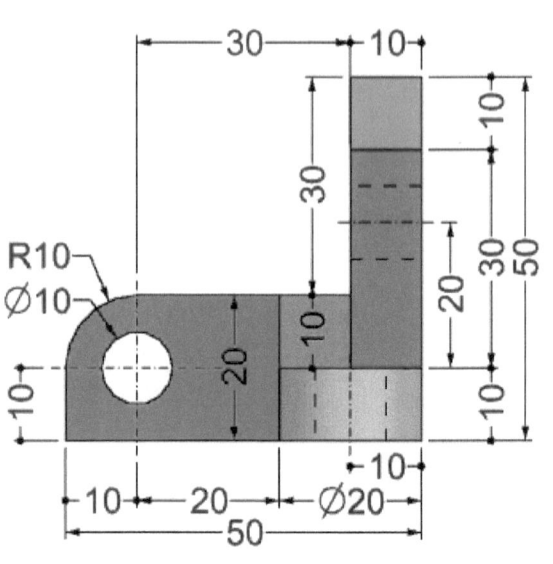

EXERCISE-69

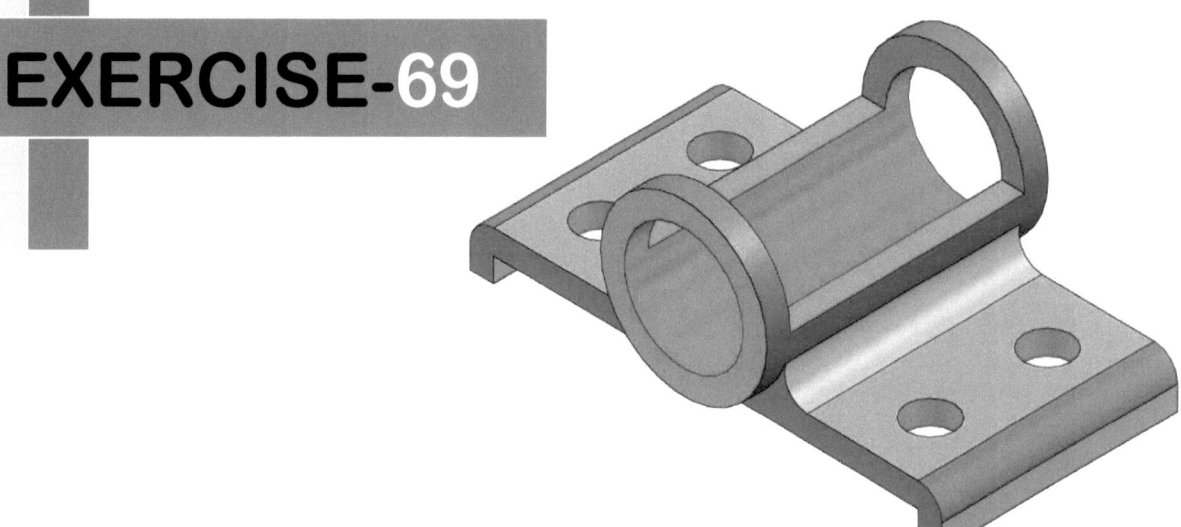

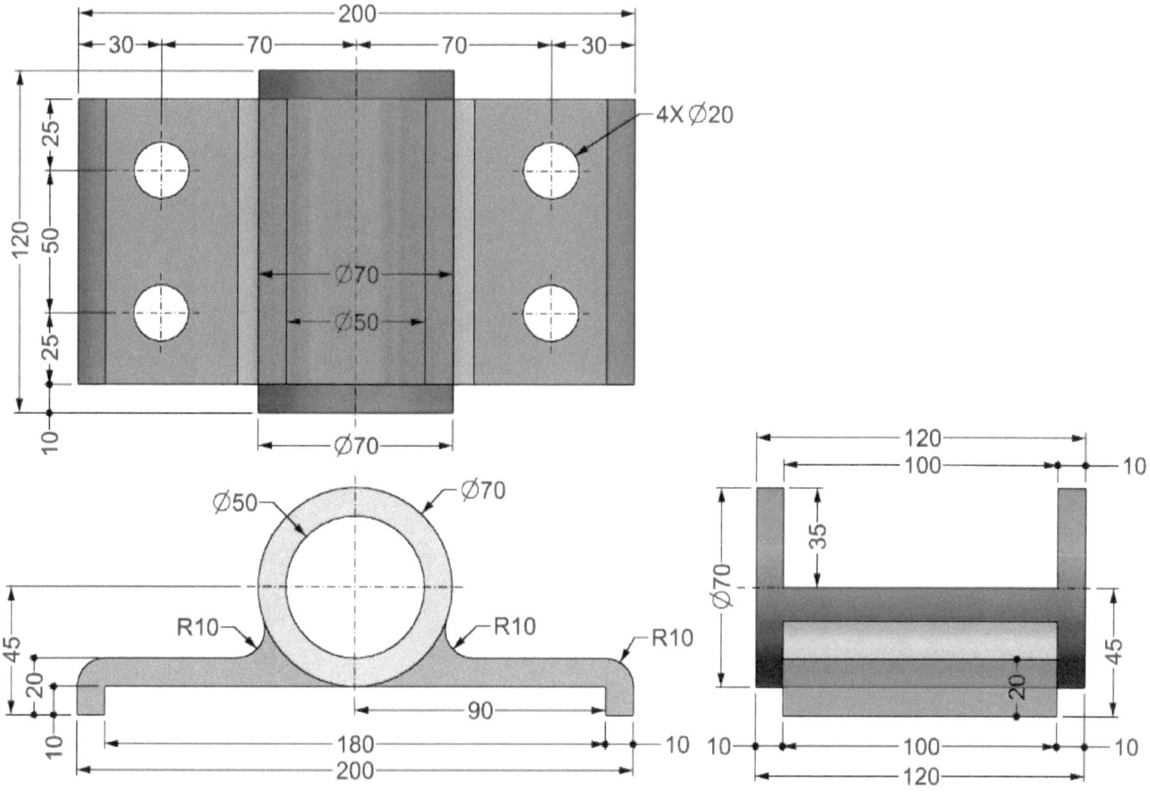
200
30
70
70
30
4X ∅20
120
25
50
25
10
∅70
∅50
∅70
∅50
∅70
R10
R10
R10
45
20
10
90
180
10
200
120
100
10
35
∅70
45
20
10
100
10
120

EXERCISE-70

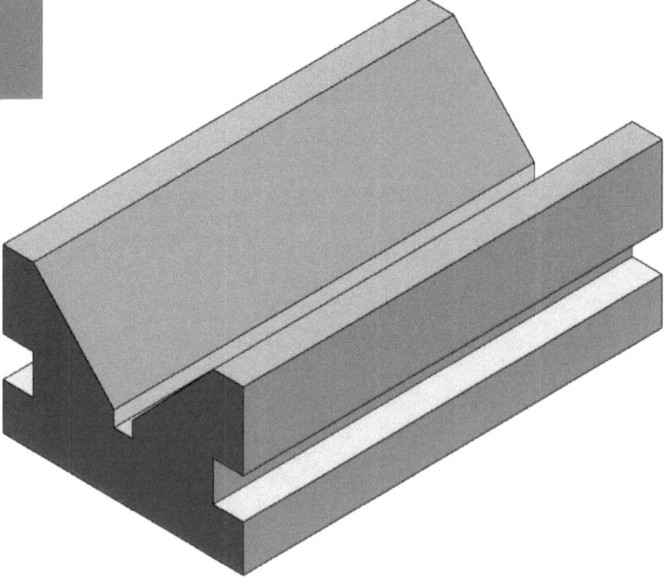

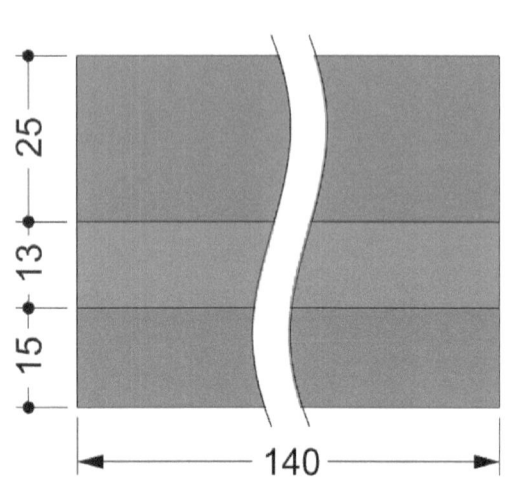

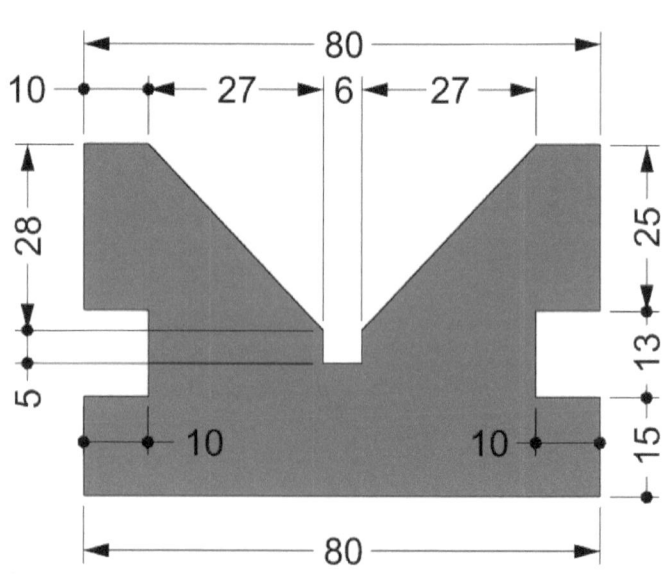

EXERCISE-71

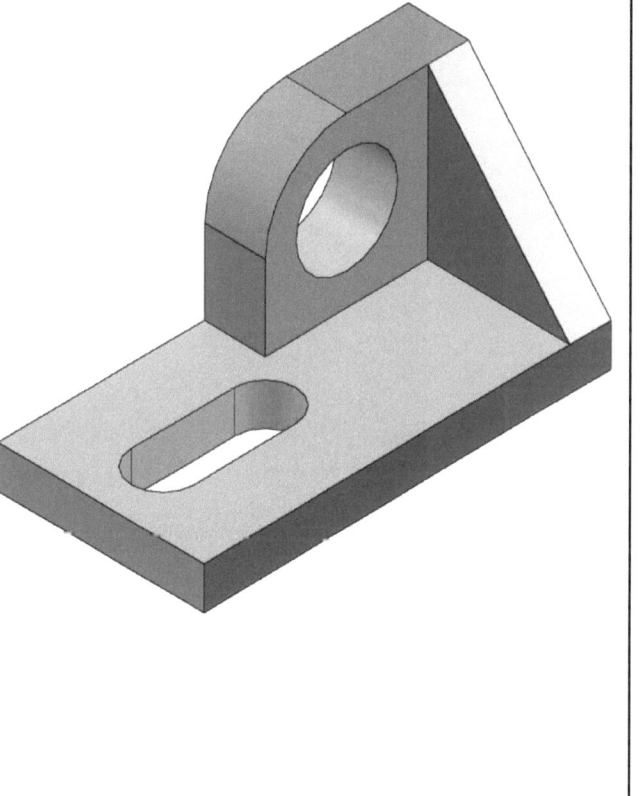

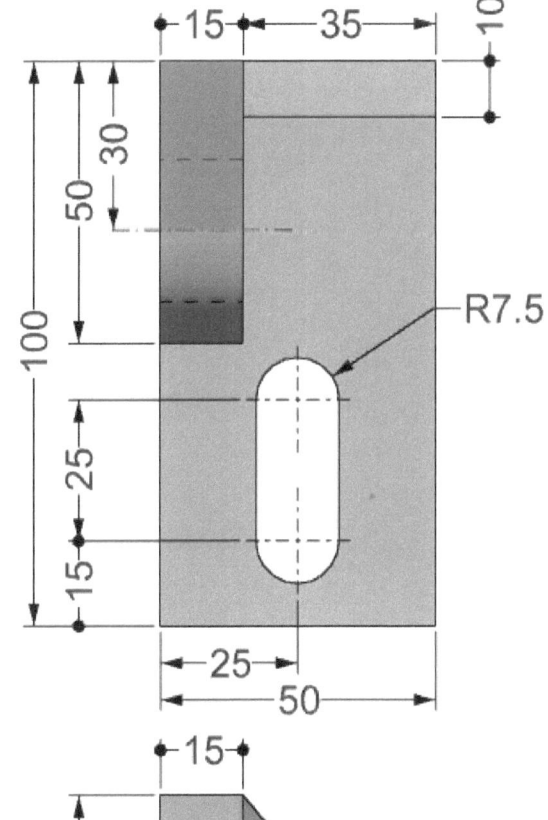

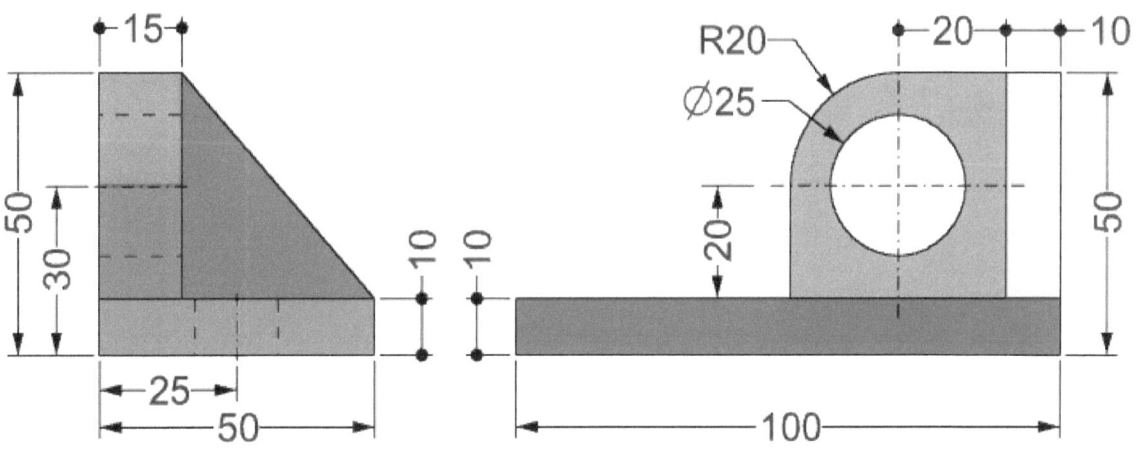

EXERCISE-72

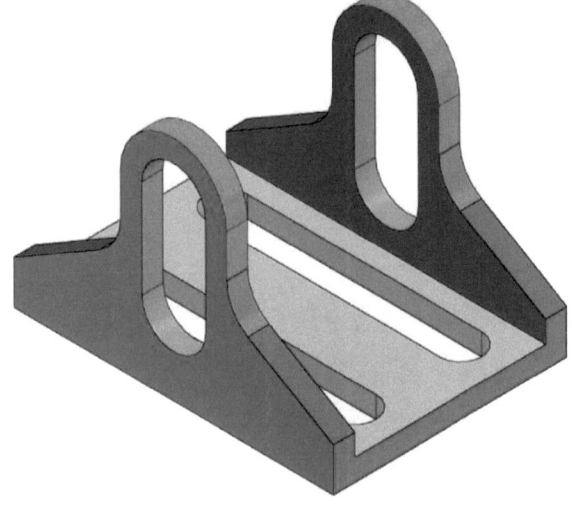

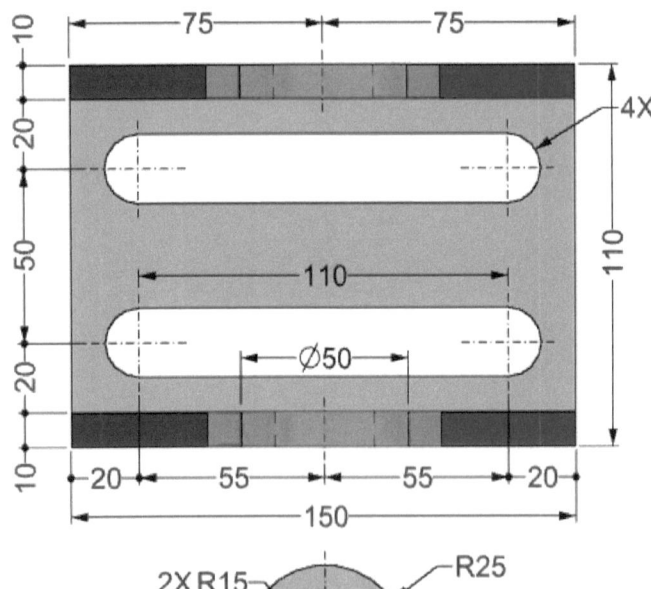

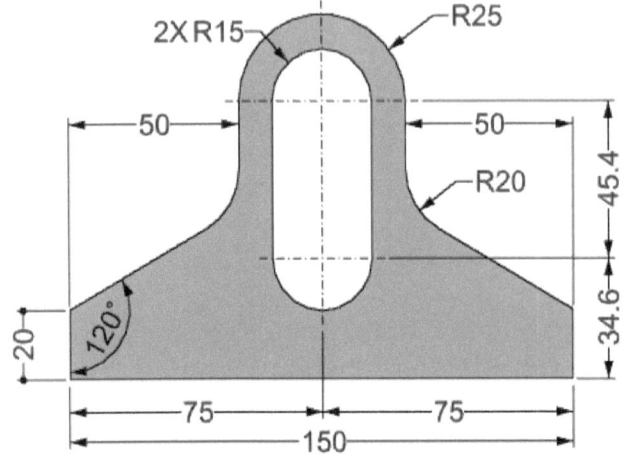

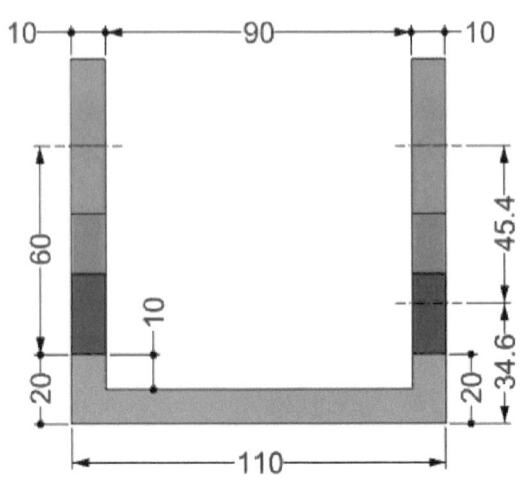

EXERCISE-73

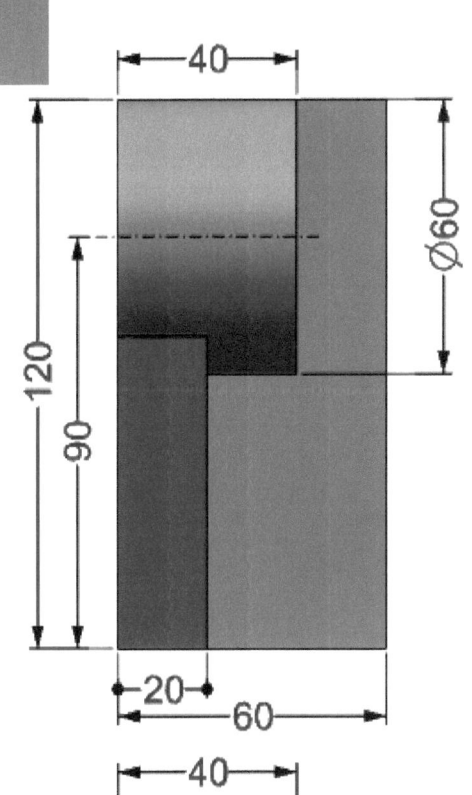
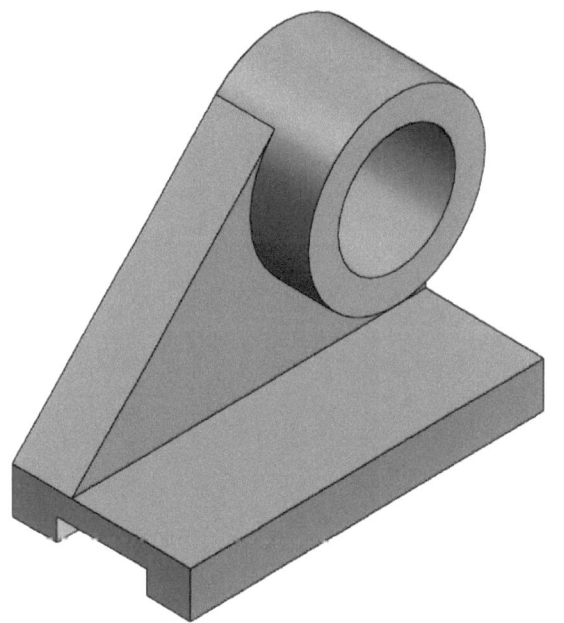
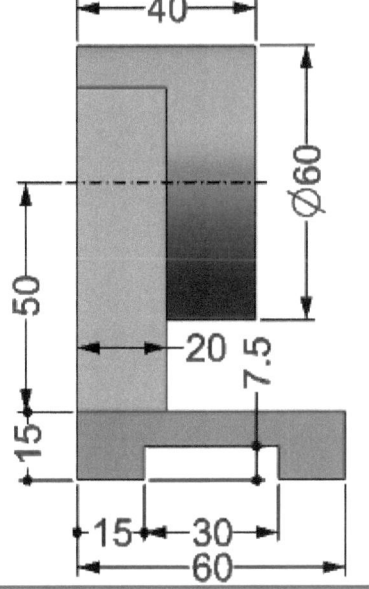
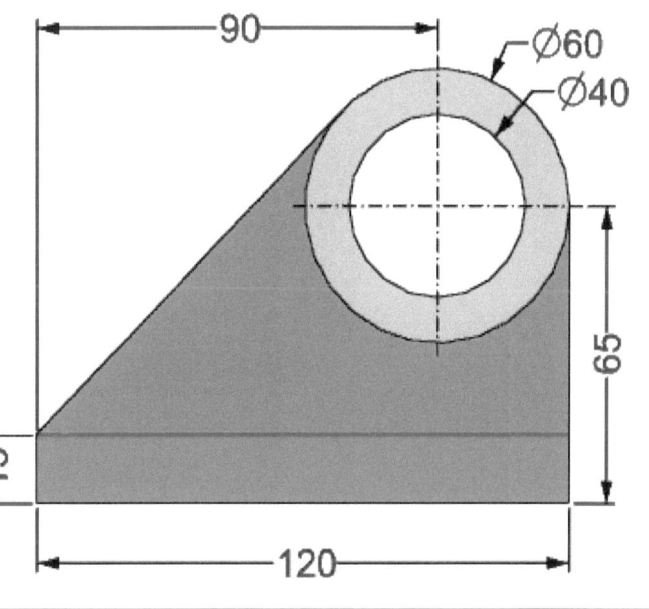

EXERCISE-74

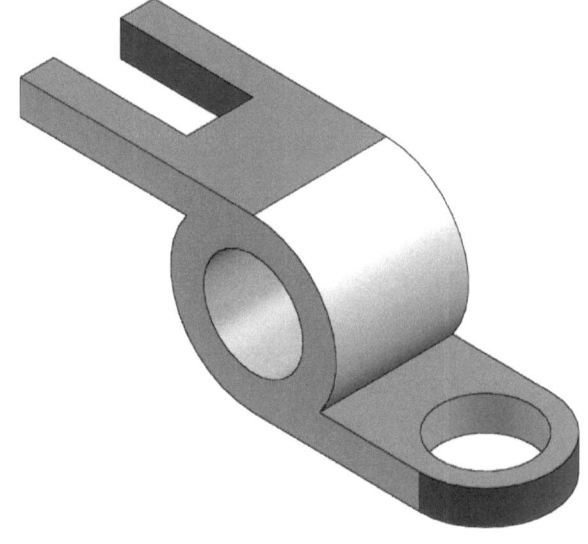

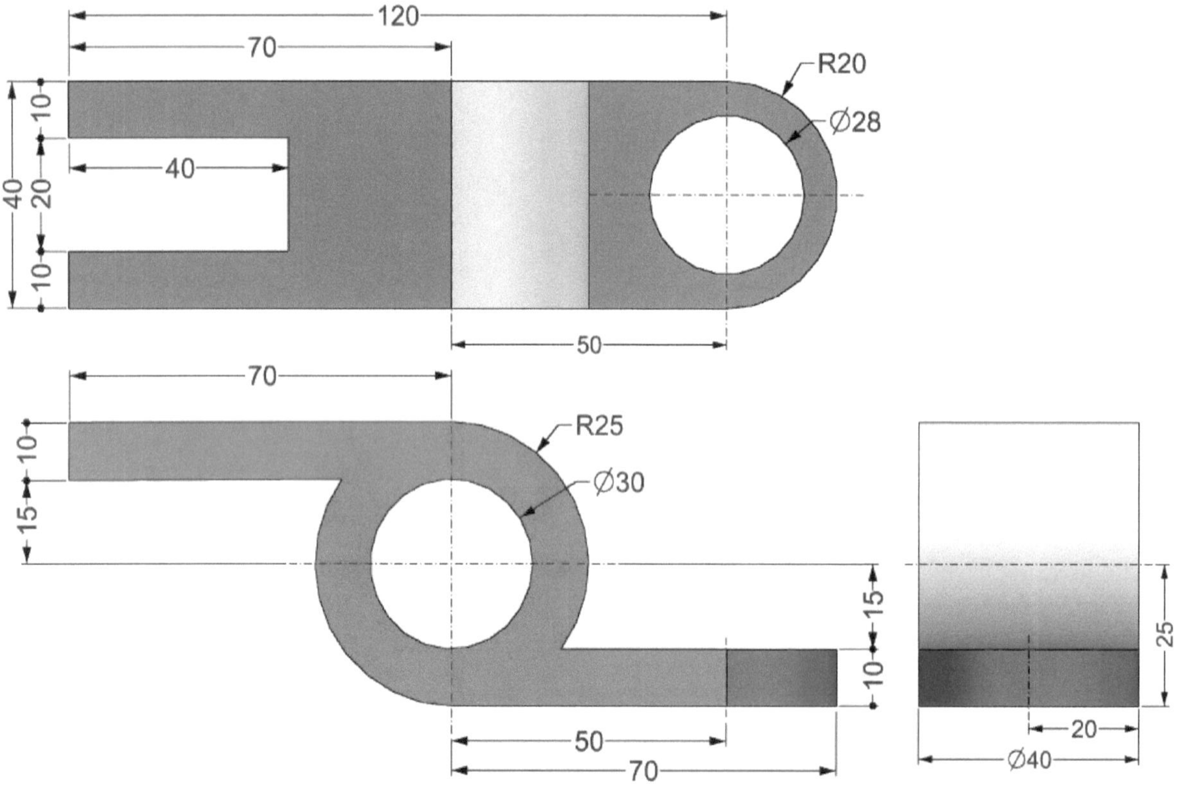
120
70
R20
Ø28
40
10
20
10
40
50
70
R25
Ø30
10
15
15
10
50
70
25
20
Ø40

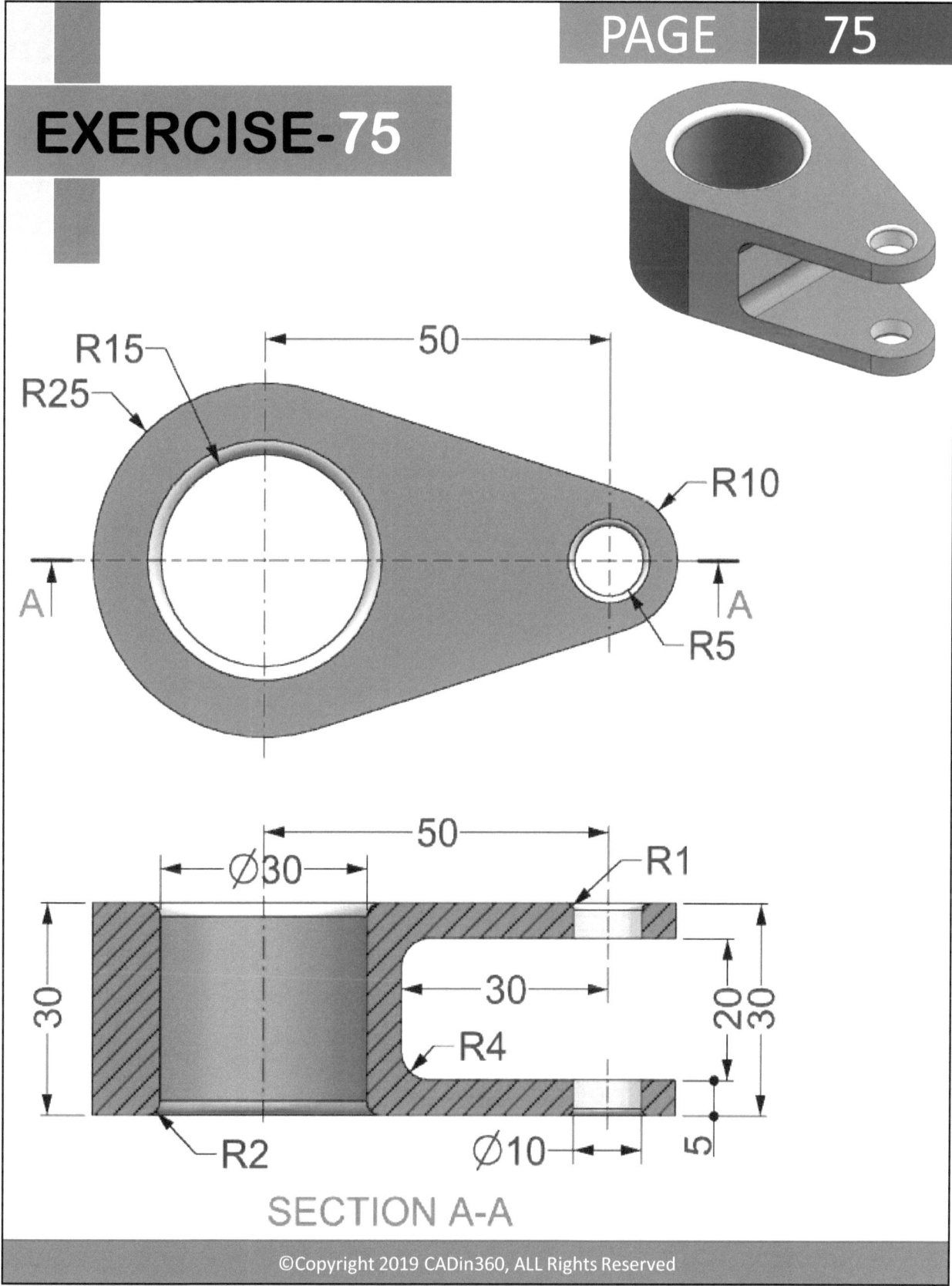

EXERCISE-76

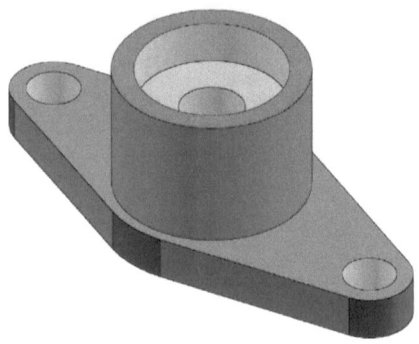

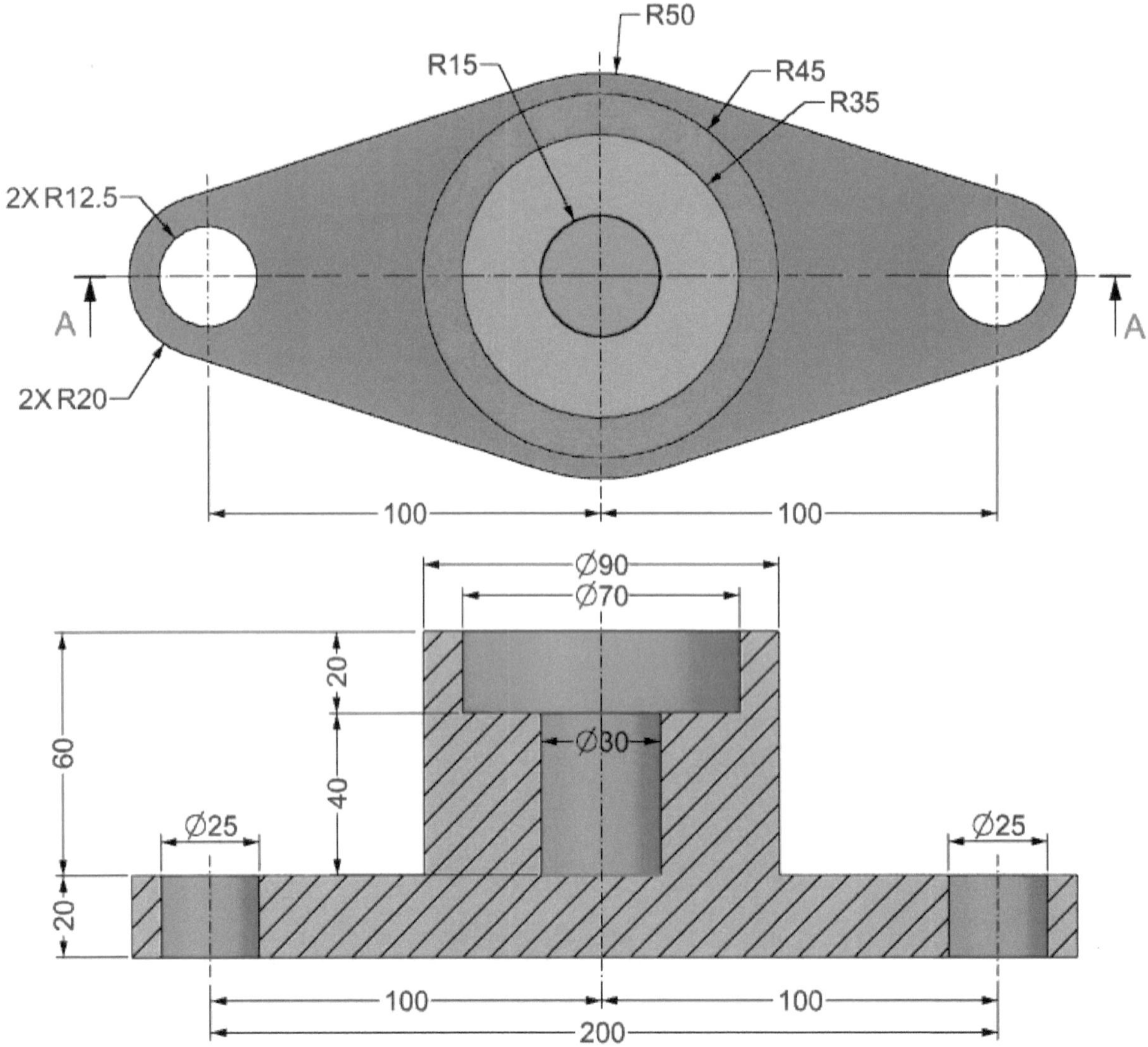

EXERCISE-77

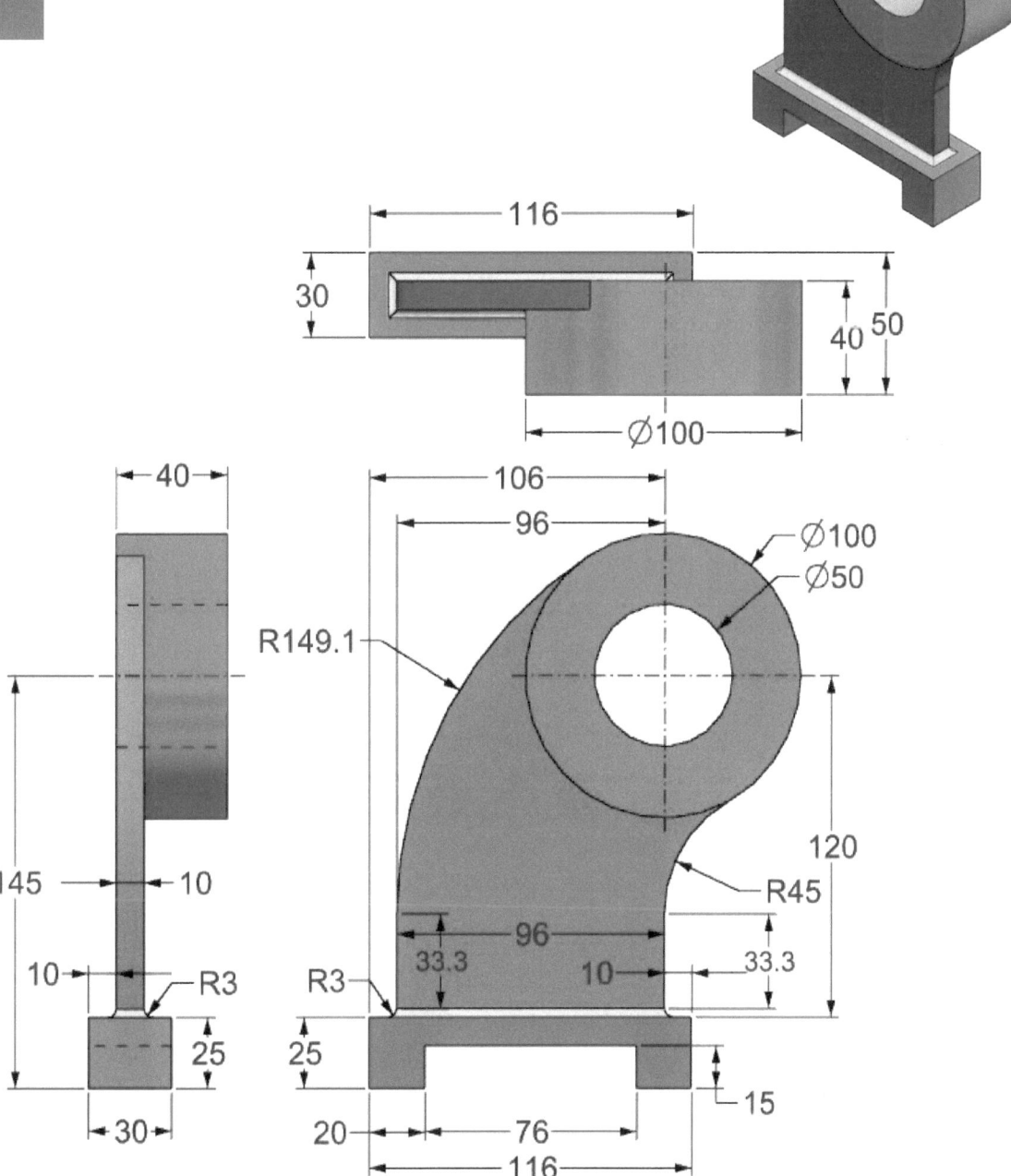

EXERCISE-78

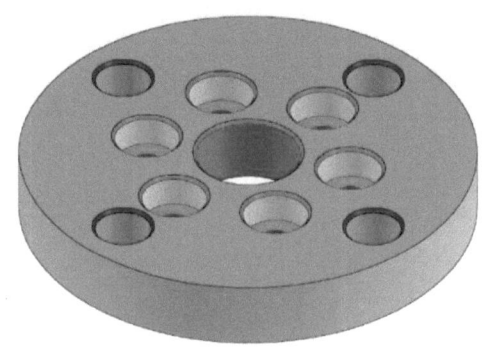

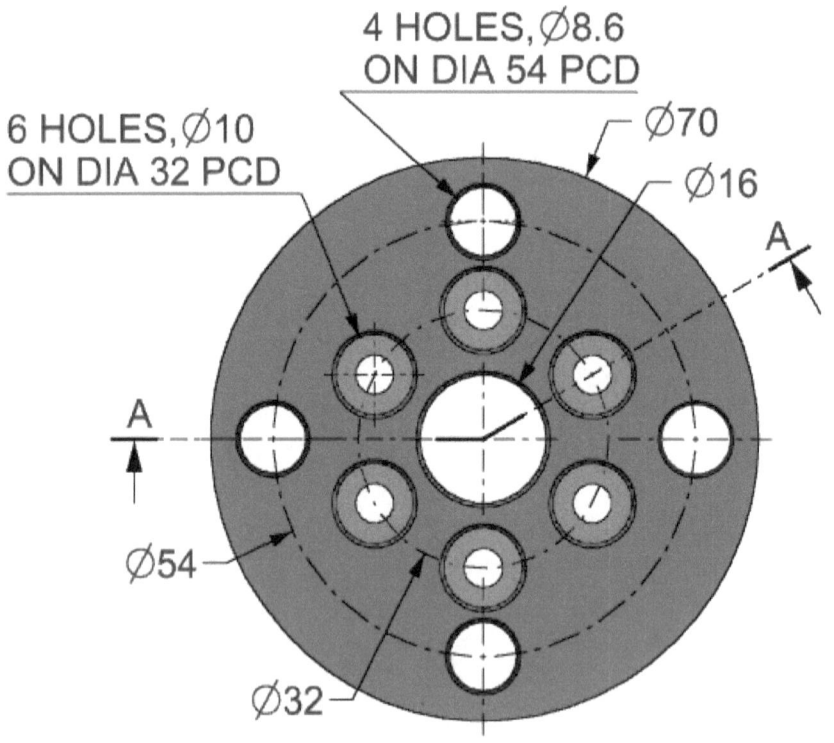

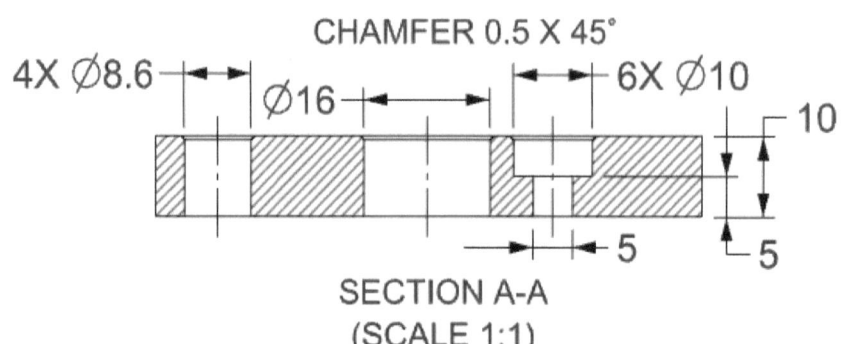

SECTION A-A
(SCALE 1:1)

EXERCISE-79

207.2
171.6
17.8
10
6X Ø8.4
87.2
4X R19.4
19.2
9.6
106
254
254
233.6
190.4
109.8
56.4
36.6
38
28
10
2X R11.6
60
10
103.6
147.2

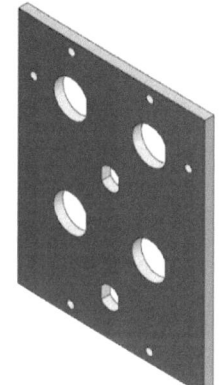

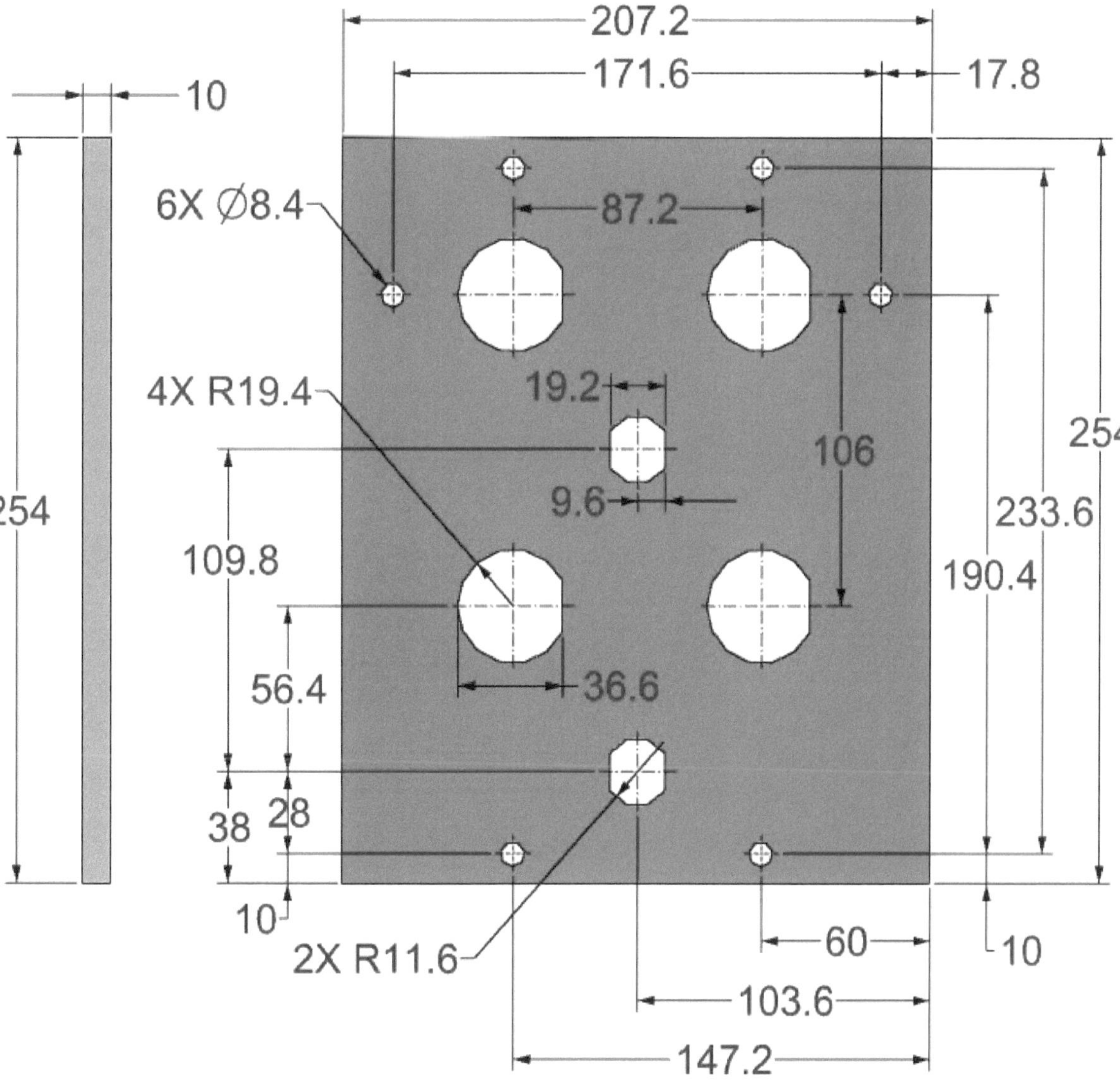

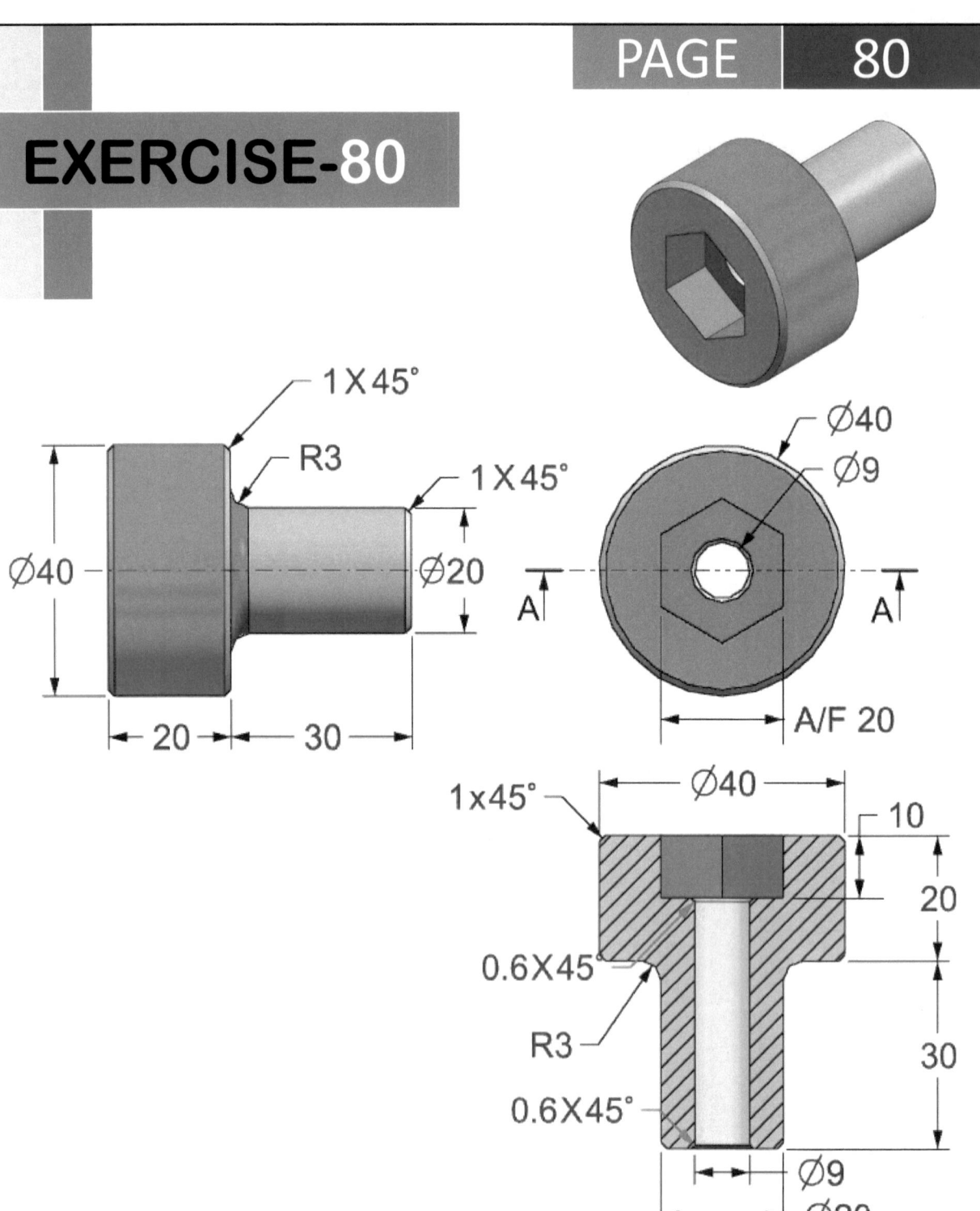

EXERCISE-81

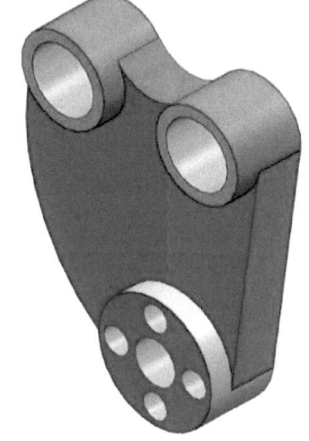

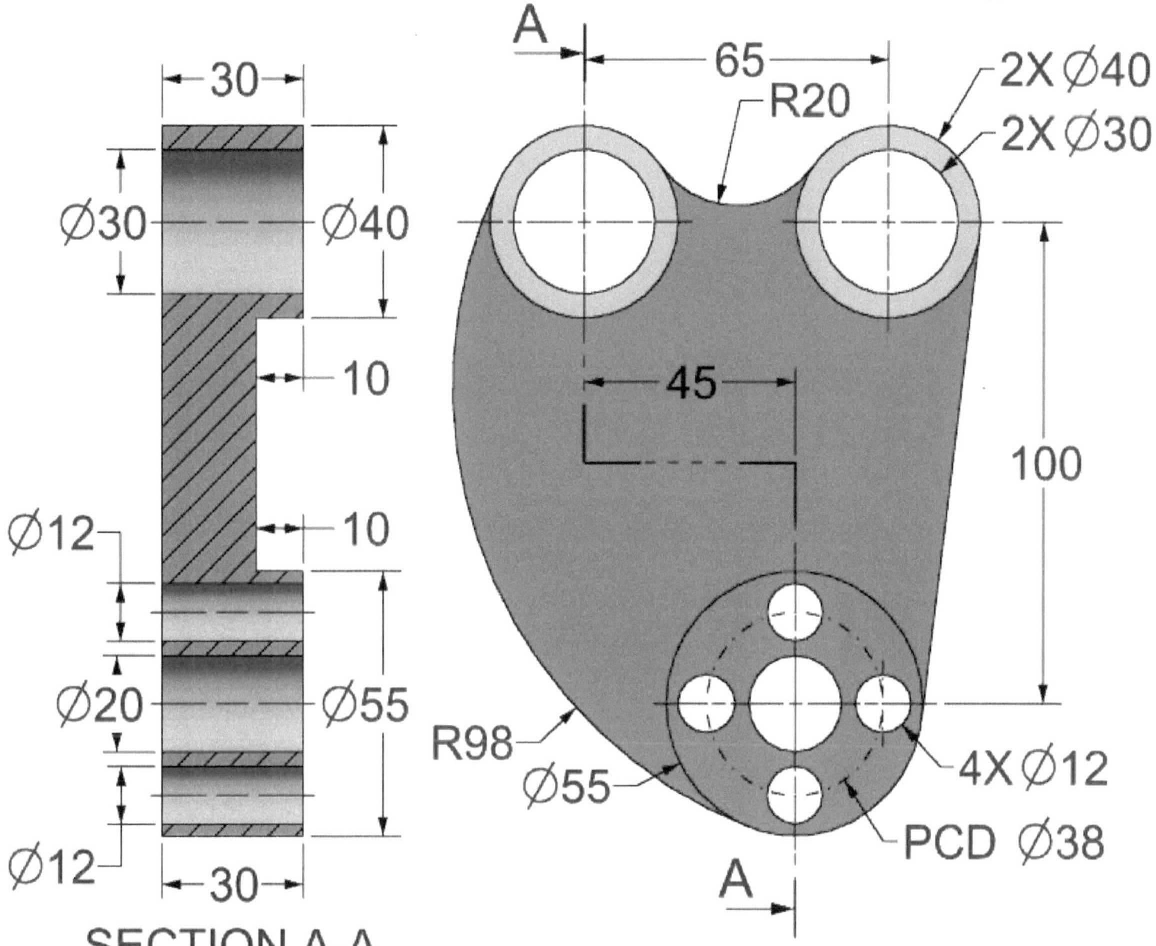

PAGE 81

EXERCISE-82

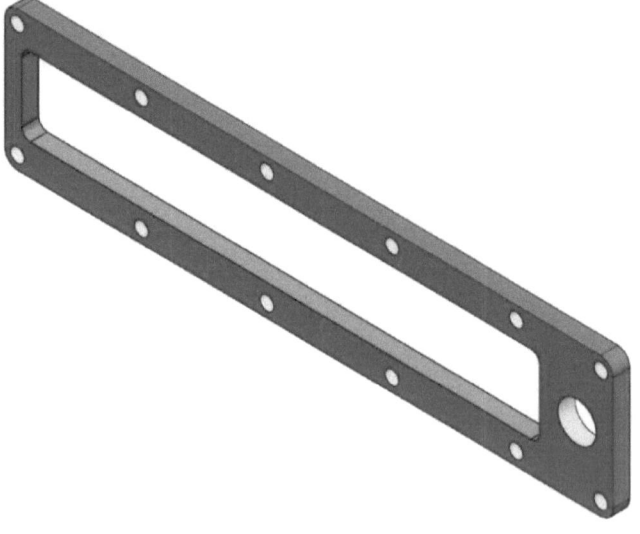

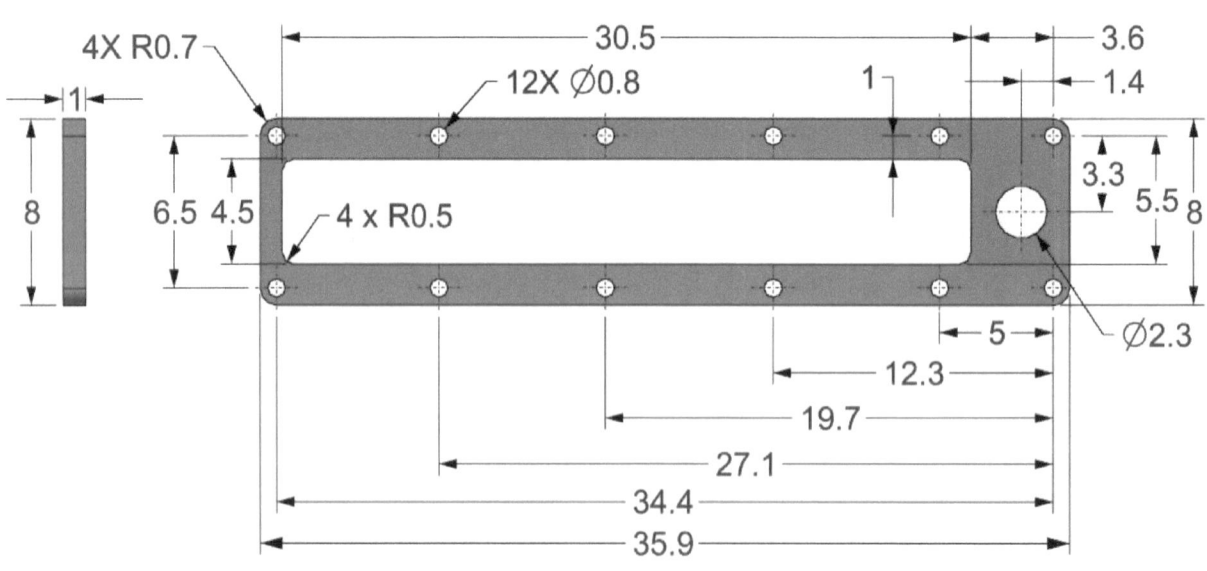

EXERCISE-83

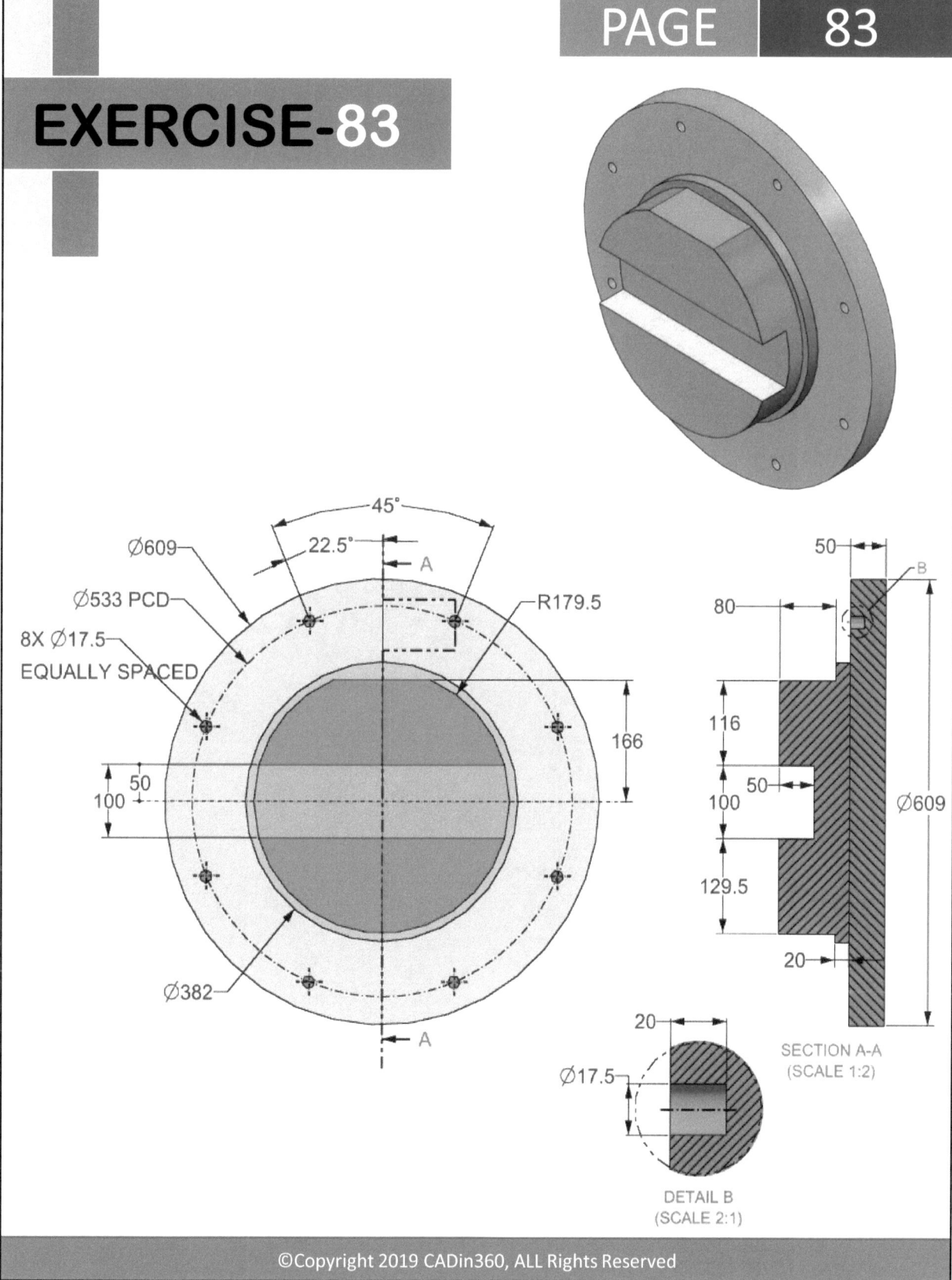

EXERCISE-84

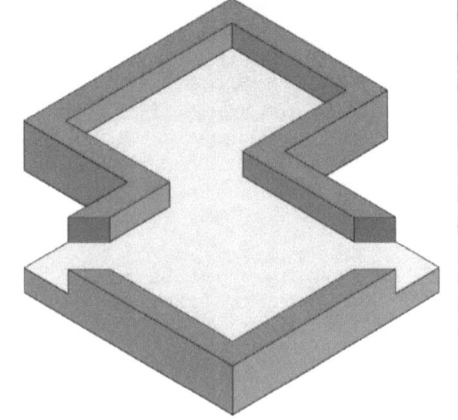

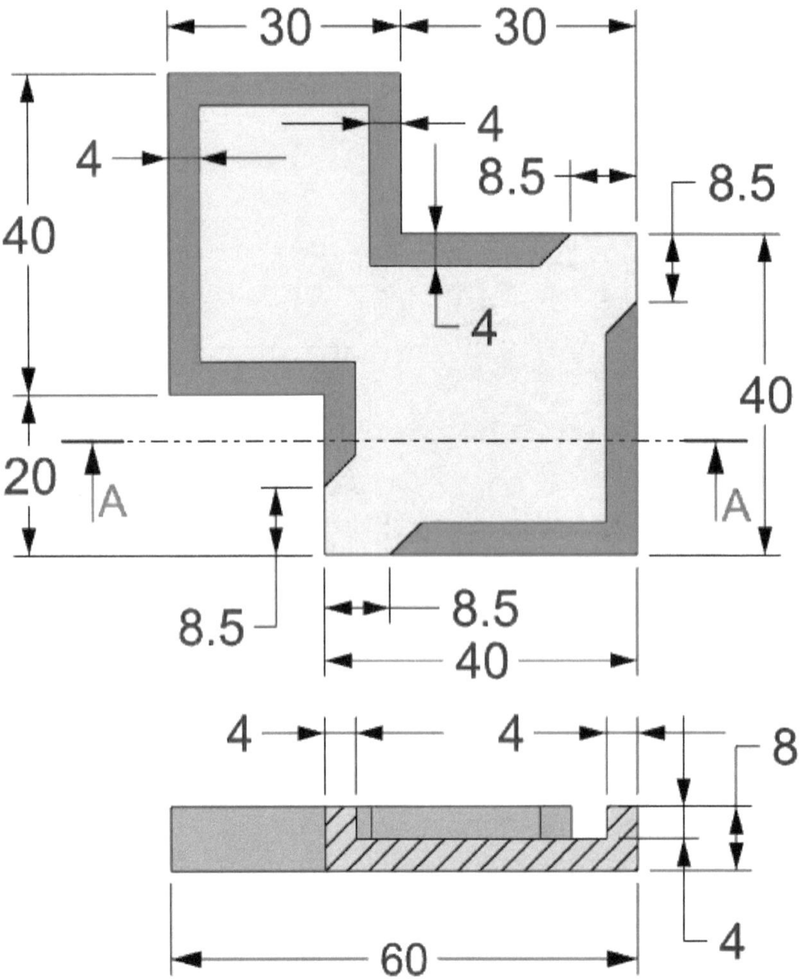

EXERCISE-85

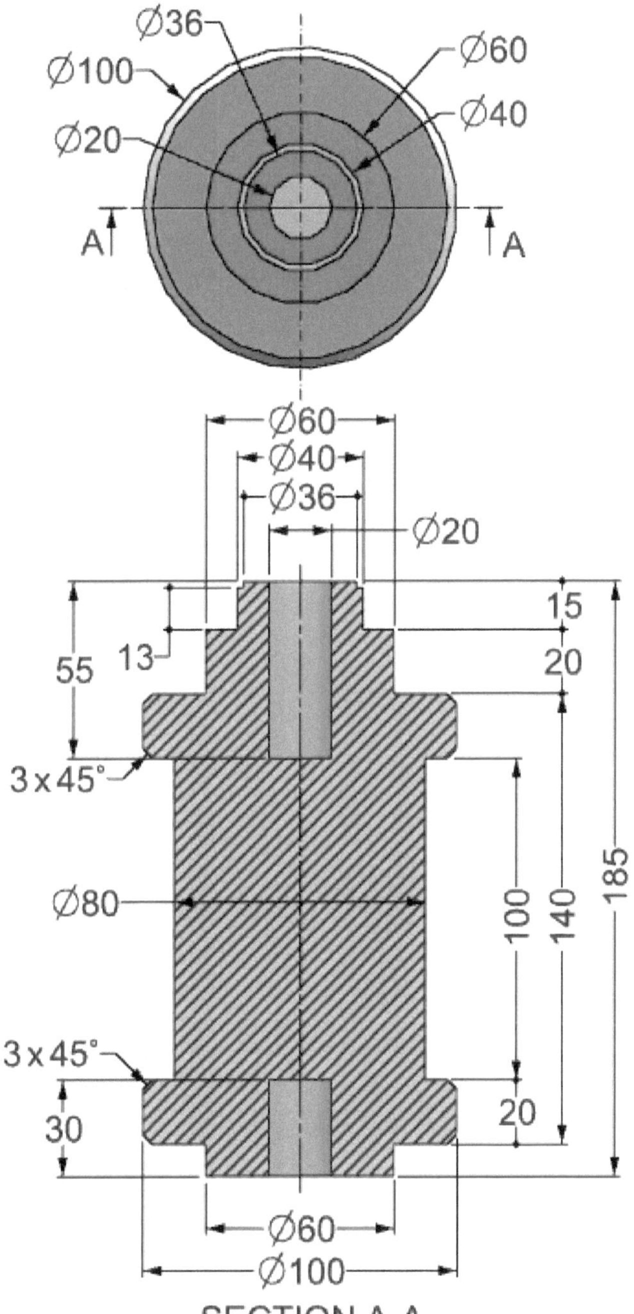

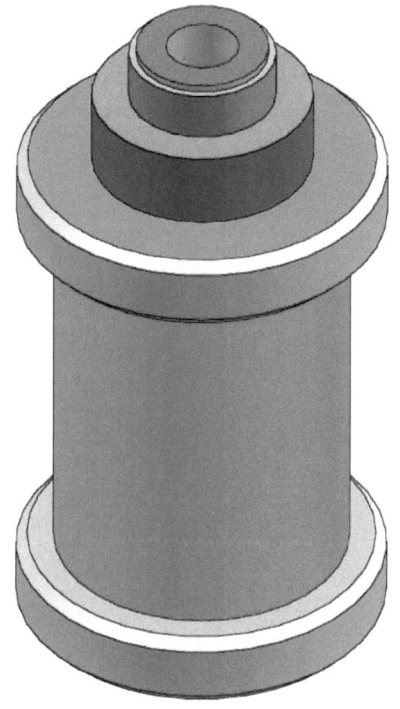

SECTION A-A

EXERCISE-86

15
94
Ø10
SECTION B-B
B
16
R26.9
R30
R12
22.2
36
Ø15
47
R26.9
A
A
18
47
2X R5
R24
R26.9
Ø41.7
100
B
Ø10
7.5
15
Ø15
Ø41.7
100
SECTION A-A

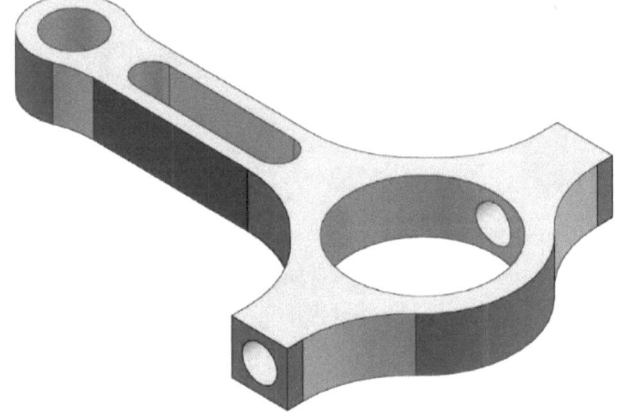

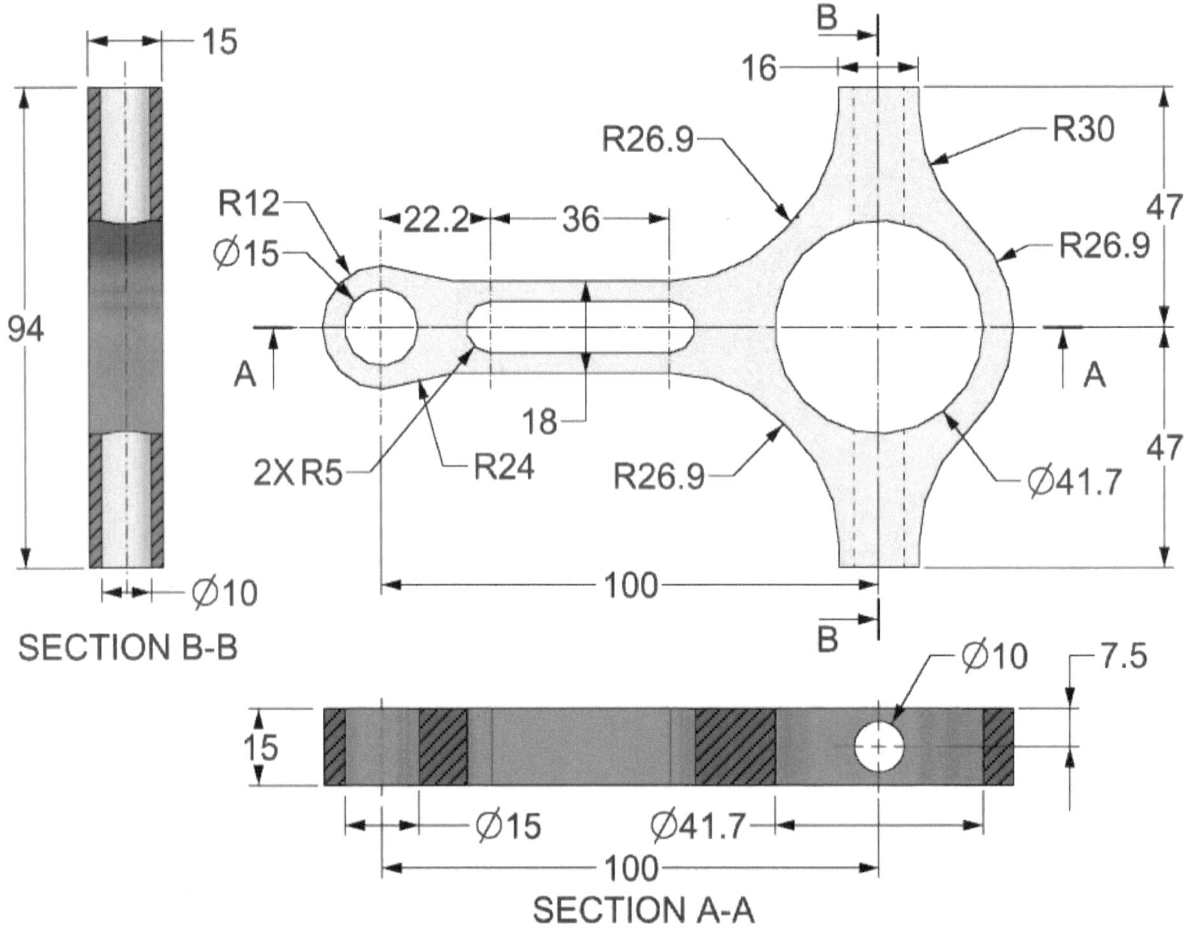

EXERCISE-87

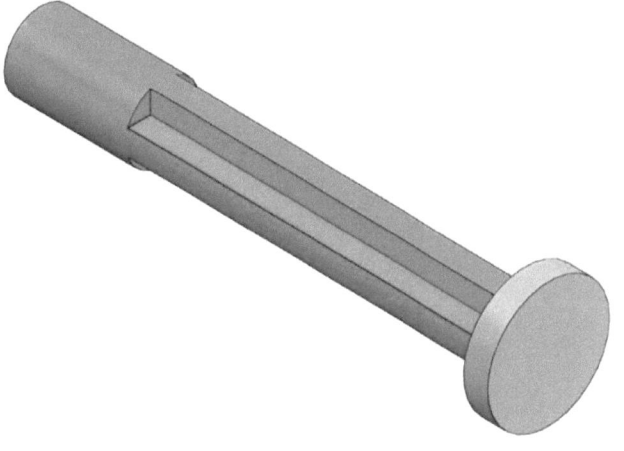

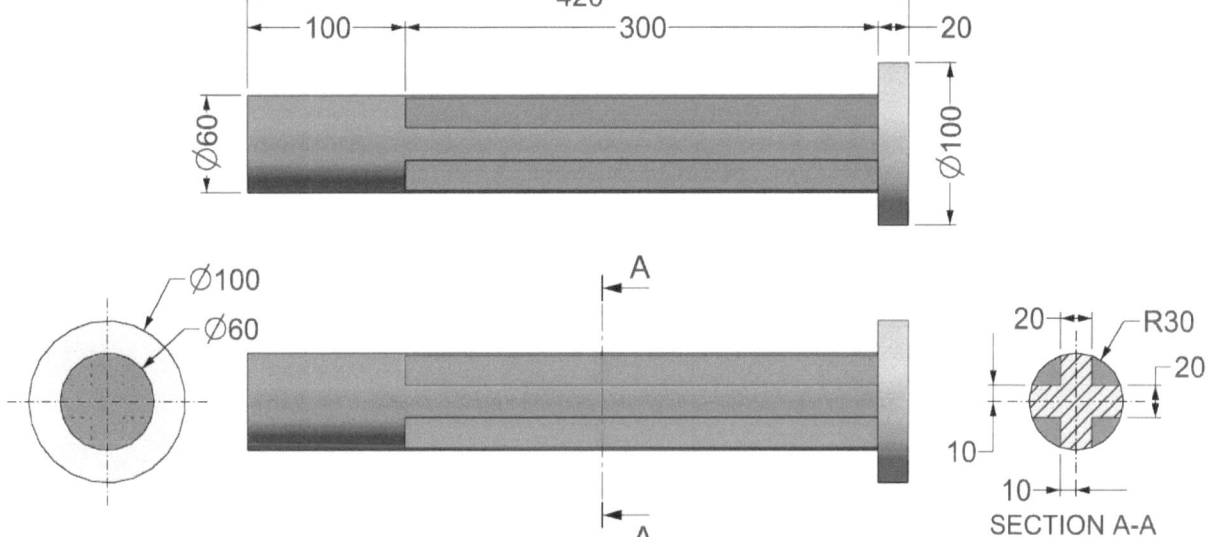

SECTION A-A

EXERCISE-88

2X Ø32
2X Ø40
20
60
20
20
36.2
10
40
60
Ø20
10
18.1
38
60
56.2
Ø40
5
20
10
20
60
56.2
116.2
100
Ø20
10
15
20
10
40
10
60

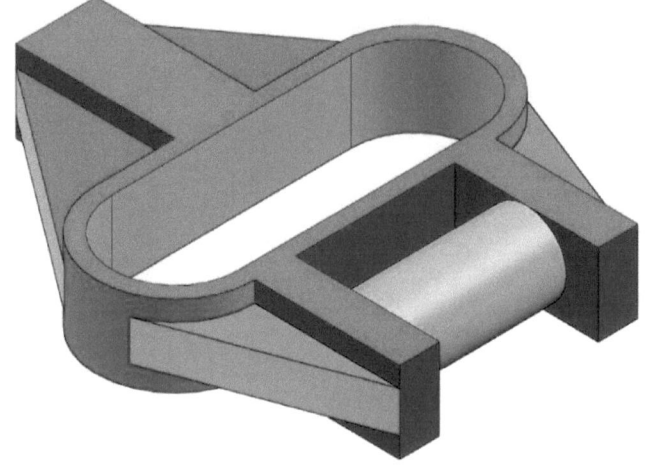

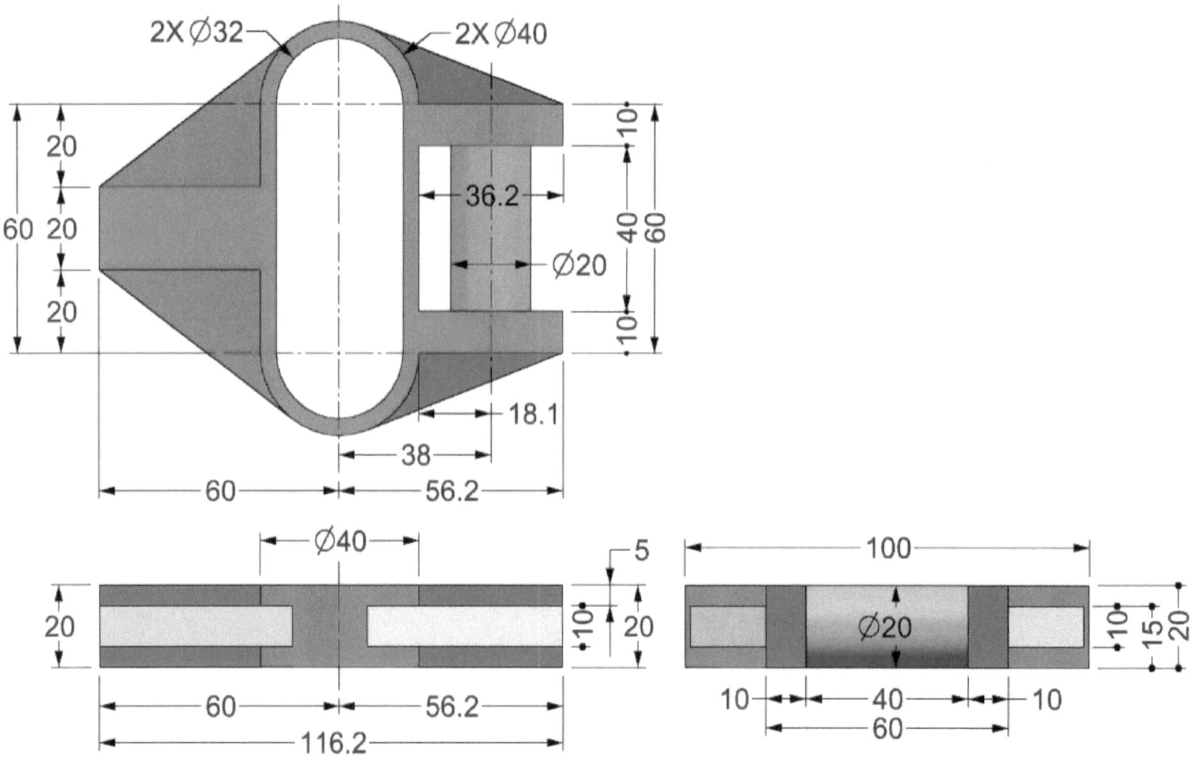

EXERCISE-89

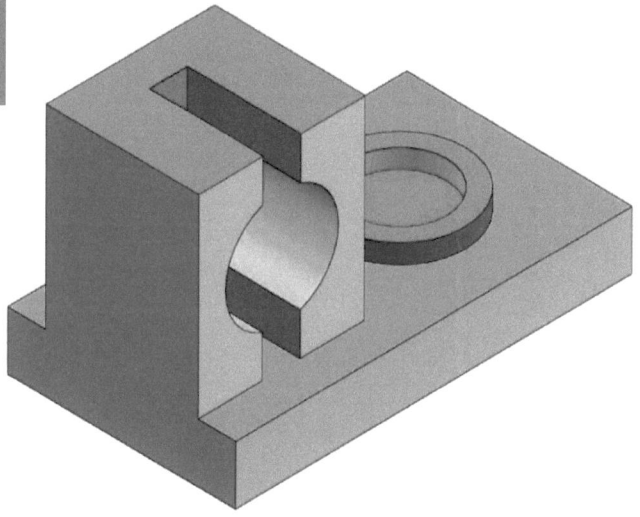

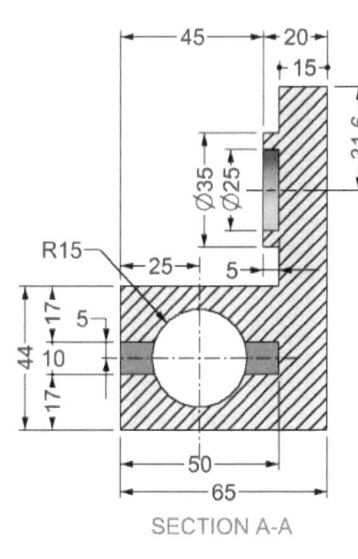

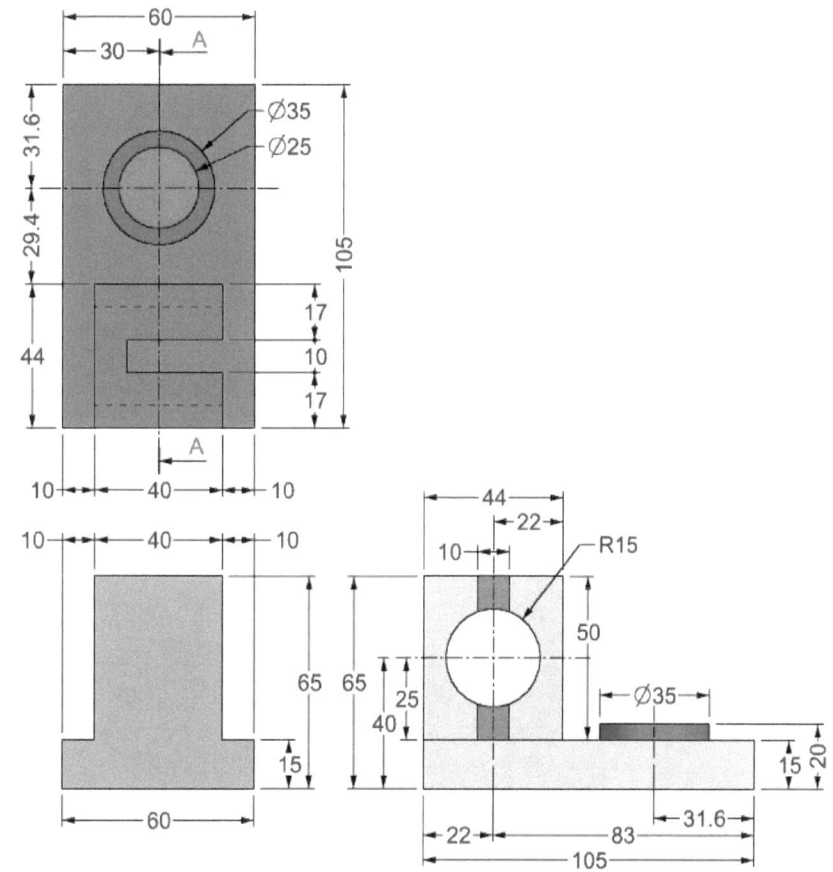

EXERCISE-90

65
55
2X Ø20
2X R20
2X Ø16
2X R10
2X Ø12
2X R10
R10
30
20
30
40
60
100
R10
2X R6
50
20
R10
20
25
40
50
30
5
Ø15
11.5
23
15
25
25
50

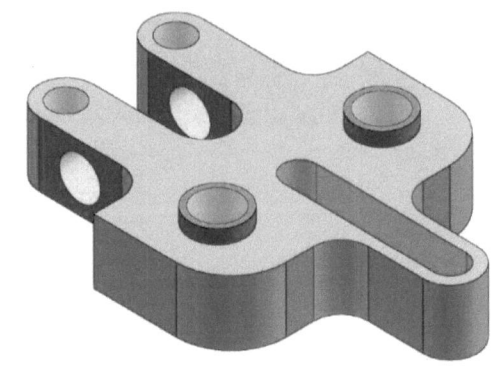

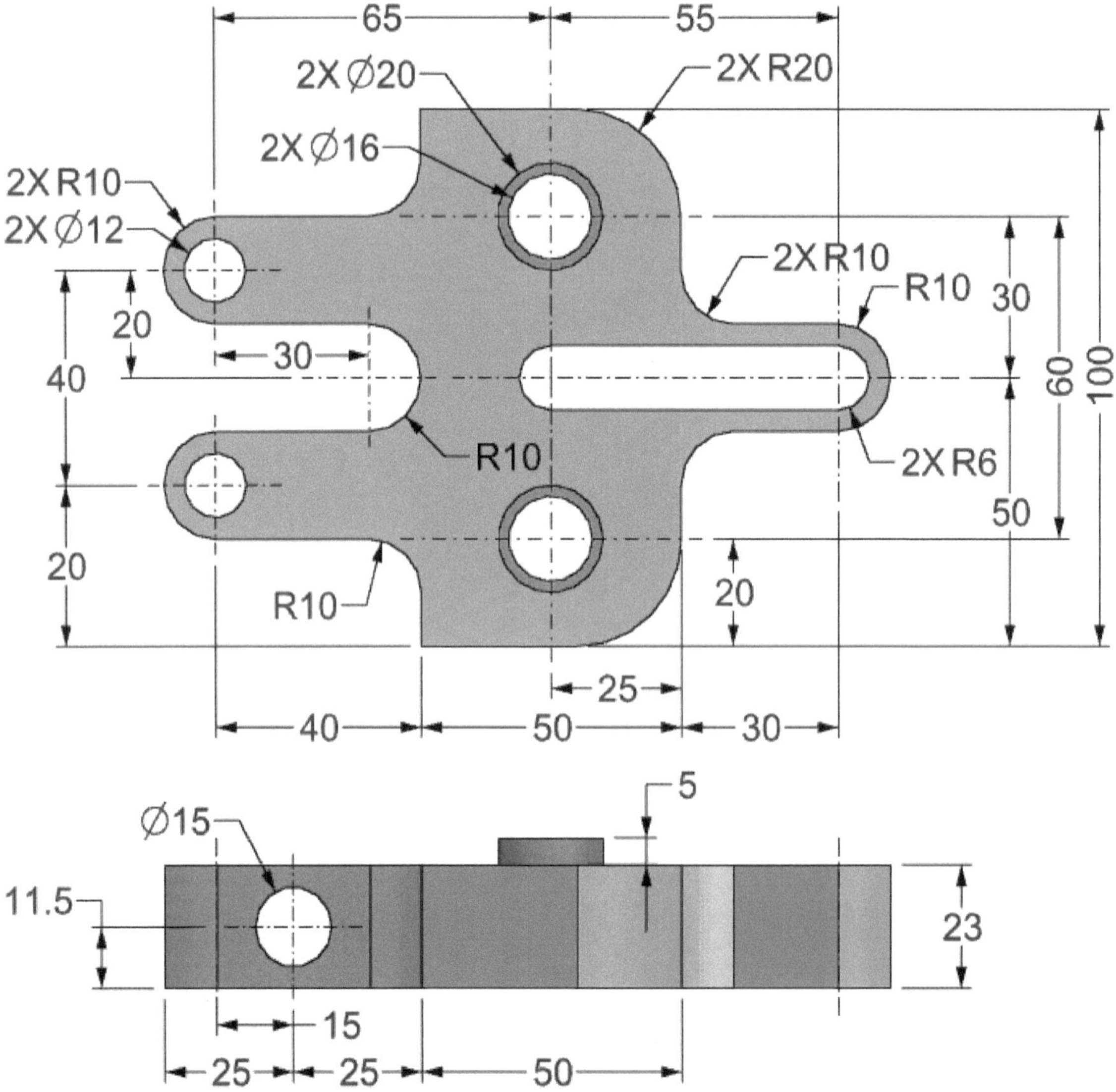

EXERCISE-91

30
Ø21.3
Ø15.7
2X R25
Ø13.8
R10
2X R20
Ø10
40
2X Ø11.7
2X Ø7.5
17
15
7.5
7.5
2X R5
7
23
23
7
46
60
Ø11.7
Ø13.8
Ø11.7
10
5
7
23
23
7
60
17
15
Ø11.7
10
5
10
7.5
25
40

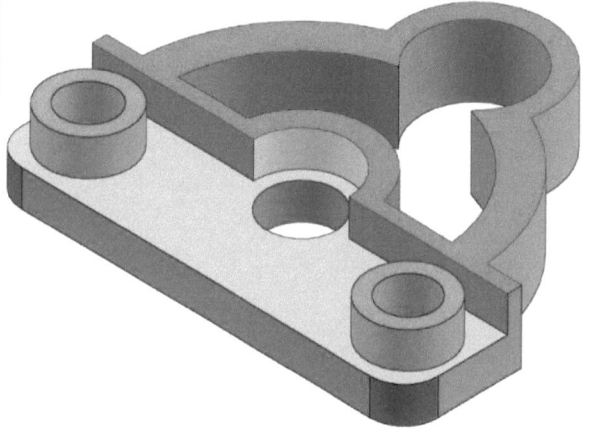

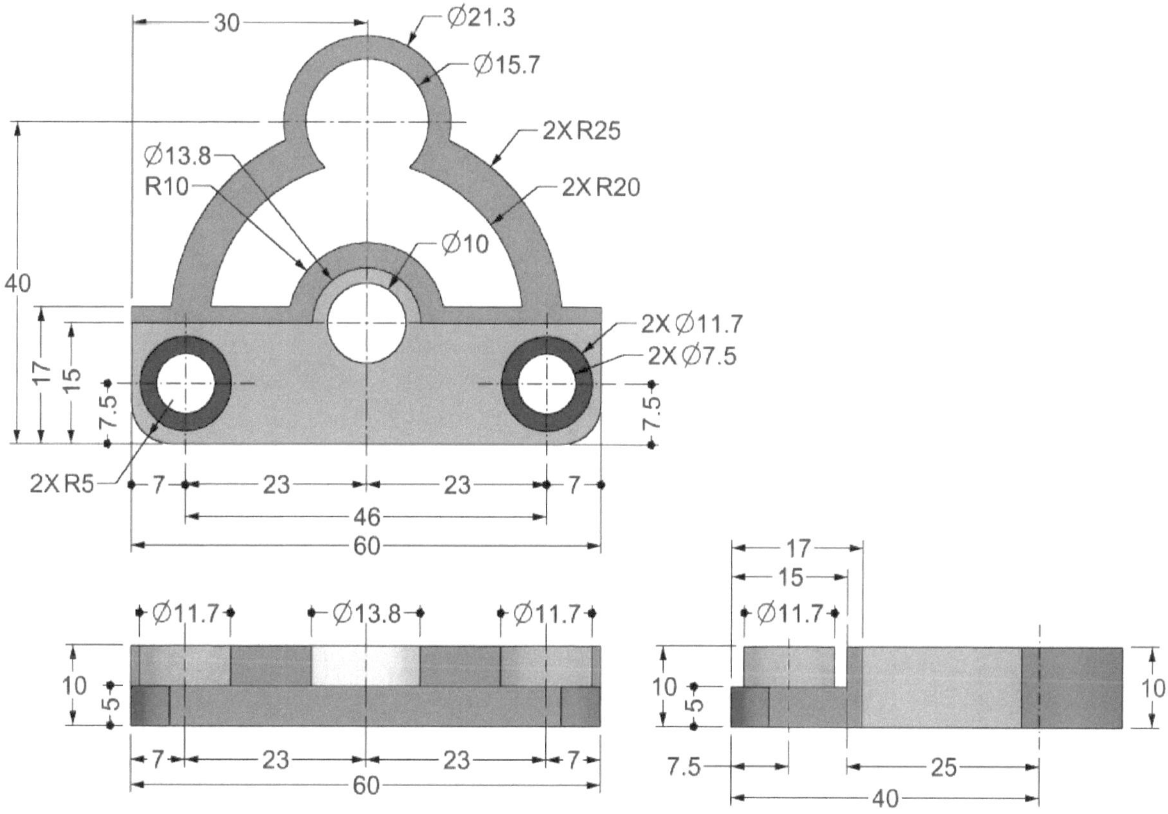

EXERCISE-92

A
10
R7.8
R10.7
2X R25
2X R20
R10
Ø12
25
40
2
Ø12
17
15
R5
R5
15
30
30
A
SECTION A-A

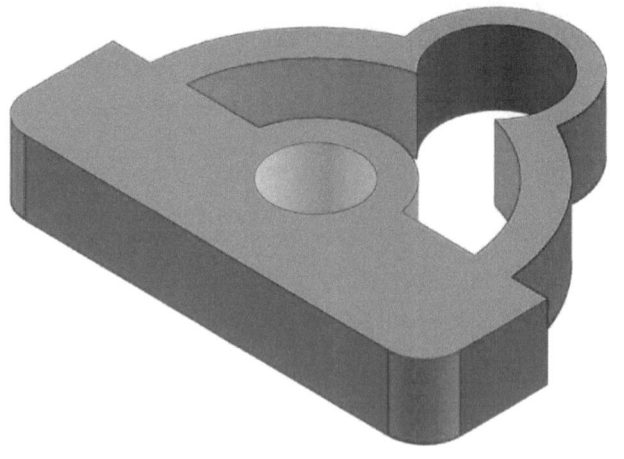

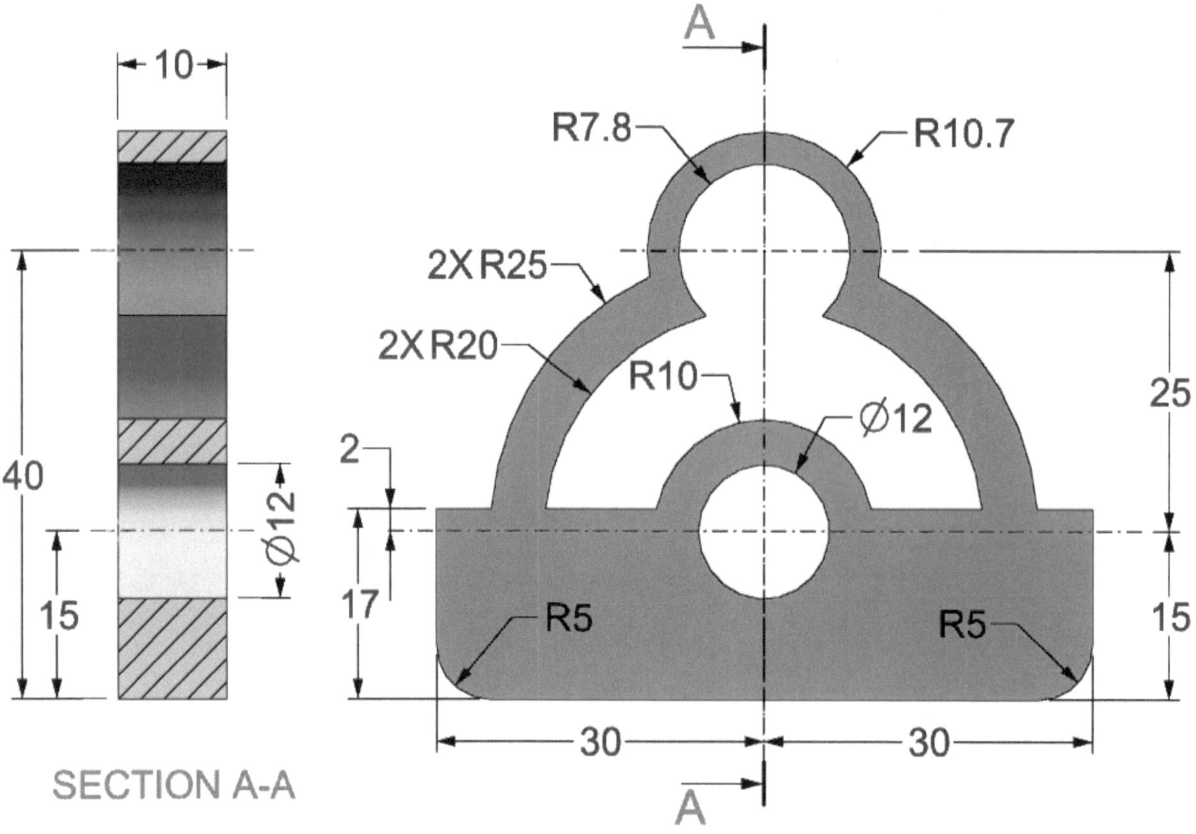

EXERCISE-93

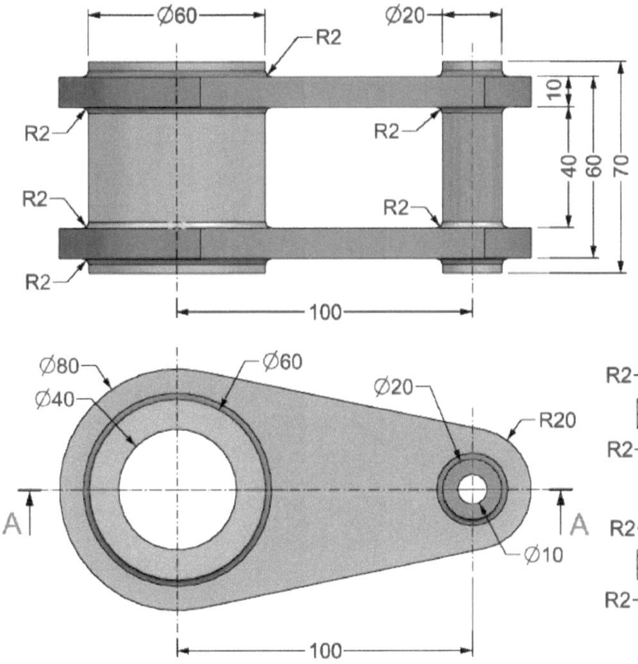

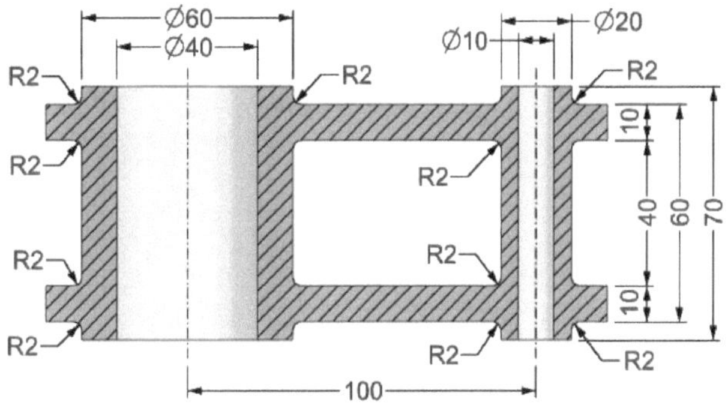

EXERCISE-94

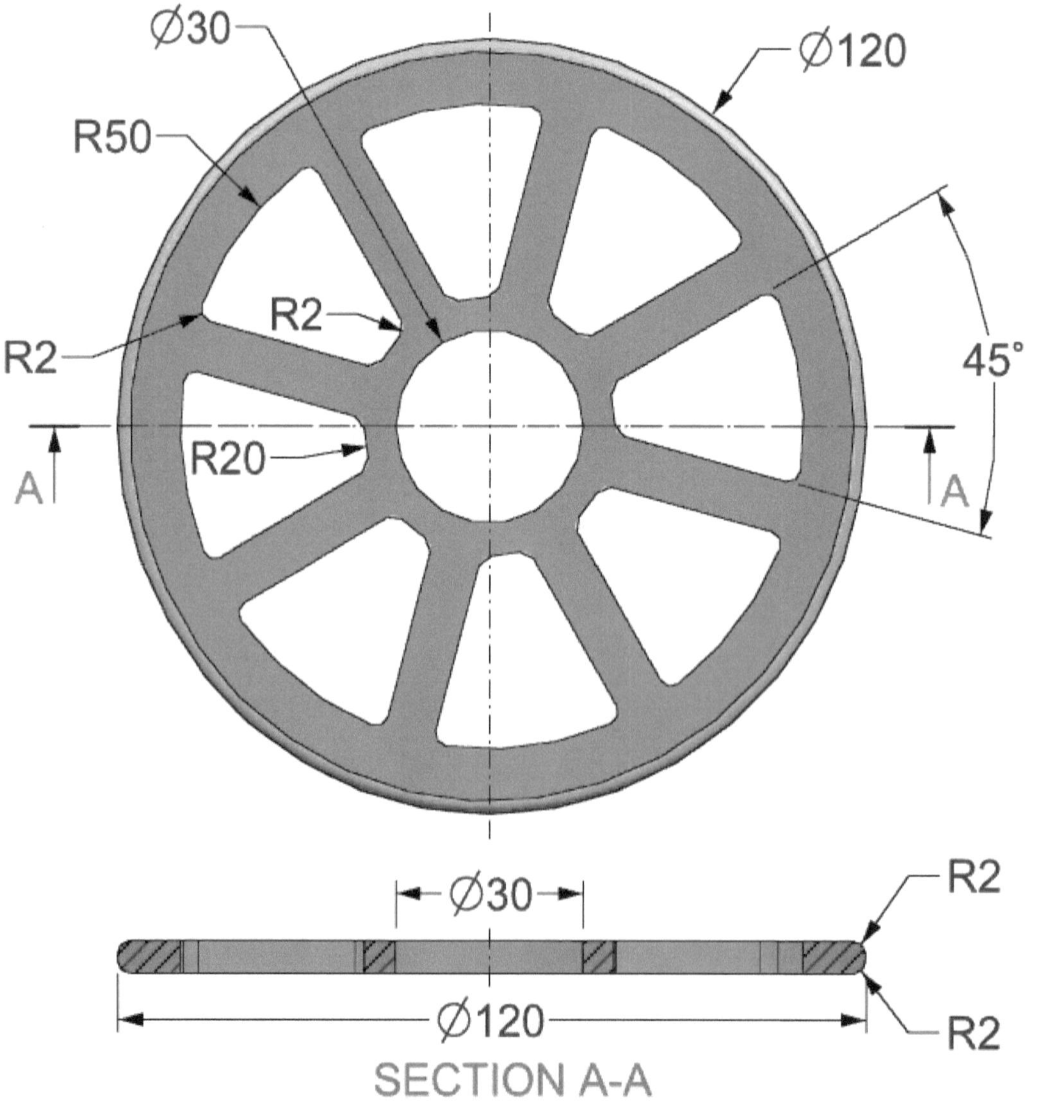

EXERCISE-95

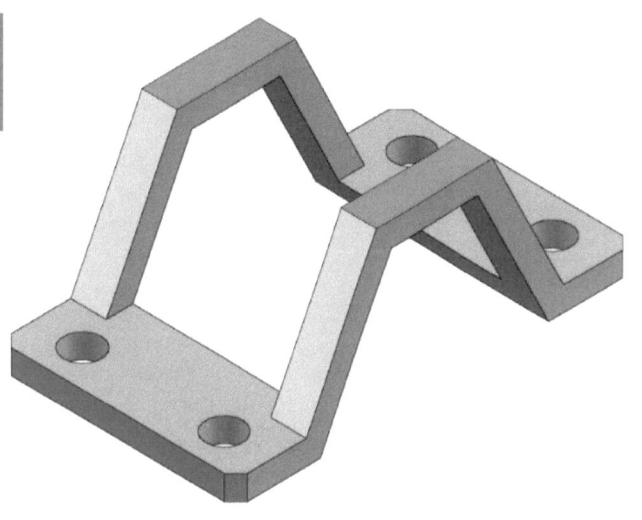

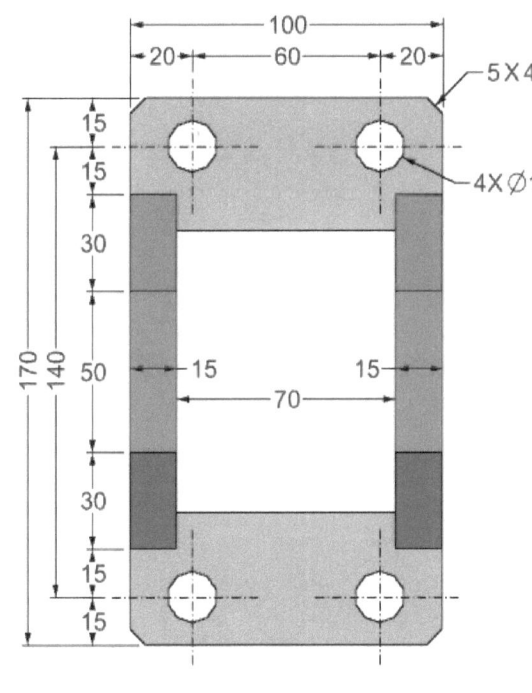

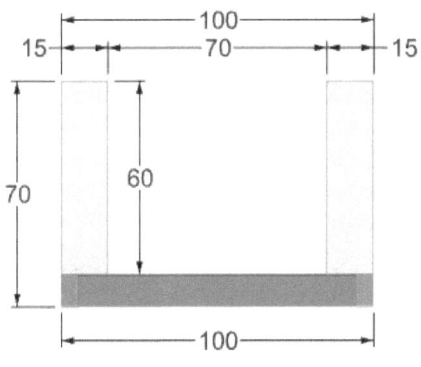

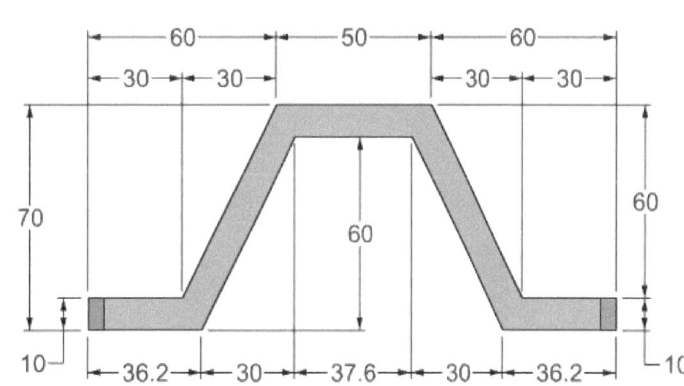

EXERCISE-96

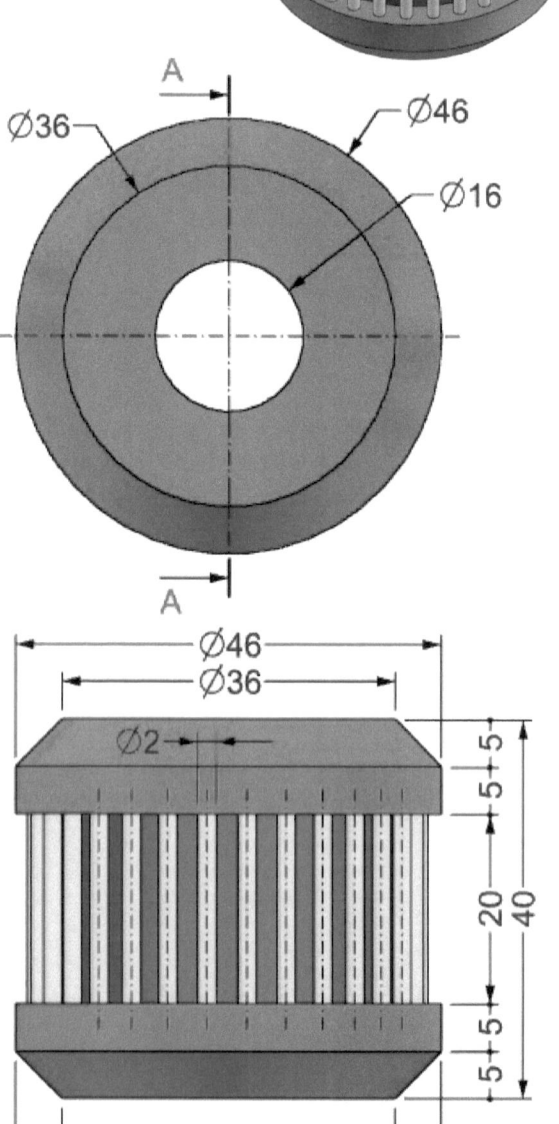

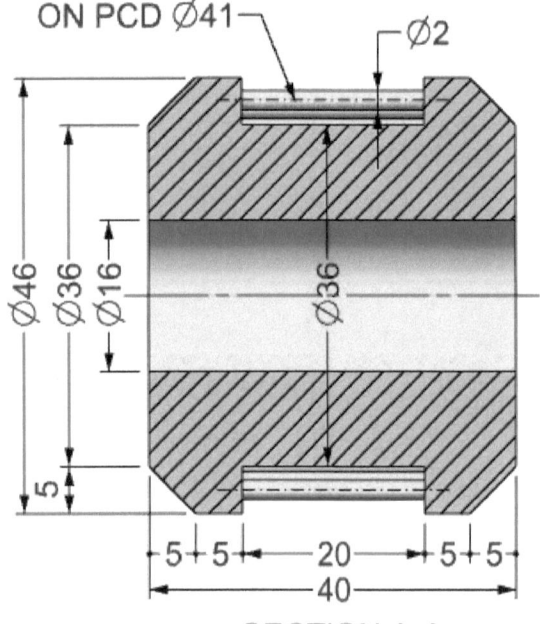

EXERCISE-97

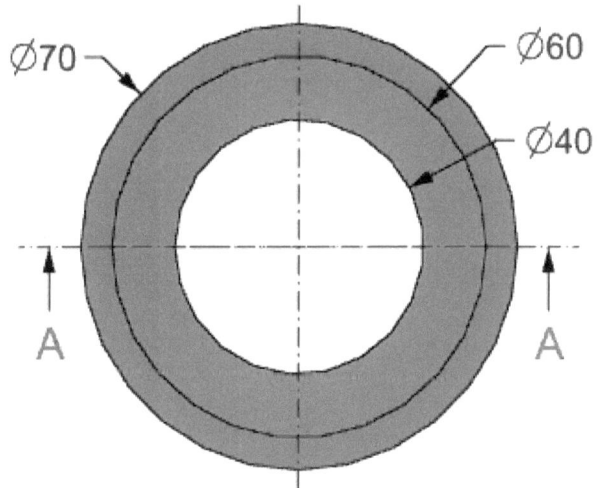
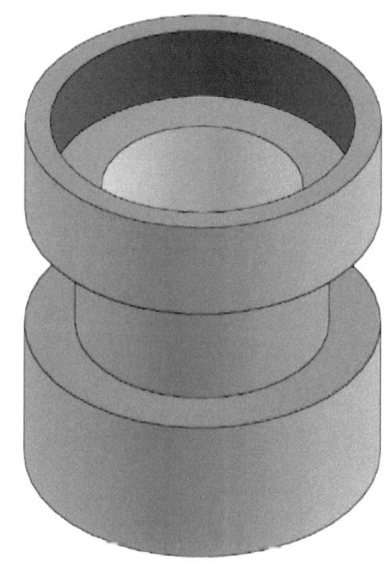
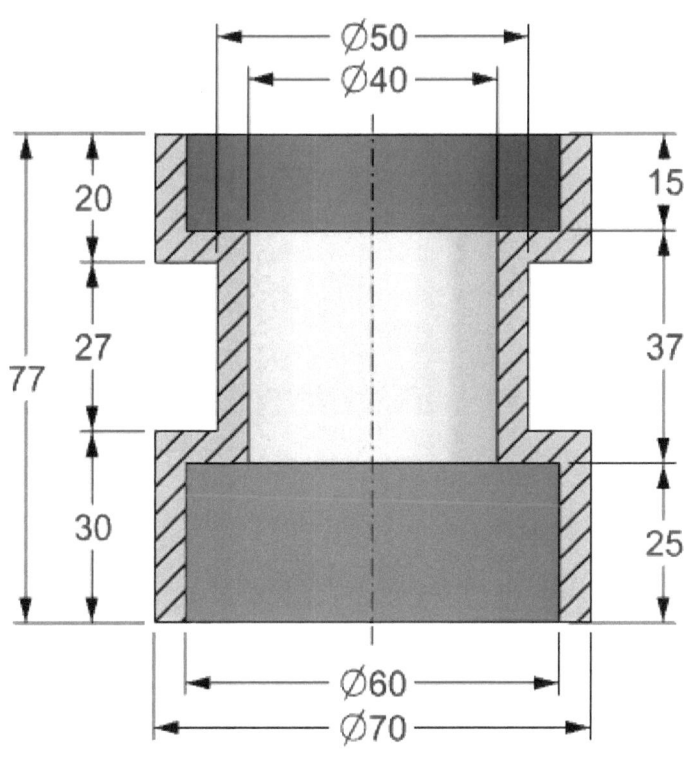

(SCALE 1:1) SECTION A-A

EXERCISE-98

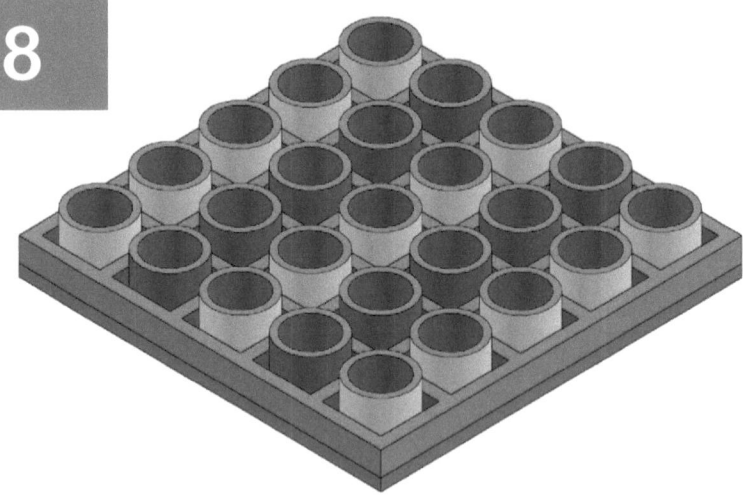

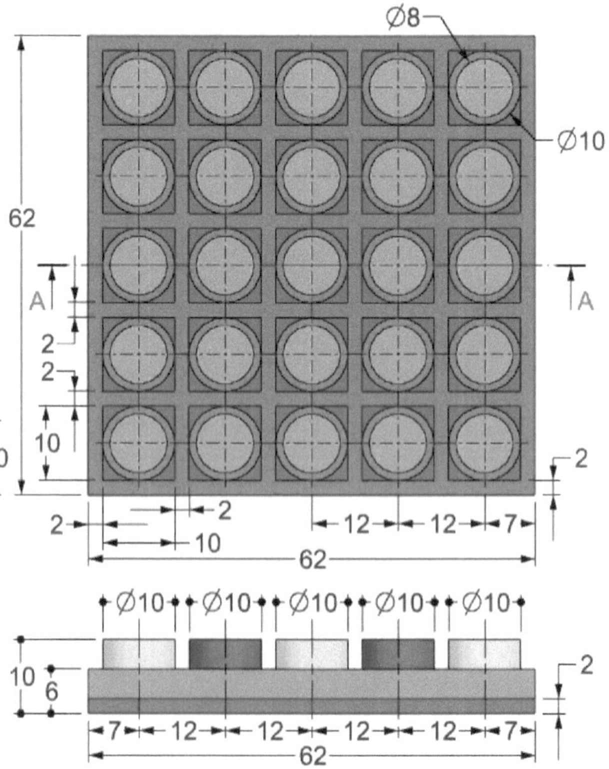

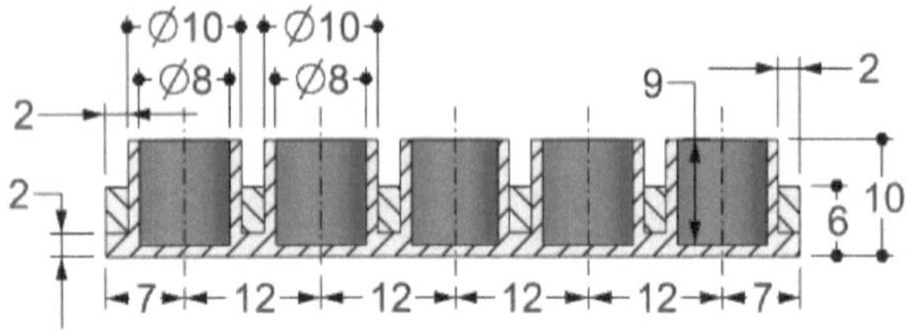

EXERCISE-99

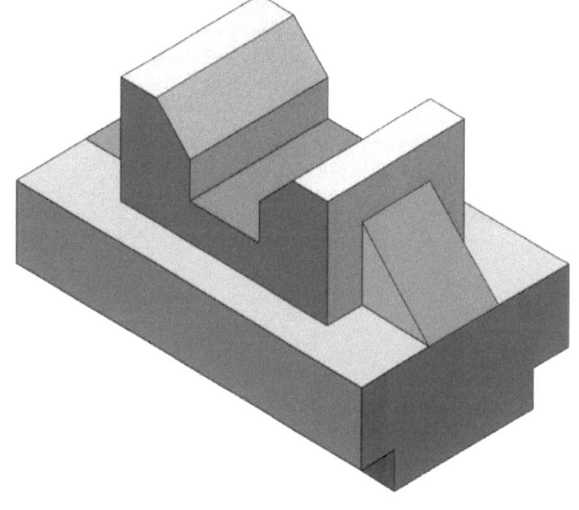

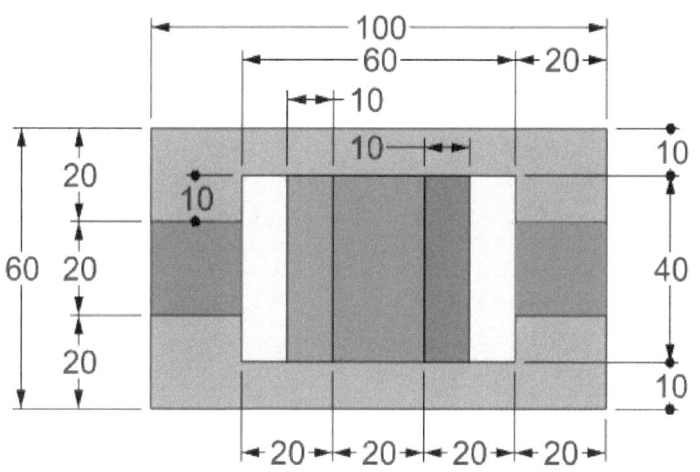

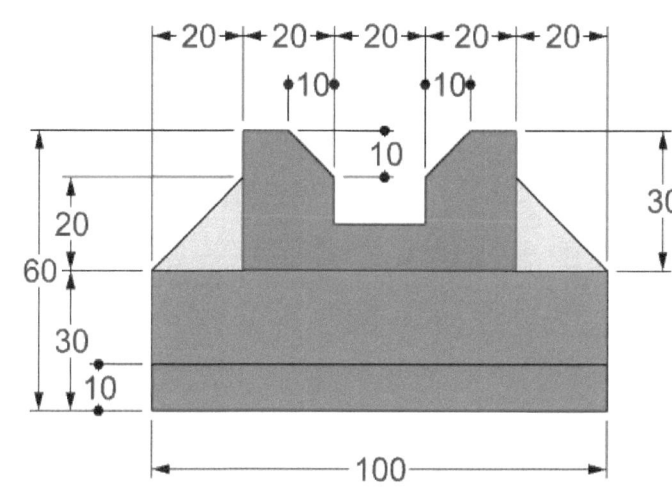

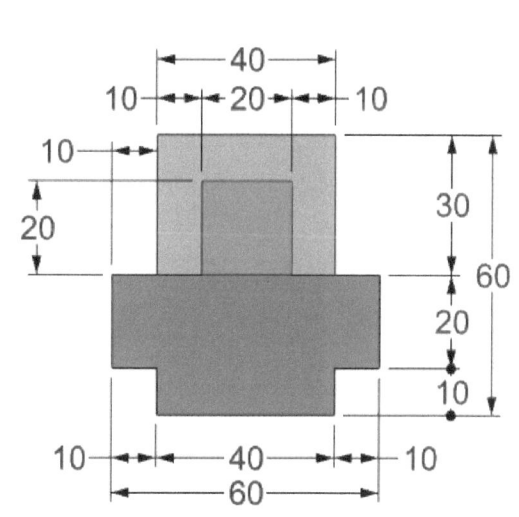

EXERCISE-100

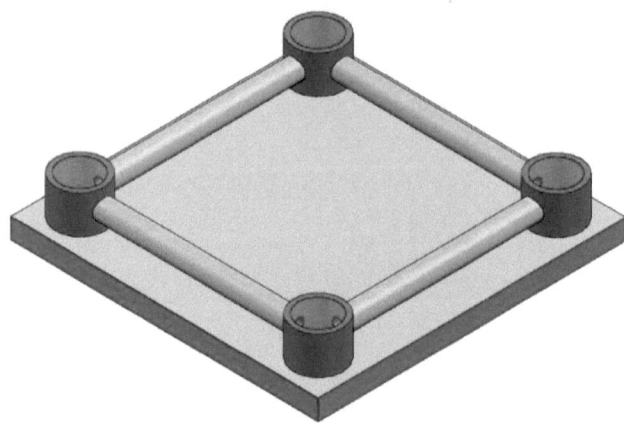
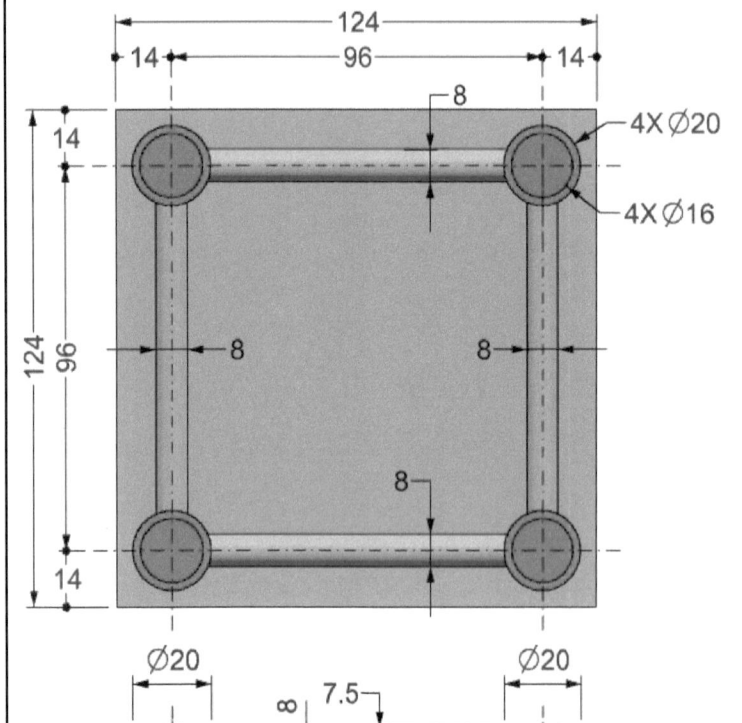
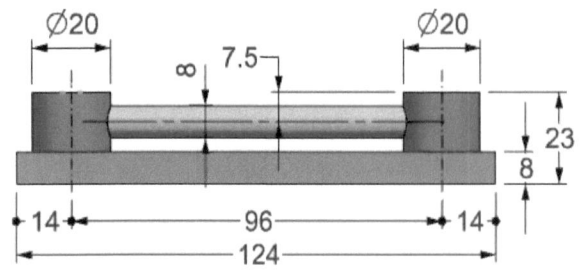
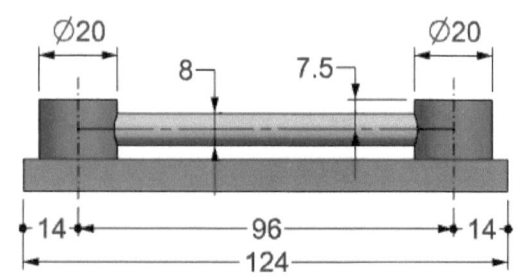

EXERCISE-101

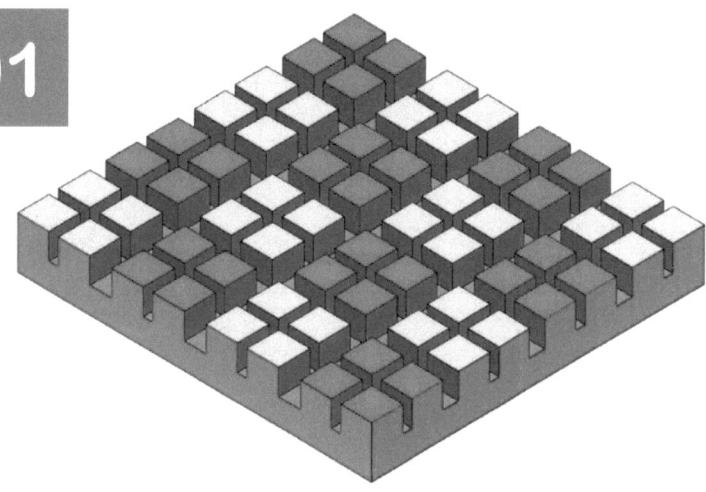

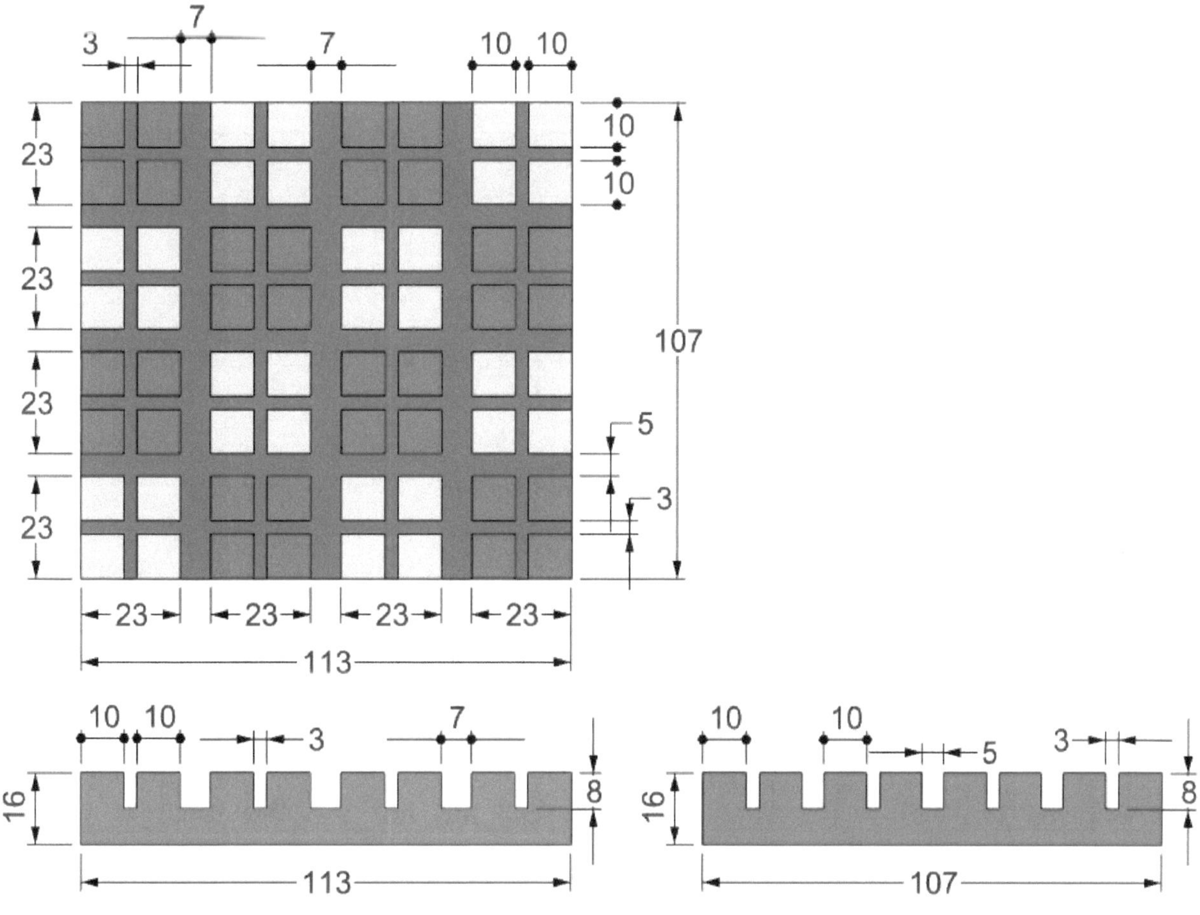

EXERCISE-102

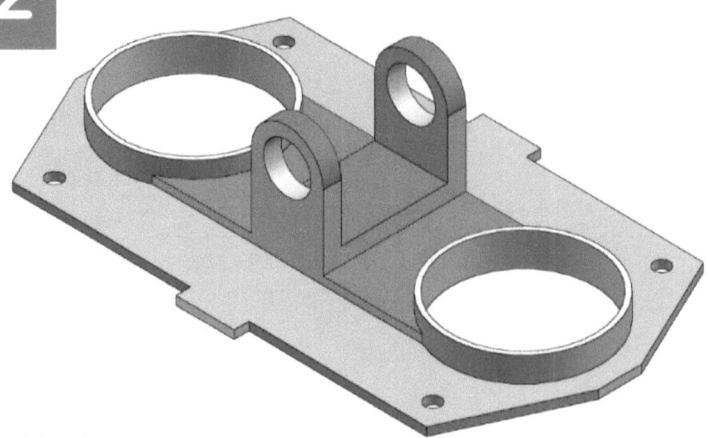

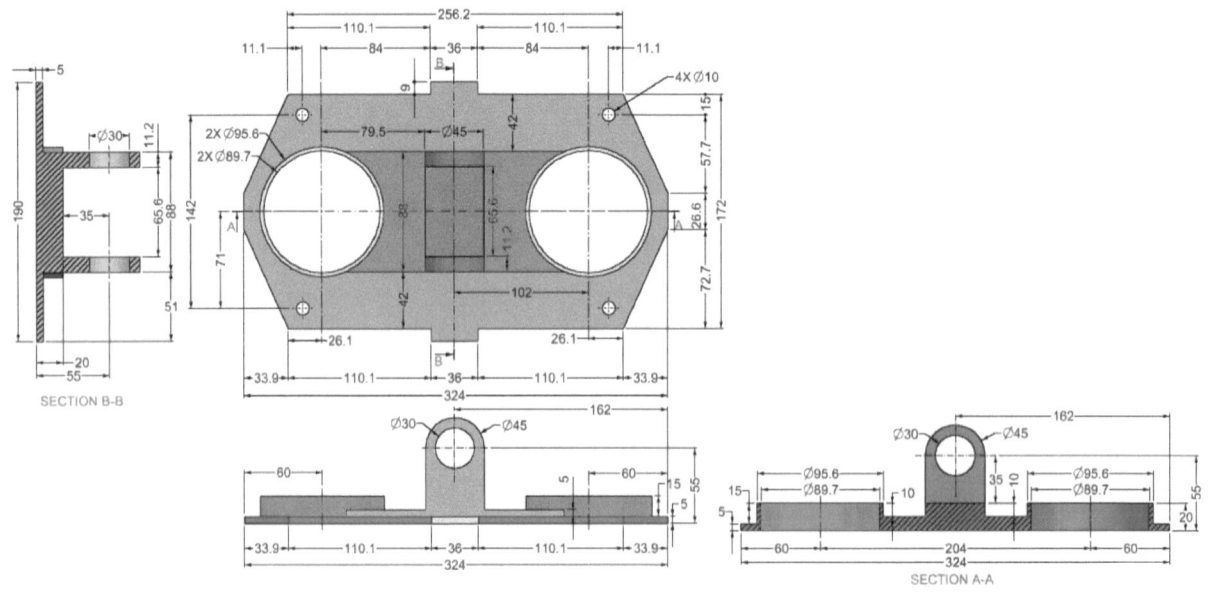

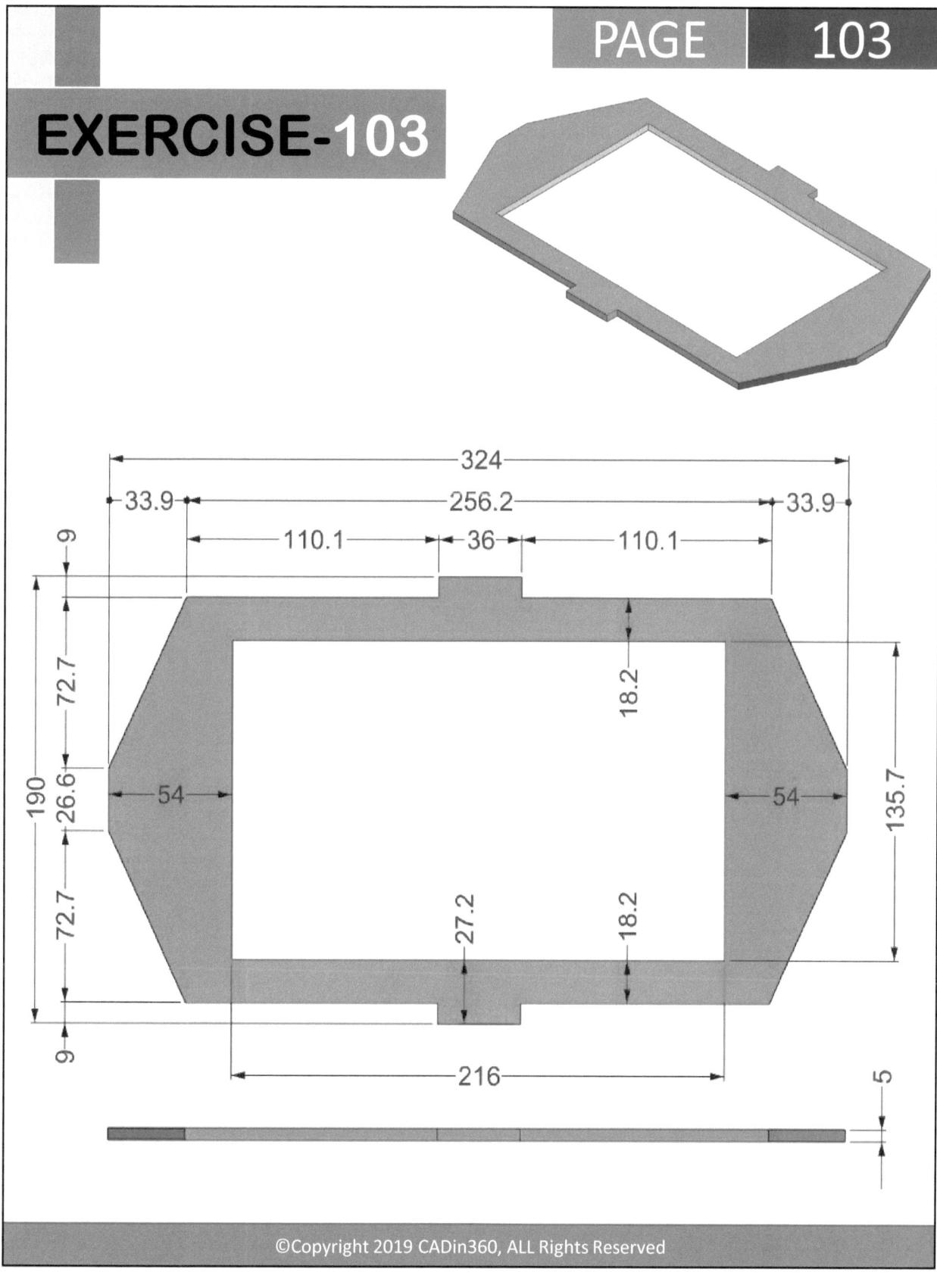

EXERCISE-104

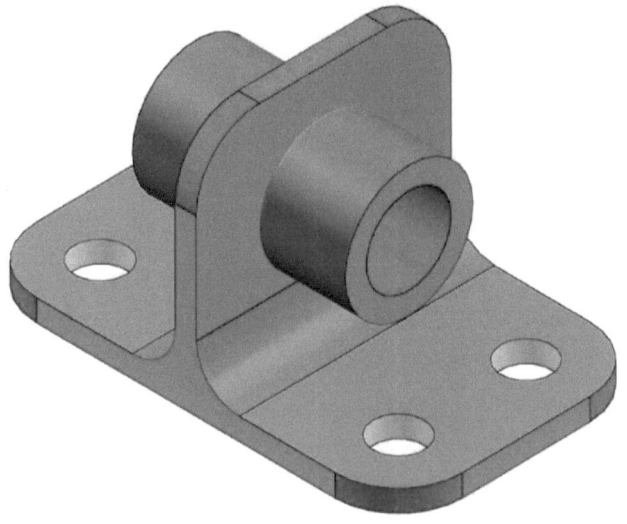

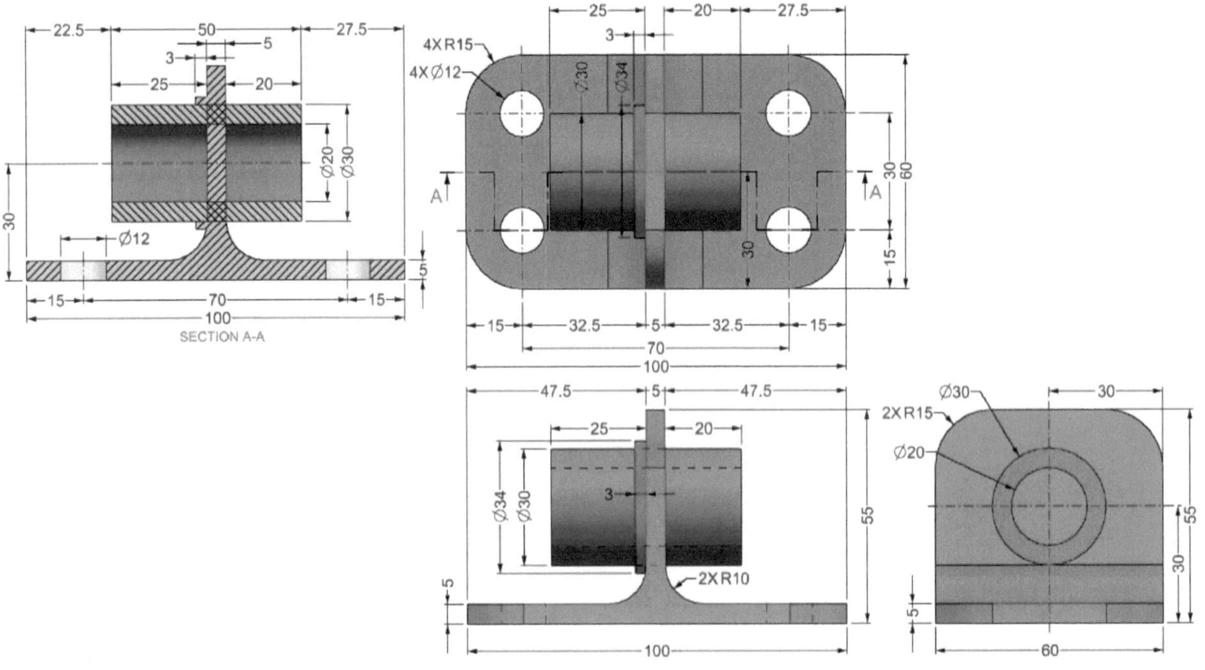

EXERCISE-105

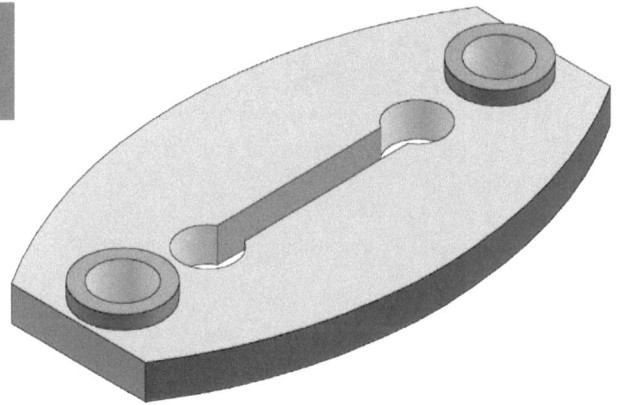

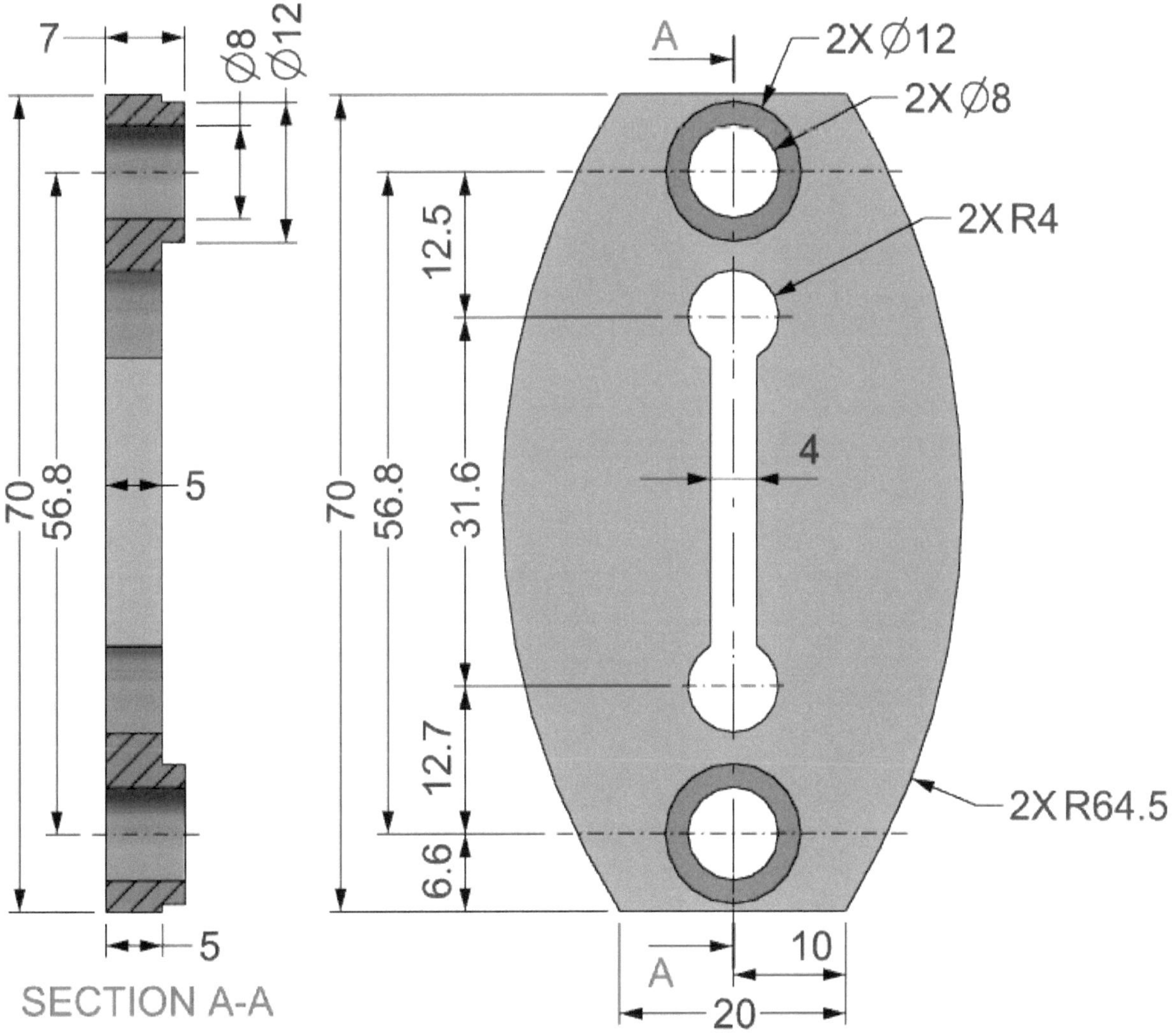

SECTION A-A

EXERCISE-106

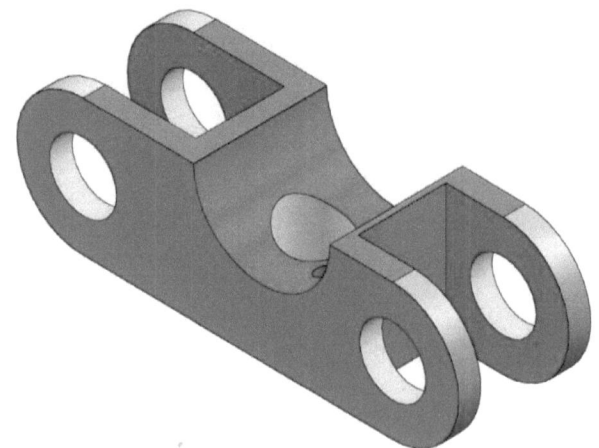

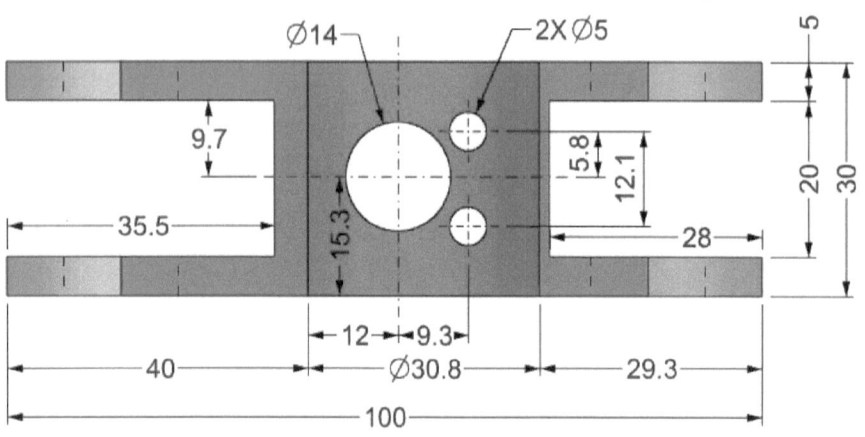

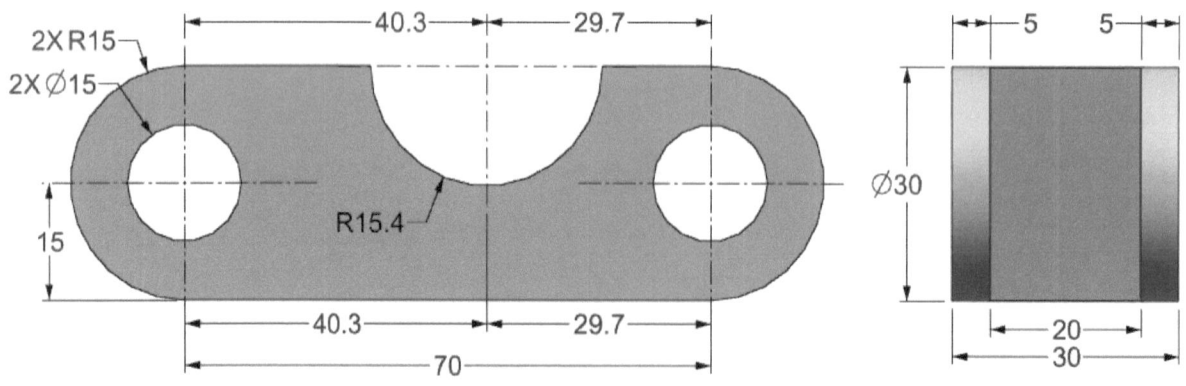

EXERCISE-107

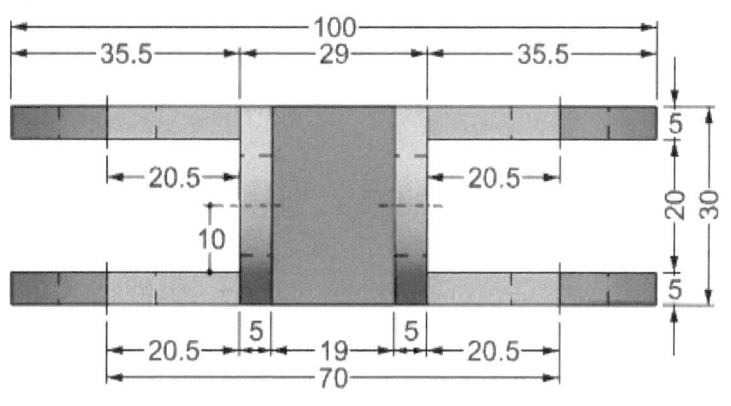
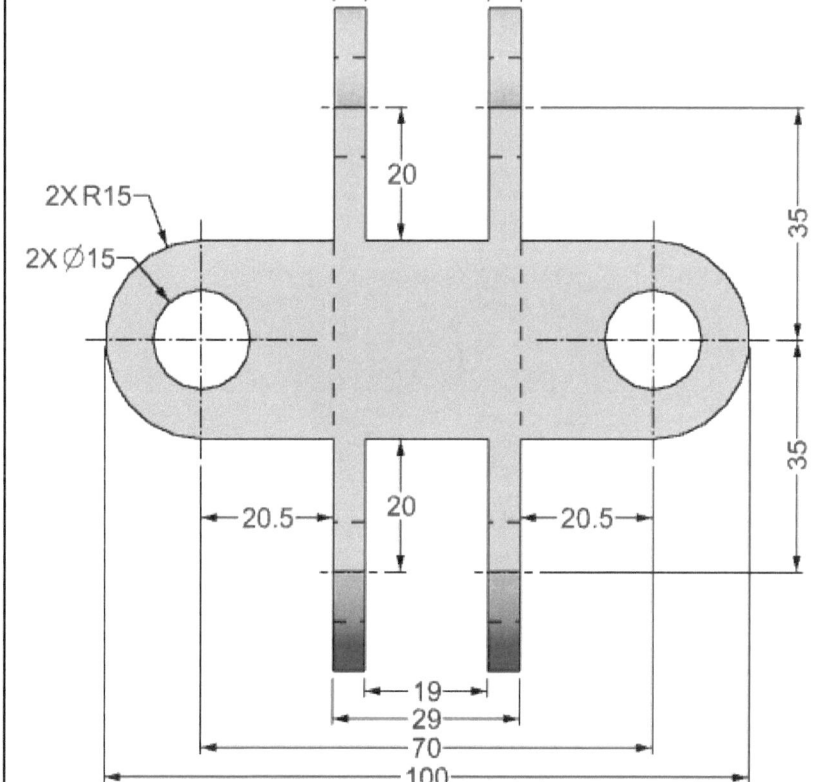
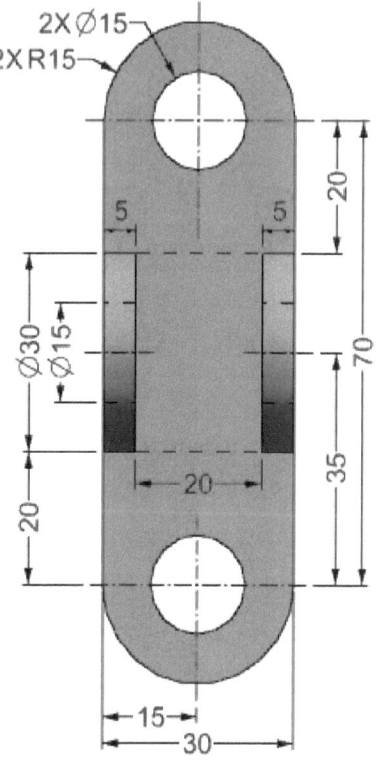

EXERCISE-108

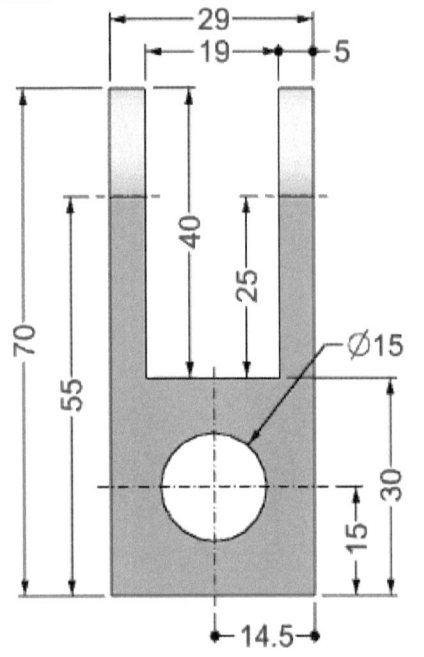
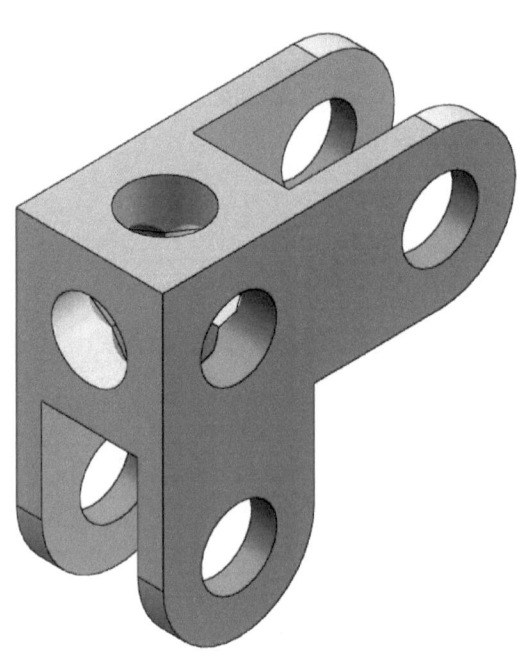
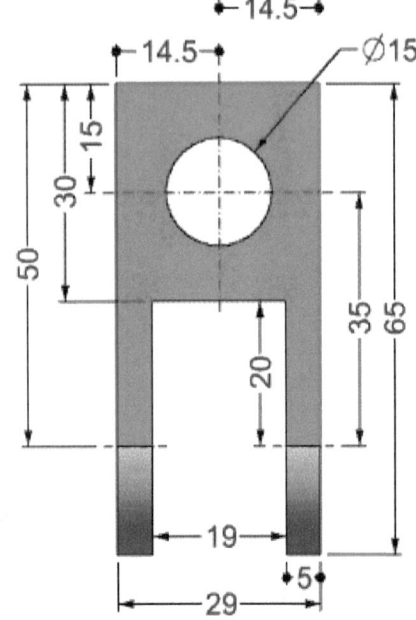
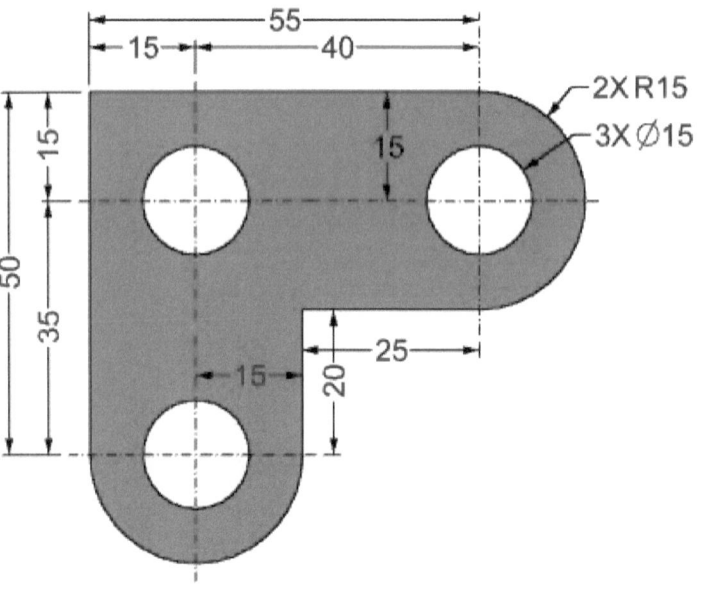

EXERCISE-109

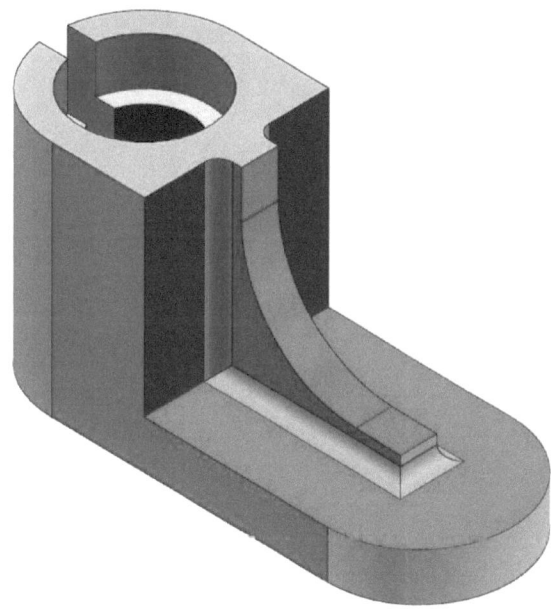

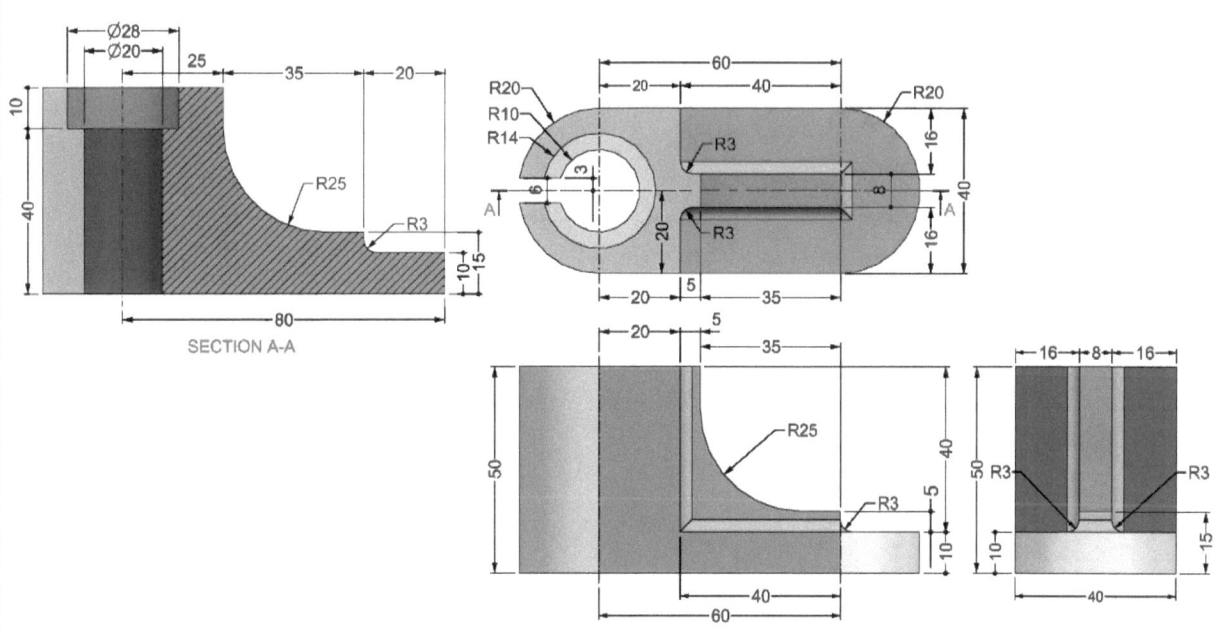

EXERCISE-110

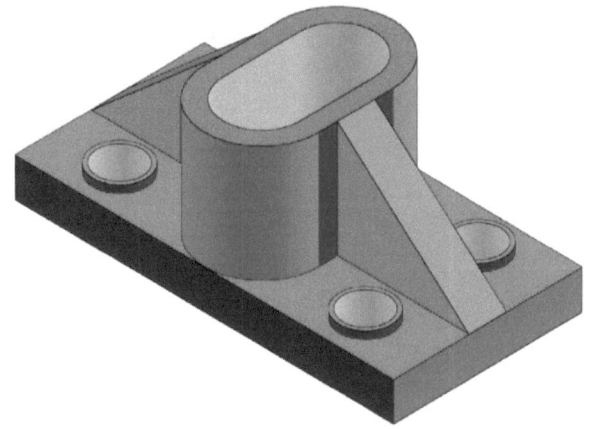

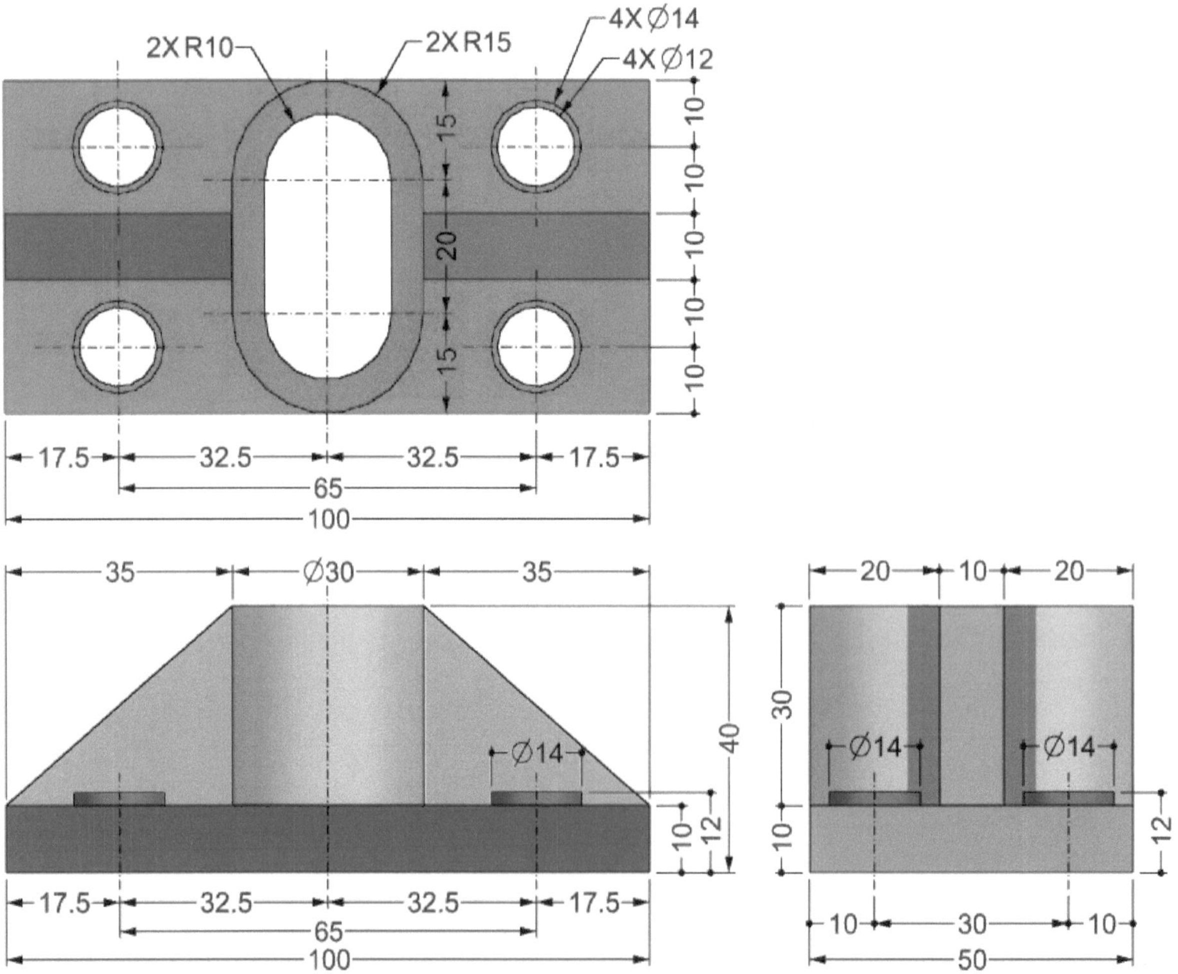

EXERCISE-111

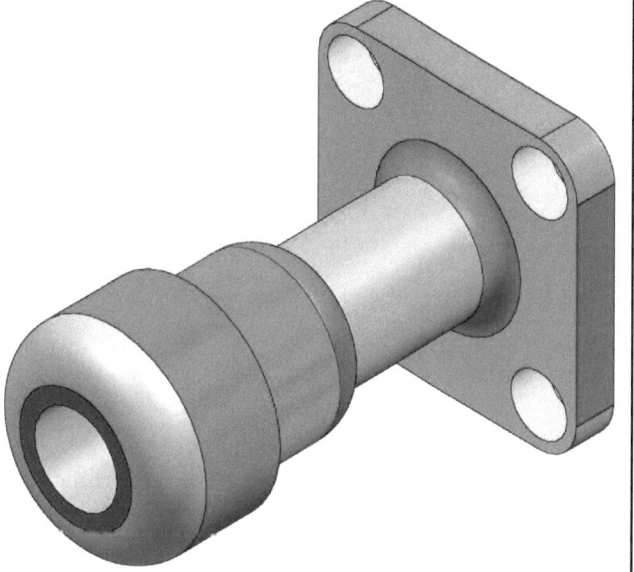

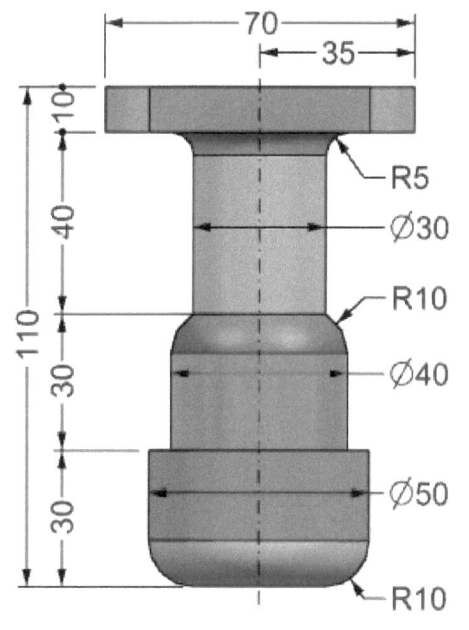

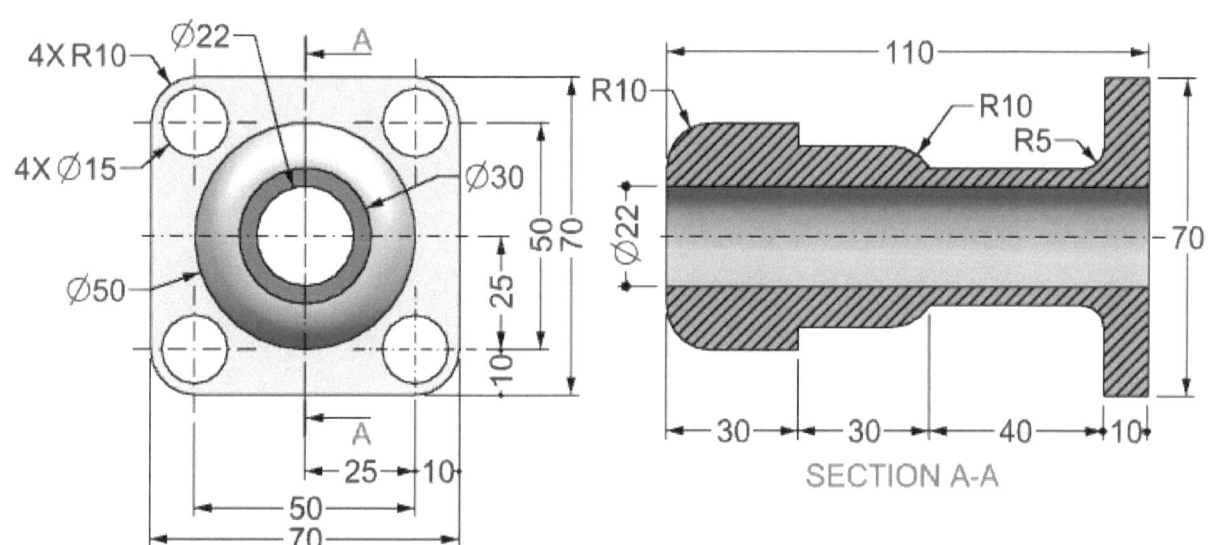

SECTION A-A

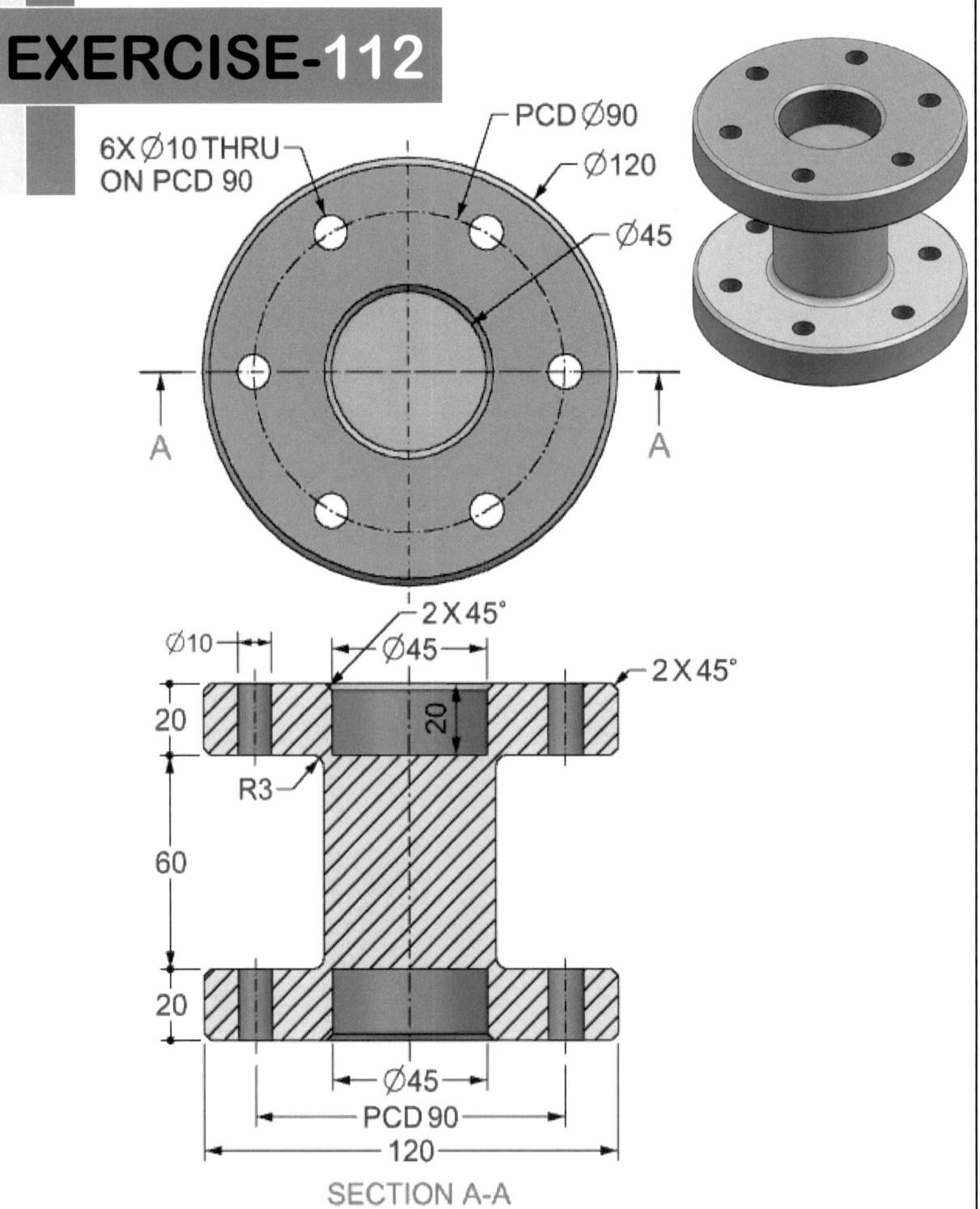

EXERCISE-113

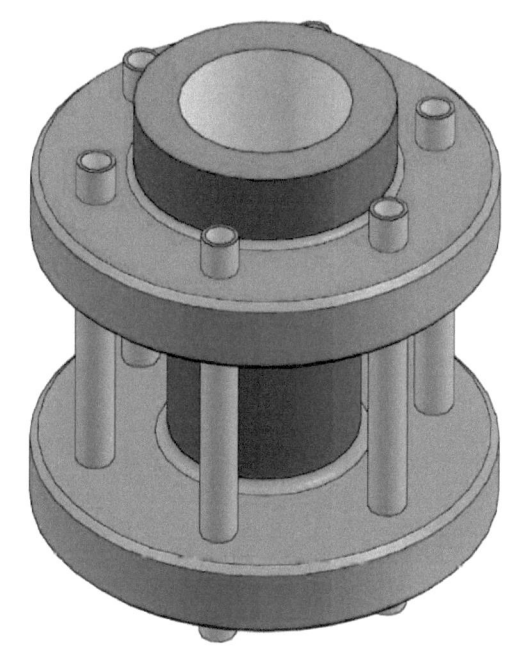

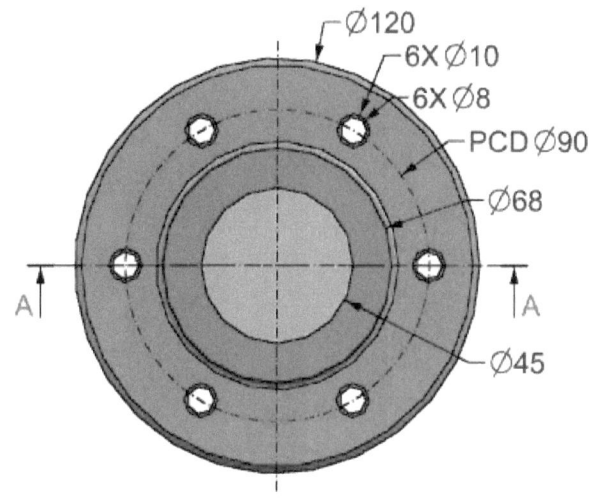

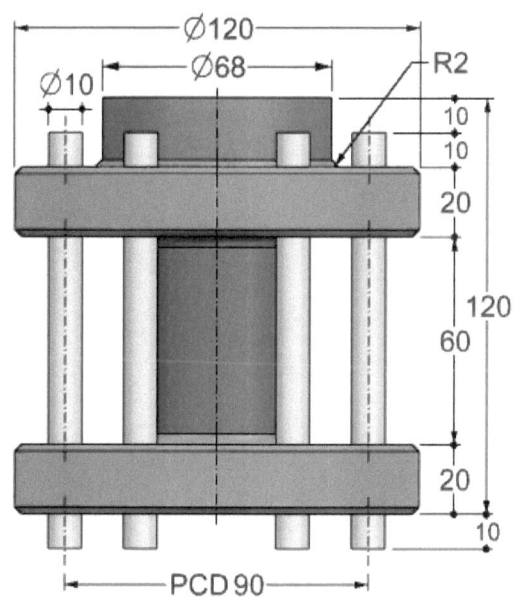

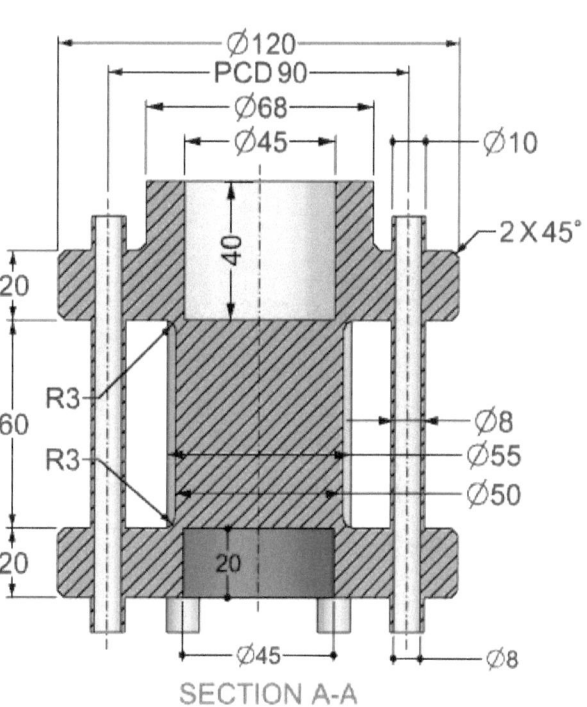

EXERCISE-114

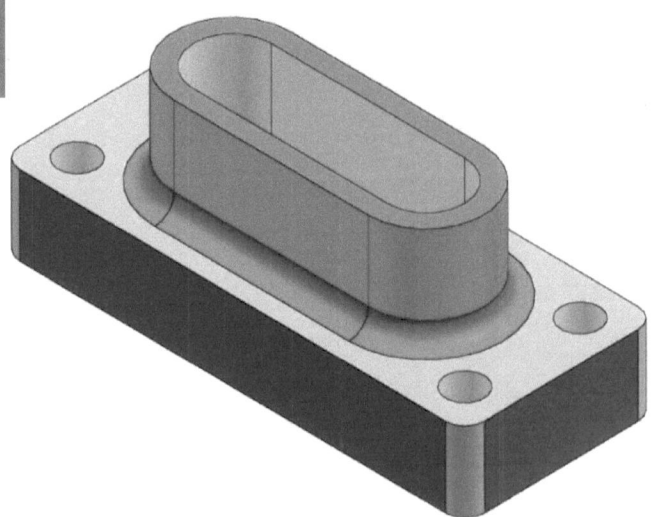

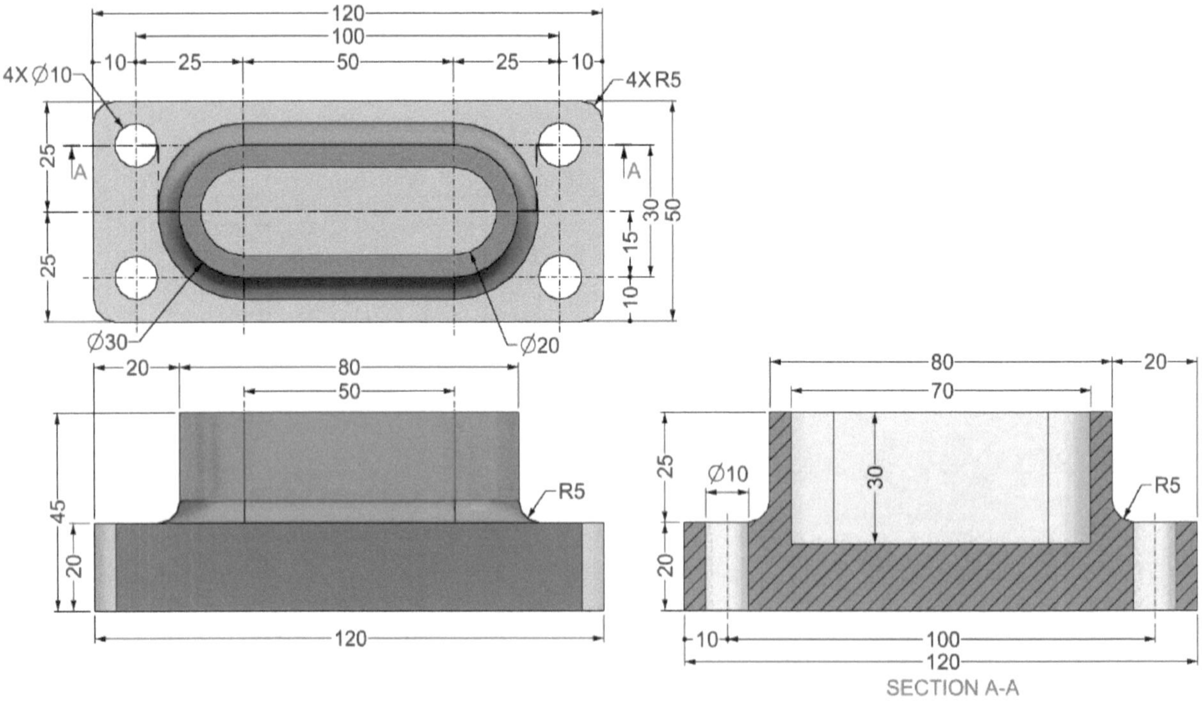

SECTION A-A

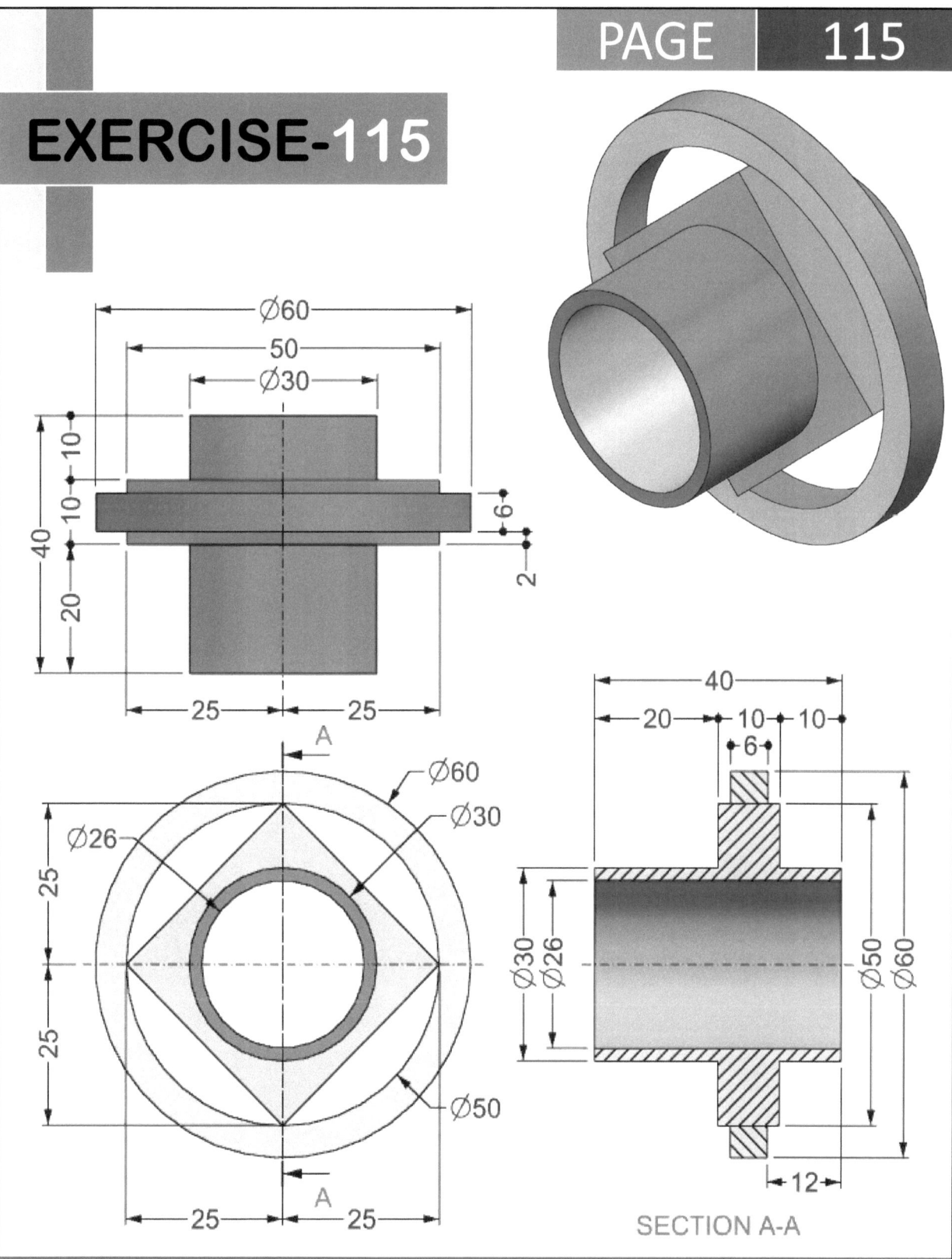

EXERCISE-116

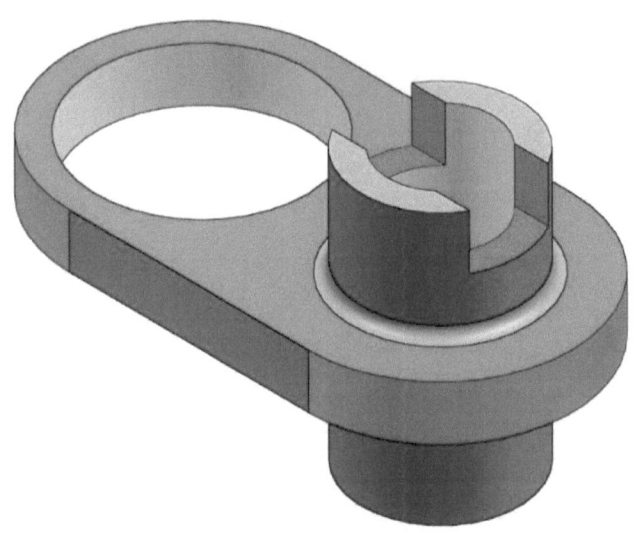

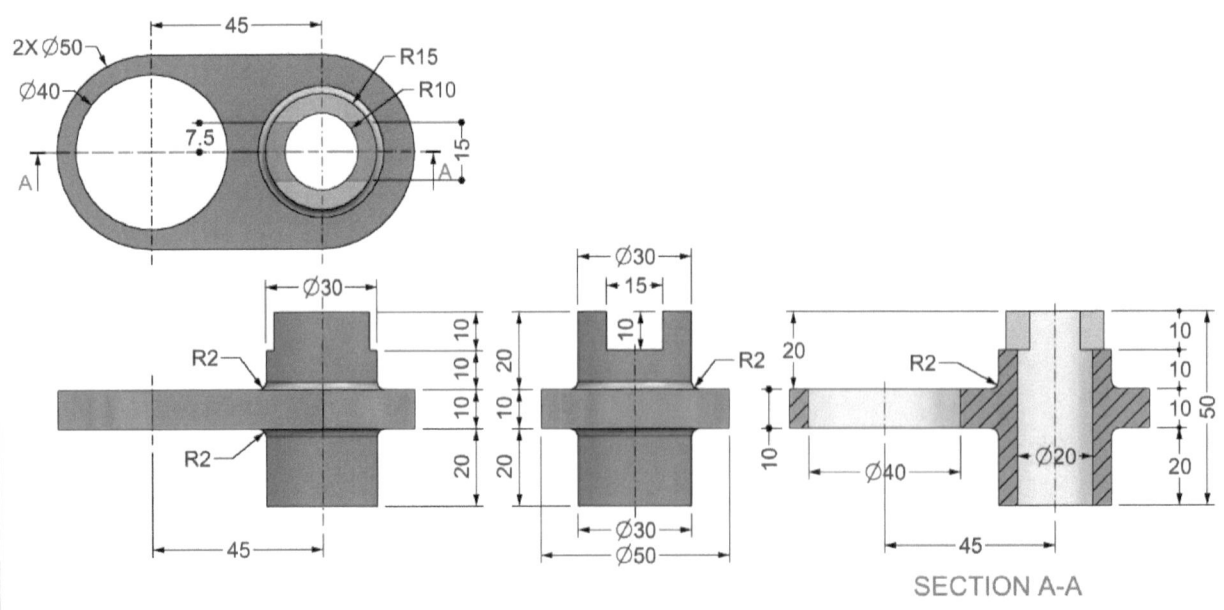

EXERCISE-117

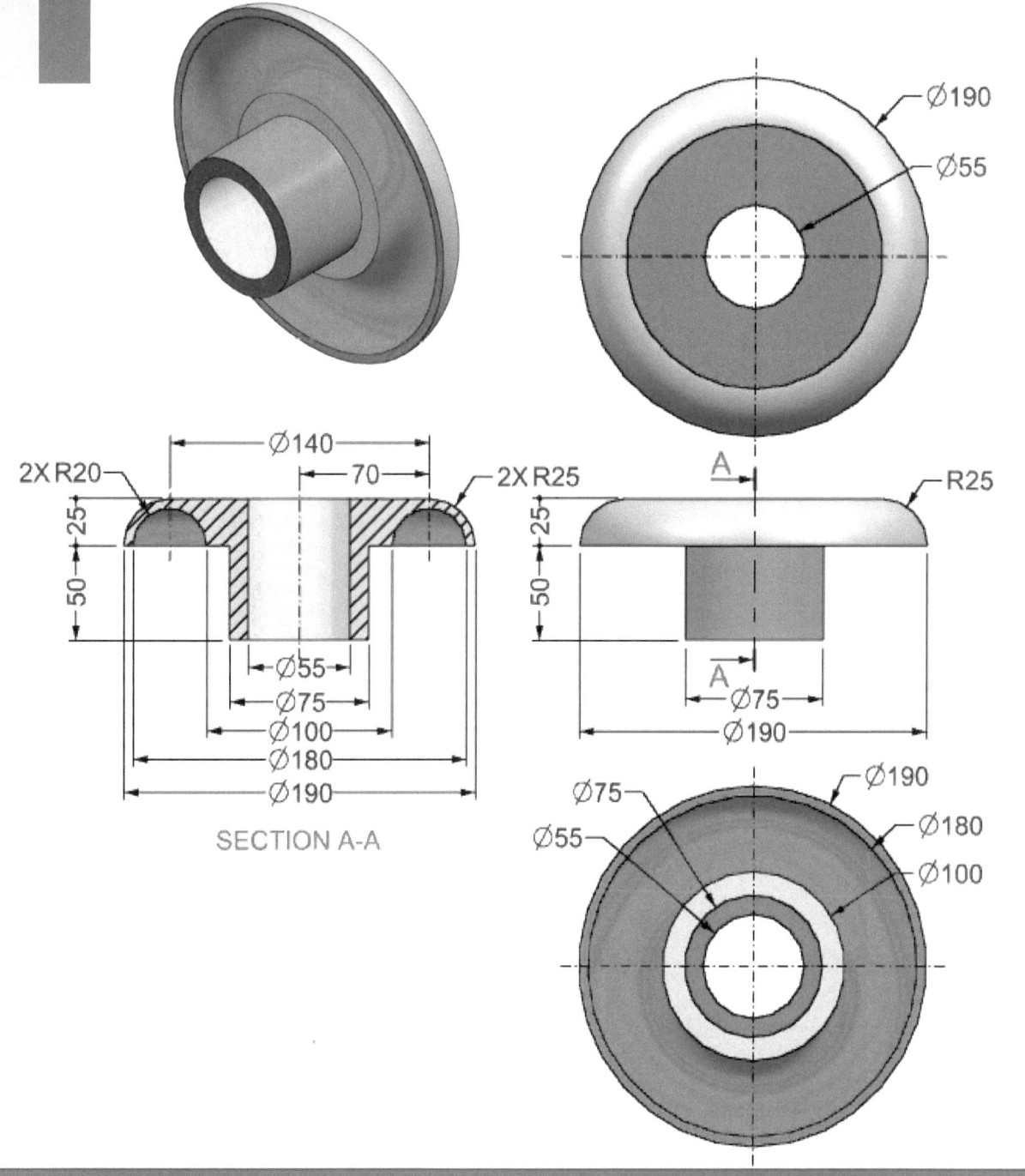

EXERCISE-118

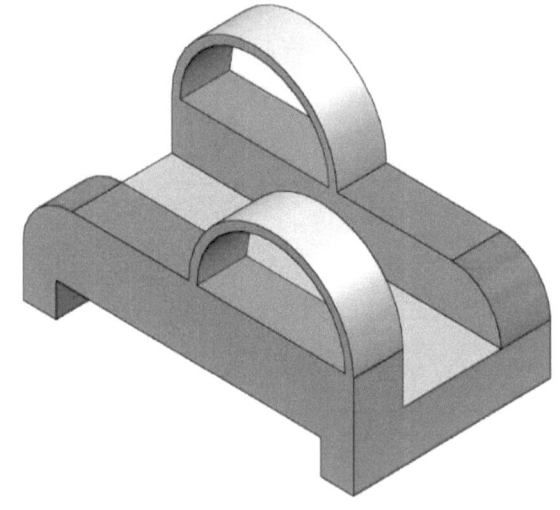
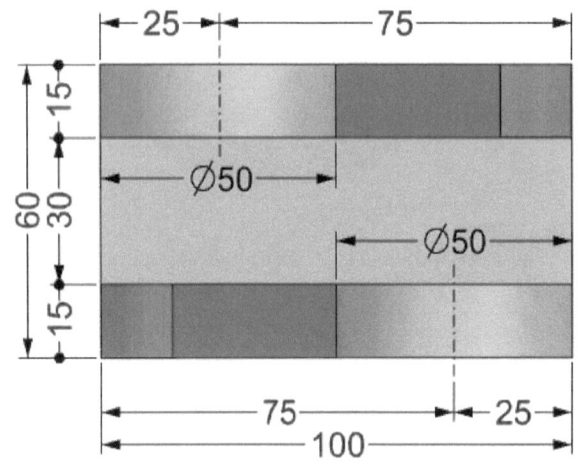
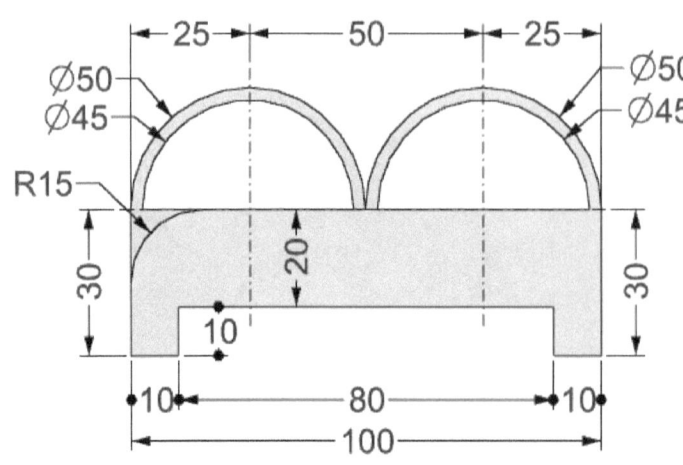
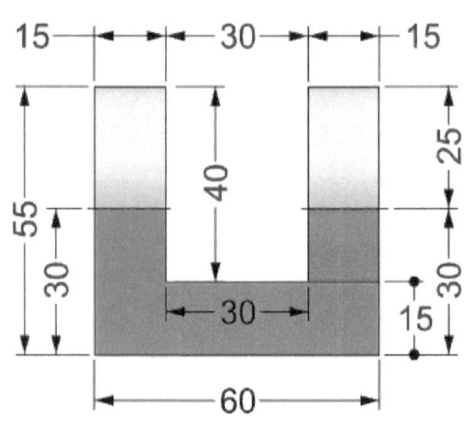

EXERCISE-119

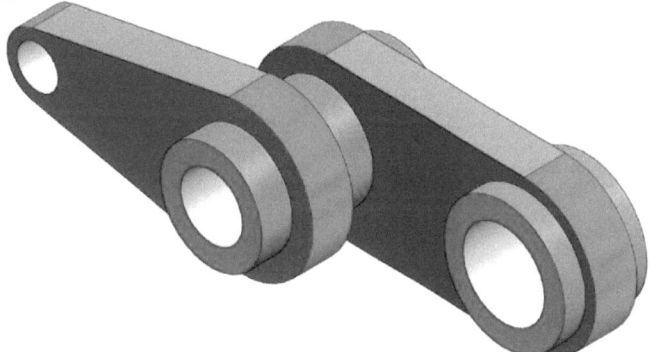

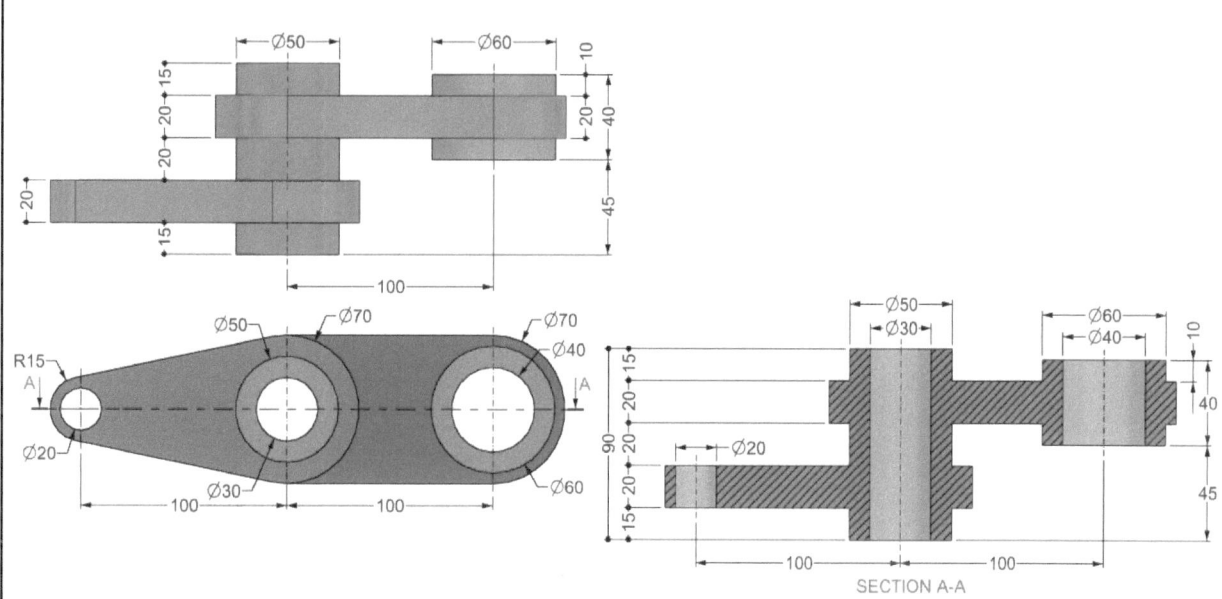

SECTION A-A

EXERCISE-120

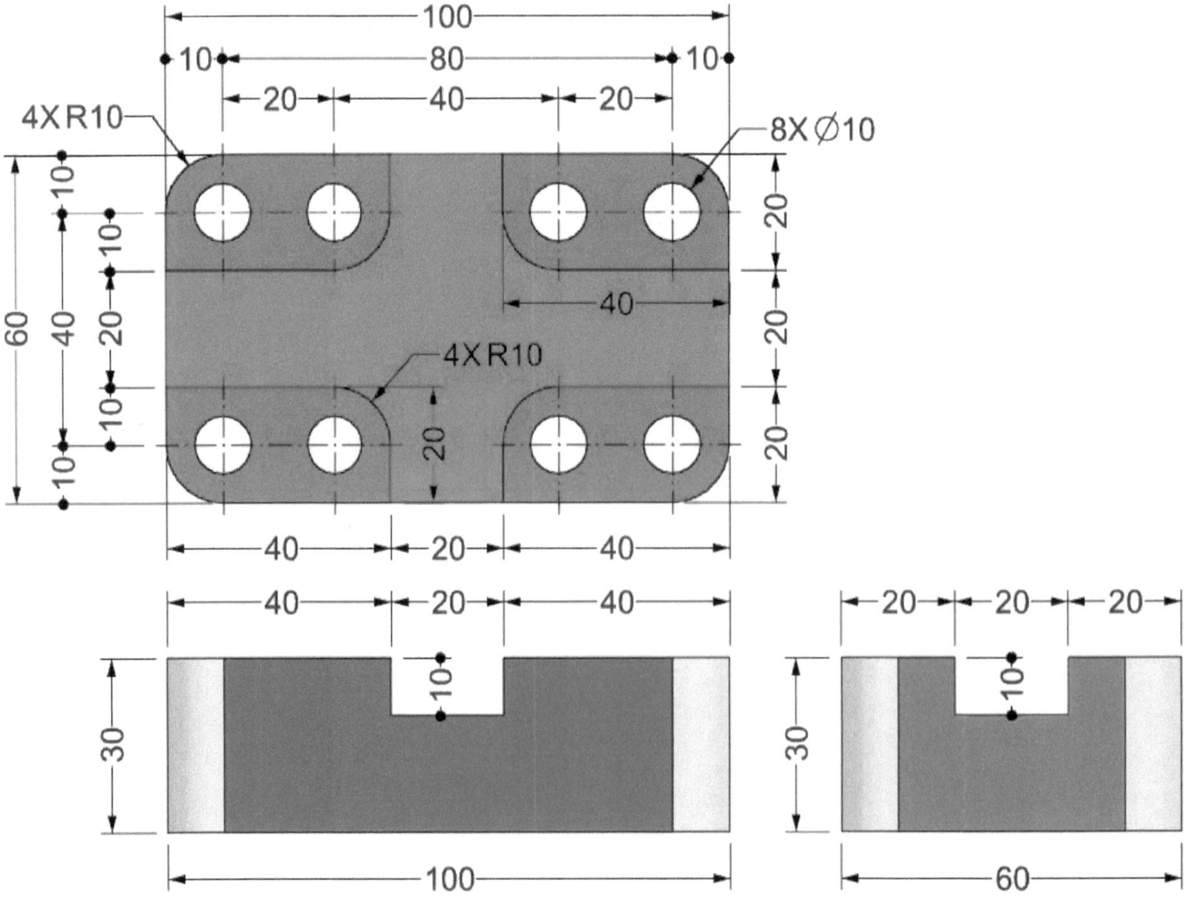

EXERCISE-121

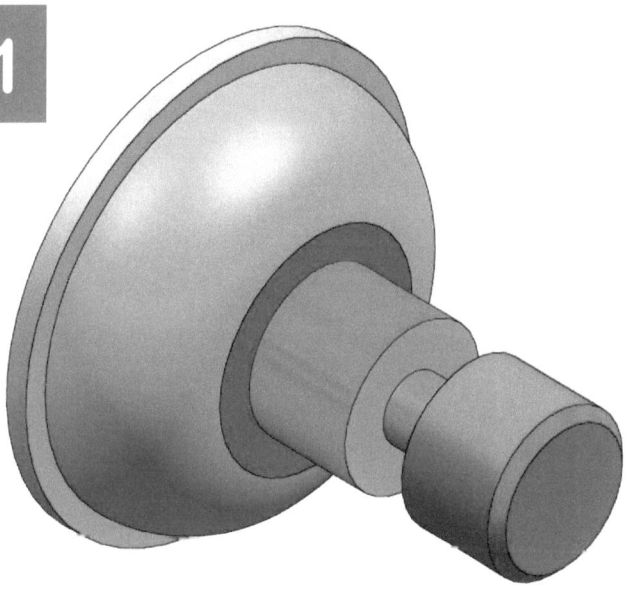

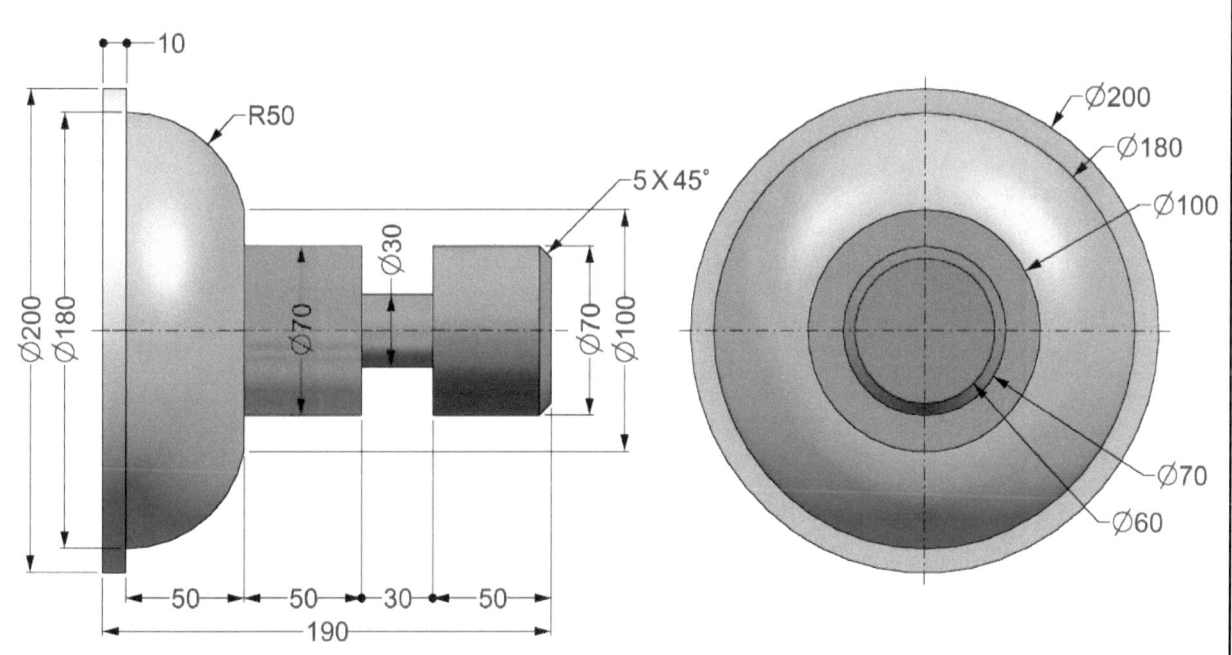

EXERCISE-122

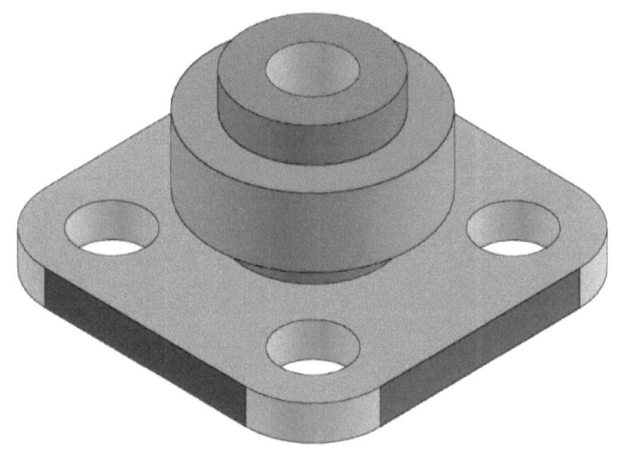

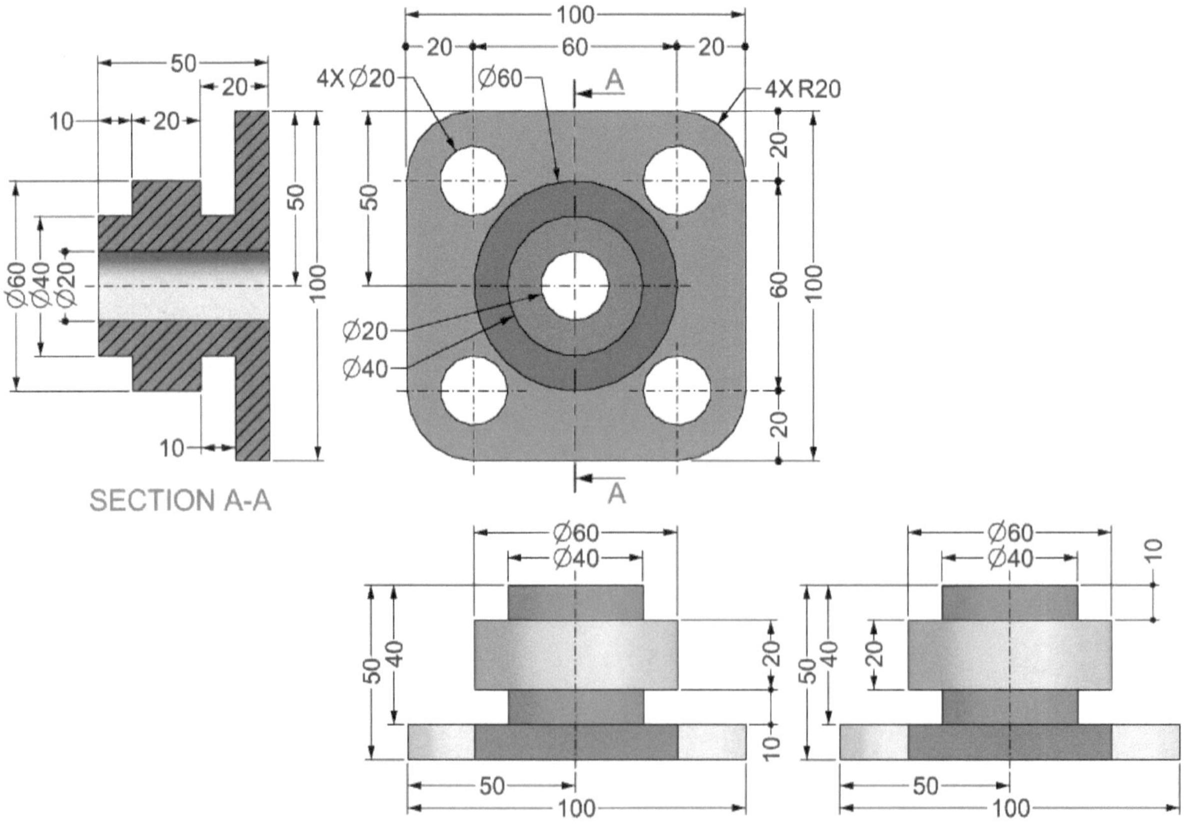

EXERCISE-123

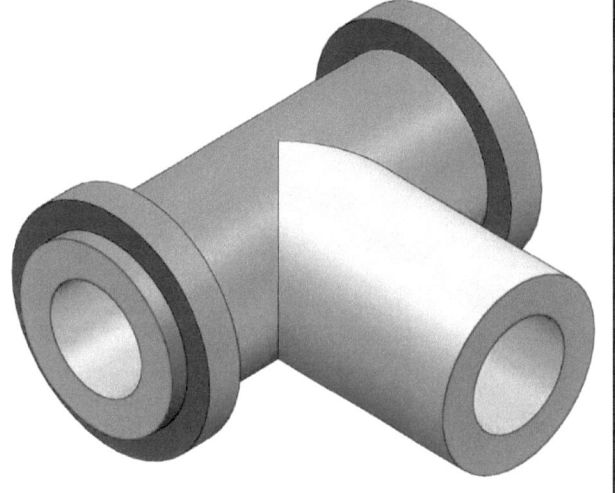

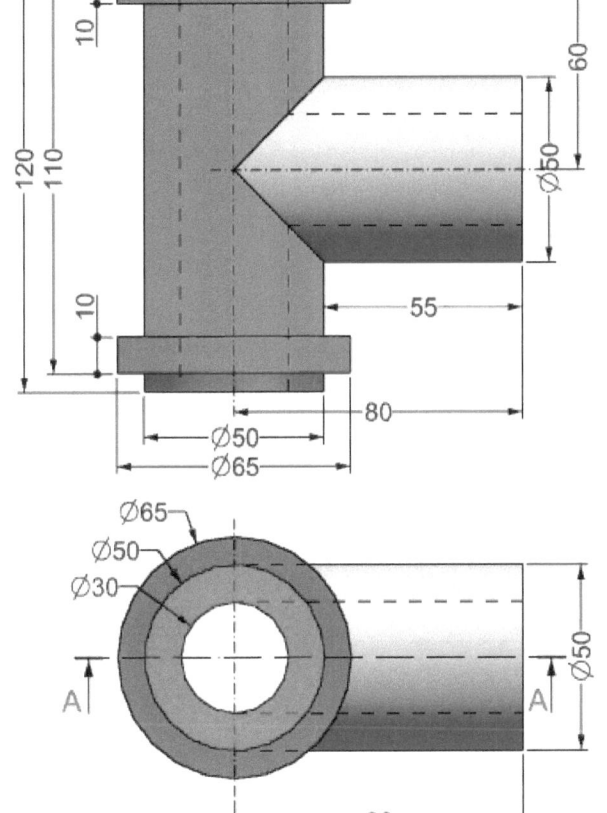

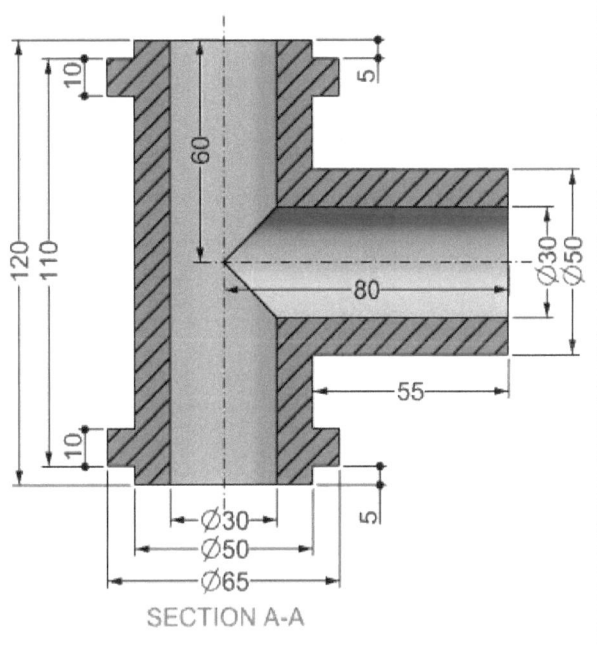

SECTION A-A

EXERCISE-124

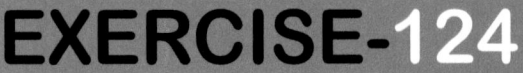

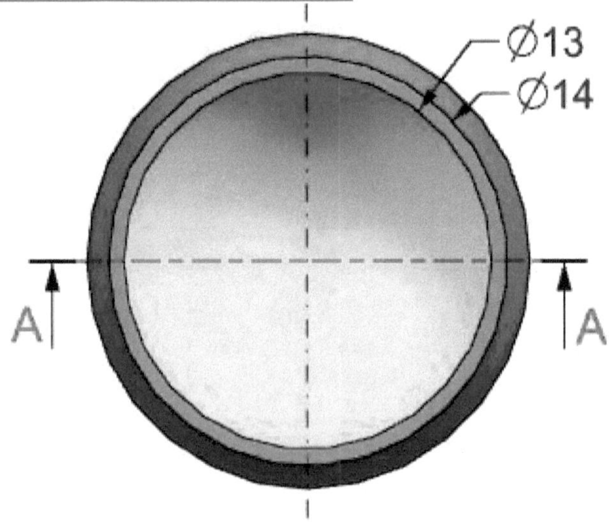

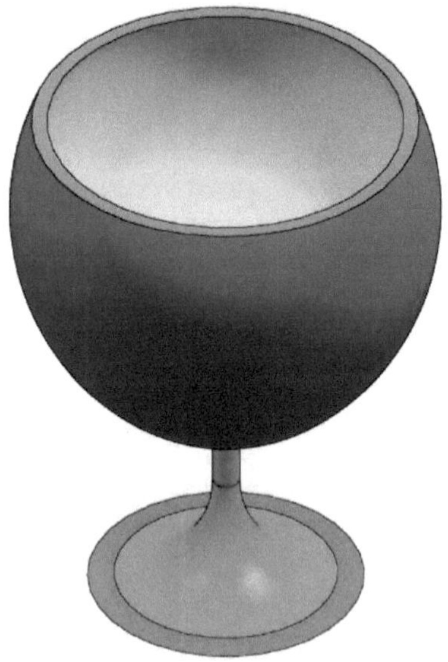

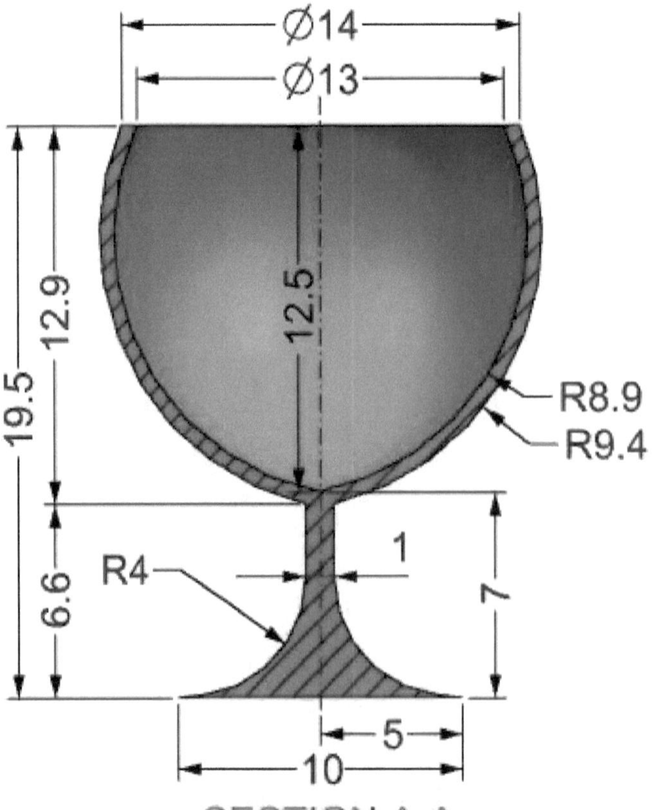

SECTION A-A

EXERCISE-125

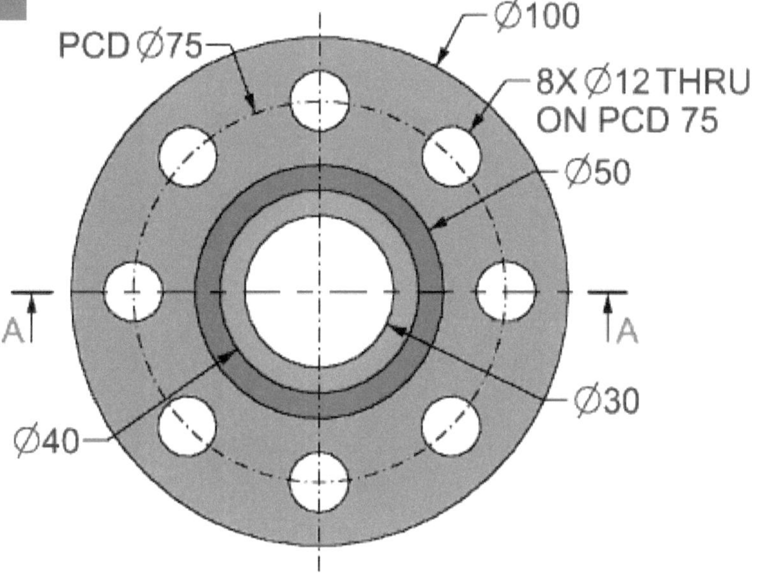

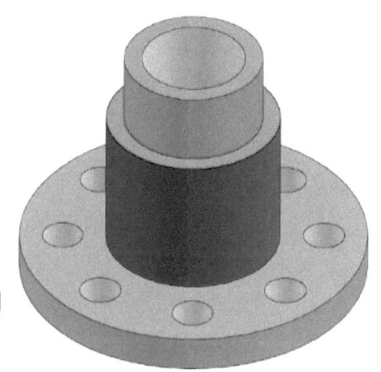

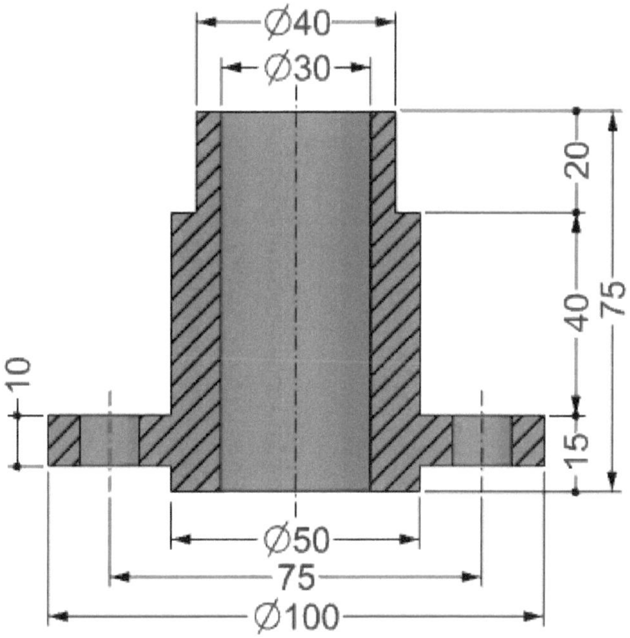

- Ø100
- PCD Ø75
- 8X Ø12 THRU ON PCD 75
- Ø50
- Ø30
- Ø40
- Ø40
- Ø30
- 20
- 40
- 75
- 10
- 15
- Ø50
- 75
- Ø100

SECTION A-A

©Copyright 2019 CADin360, ALL Rights Reserved

EXERCISE-126

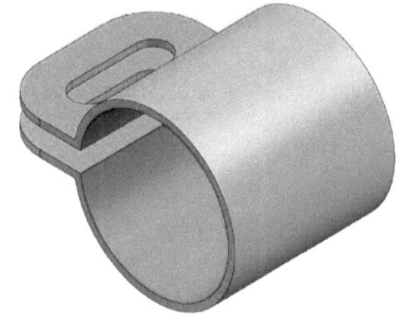

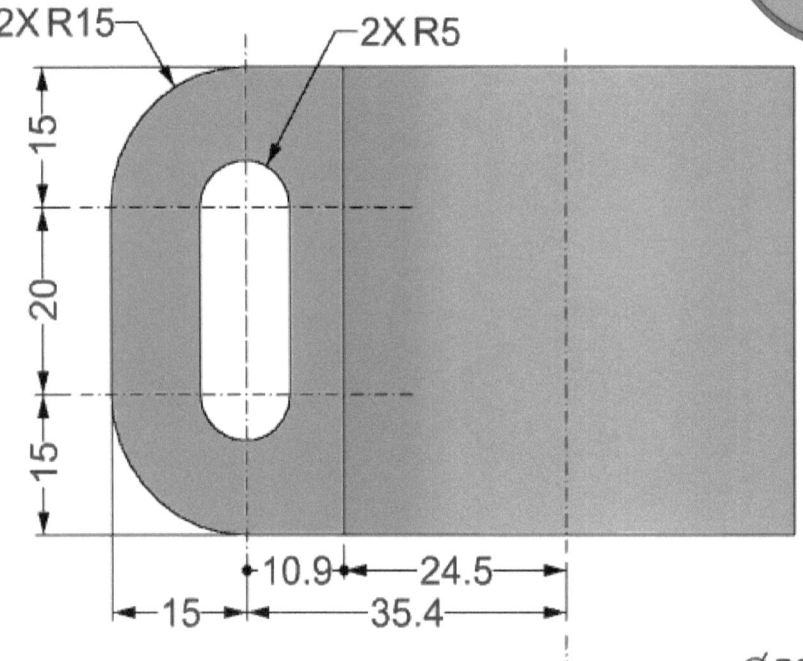

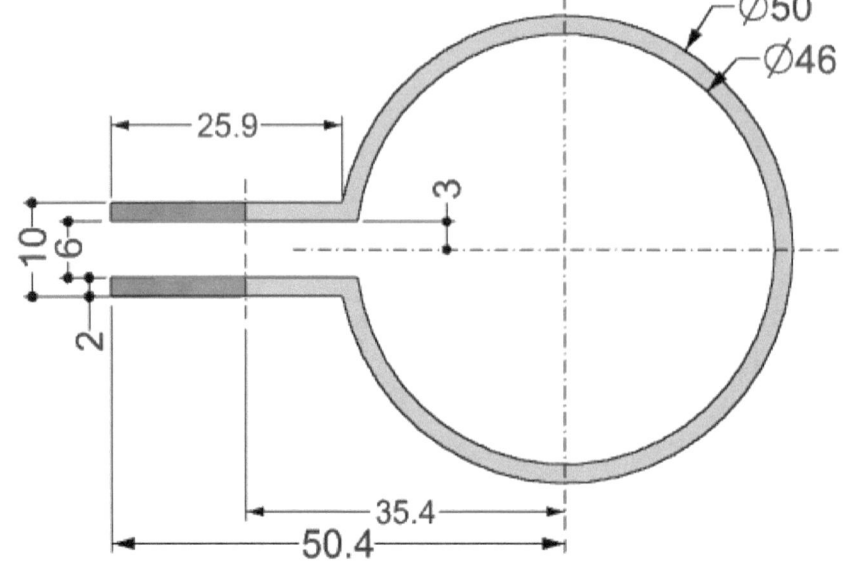

EXERCISE-127

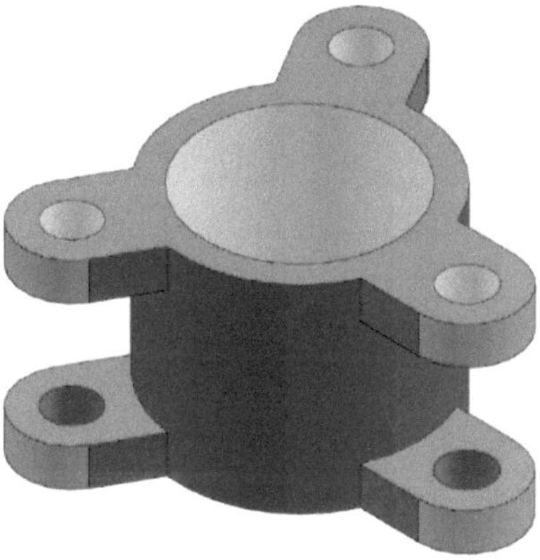

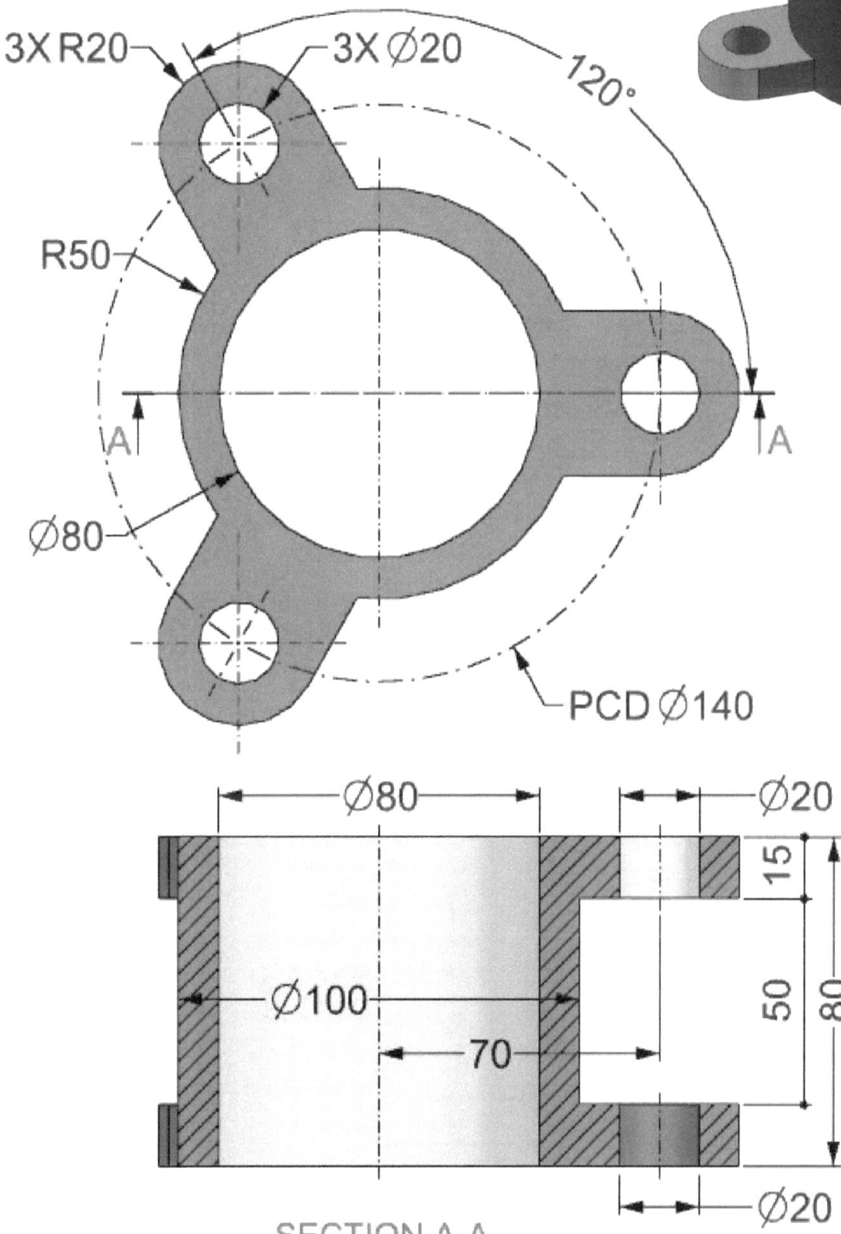

3X R20
3X Ø20
120°
R50
Ø80
PCD Ø140

Ø80
Ø20
15
Ø100
50
80
70
Ø20

SECTION A-A

EXERCISE-128

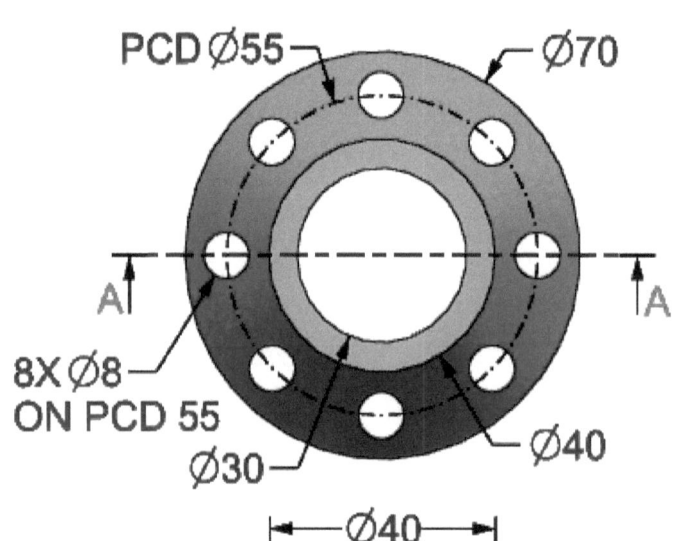
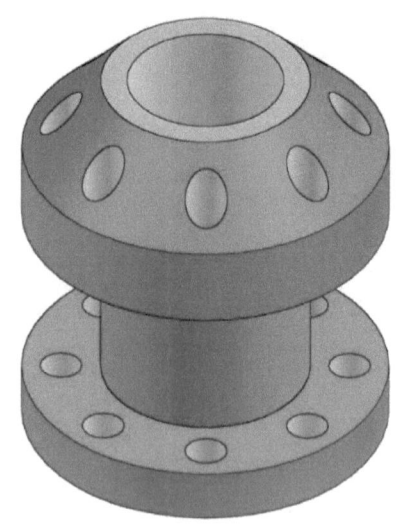
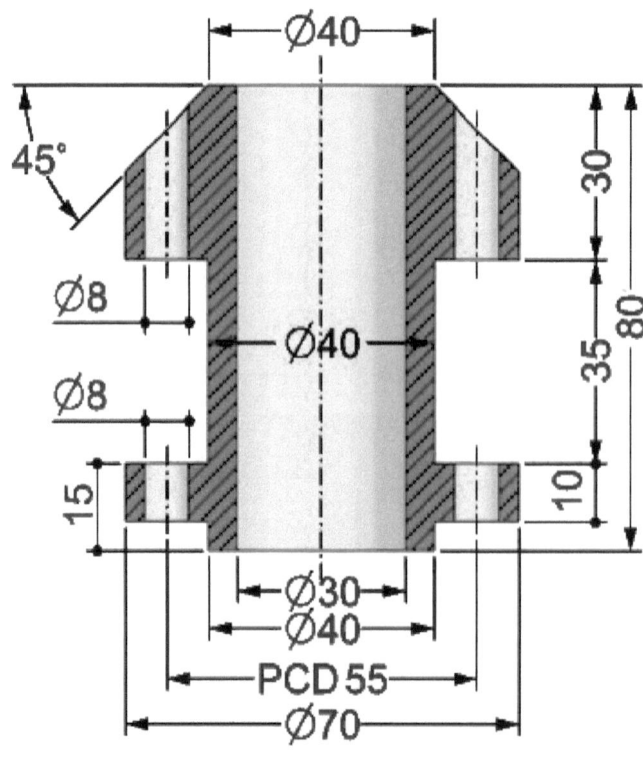

SECTION A-A

EXERCISE-129

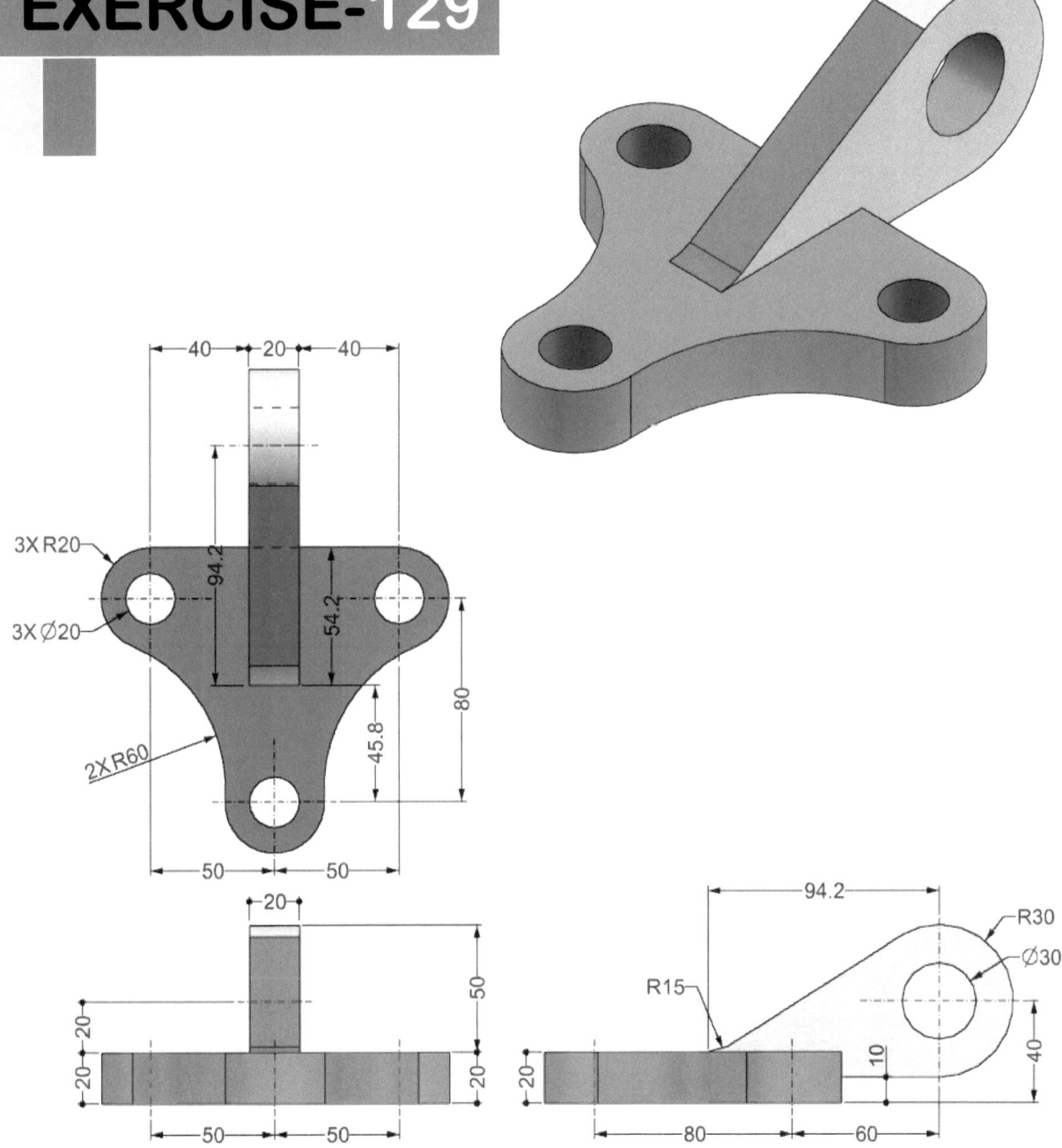

EXERCISE-130

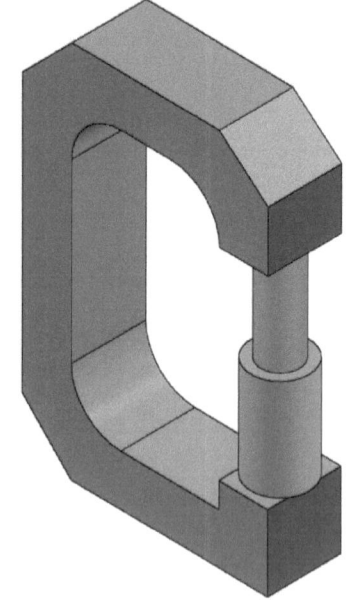
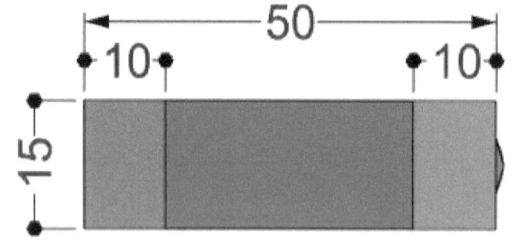
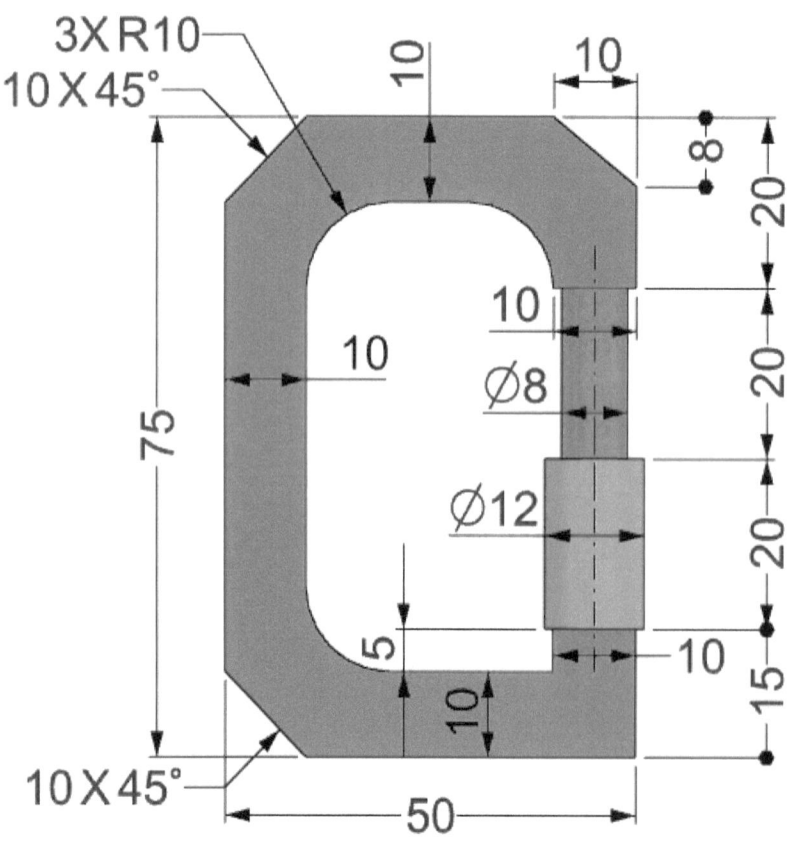
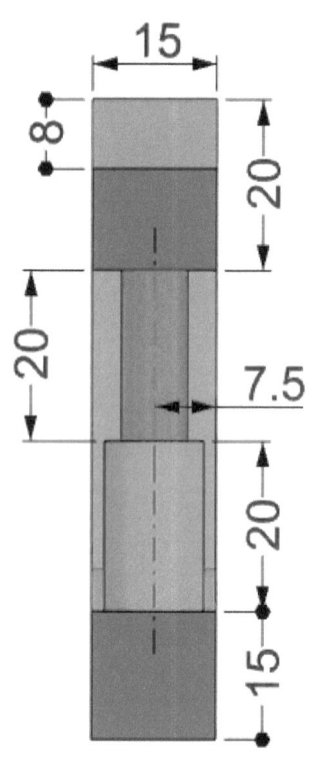

EXERCISE-131

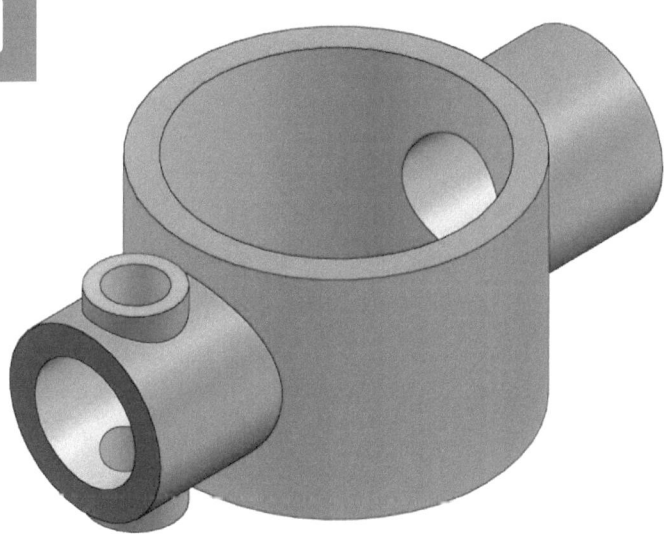

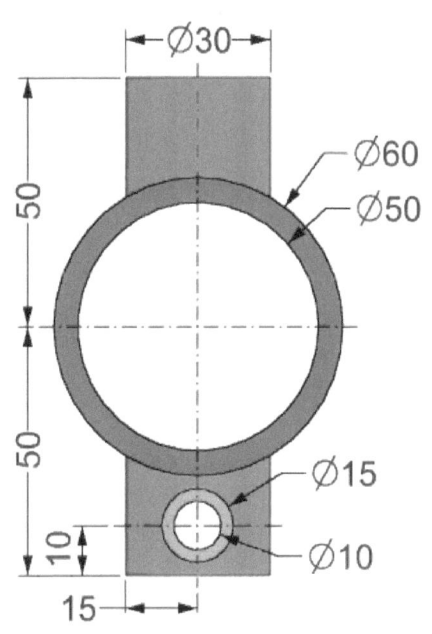

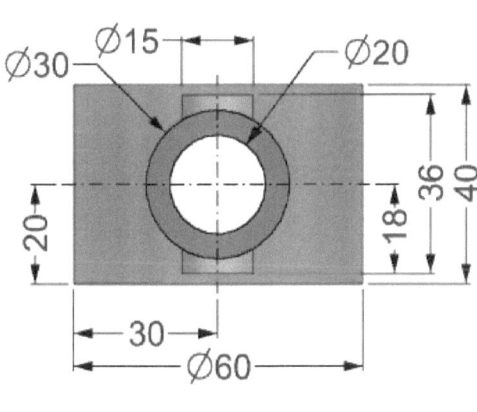

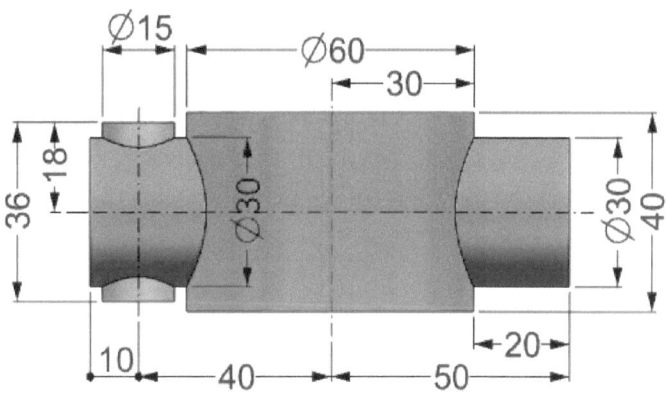

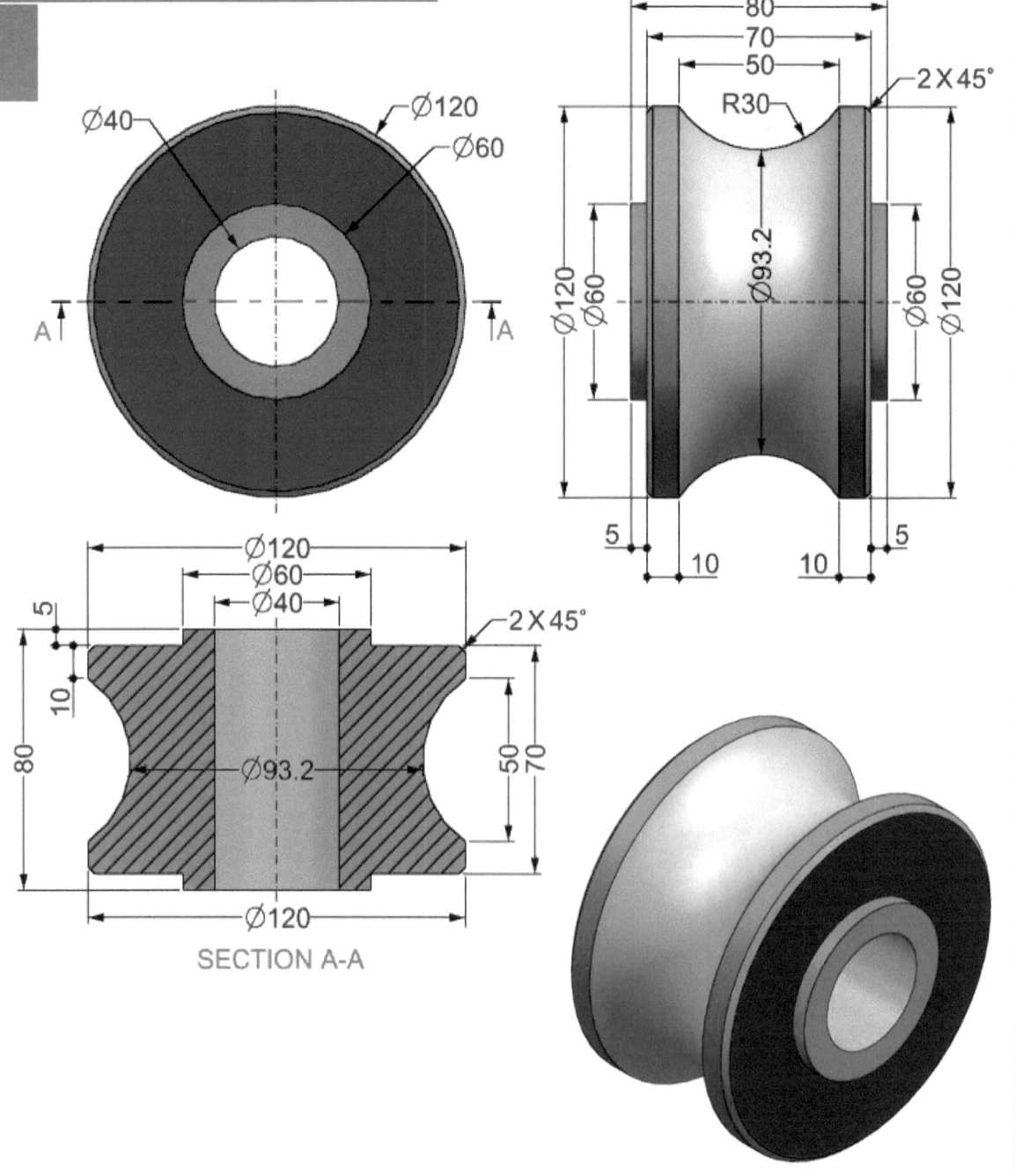

EXERCISE-133

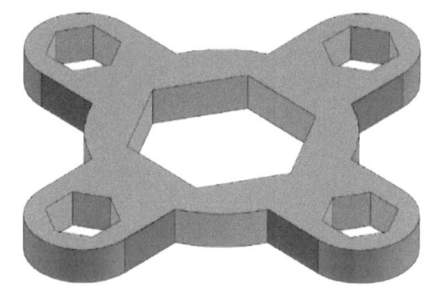

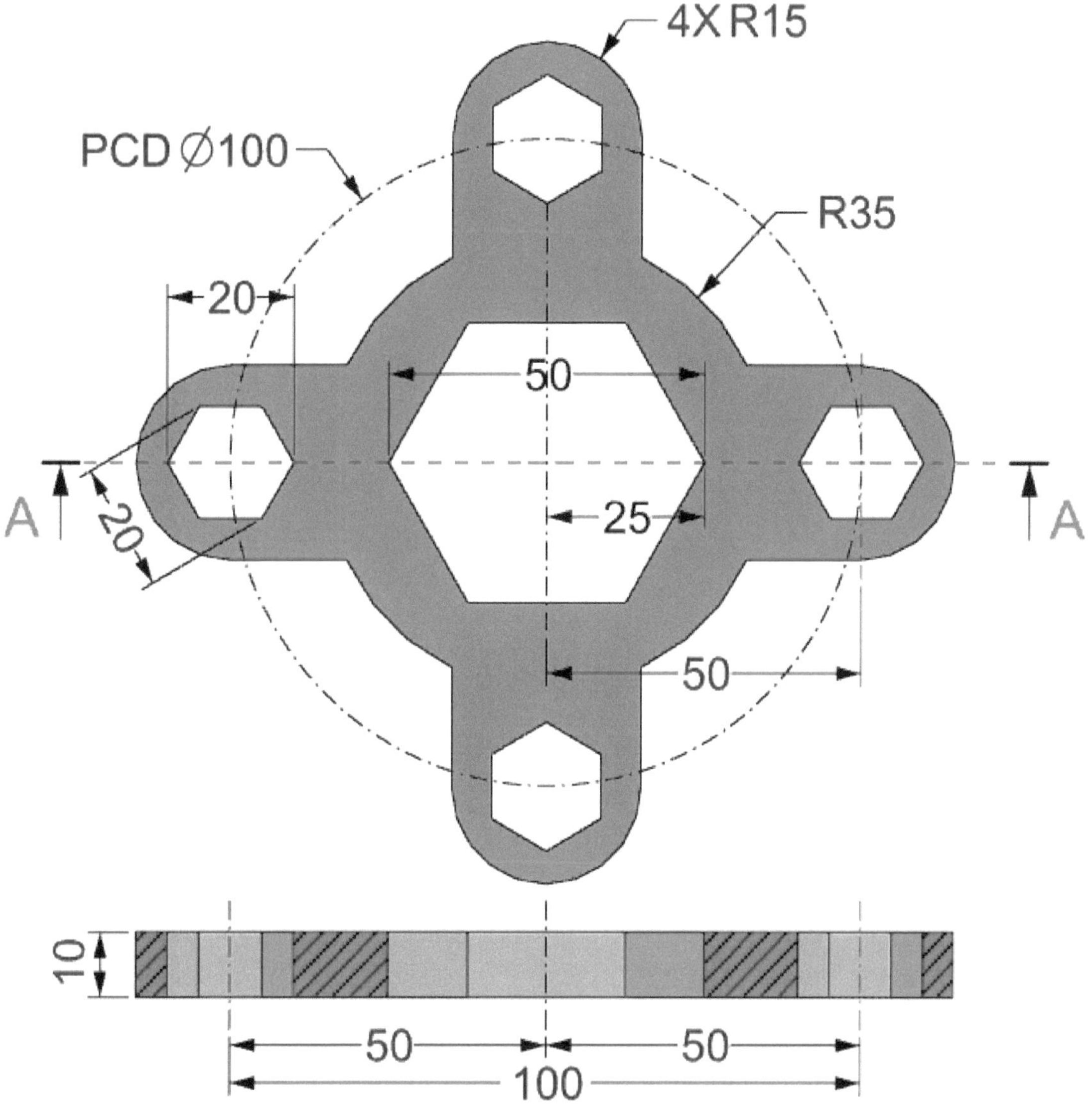

4X R15
PCD ∅100
R35
20
50
20
A
A
25
50
10
50
50
100

SECTION A-A

EXERCISE-134

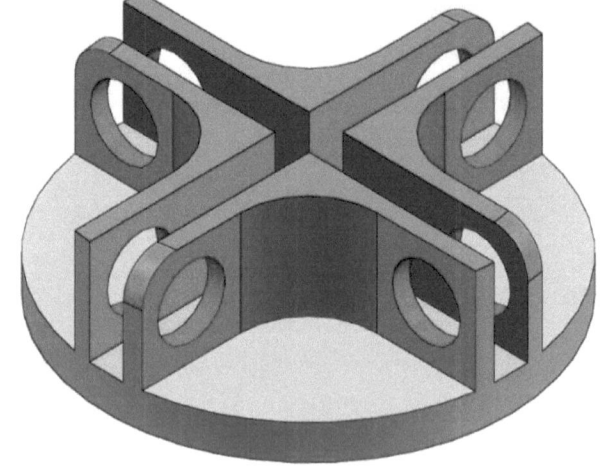
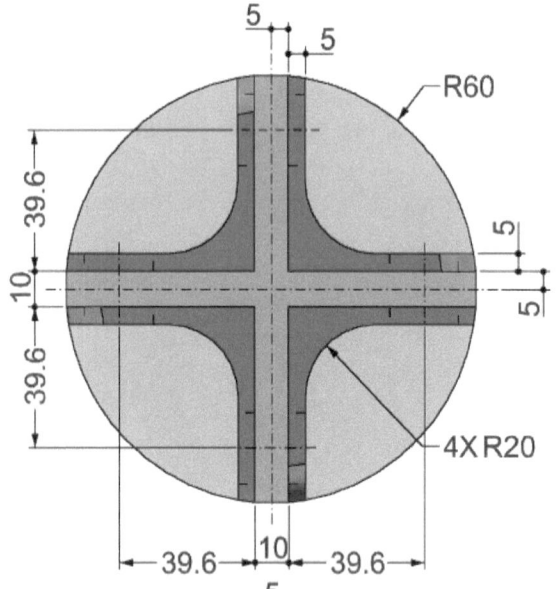
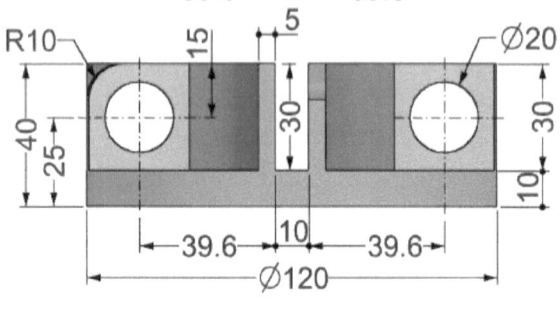
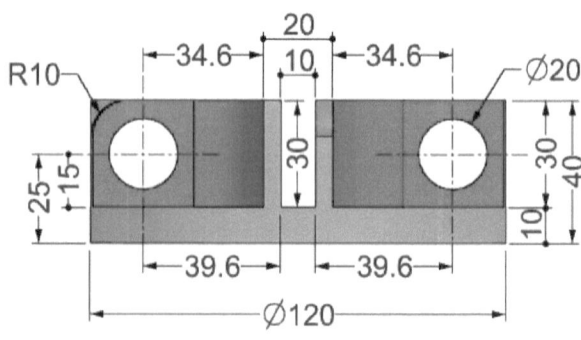

EXERCISE-135

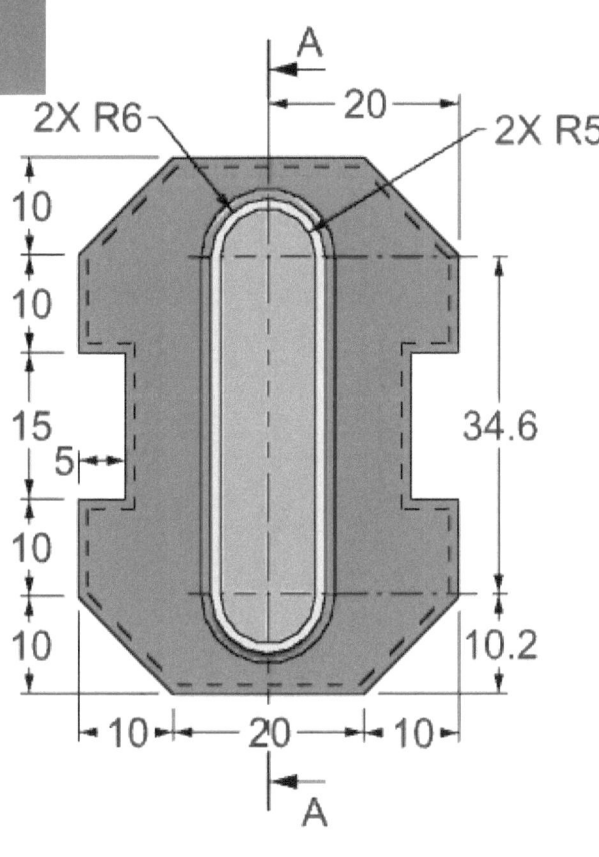

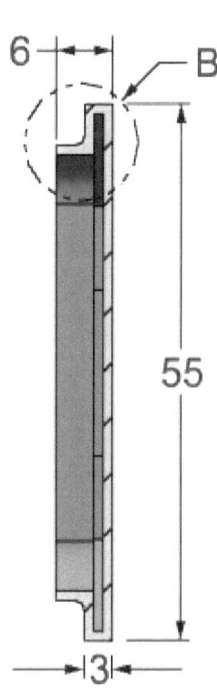

SECTION A-A
(SCALE 1:1)

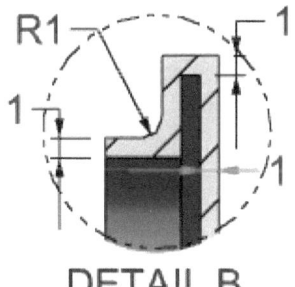

DETAIL B
(SCALE 2:1)

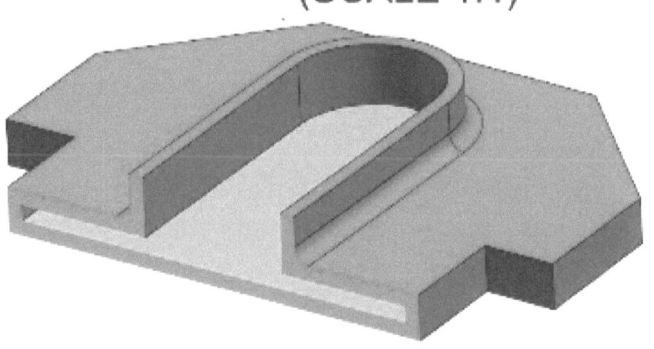

SHELL THICKNESS = 1MM
ALL INSIDE WALL THICKNESS

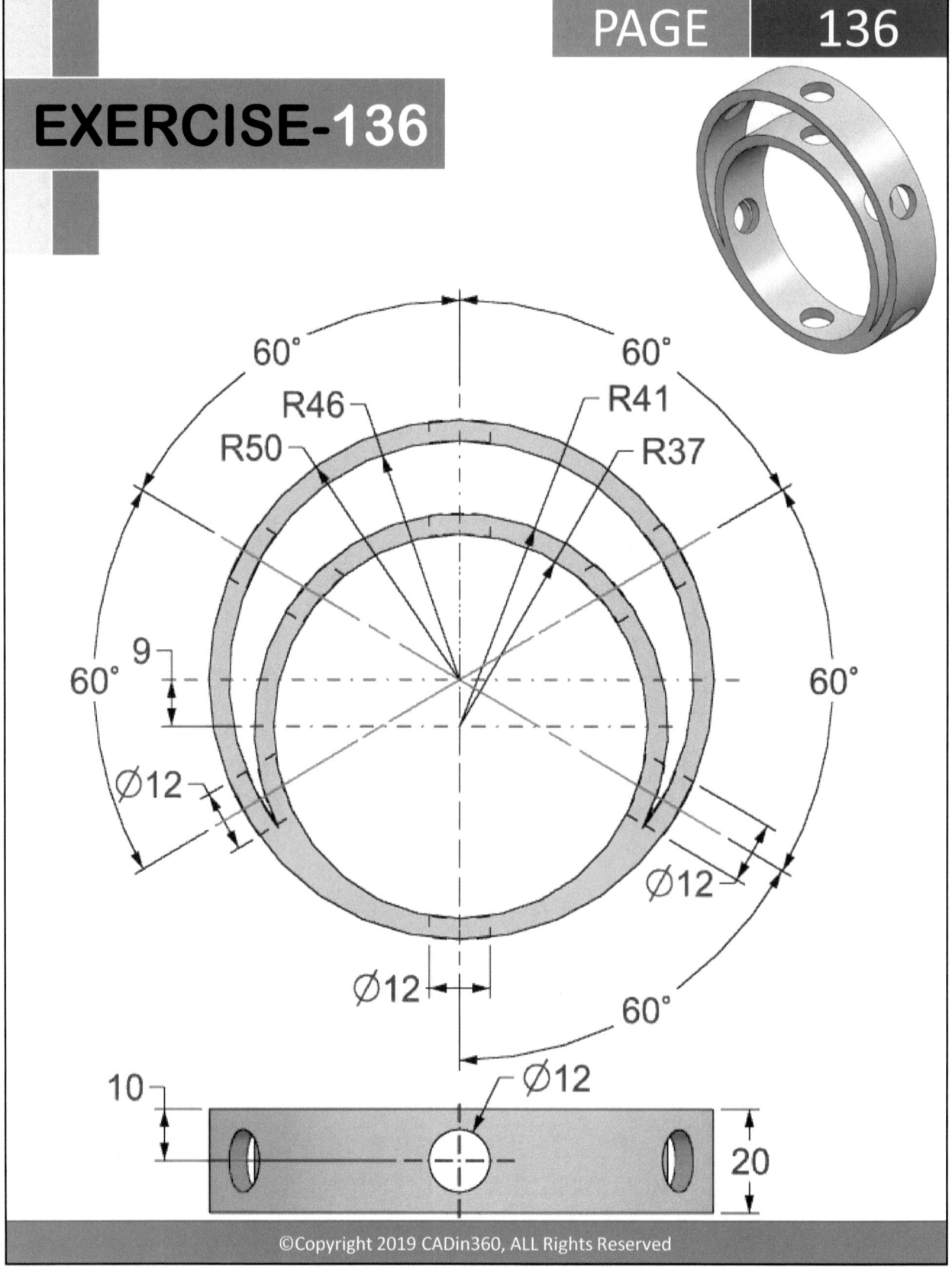

EXERCISE-137

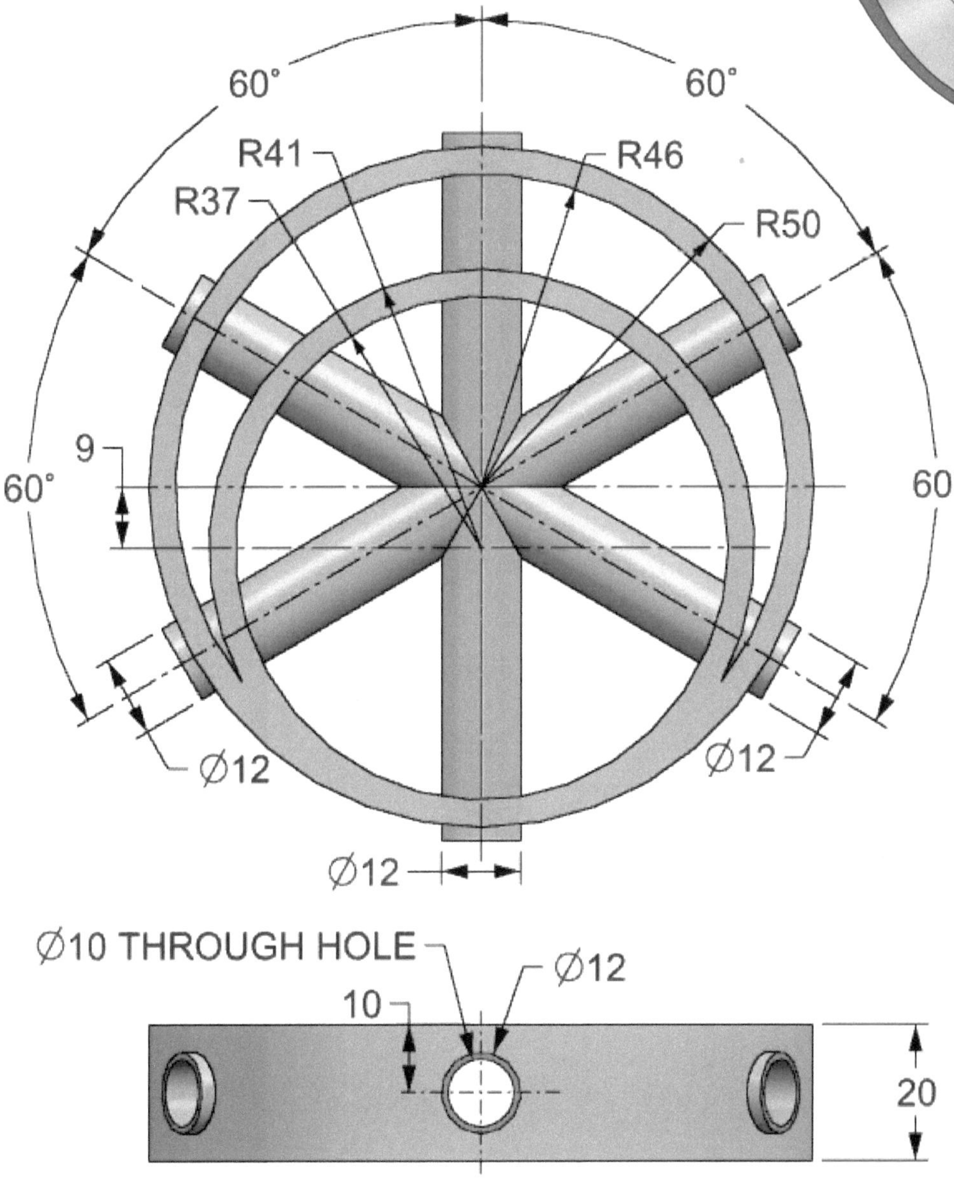

60° 60°
R41
R37 R46
R50
60° 9 60°
Ø12 Ø12
Ø12

Ø10 THROUGH HOLE — Ø12
10
20

EXERCISE-138

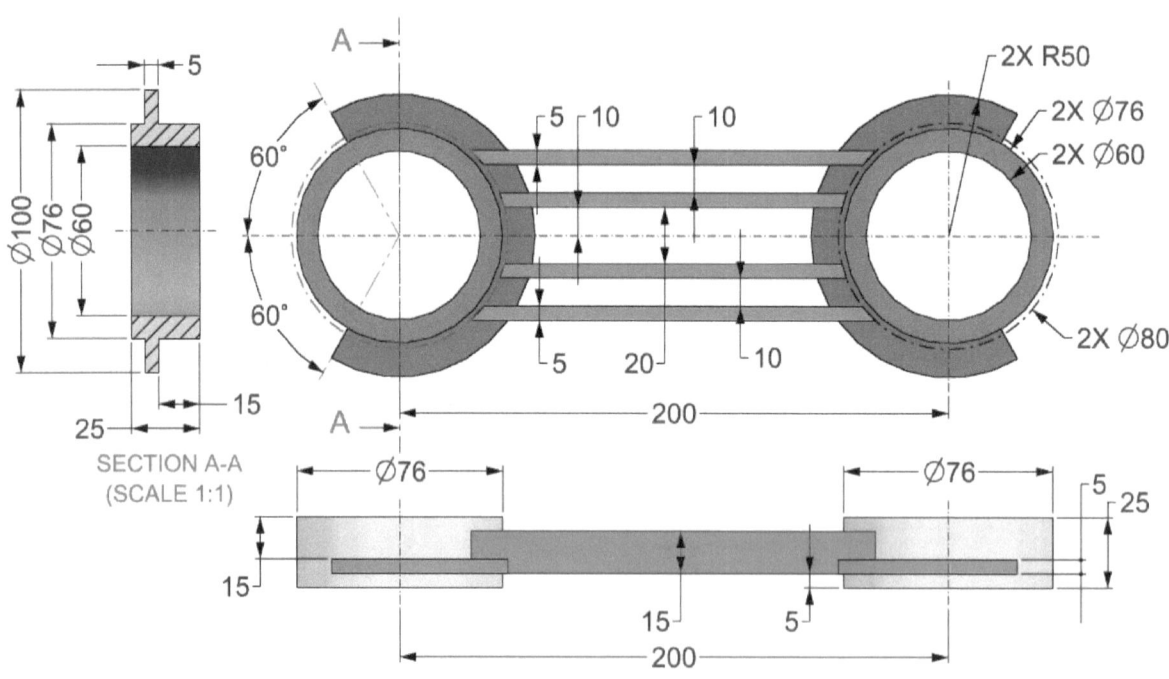

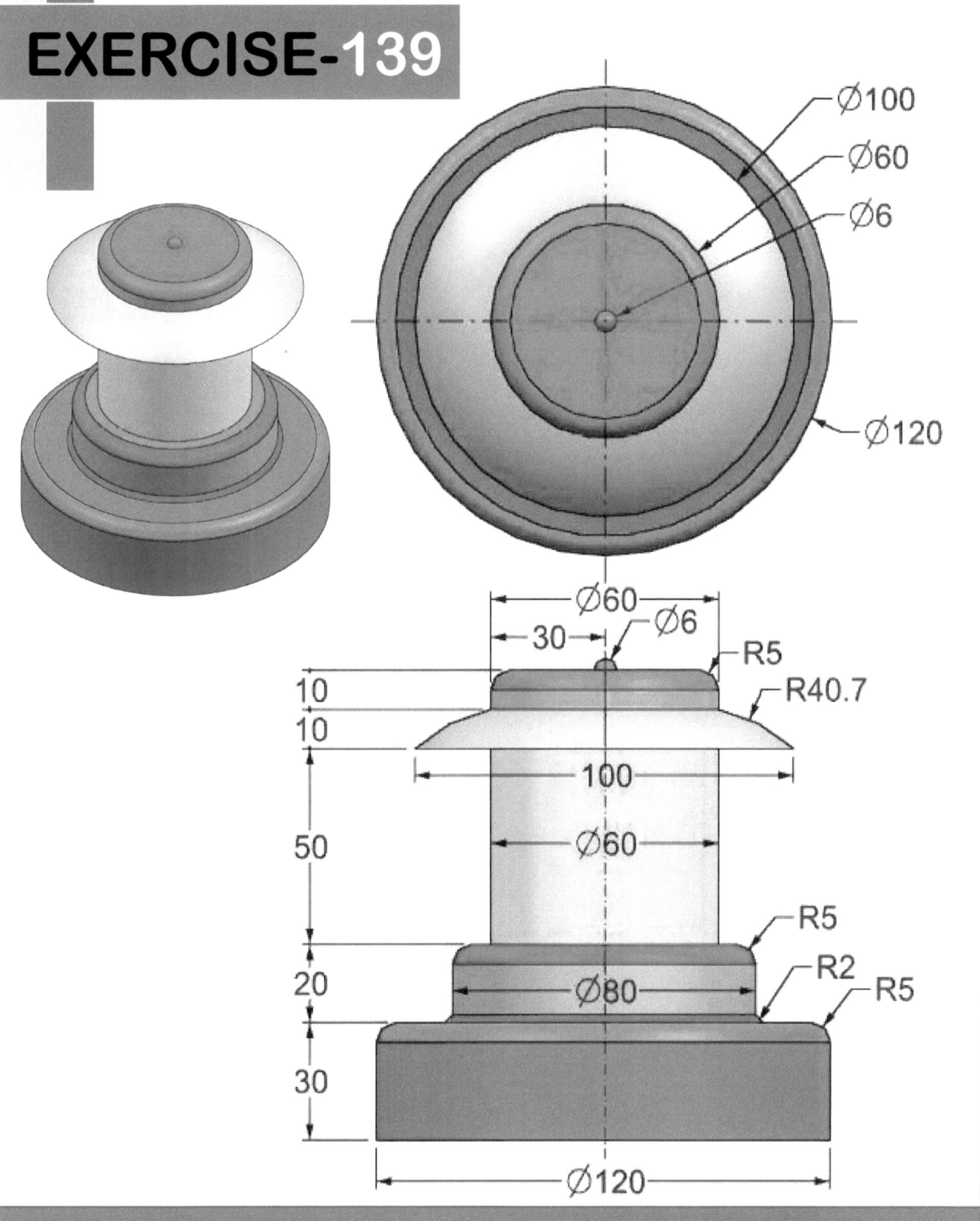

EXERCISE-140

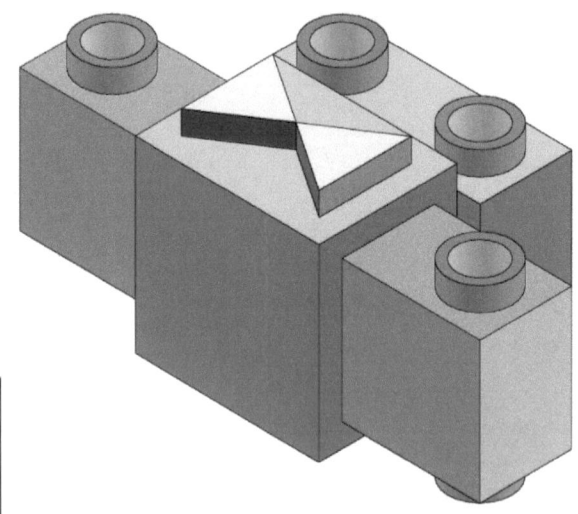
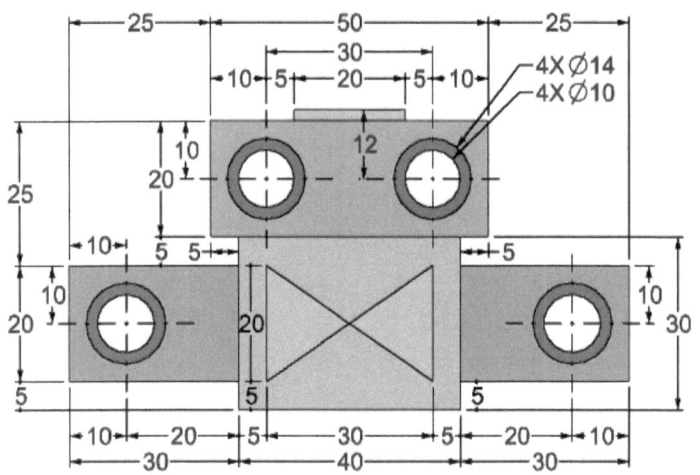
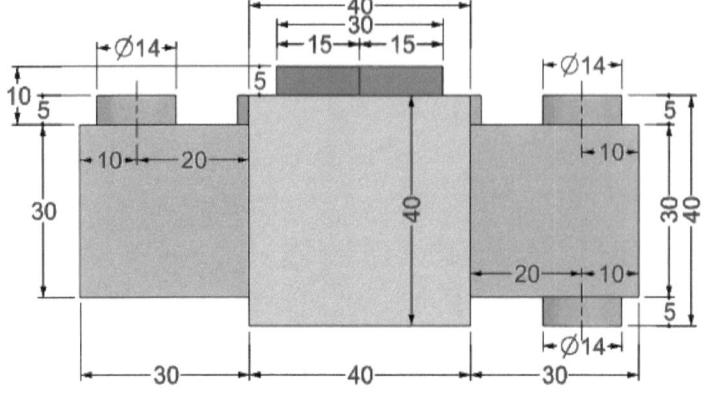
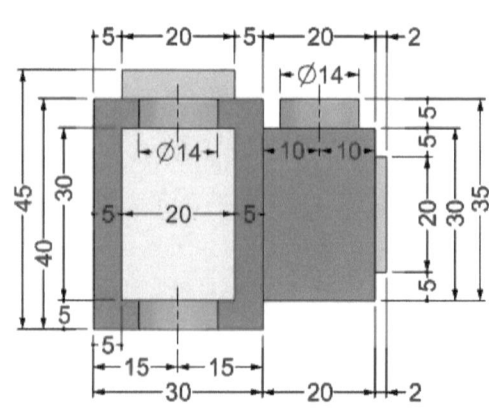

EXERCISE-141

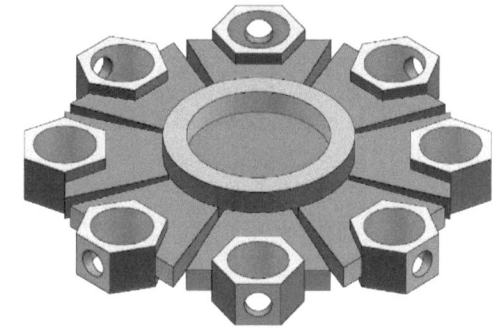

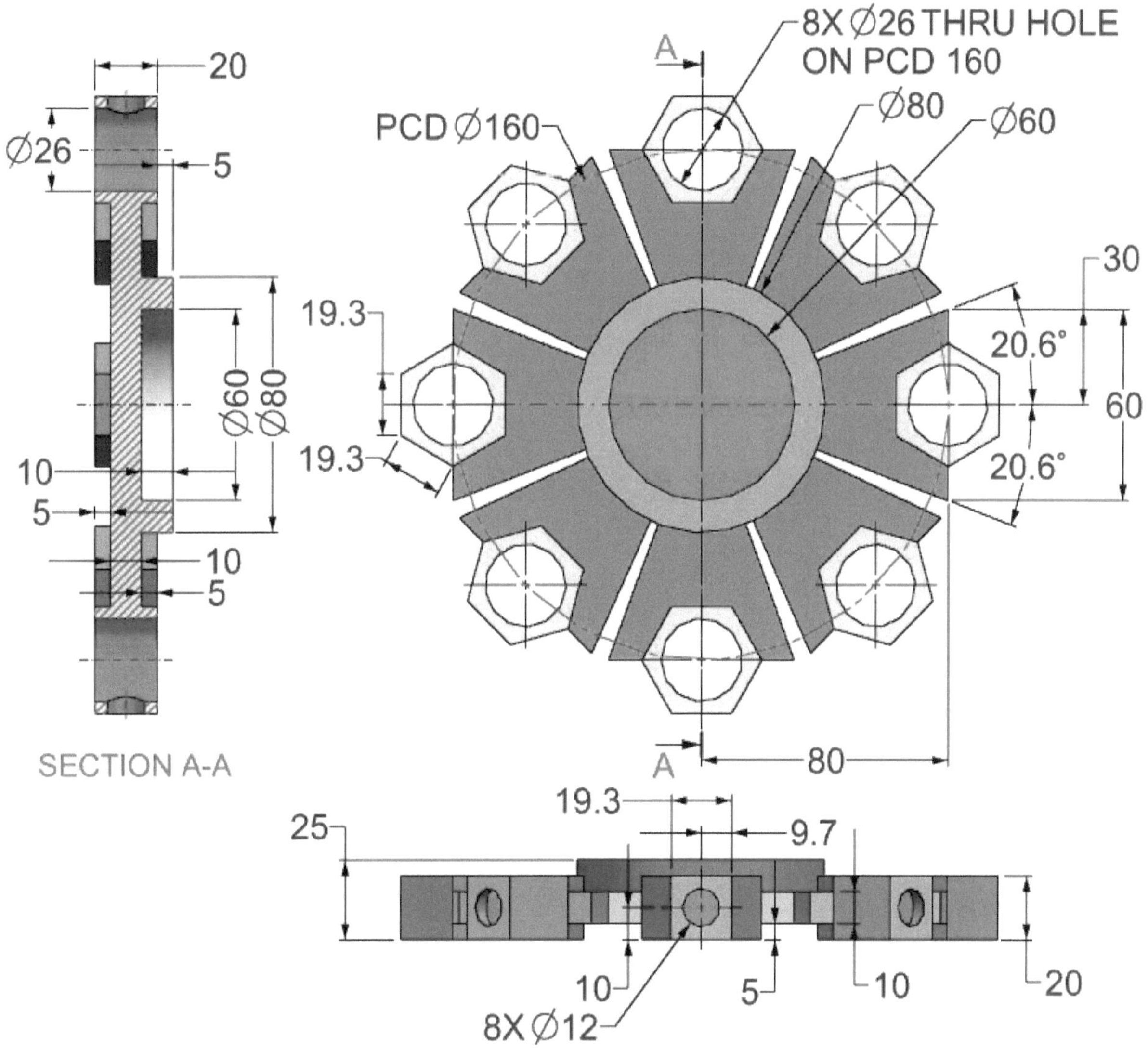

8X Ø26 THRU HOLE ON PCD 160

PCD Ø160, Ø80, Ø60

20, 5, Ø26, 10, 5, 10, 5, Ø60, Ø80

19.3, 19.3, 20.6°, 20.6°, 30, 60, 80

SECTION A-A

25, 19.3, 9.7, 10, 5, 10, 20

8X Ø12

EXERCISE-142

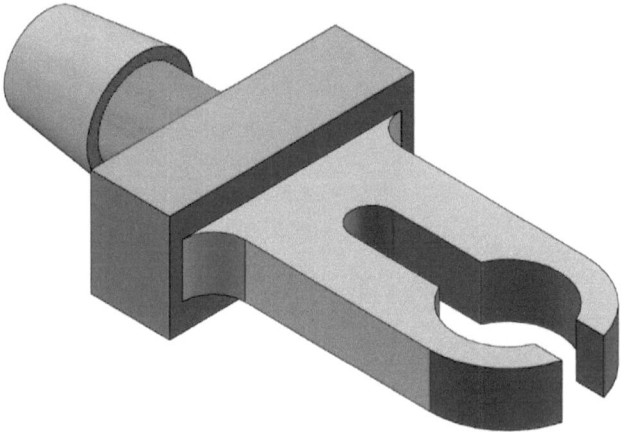

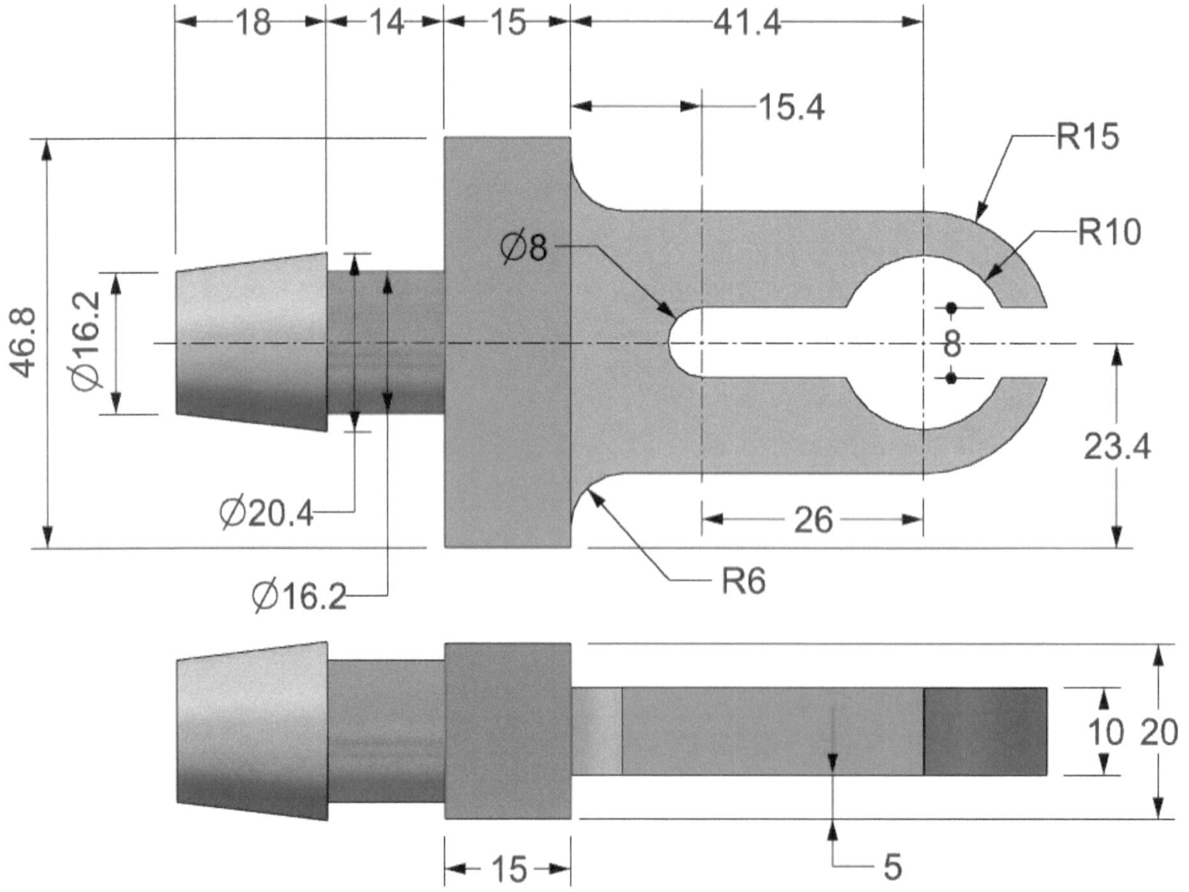

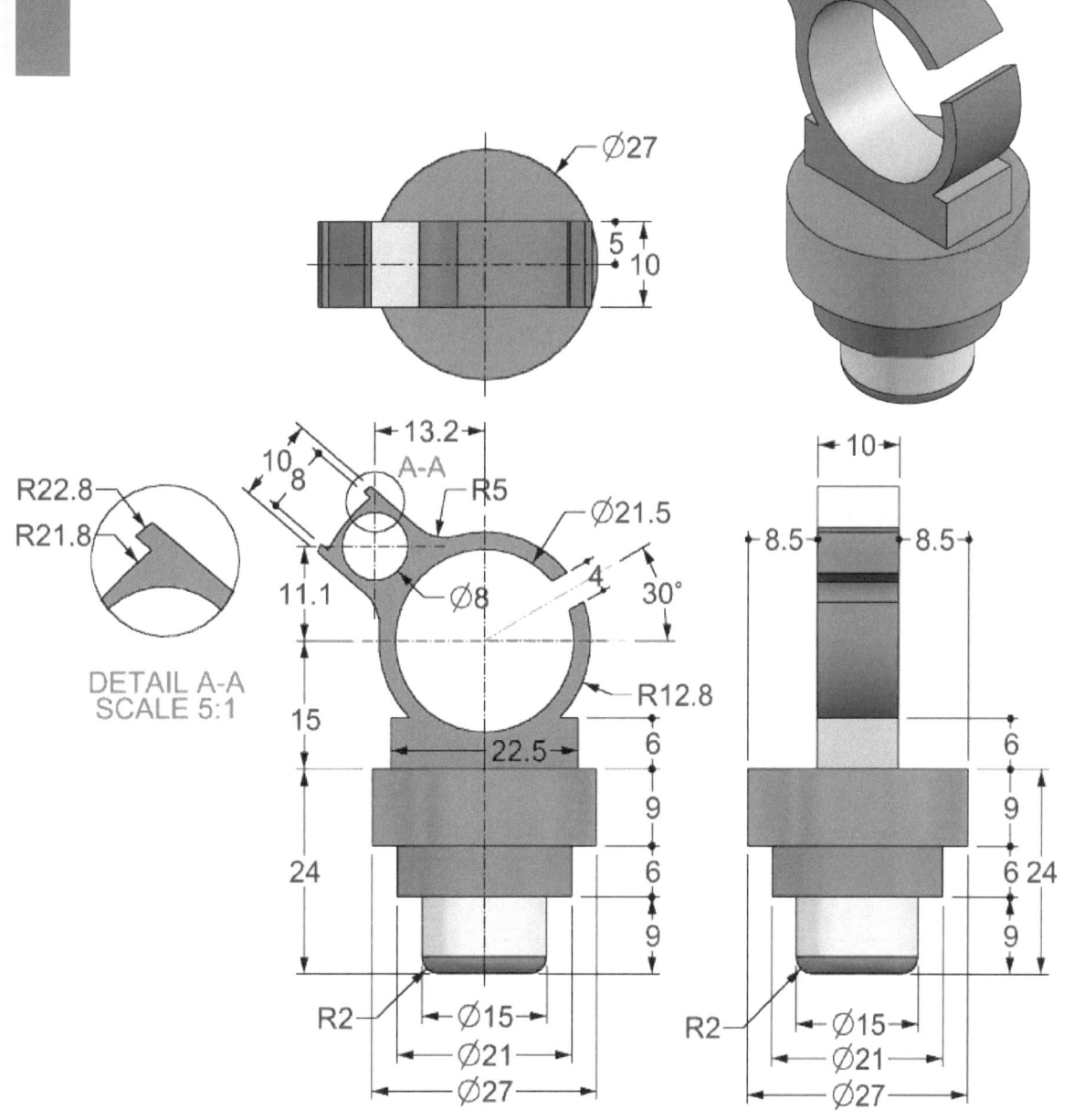

EXERCISE-144

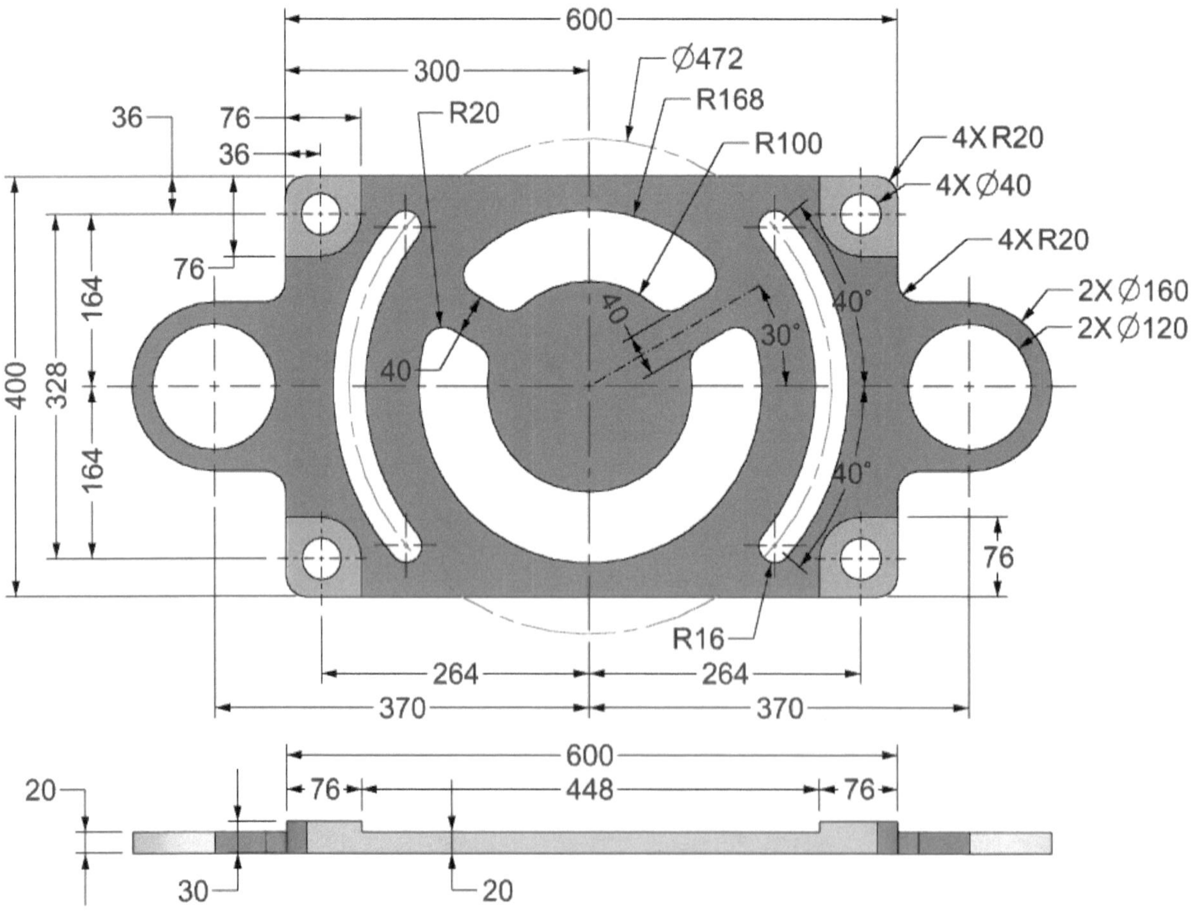

EXERCISE-145

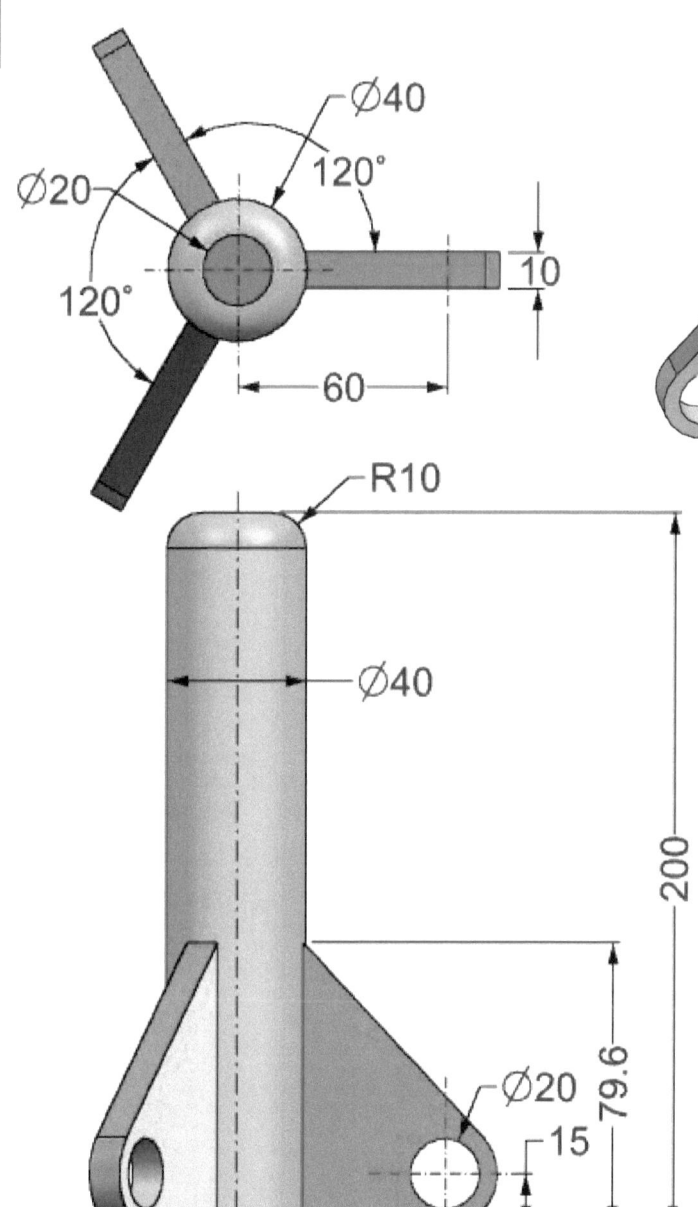

EXERCISE-146

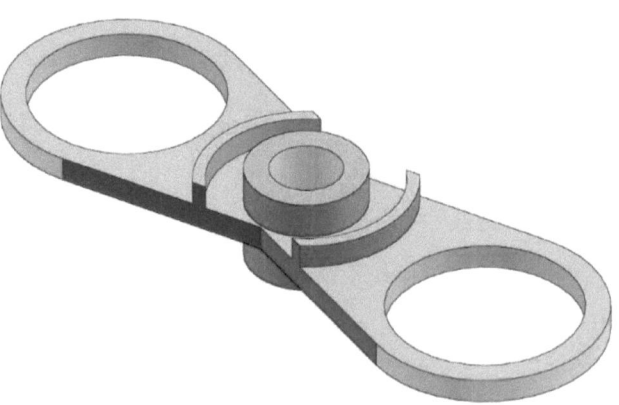

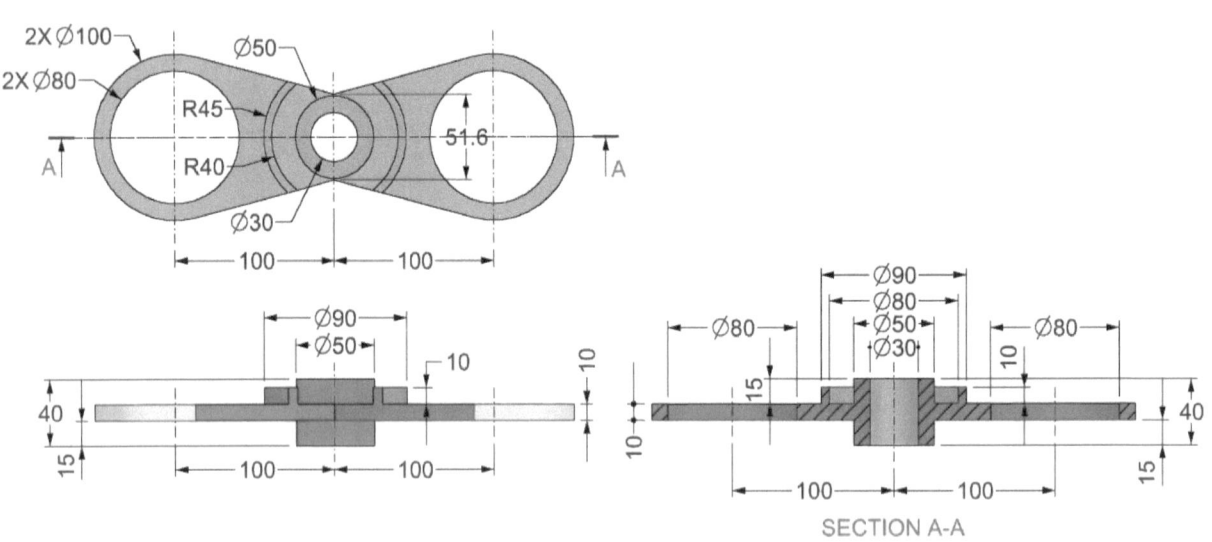

SECTION A-A

EXERCISE-147

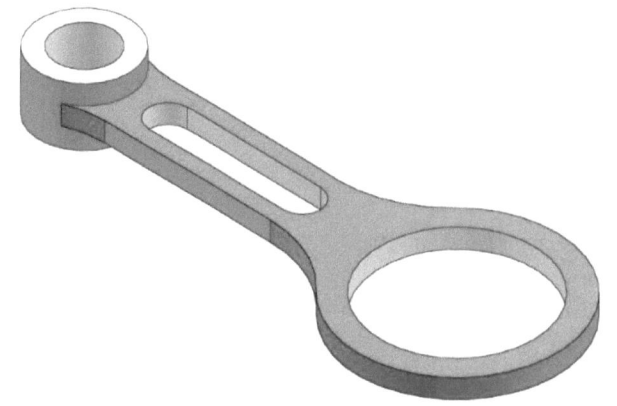

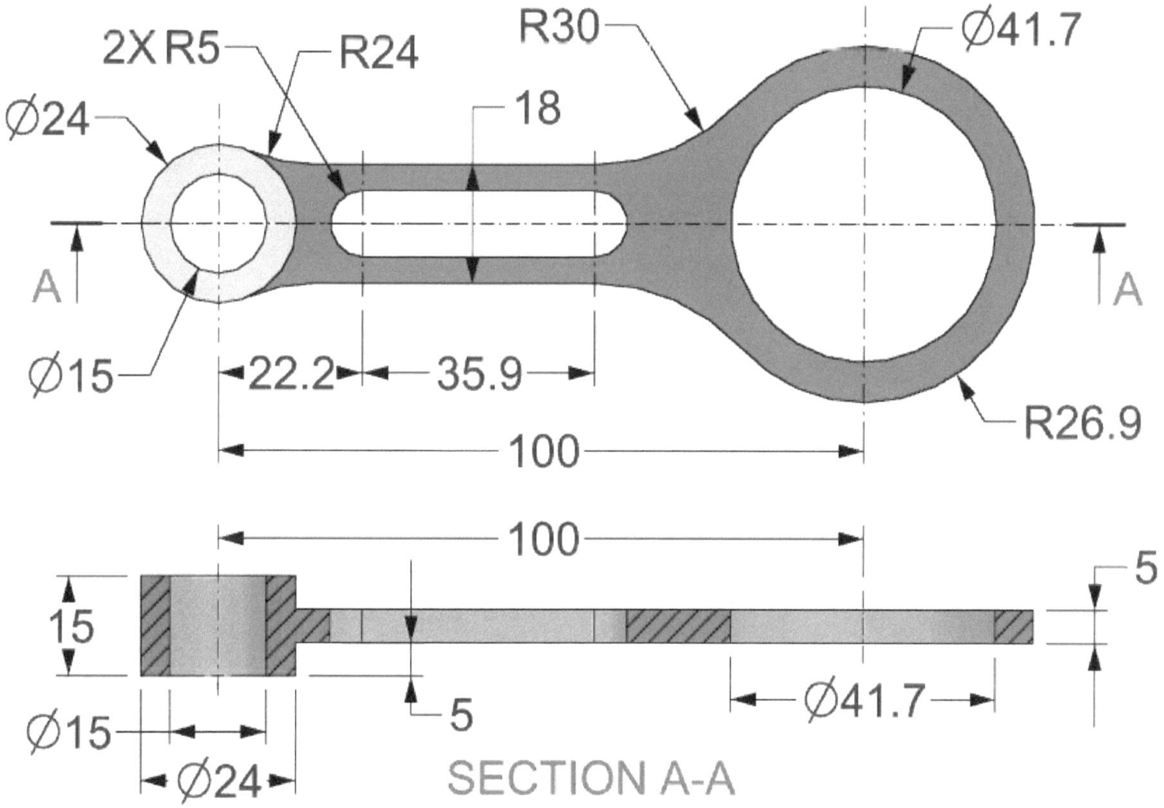

EXERCISE-148

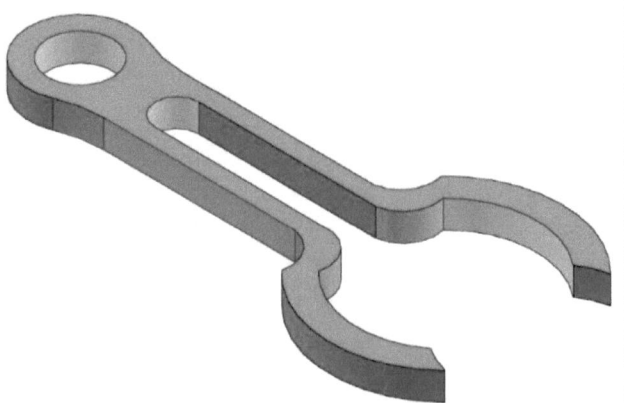

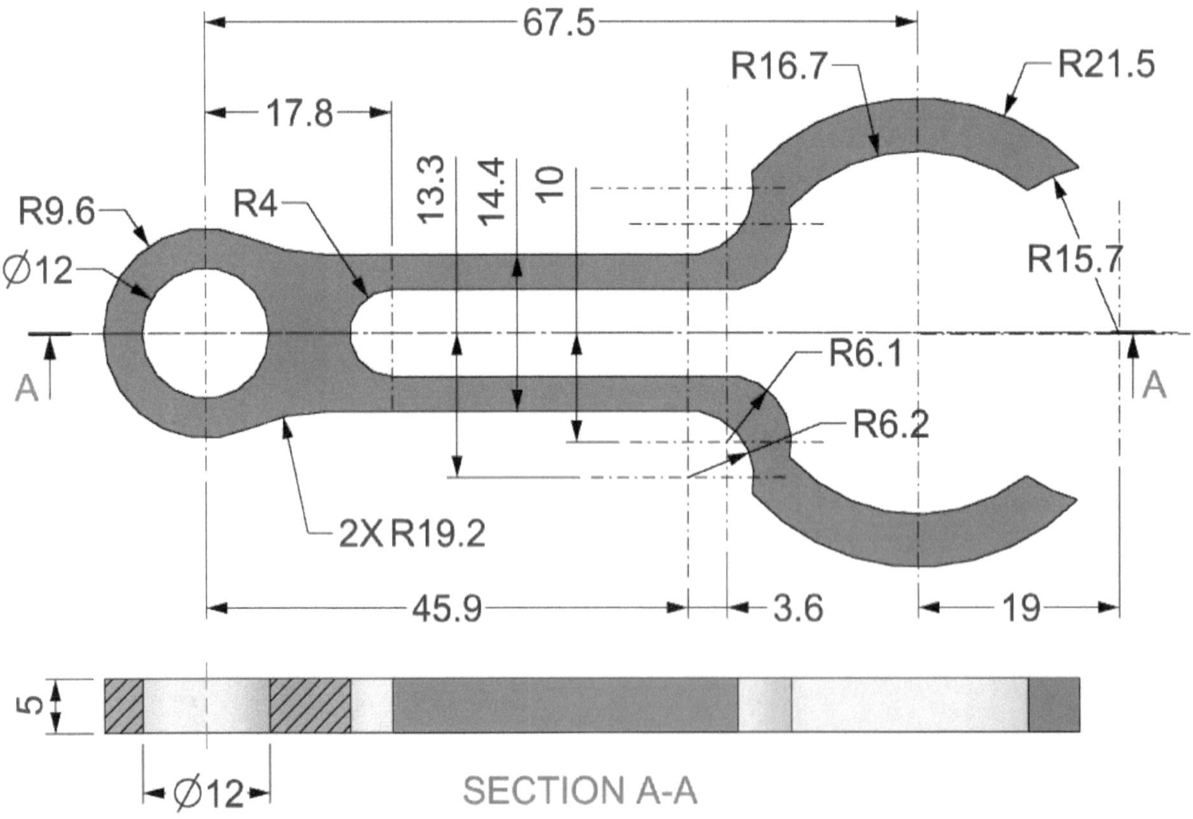

EXERCISE-149

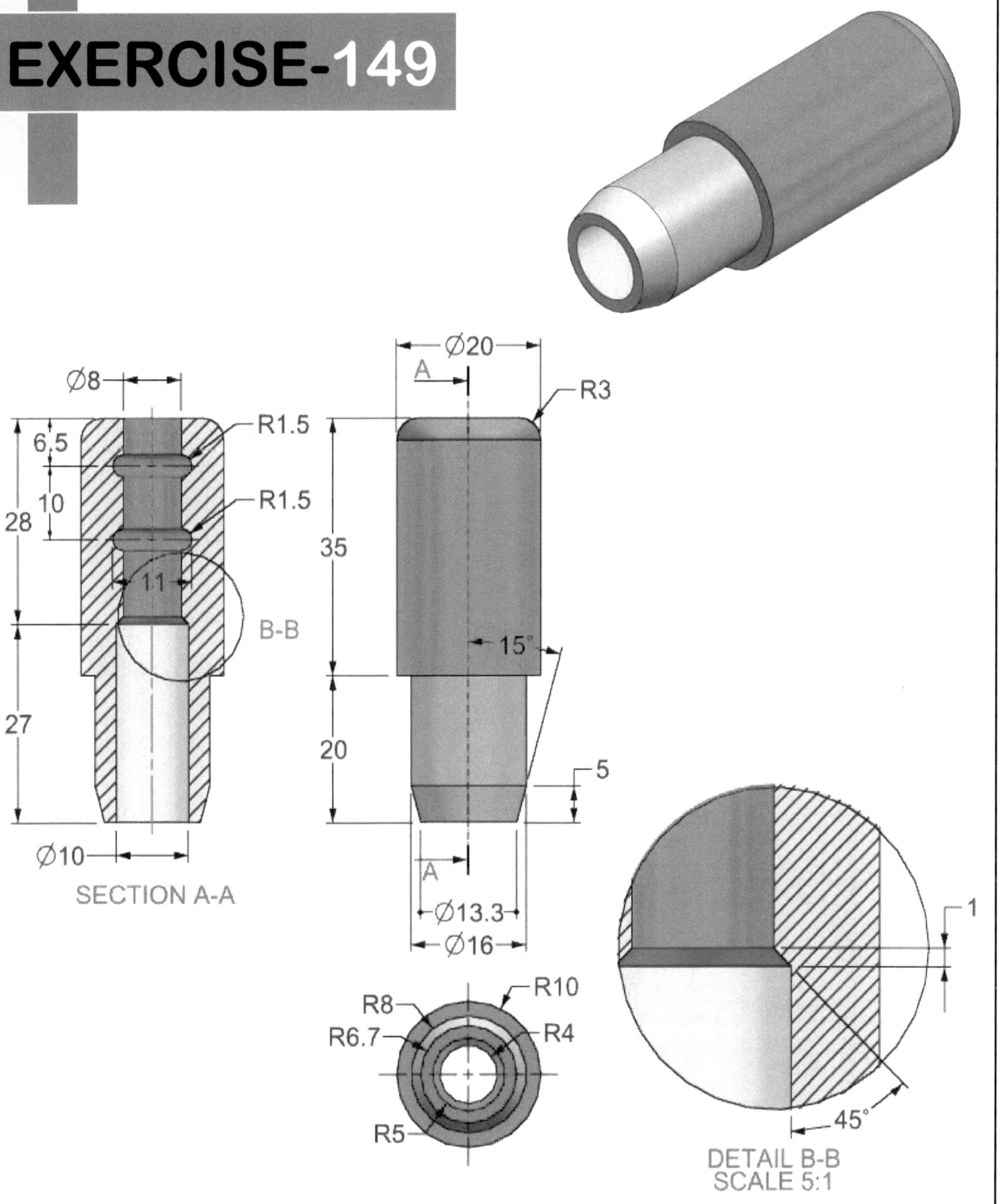

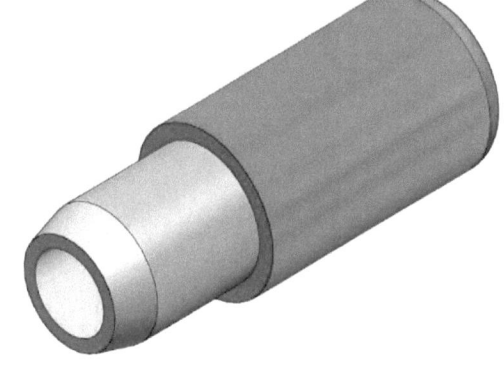

EXERCISE-150

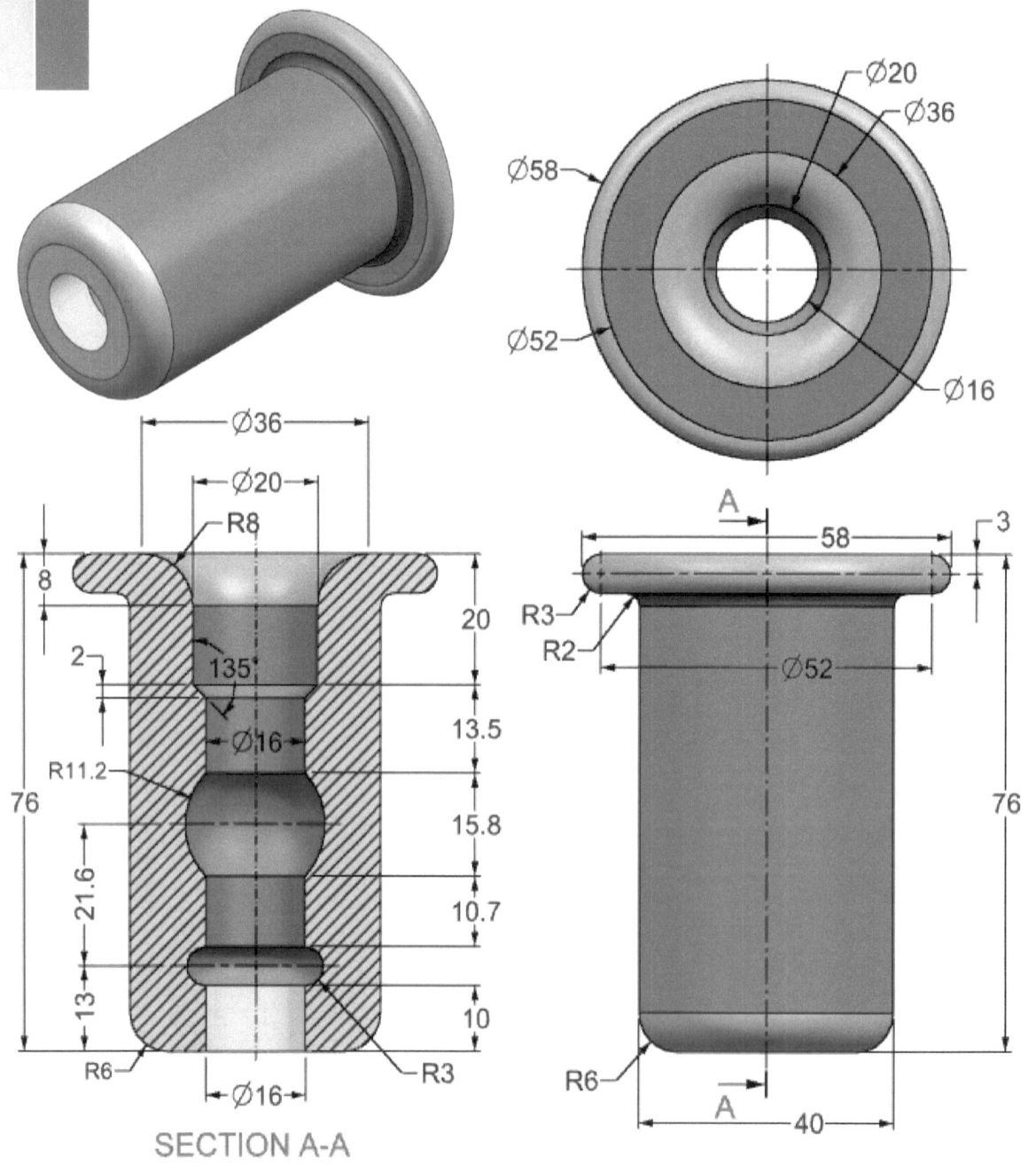

SECTION A-A

EXERCISE-151

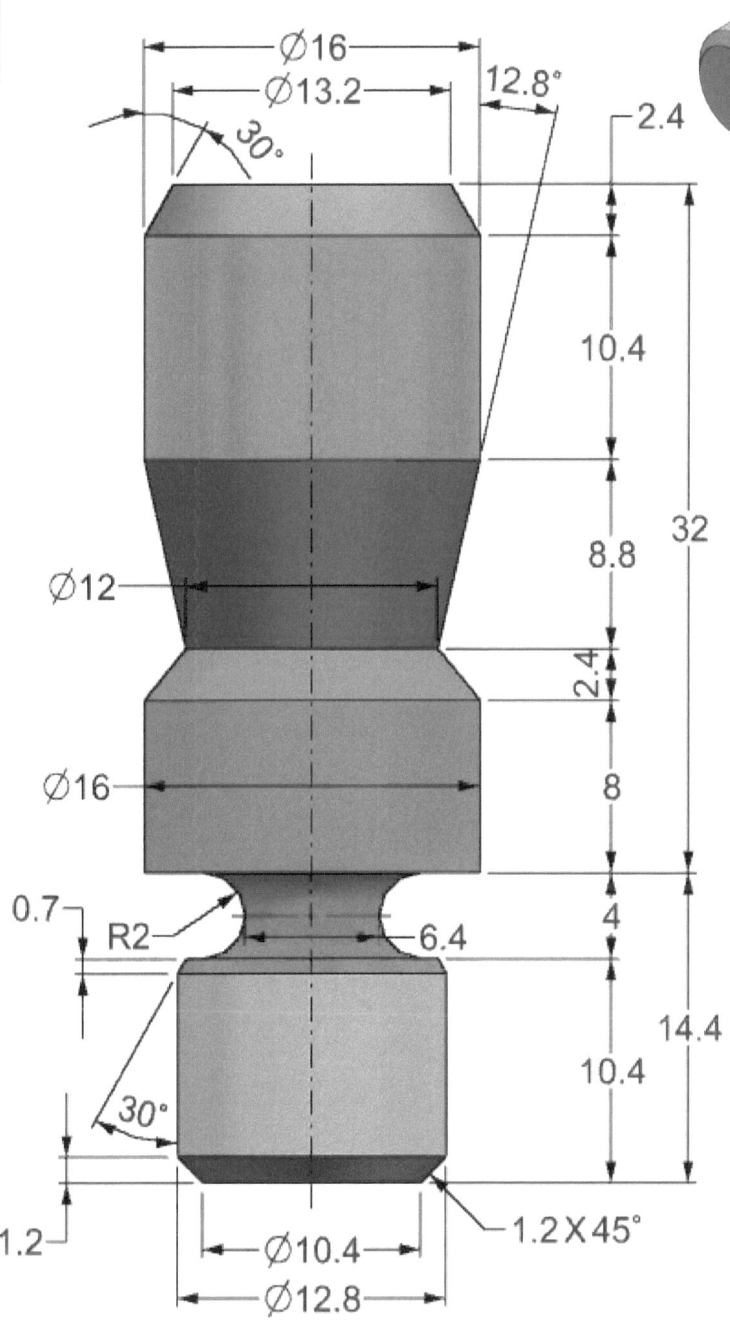

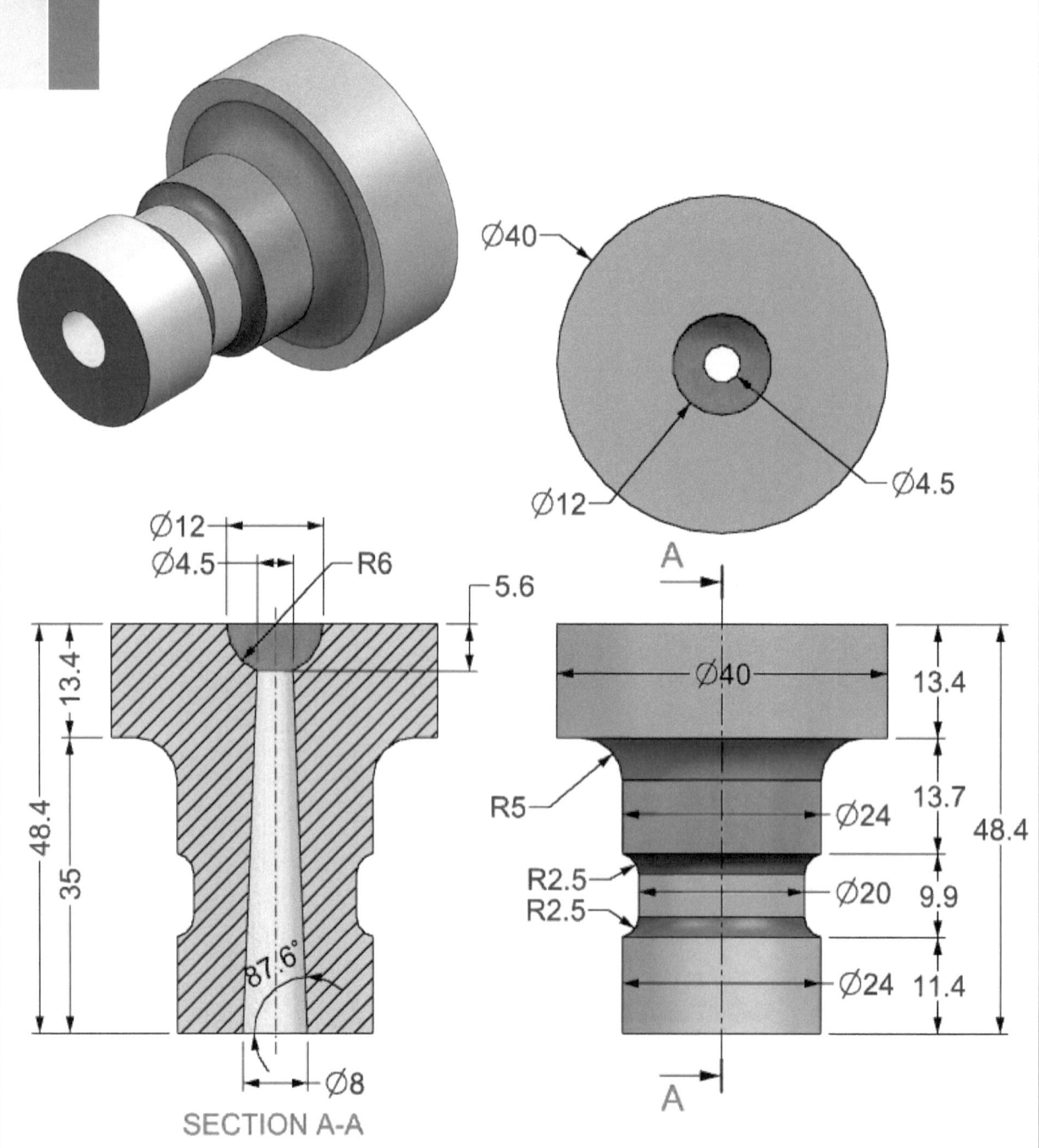

EXERCISE-153

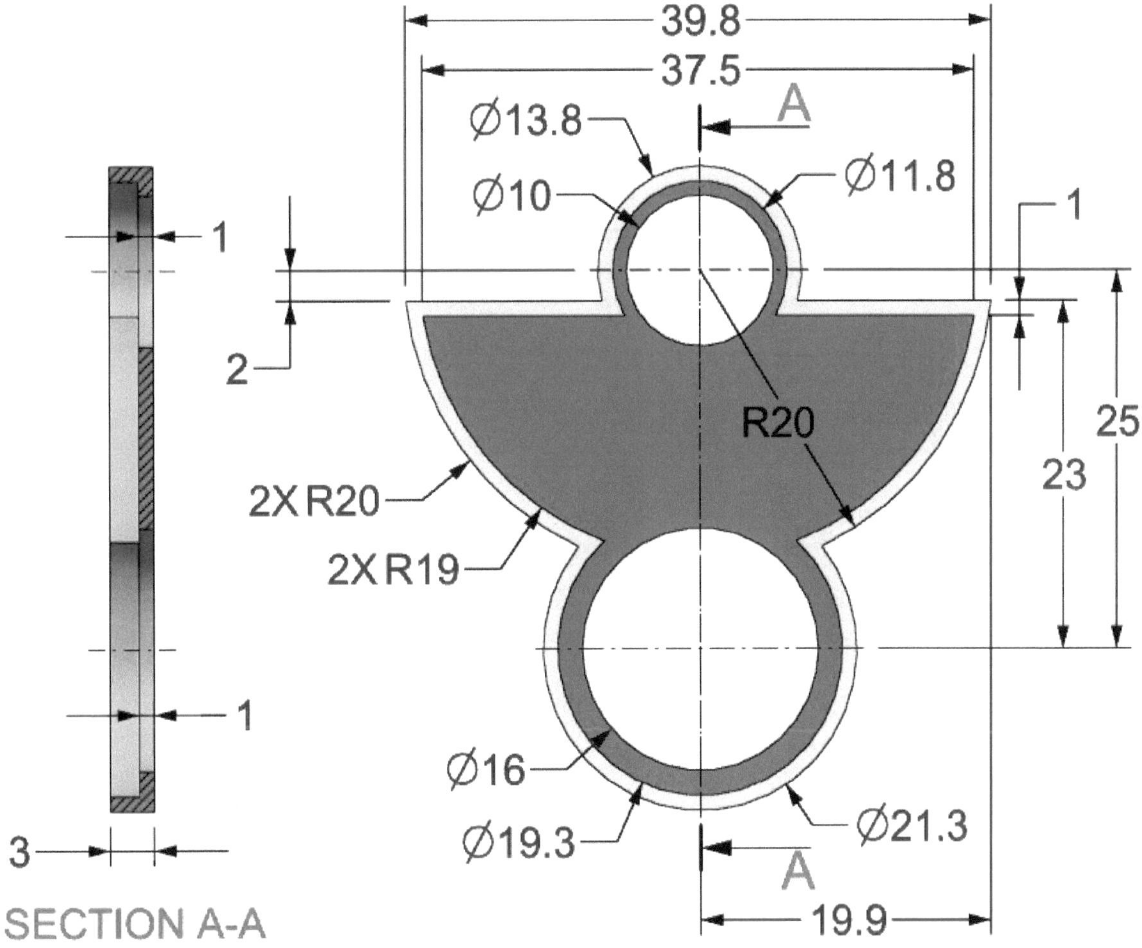

EXERCISE-154

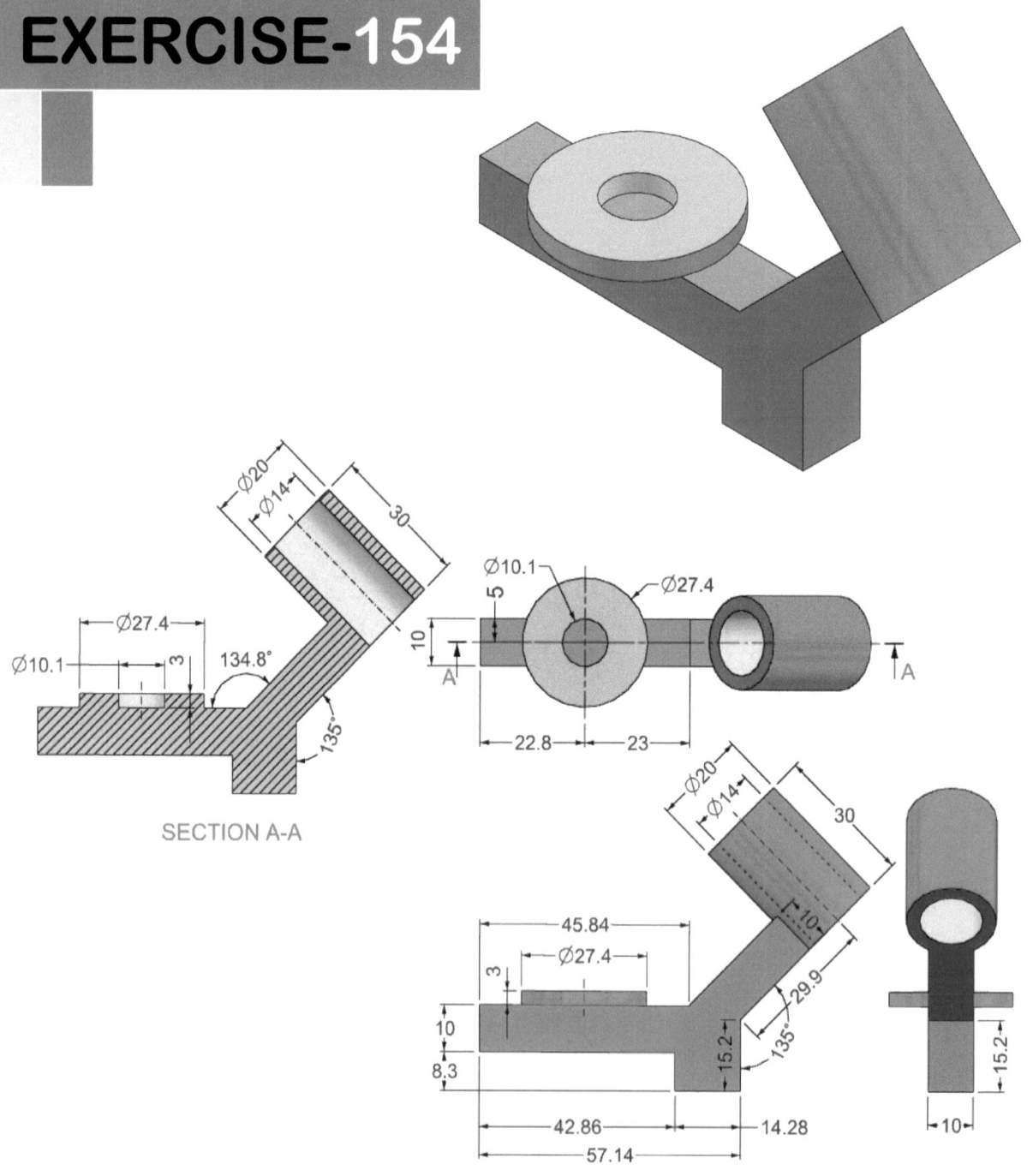

EXERCISE-155

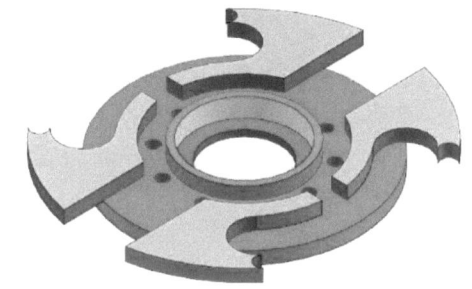

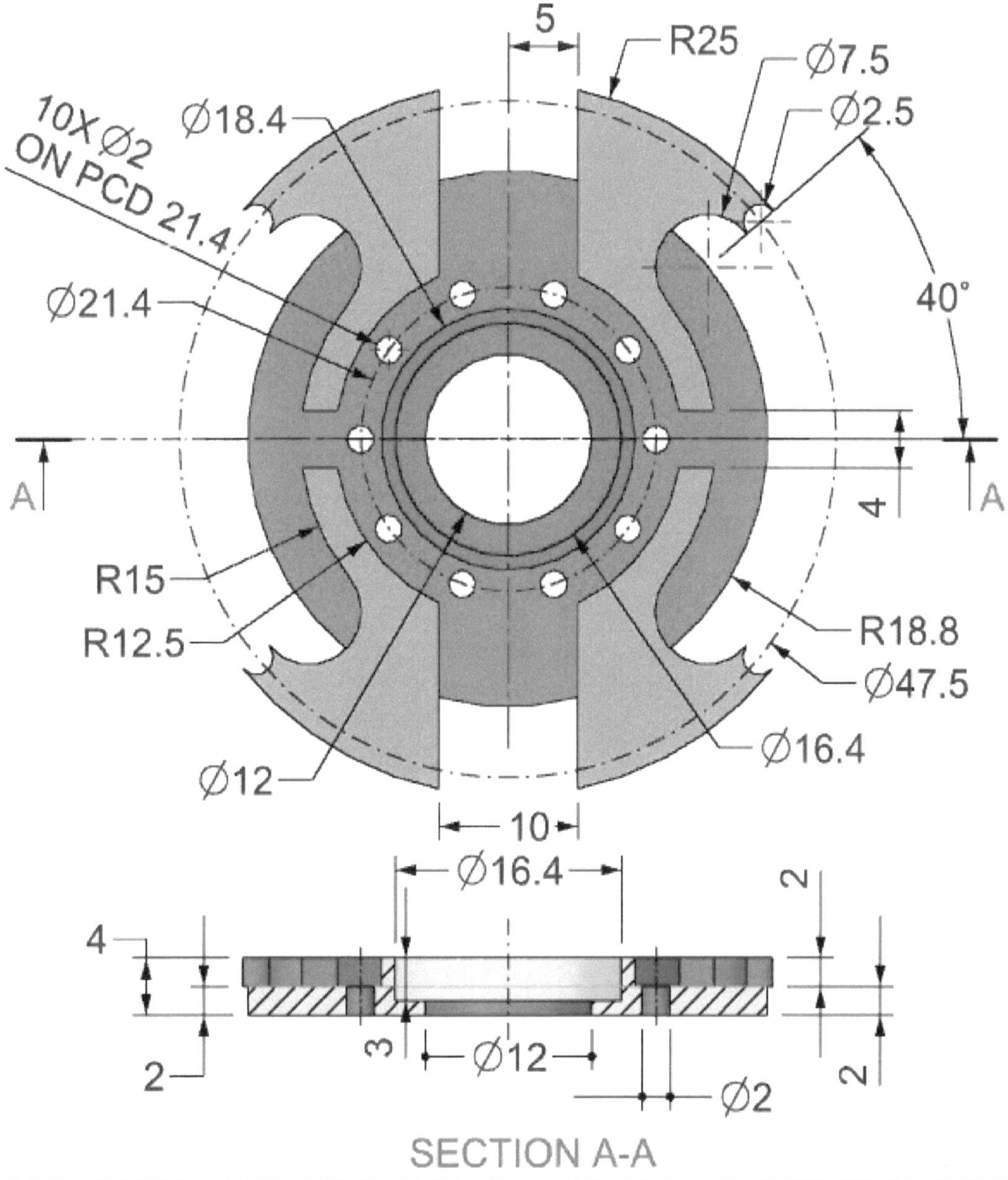

EXERCISE-156

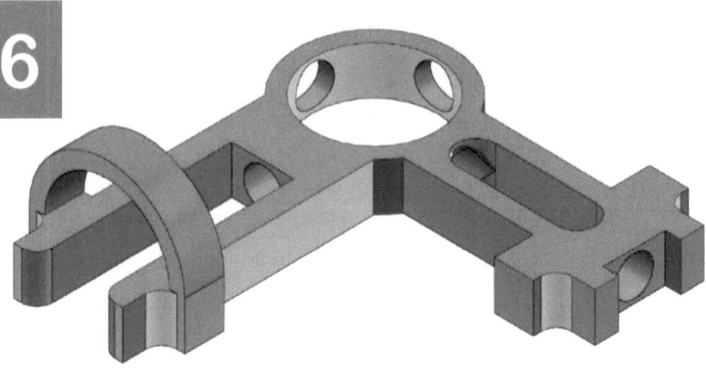
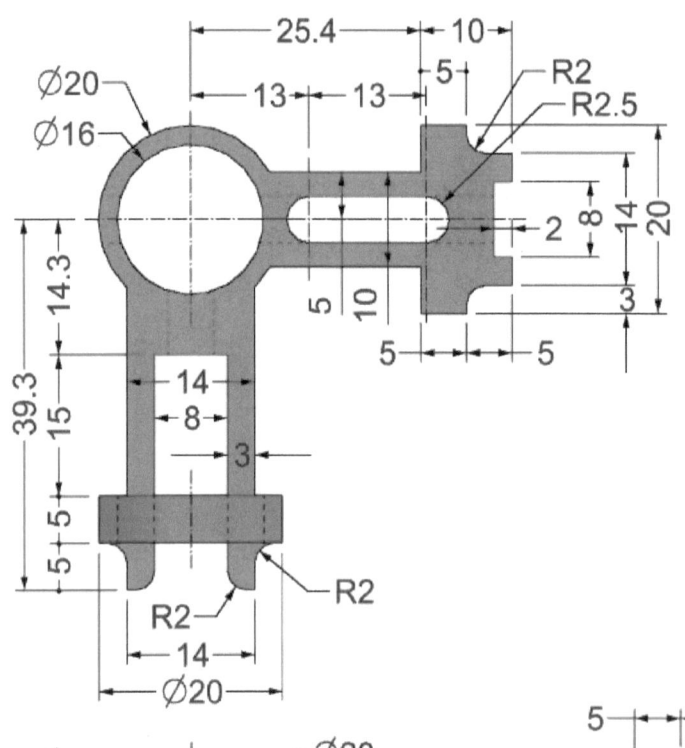
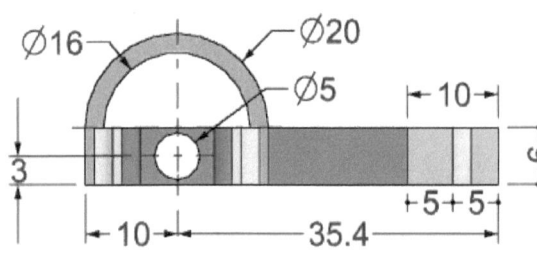
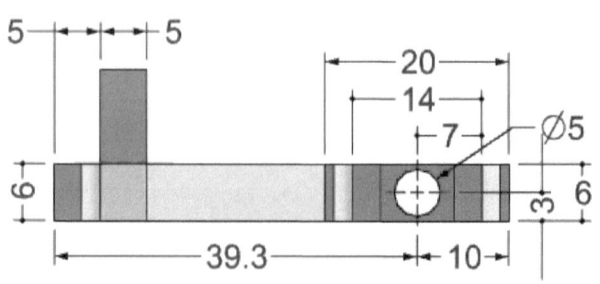

EXERCISE-157

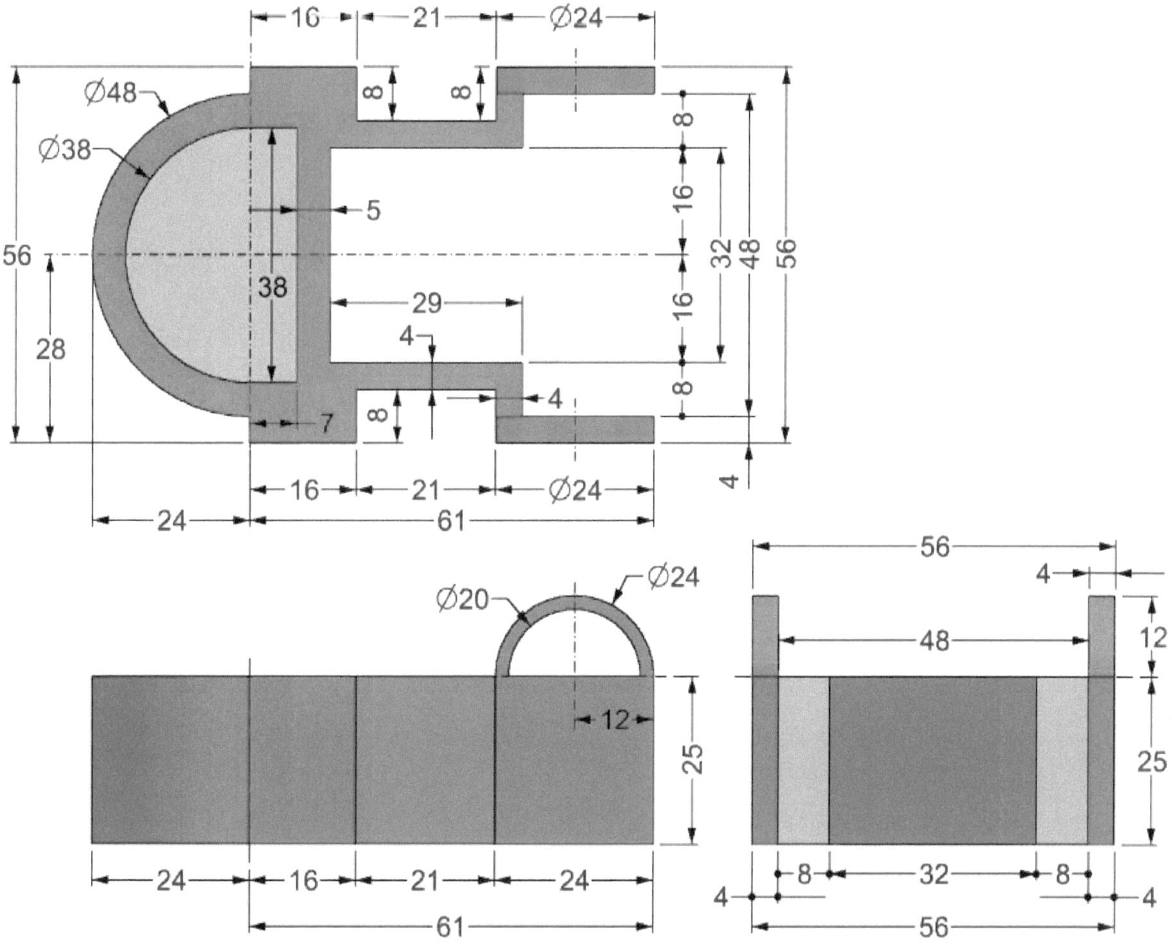

EXERCISE-158

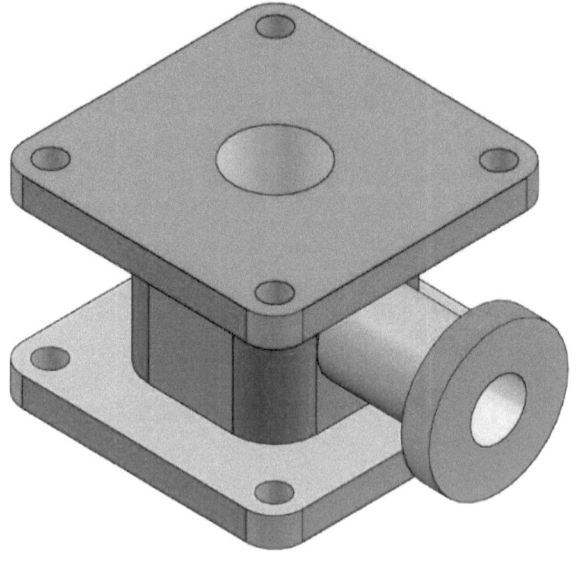

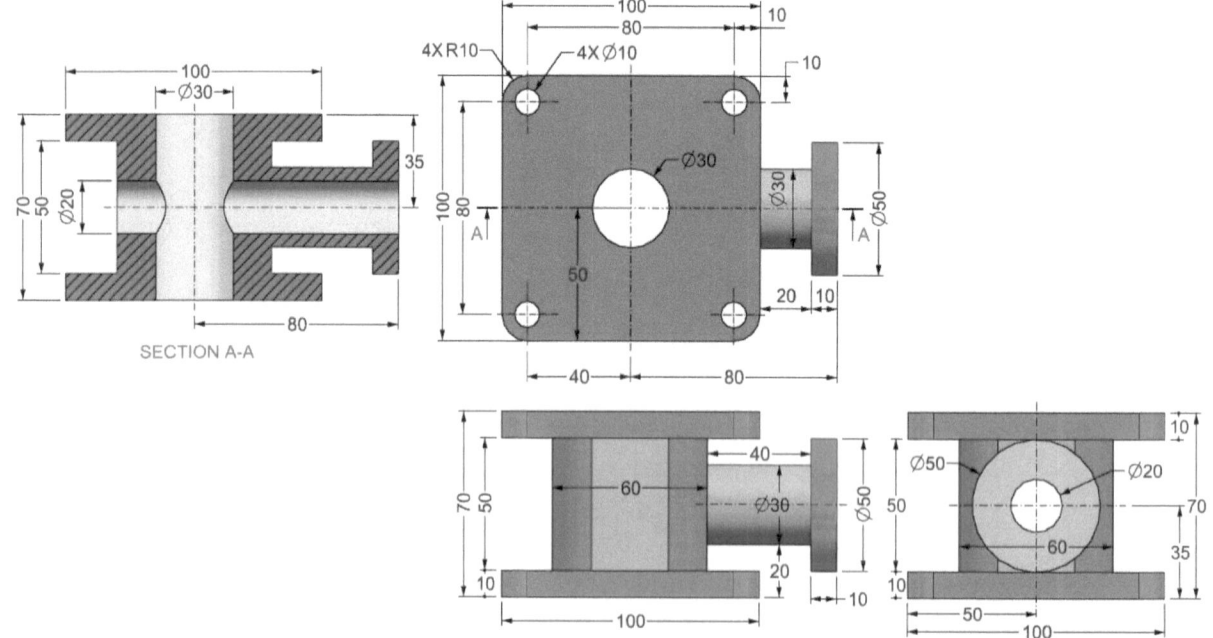

SECTION A-A

EXERCISE-159

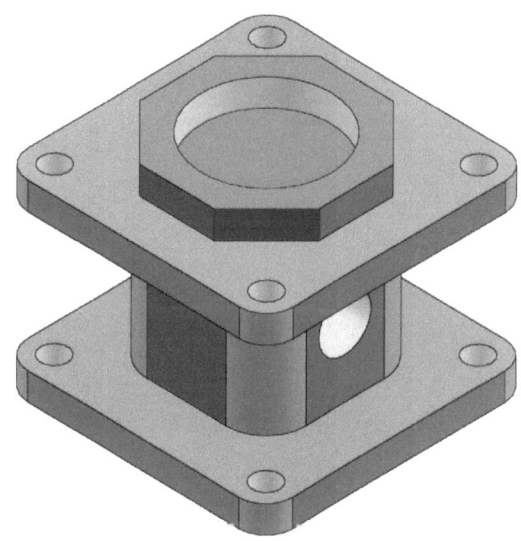

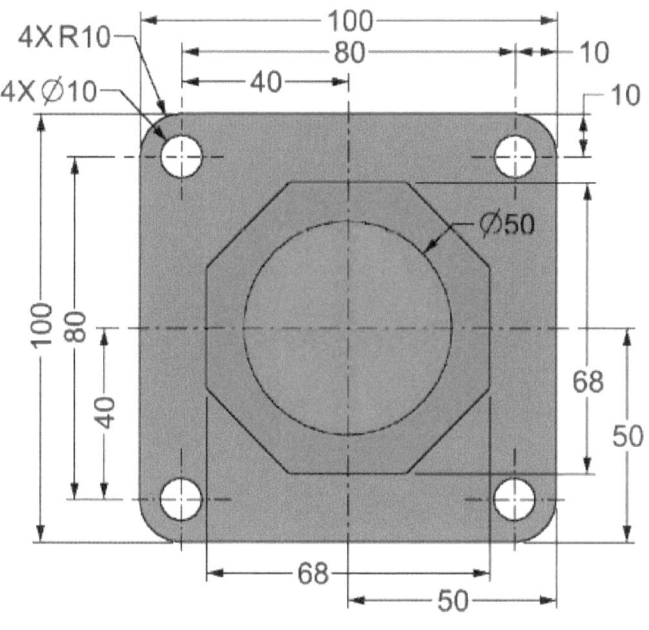

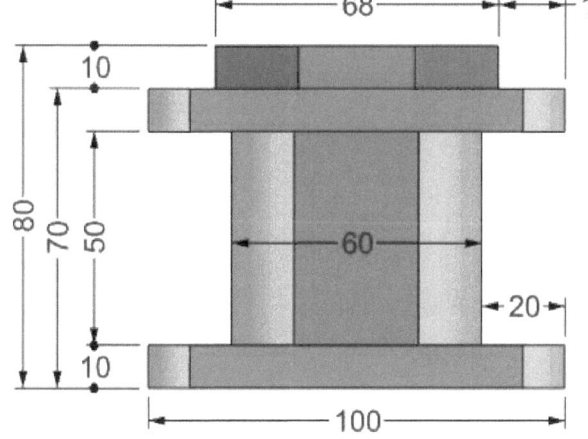

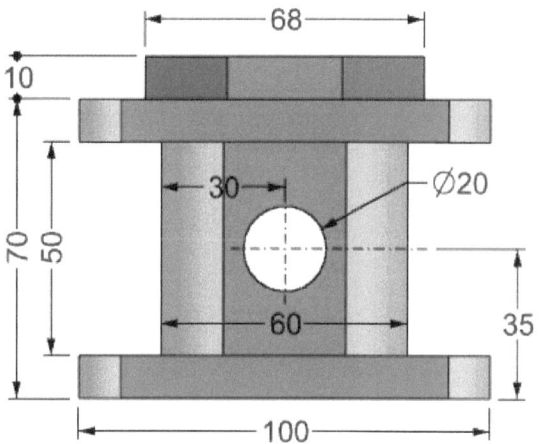

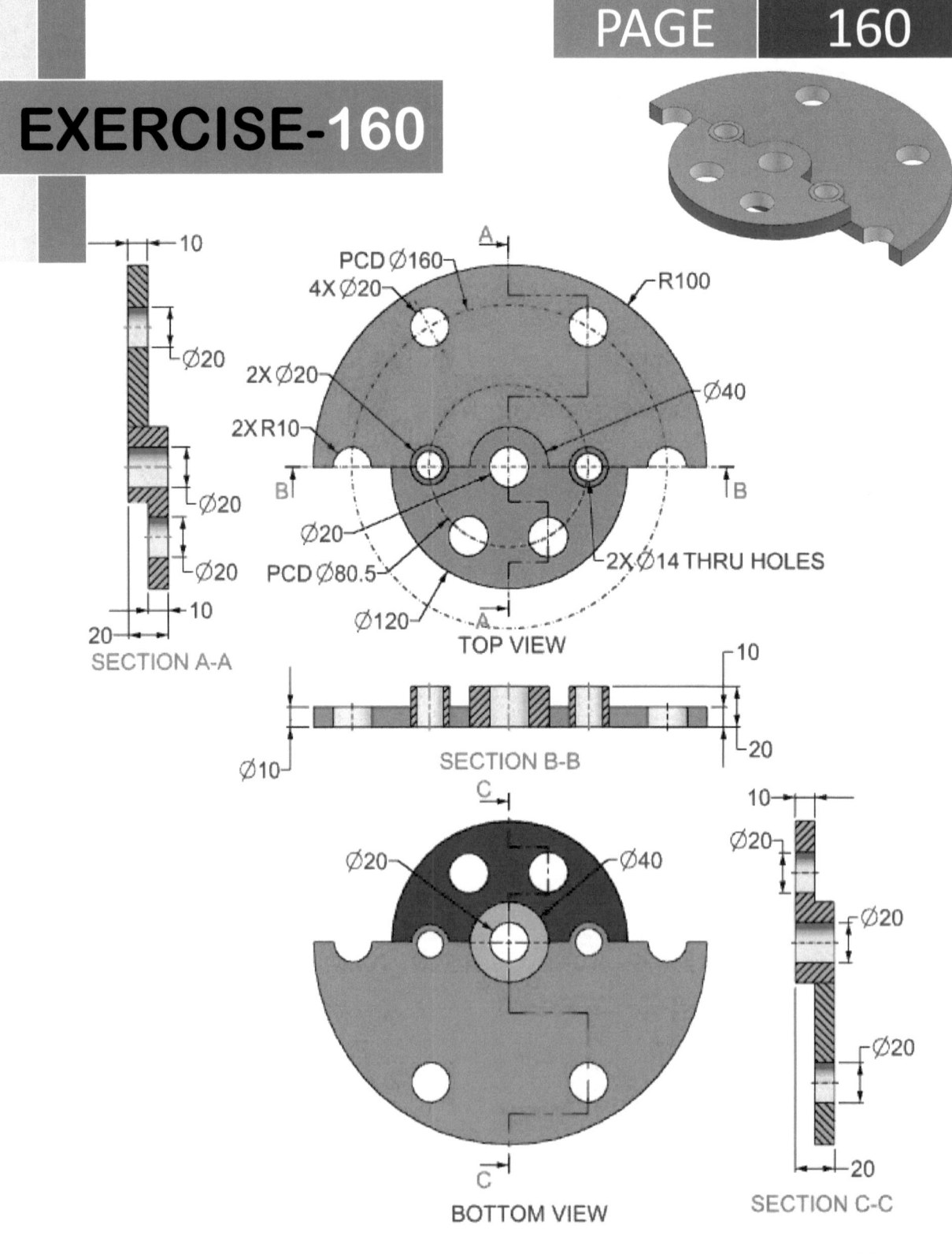

EXERCISE-161

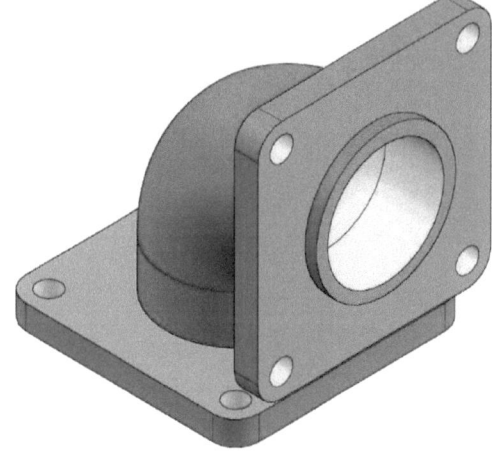

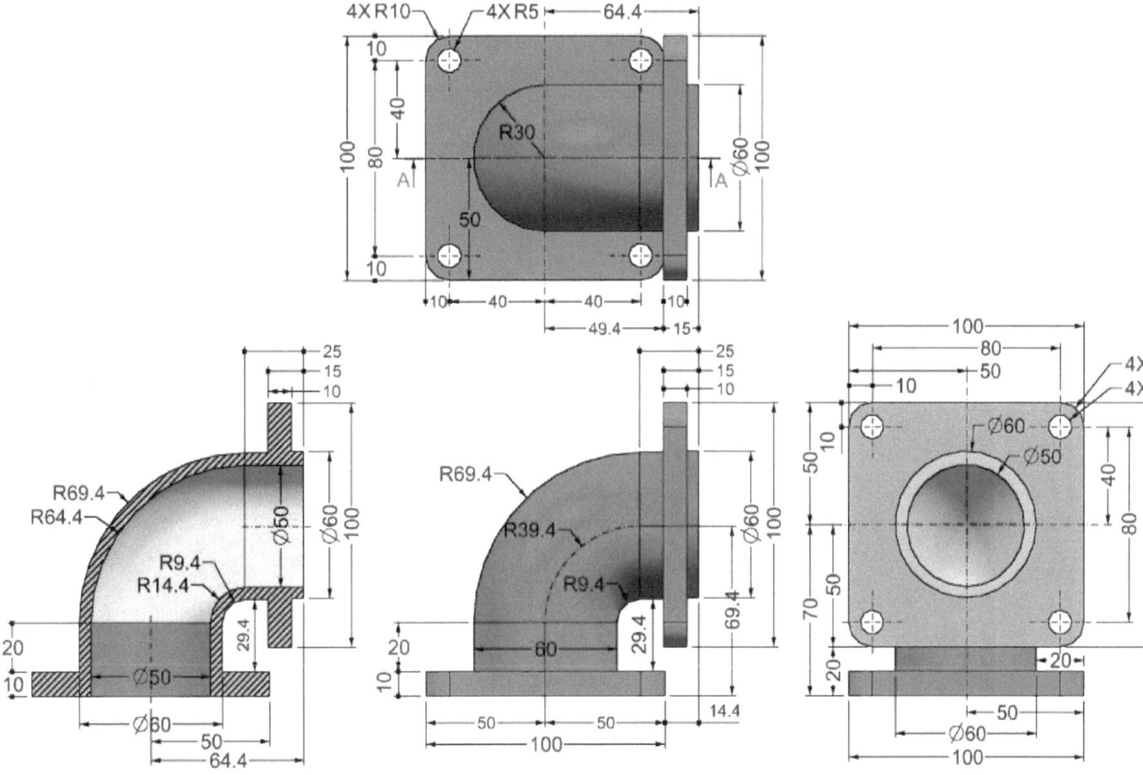

EXERCISE-162

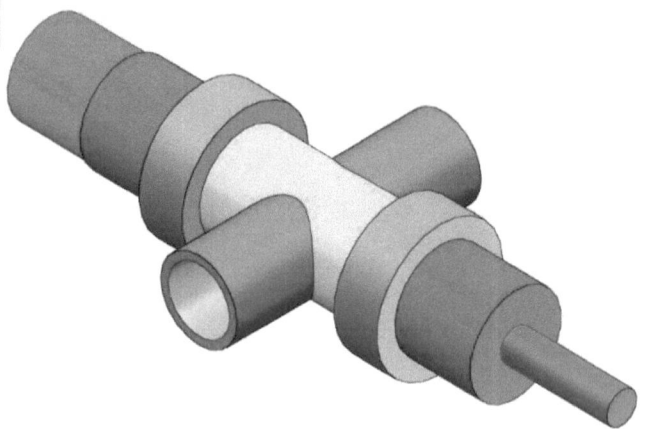

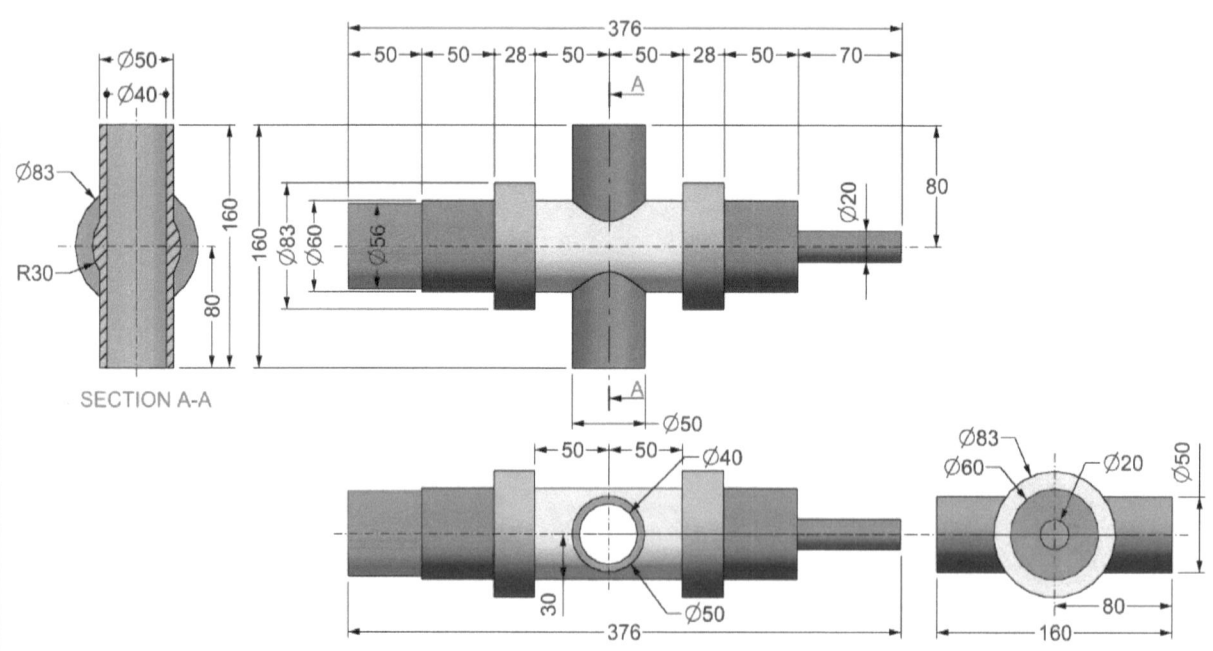

EXERCISE-163

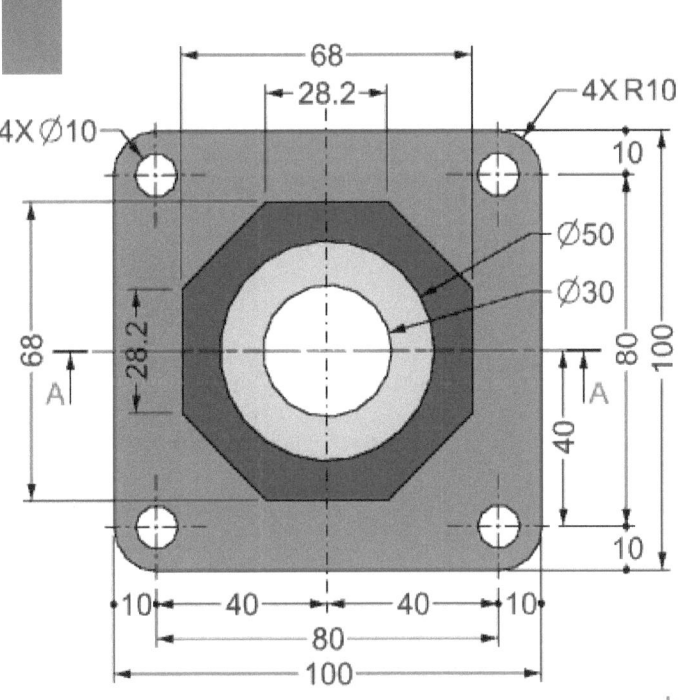
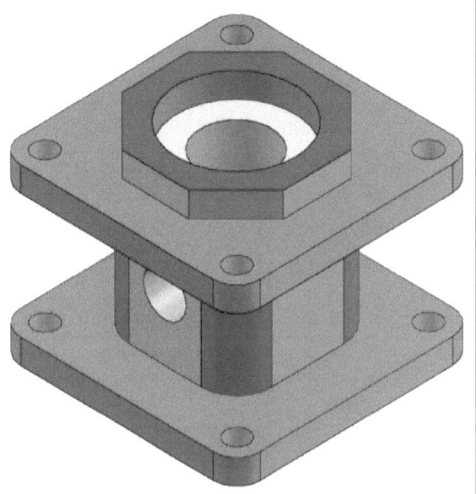
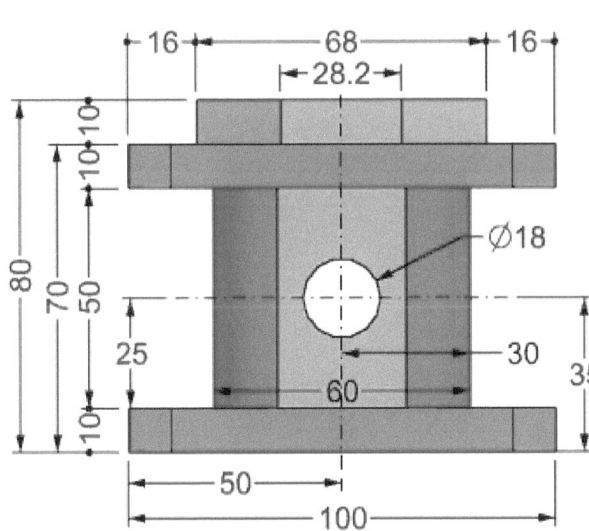
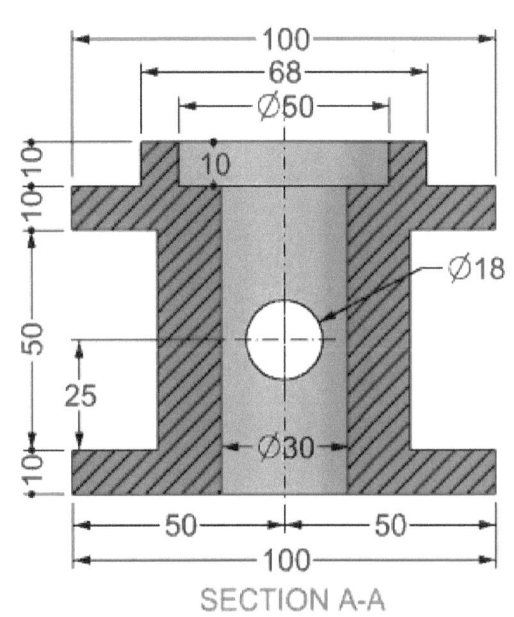

SECTION A-A

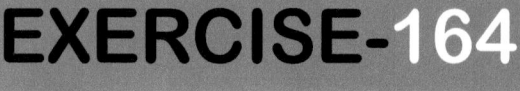

EXERCISE-164

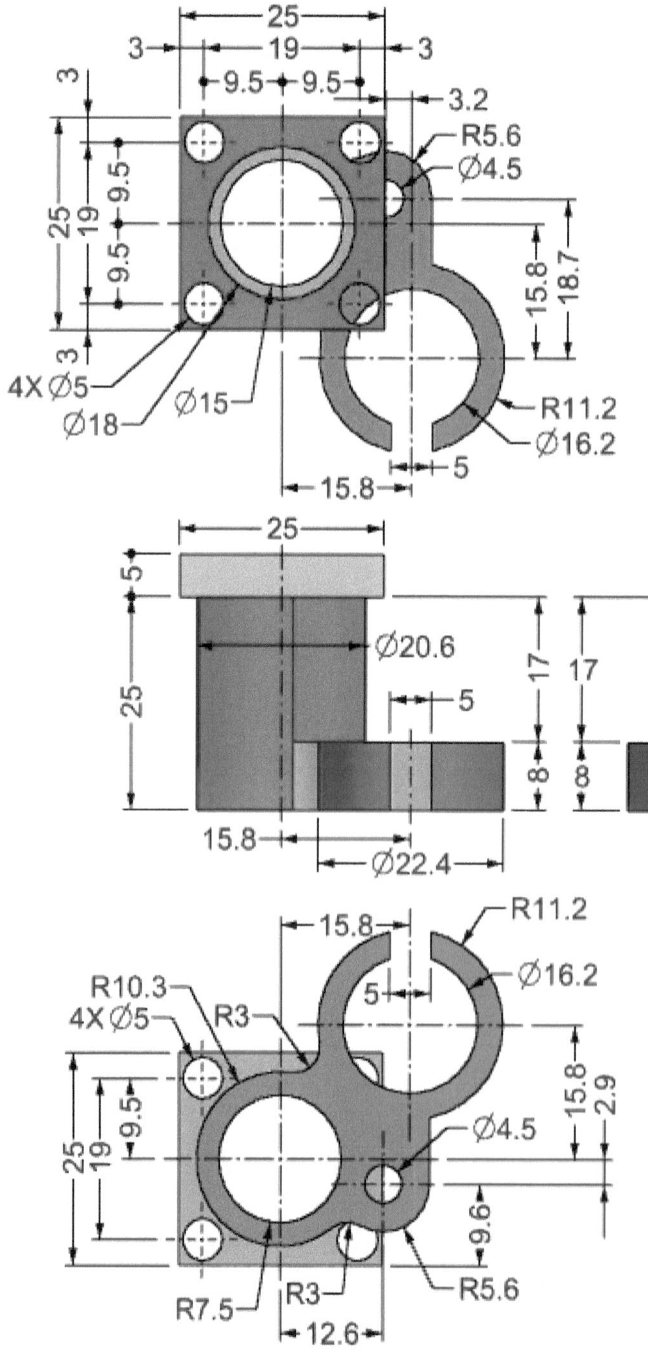

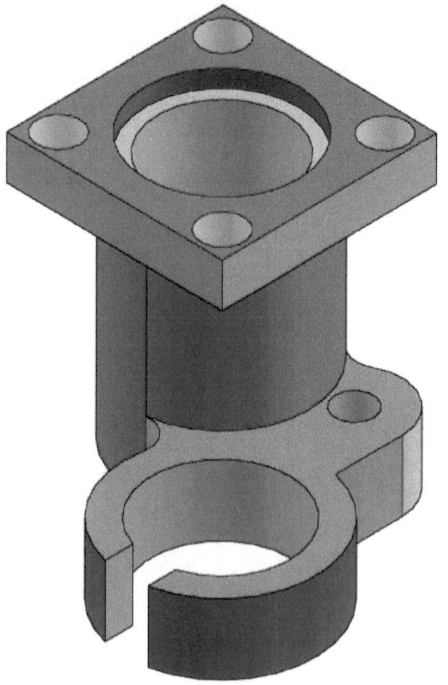

EXERCISE-165

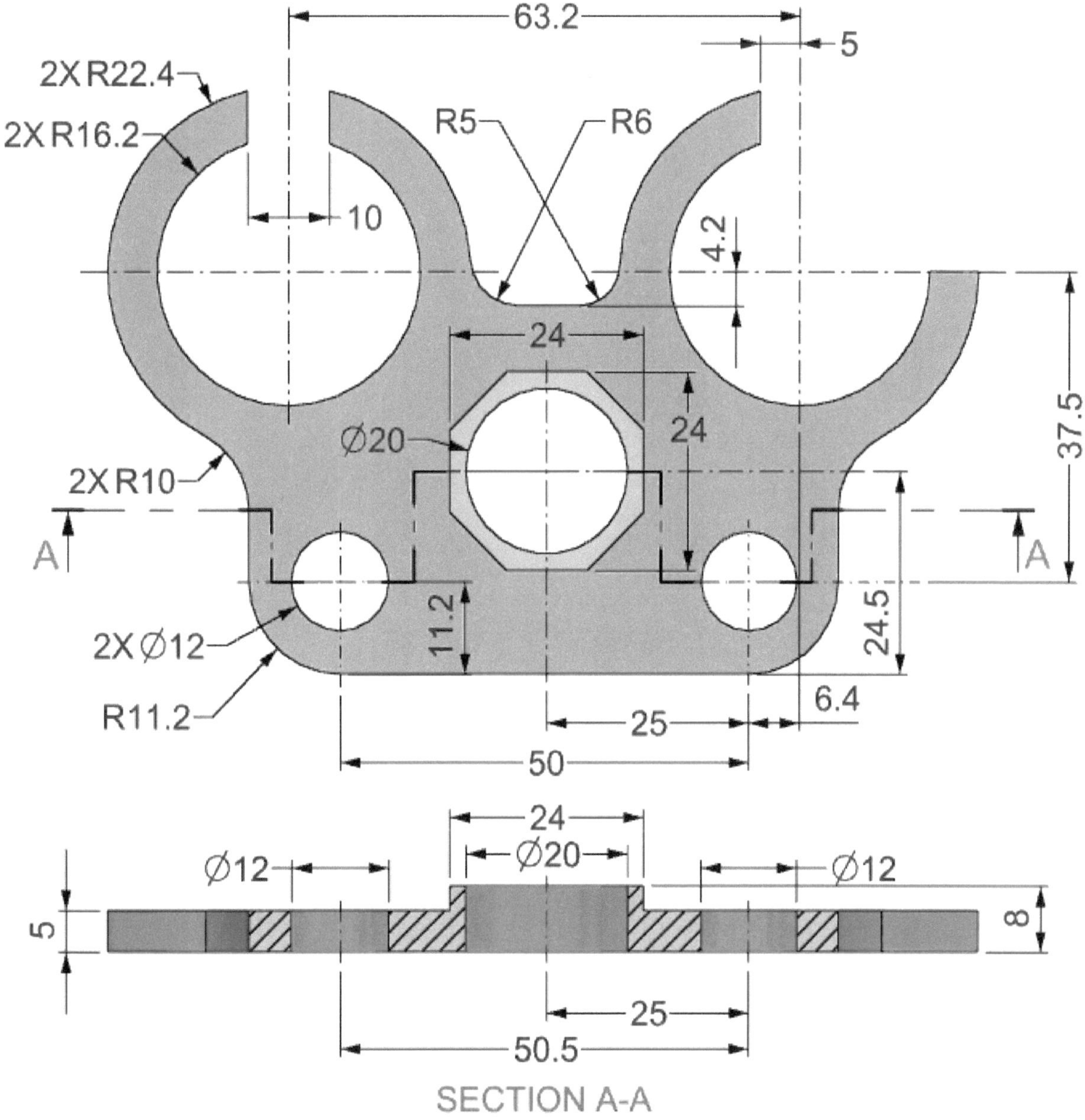

EXERCISE-166

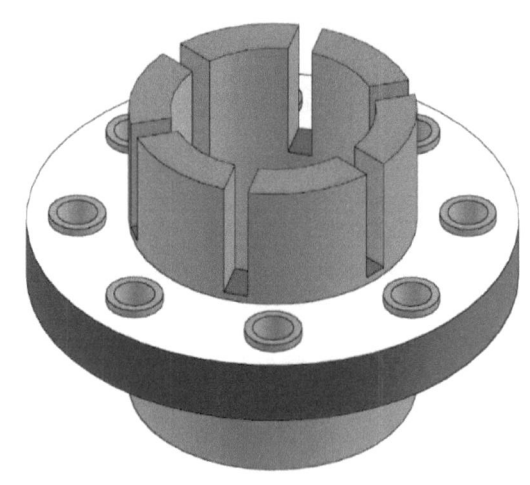

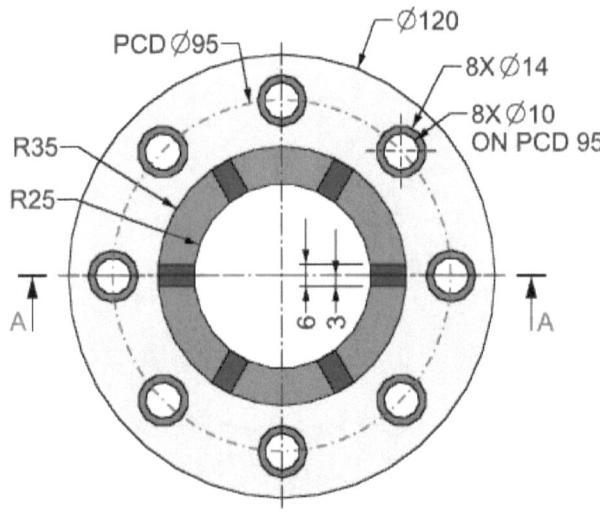

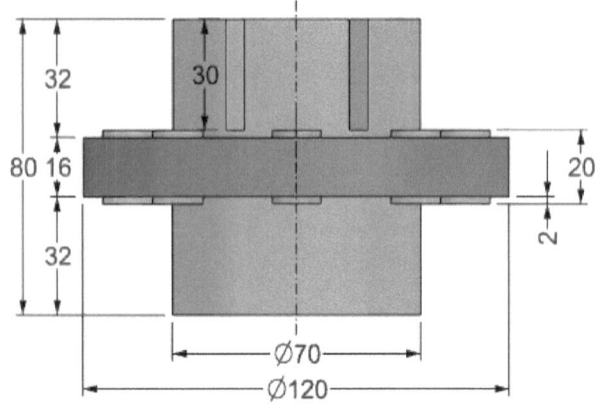

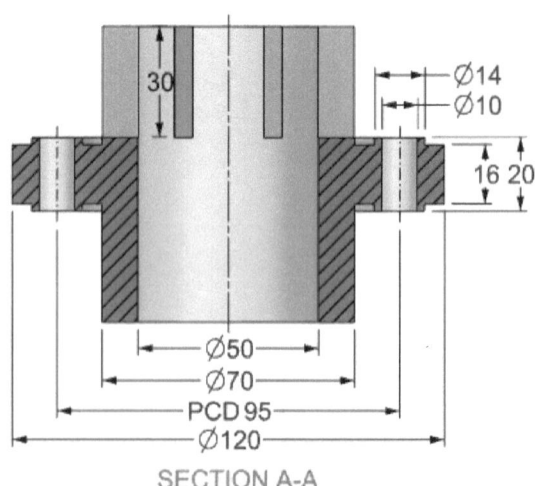

SECTION A-A

EXERCISE-167

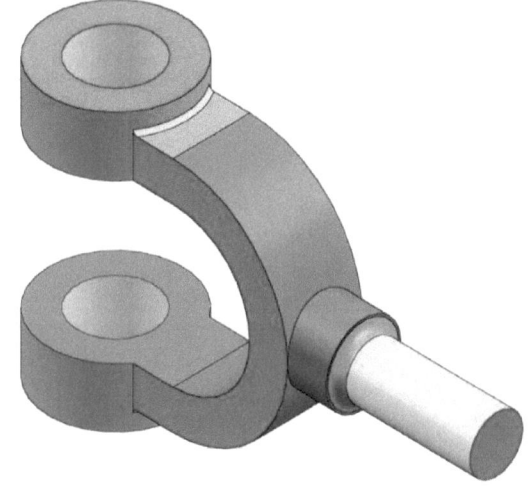
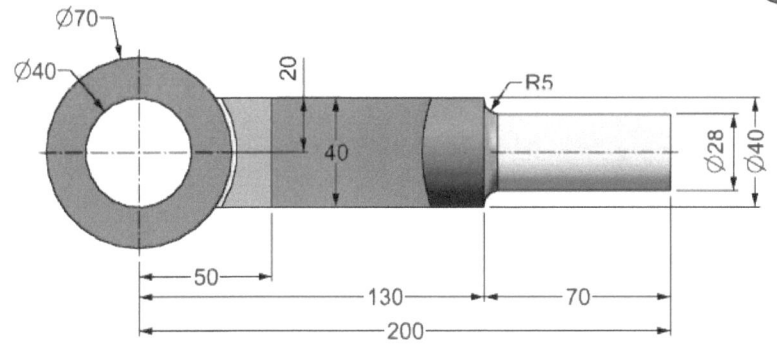
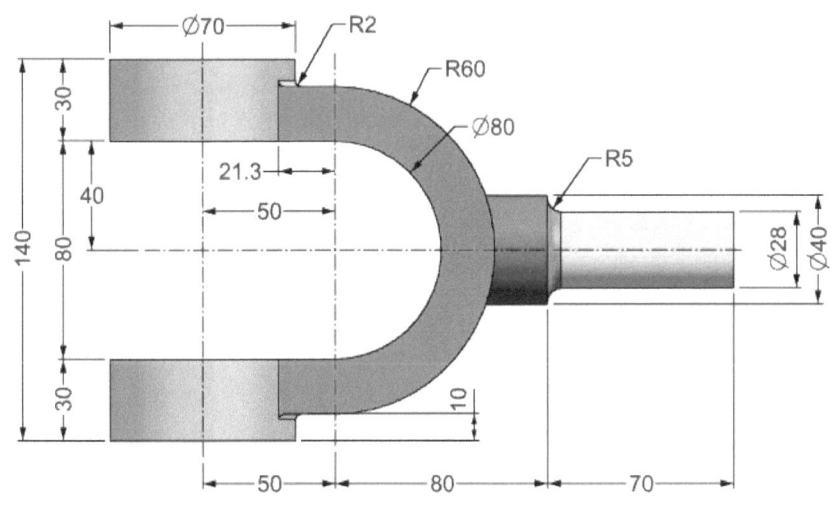
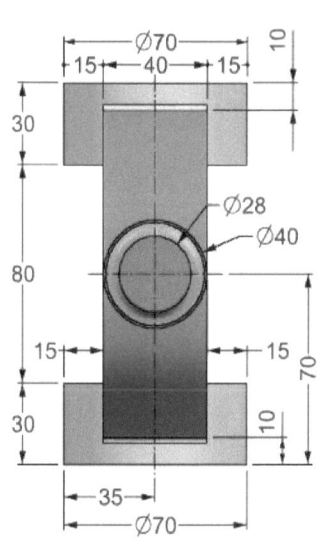

EXERCISE-168

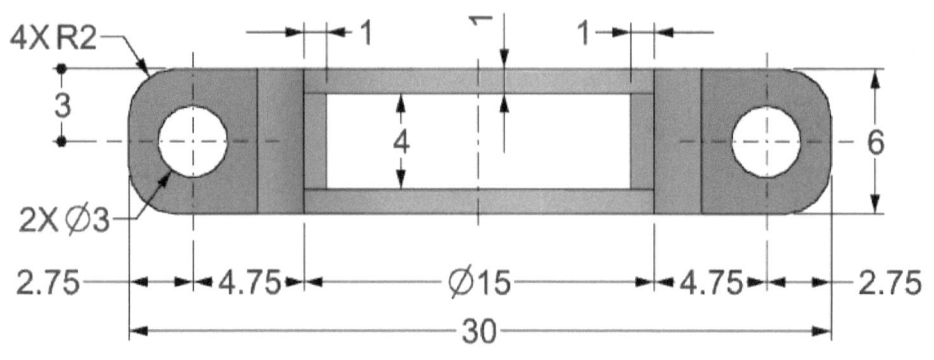

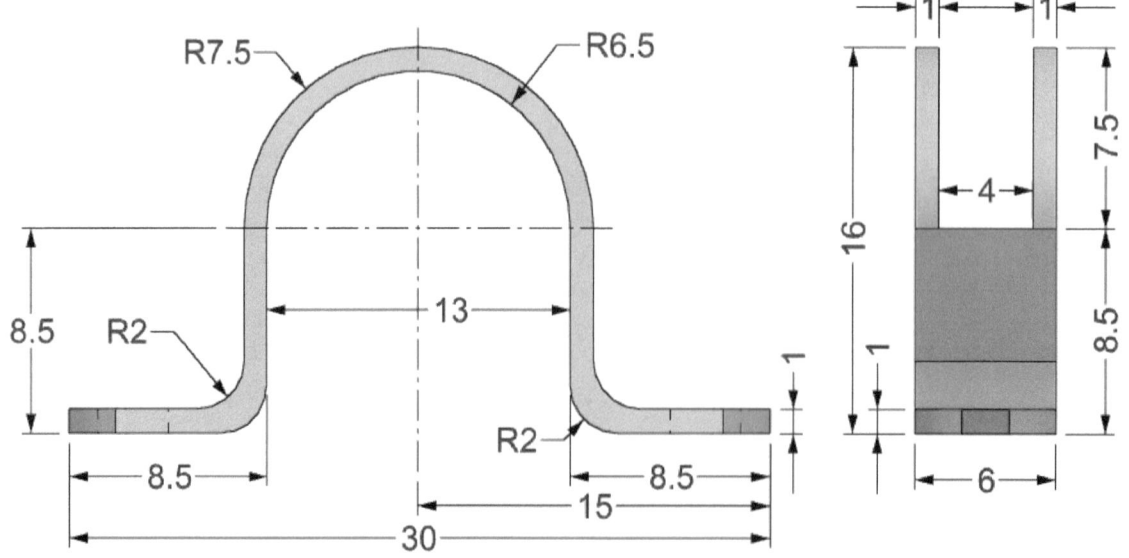

EXERCISE-169

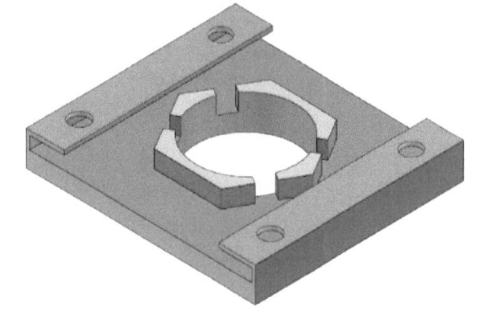

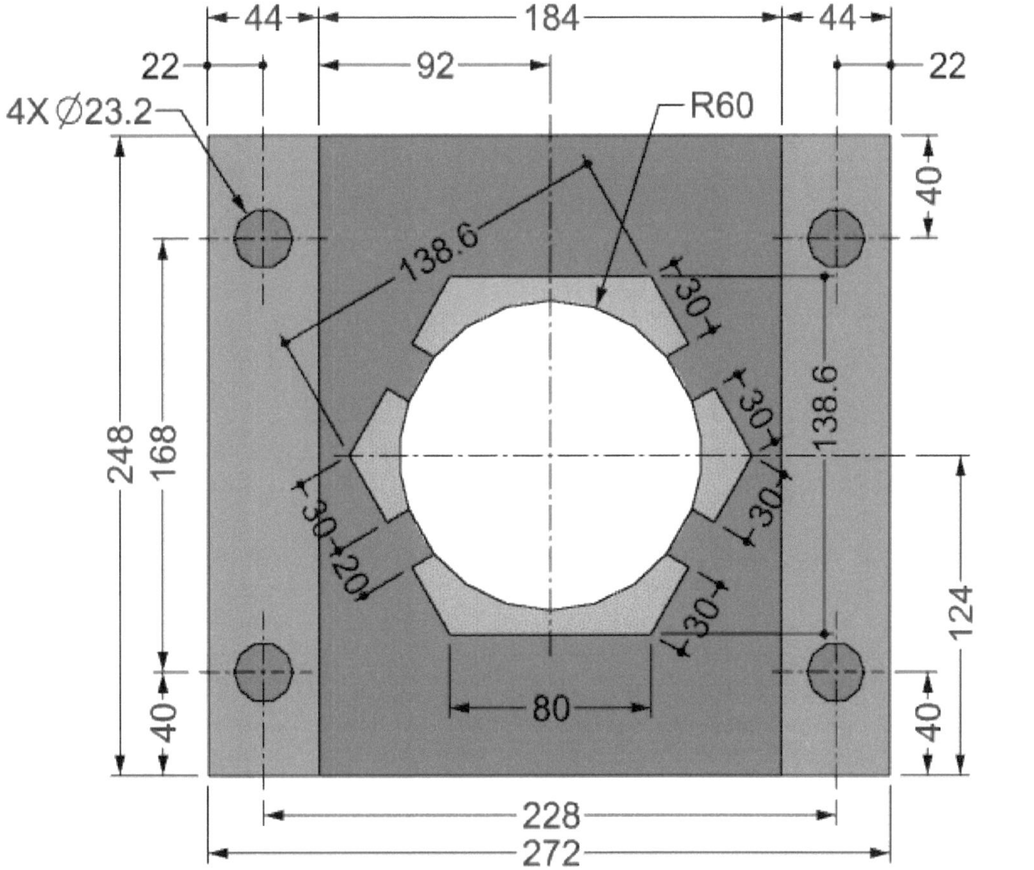

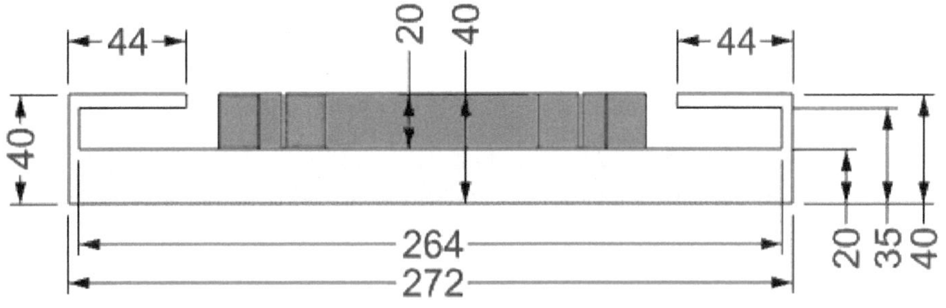

EXERCISE-170

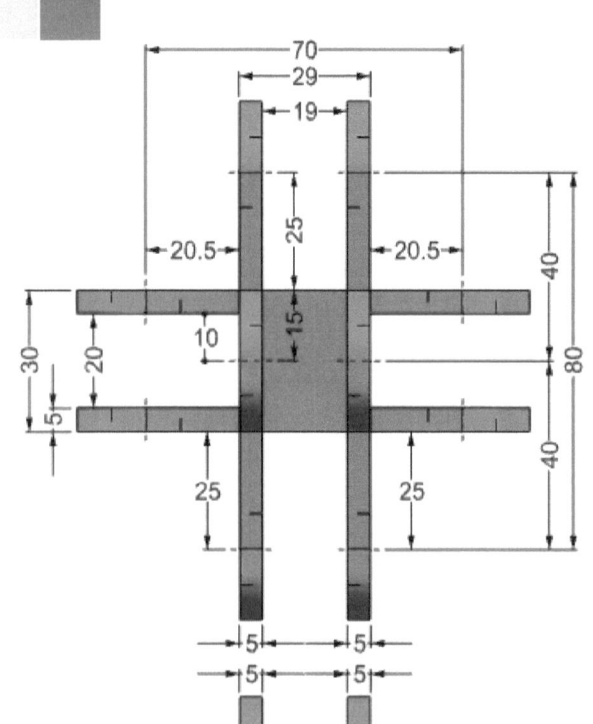

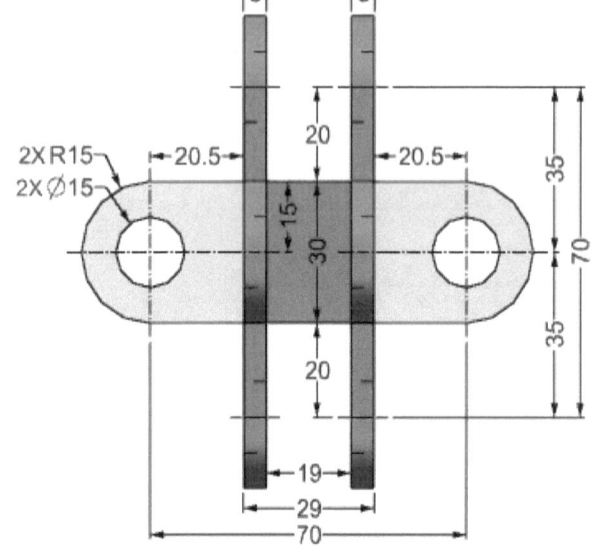
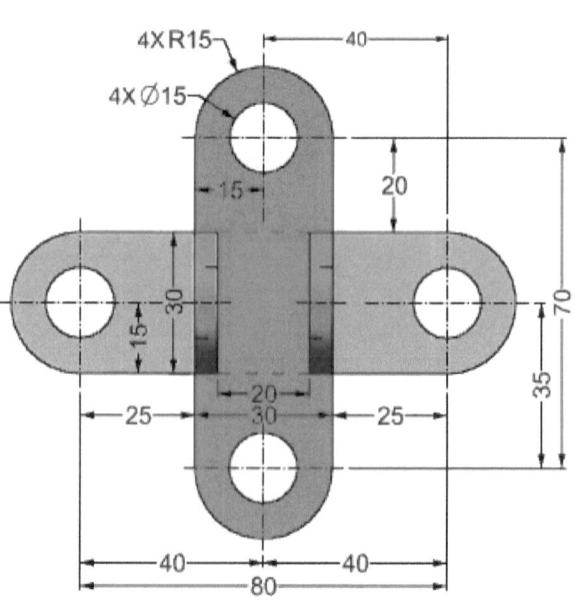

EXERCISE-171

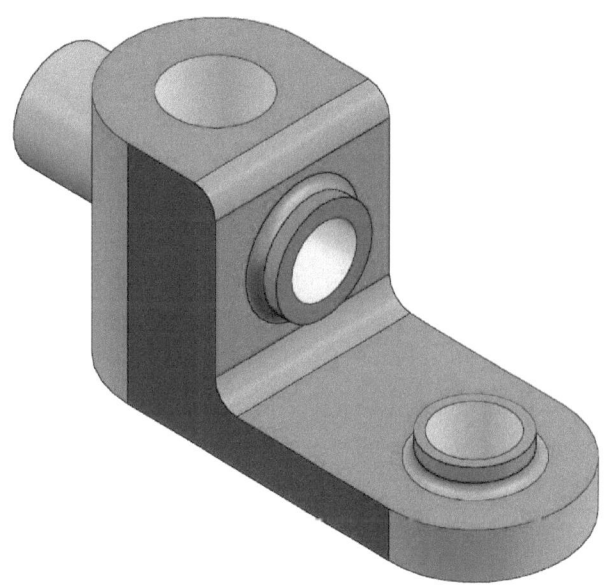

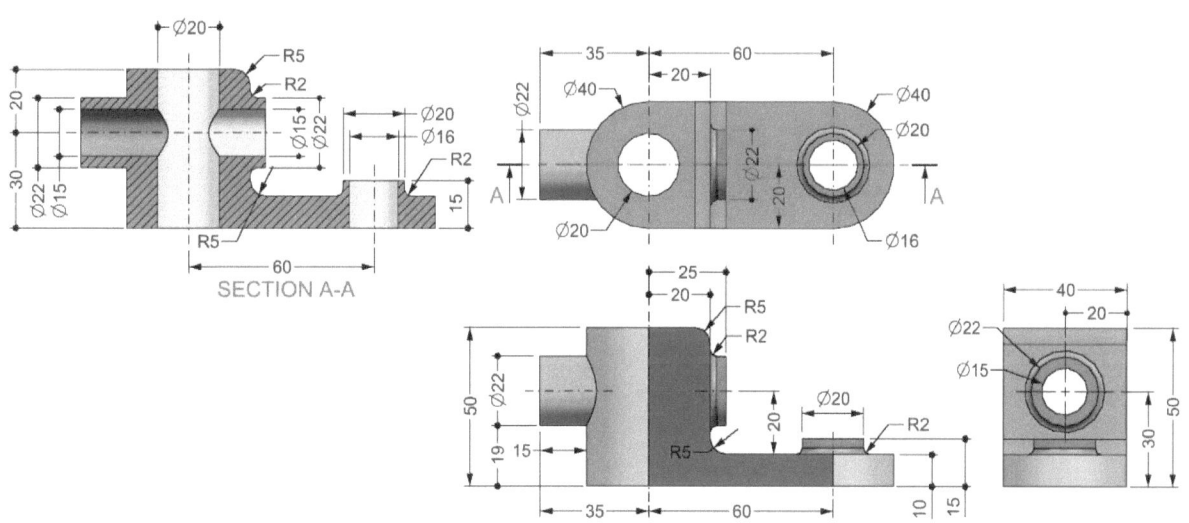

EXERCISE-172

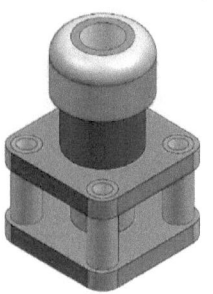

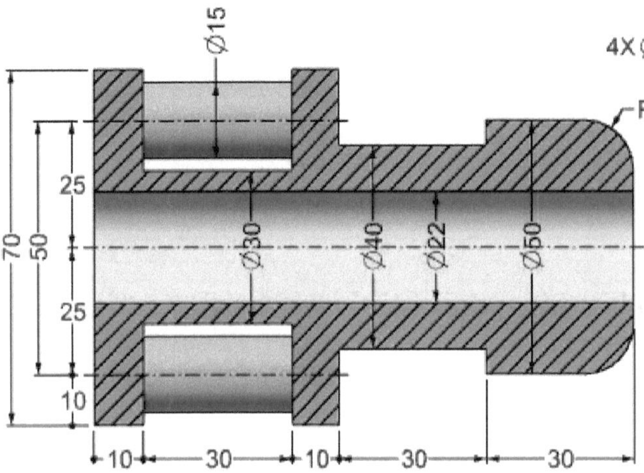

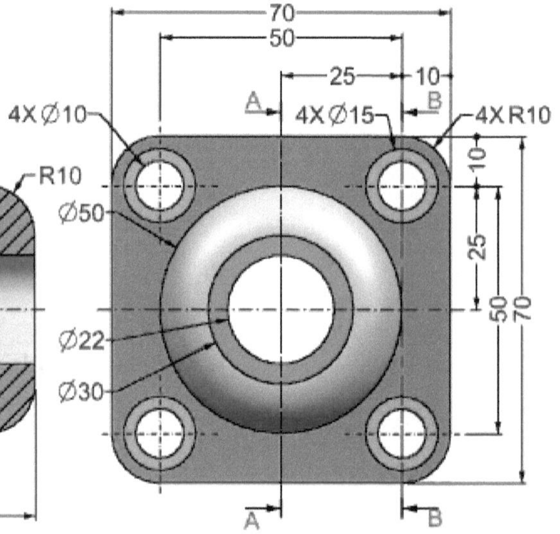

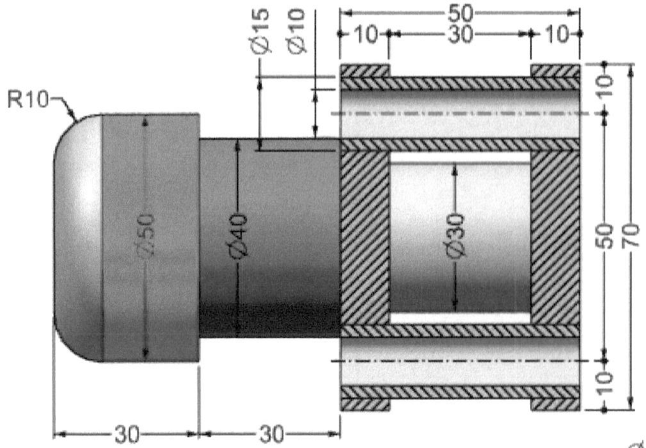

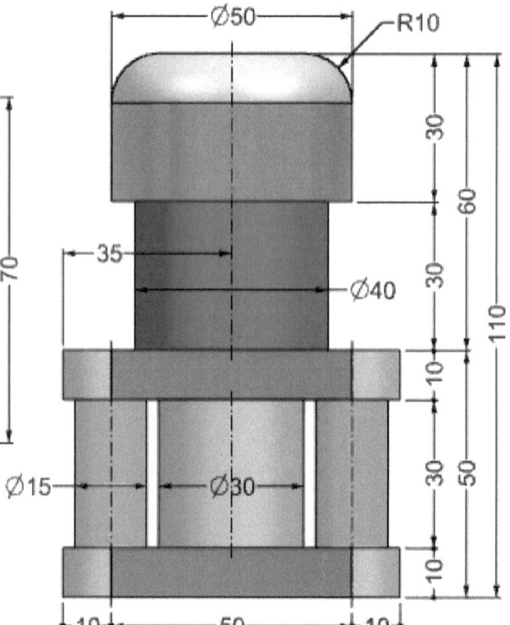

EXERCISE-173

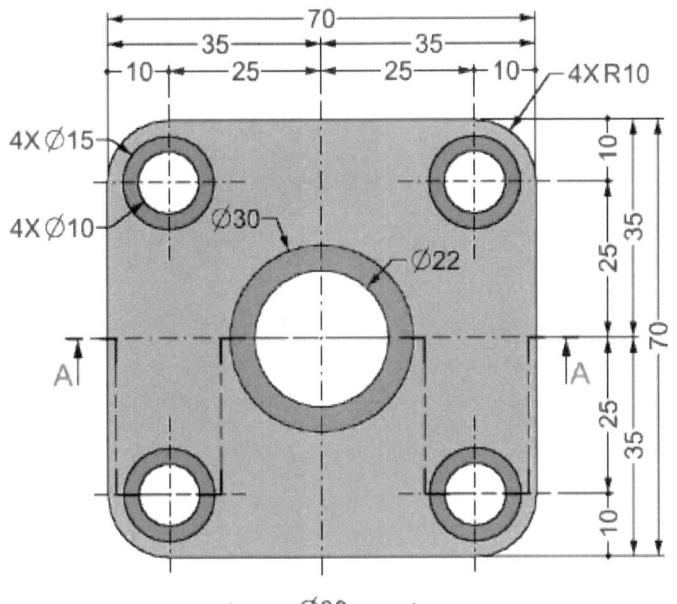
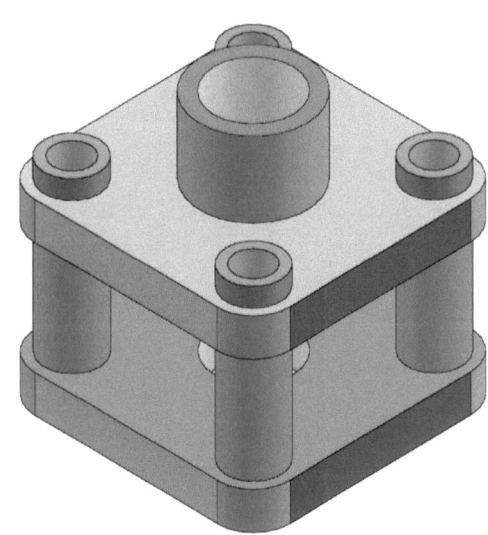
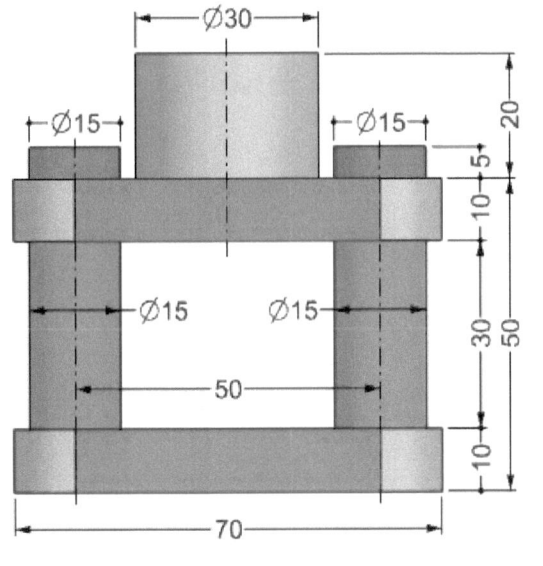
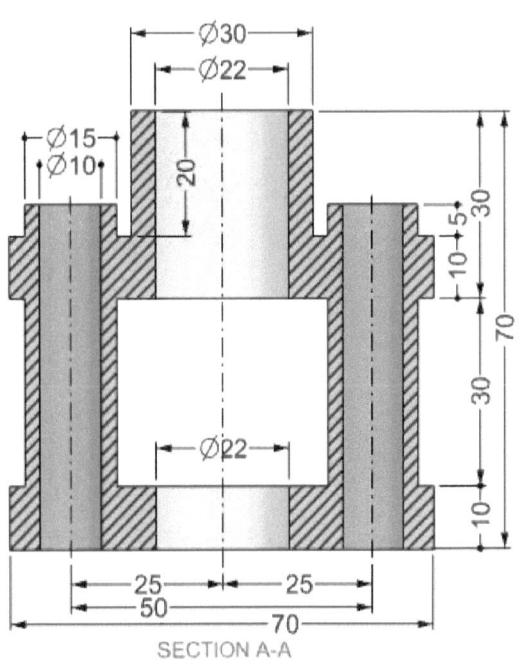

SECTION A-A

EXERCISE-174

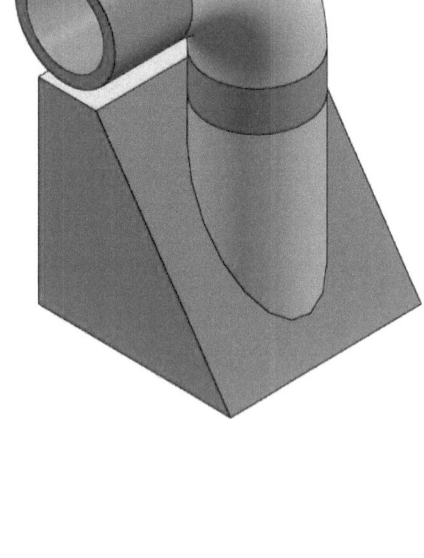

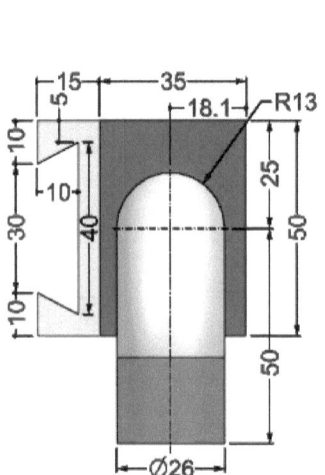

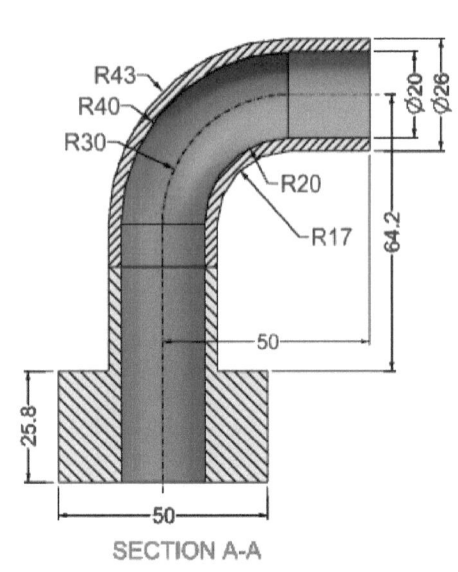

SECTION A-A

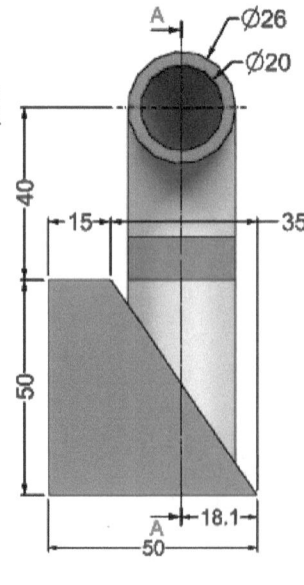

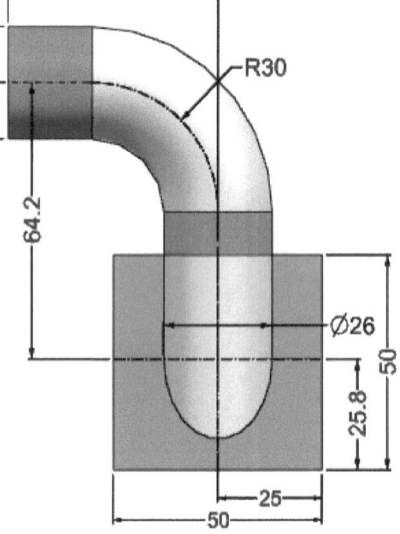

EXERCISE-175

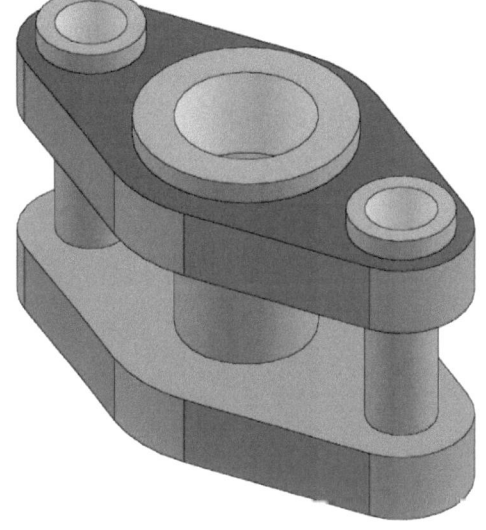

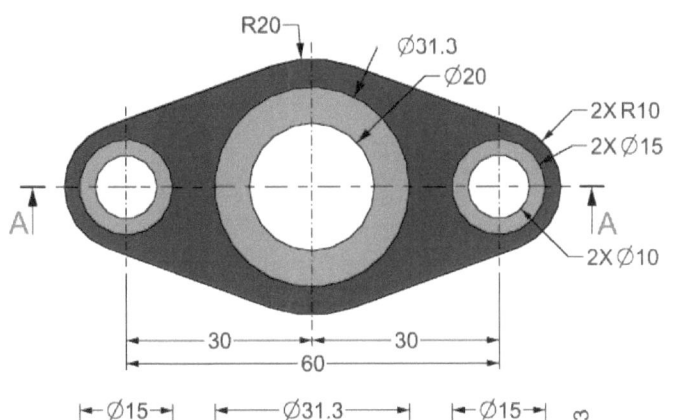

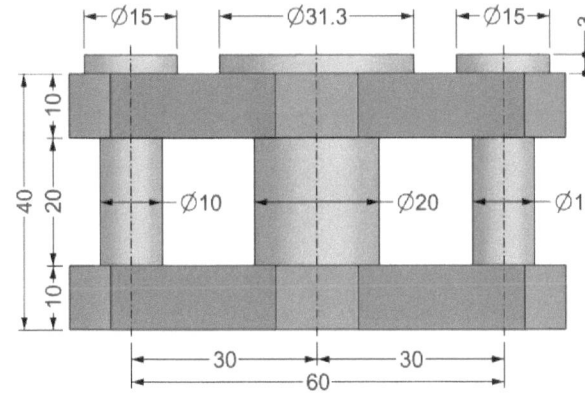 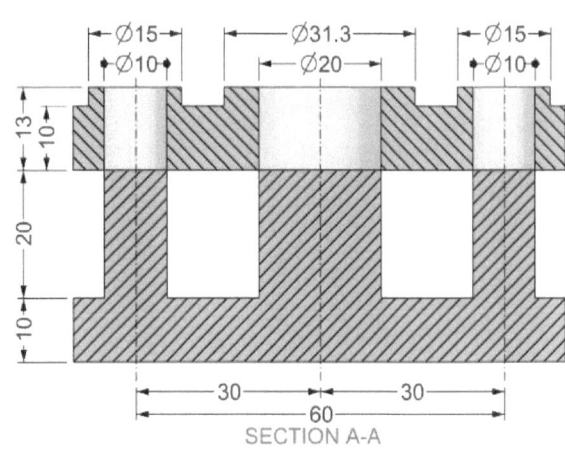

SECTION A-A

EXERCISE-176

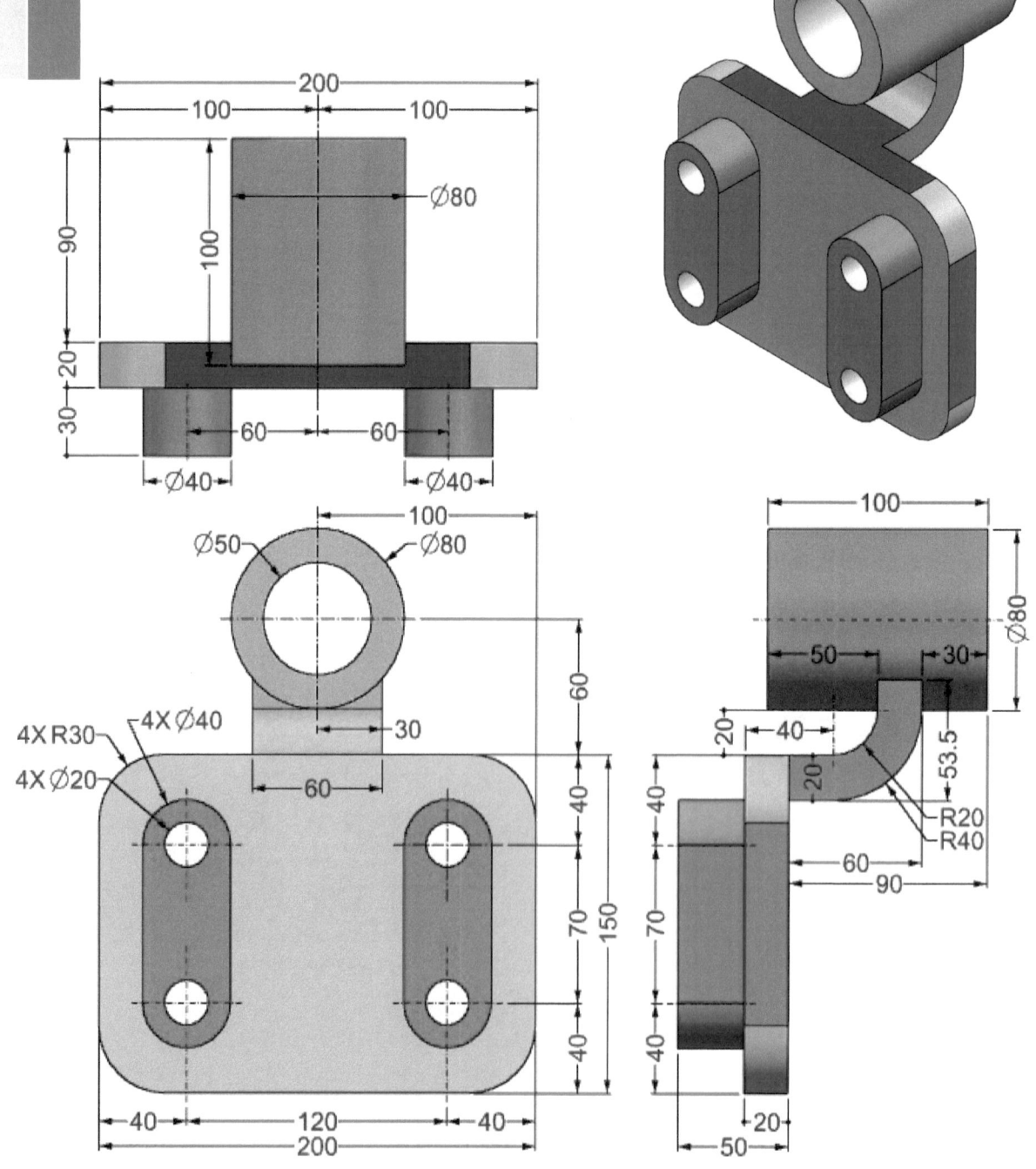

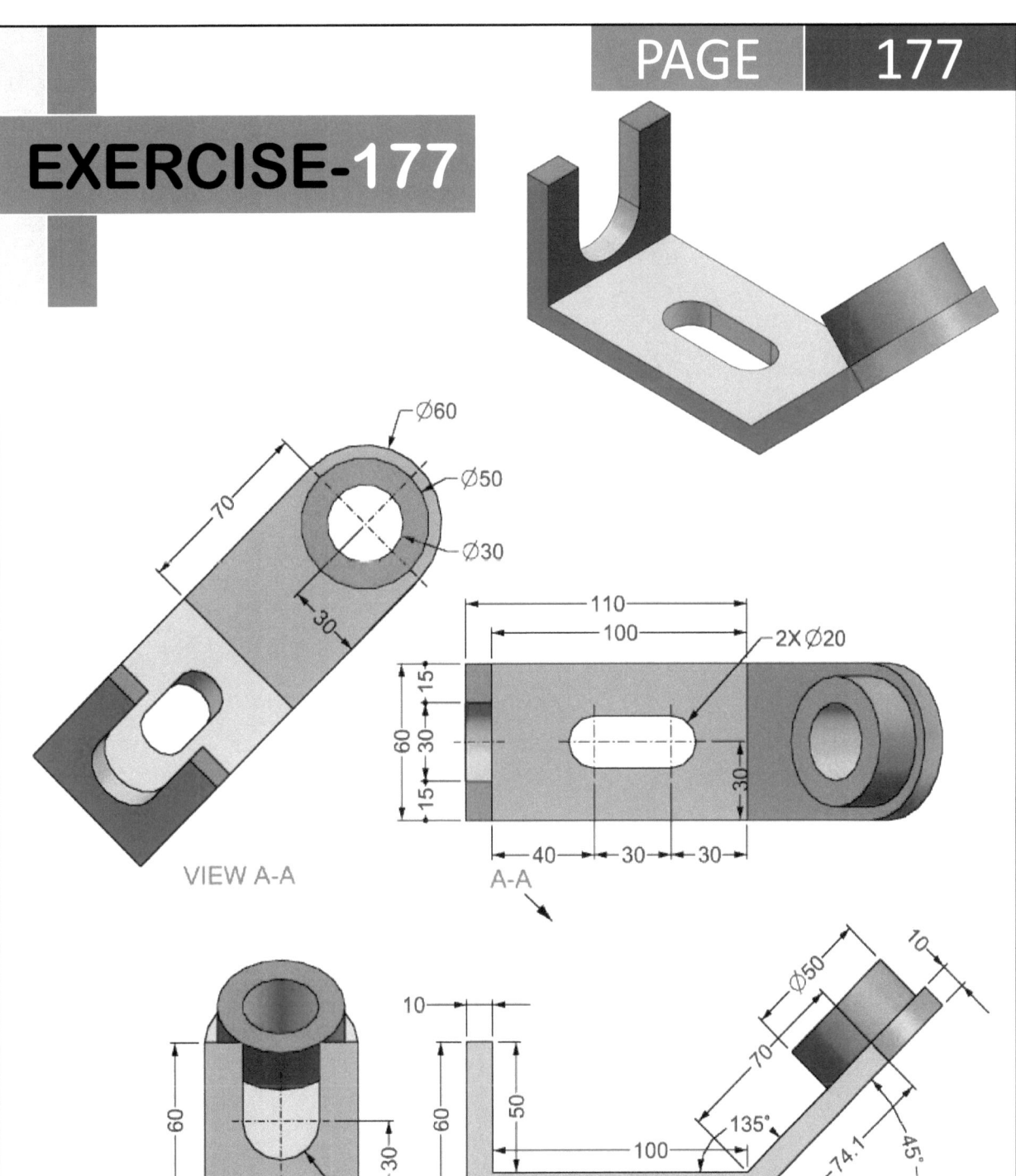

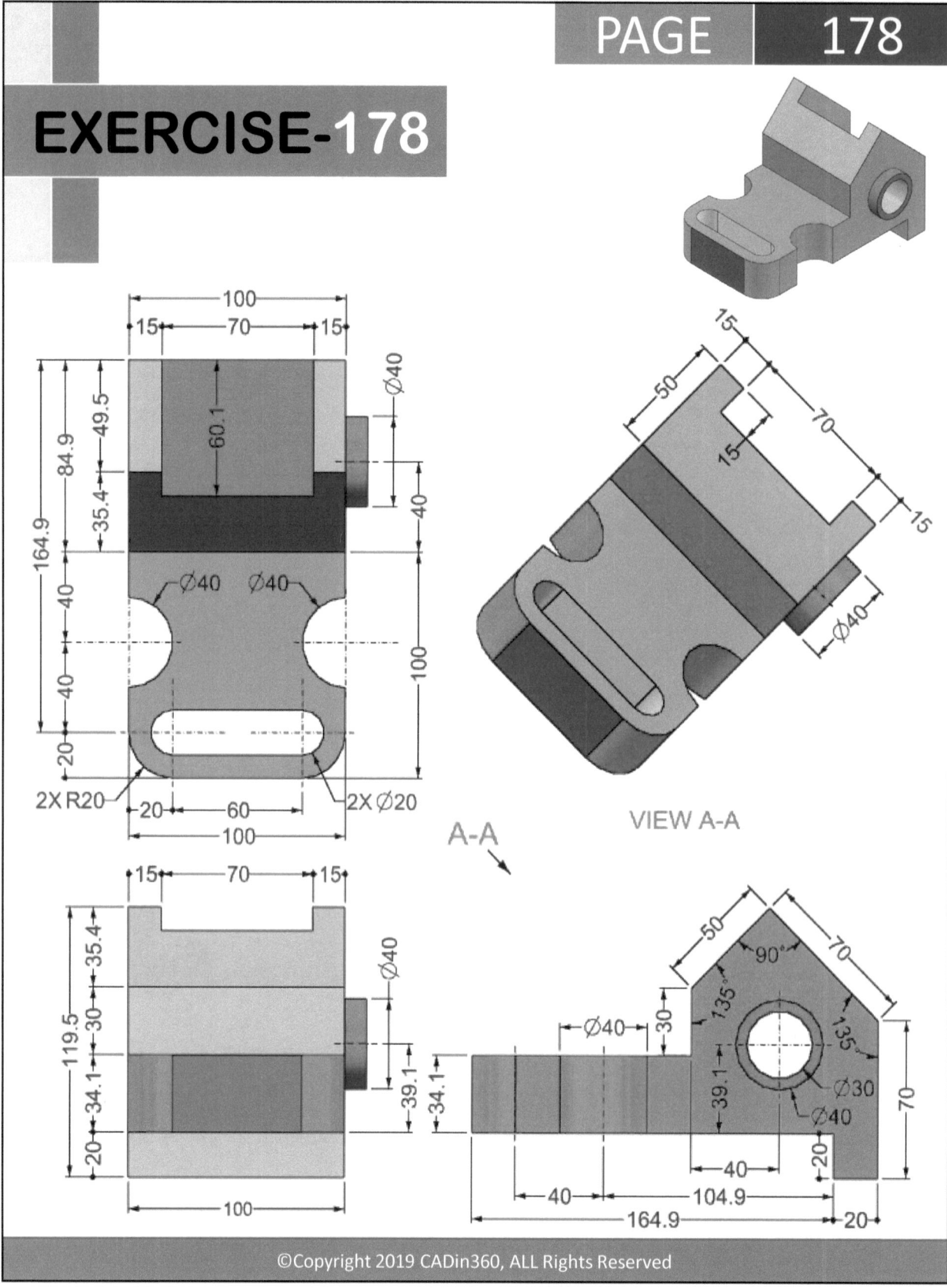

EXERCISE-179

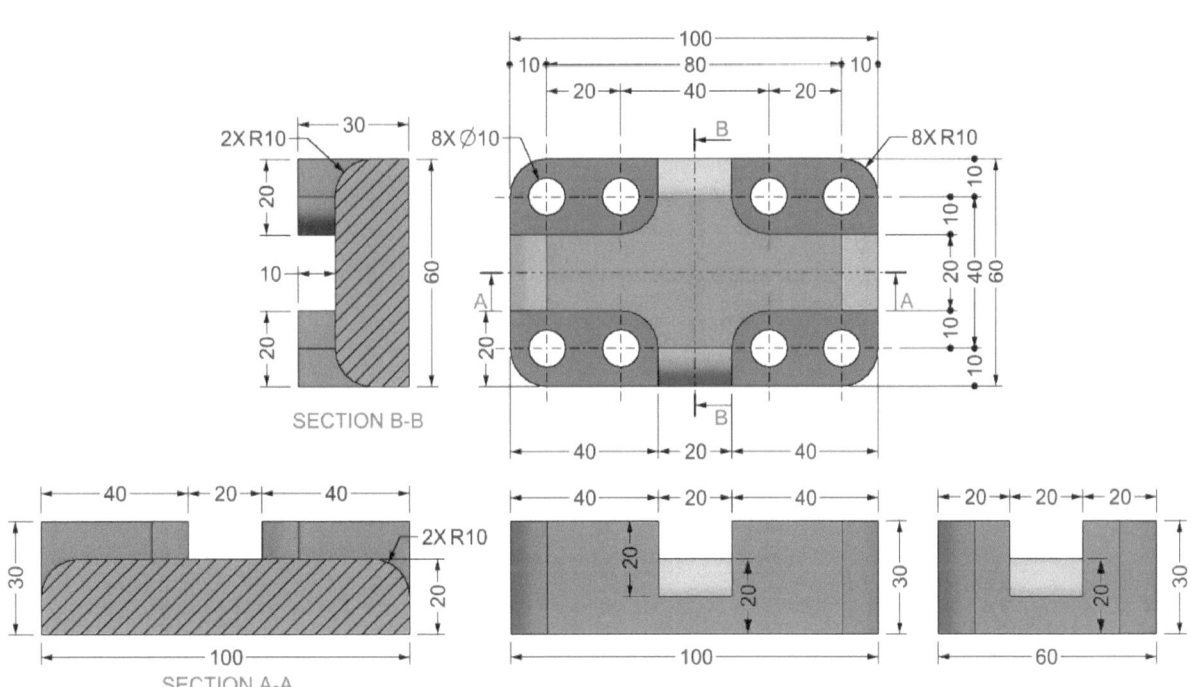

EXERCISE-180

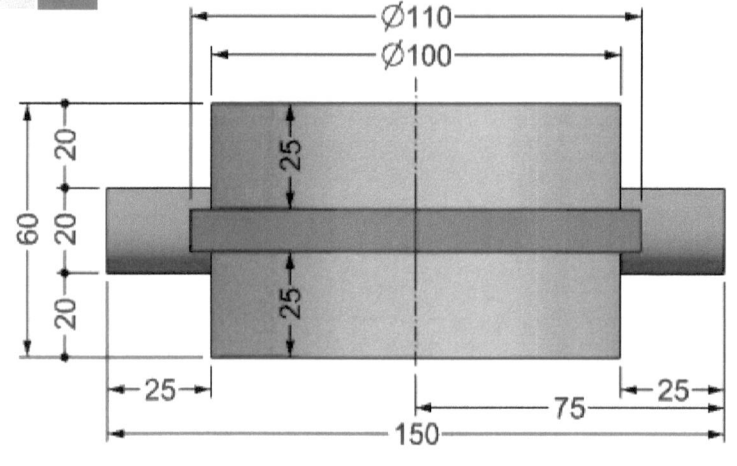
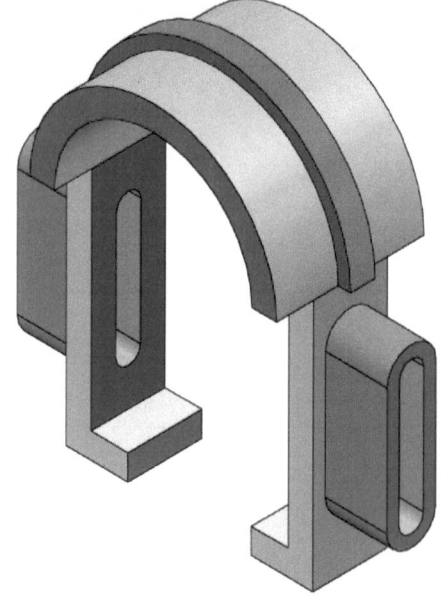
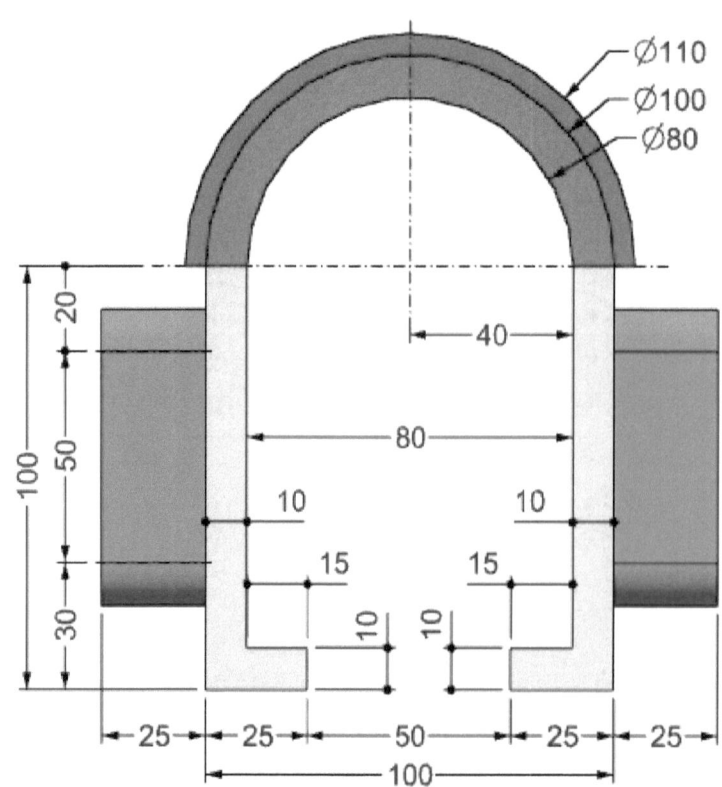
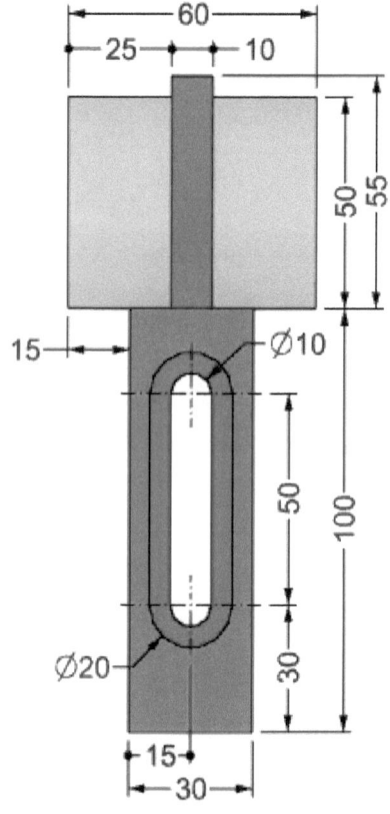

EXERCISE-181

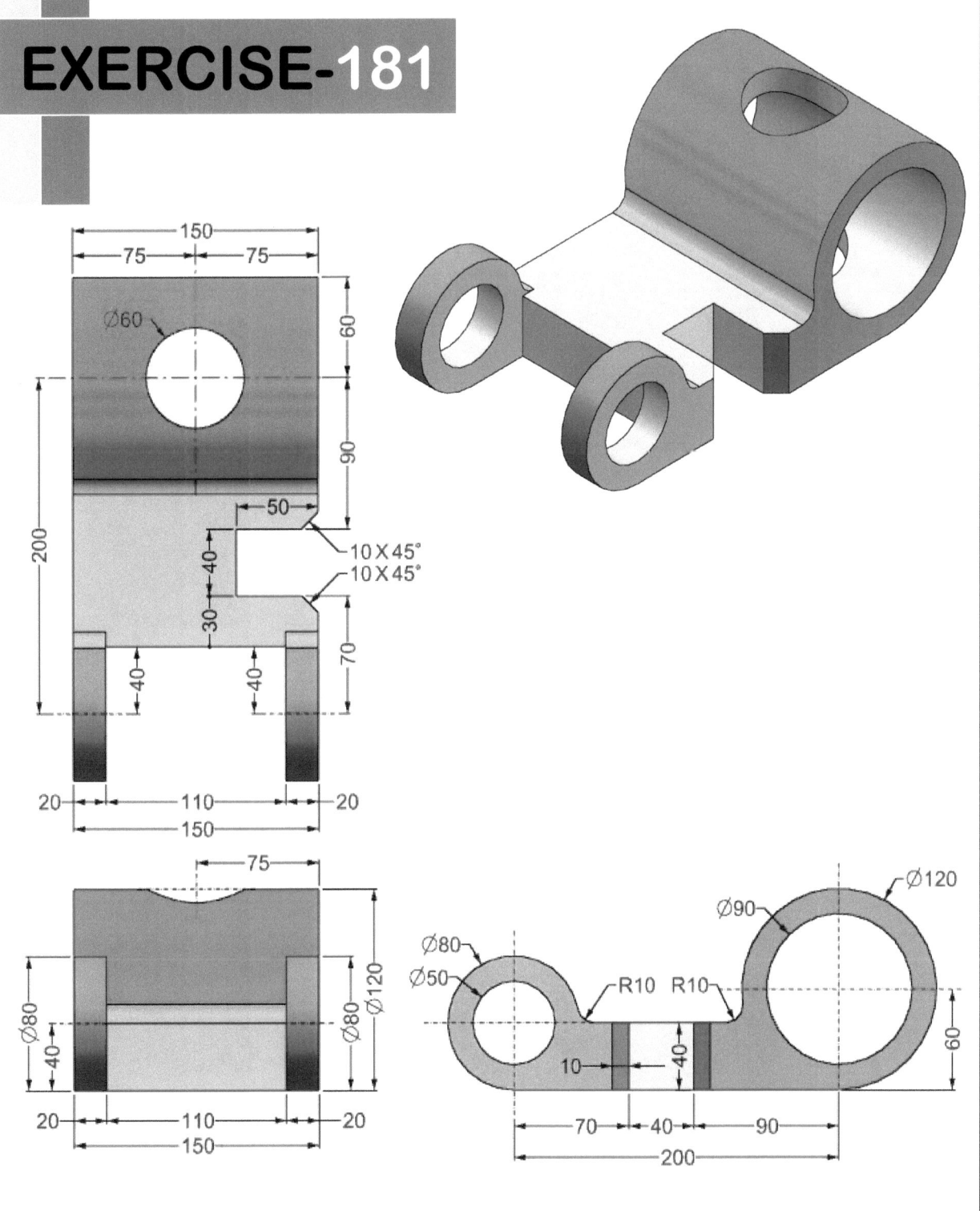

EXERCISE-182

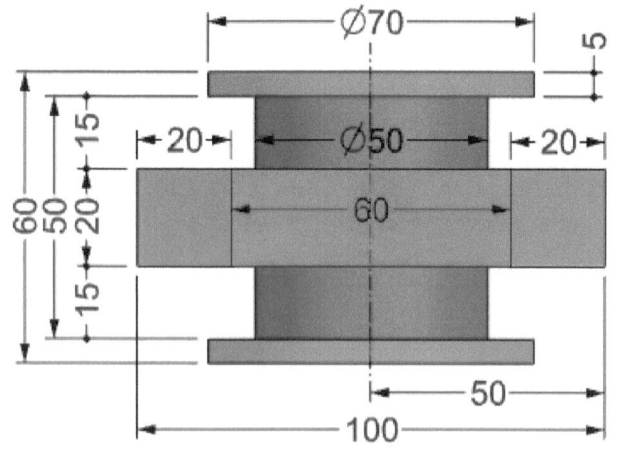
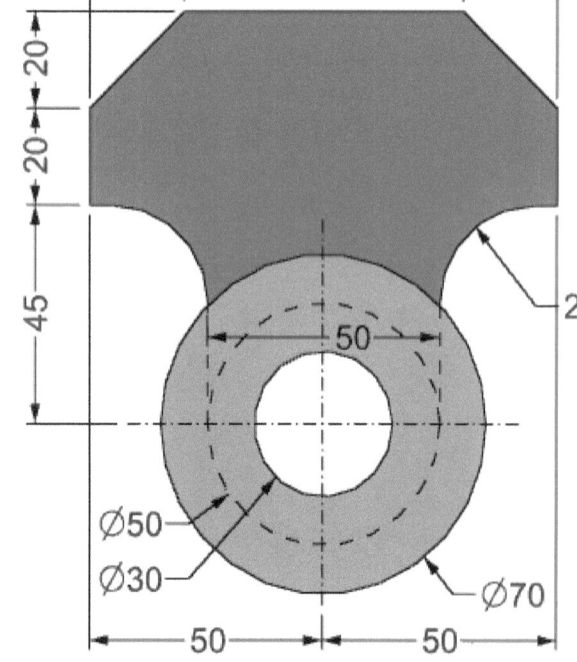
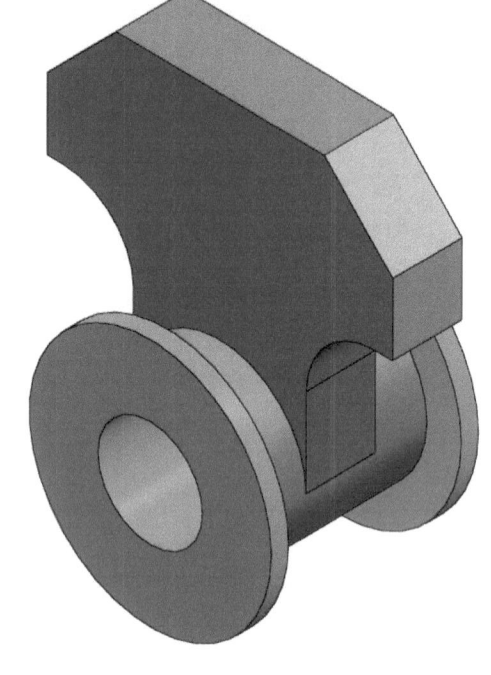
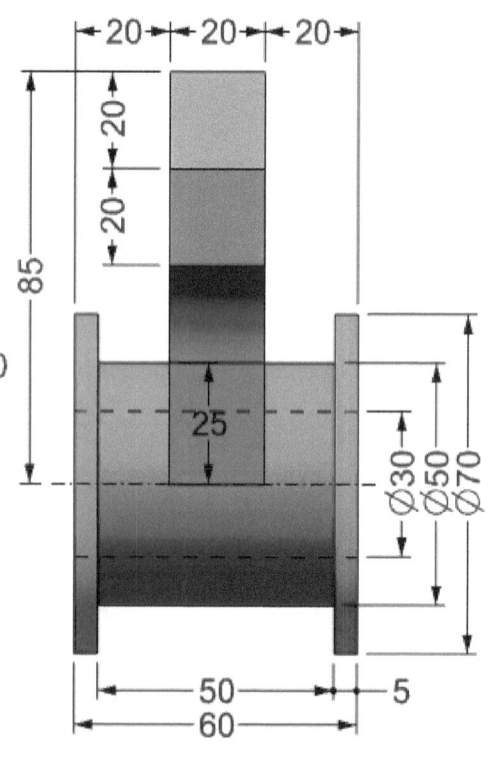

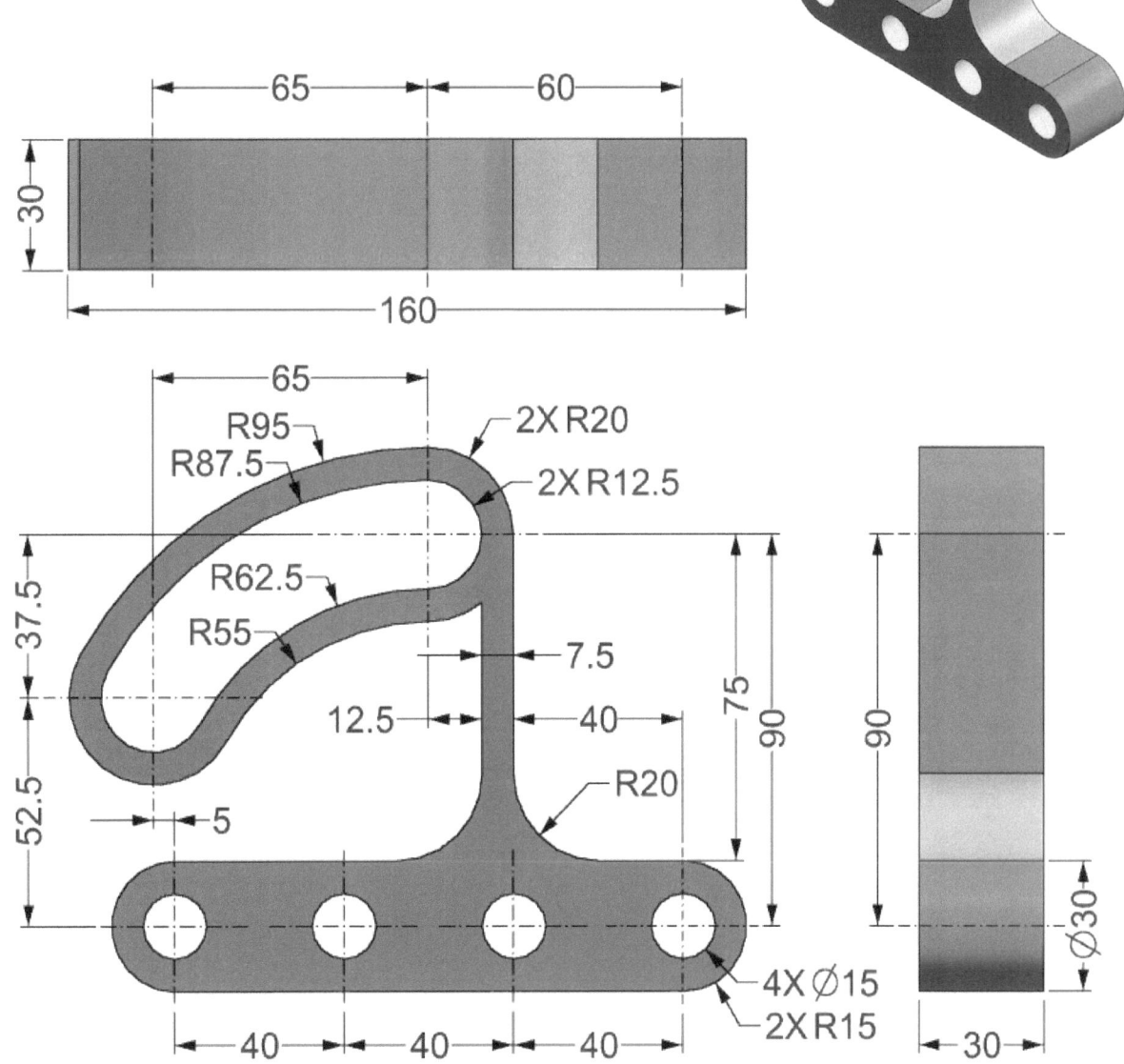

EXERCISE-184

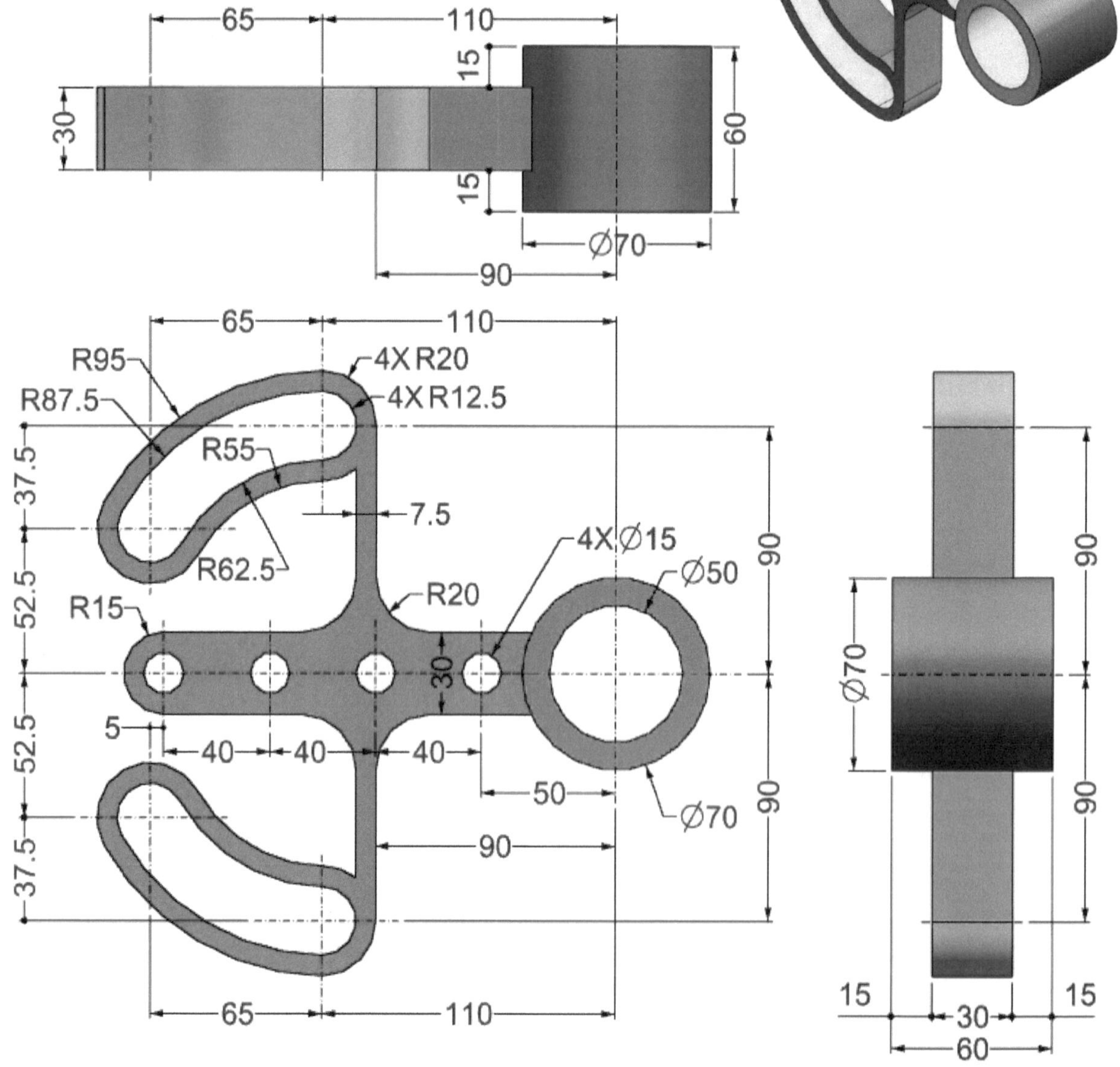

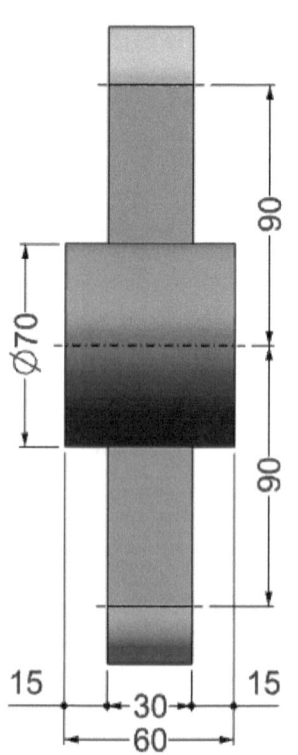

EXERCISE-185

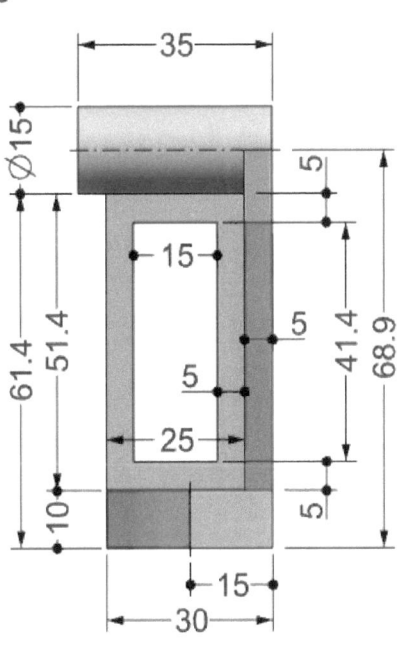

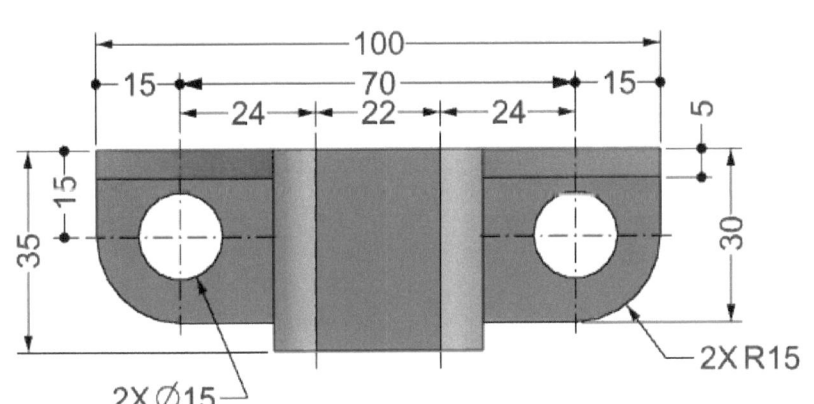

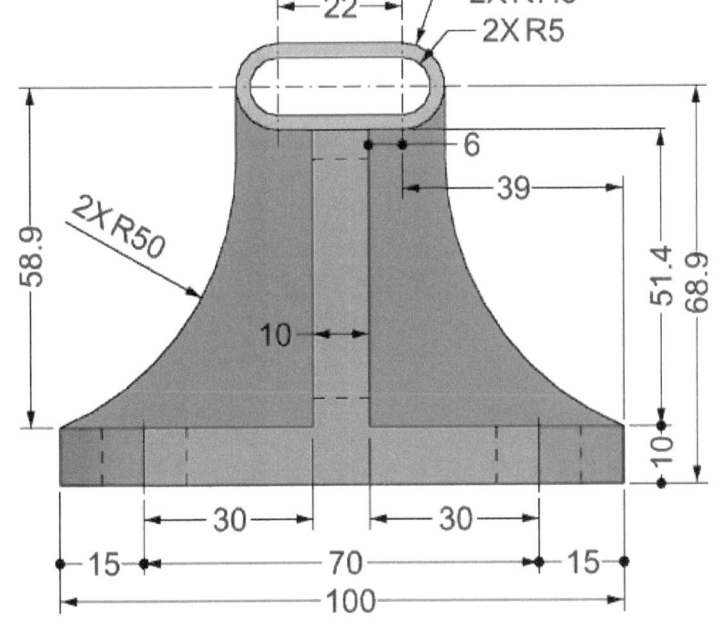

EXERCISE-186

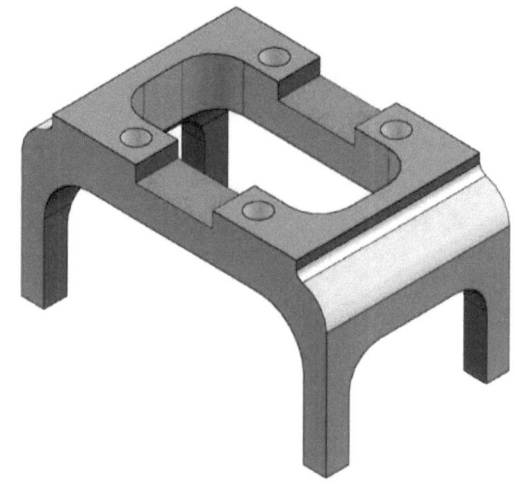
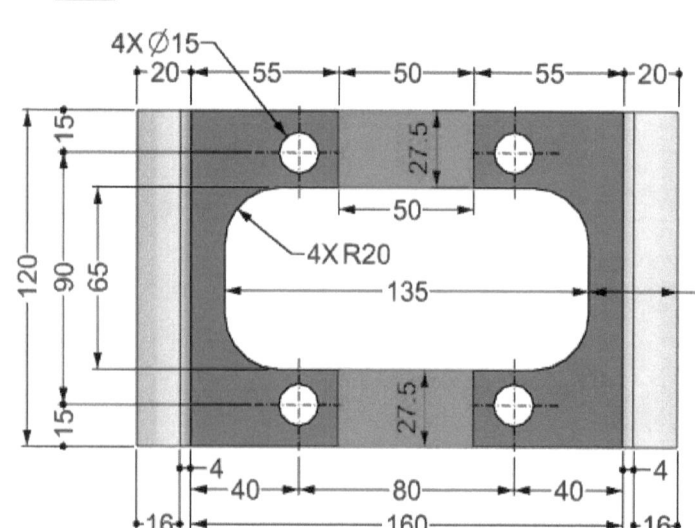
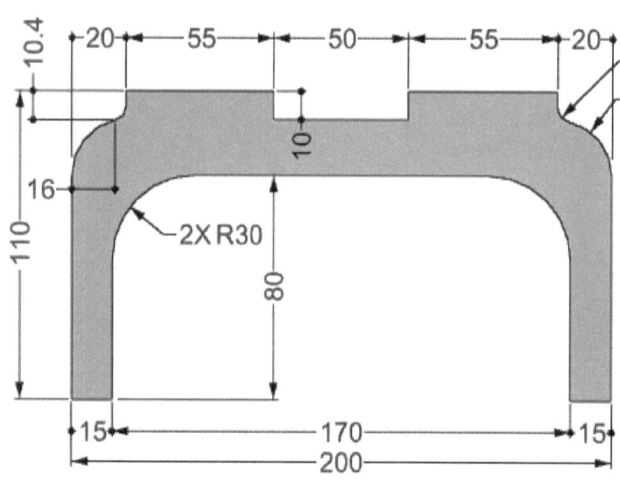
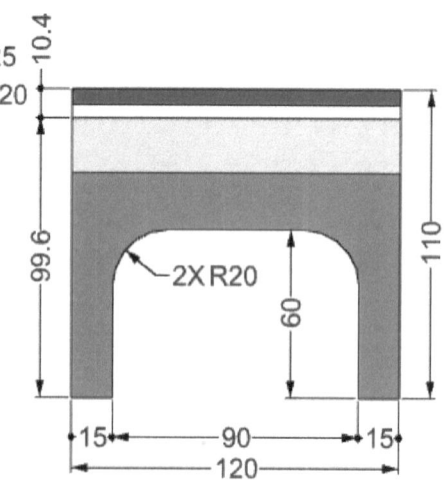

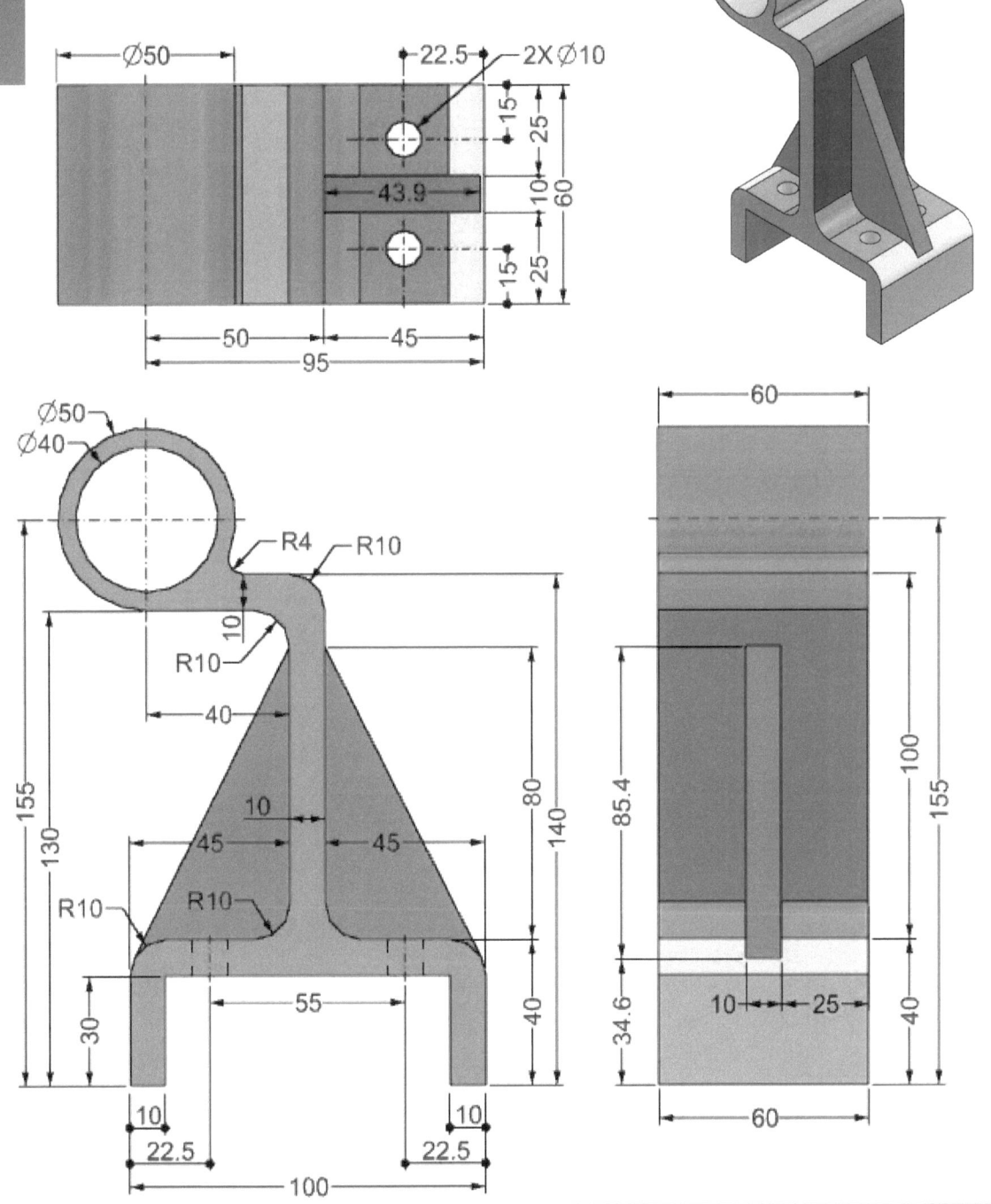

EXERCISE-188

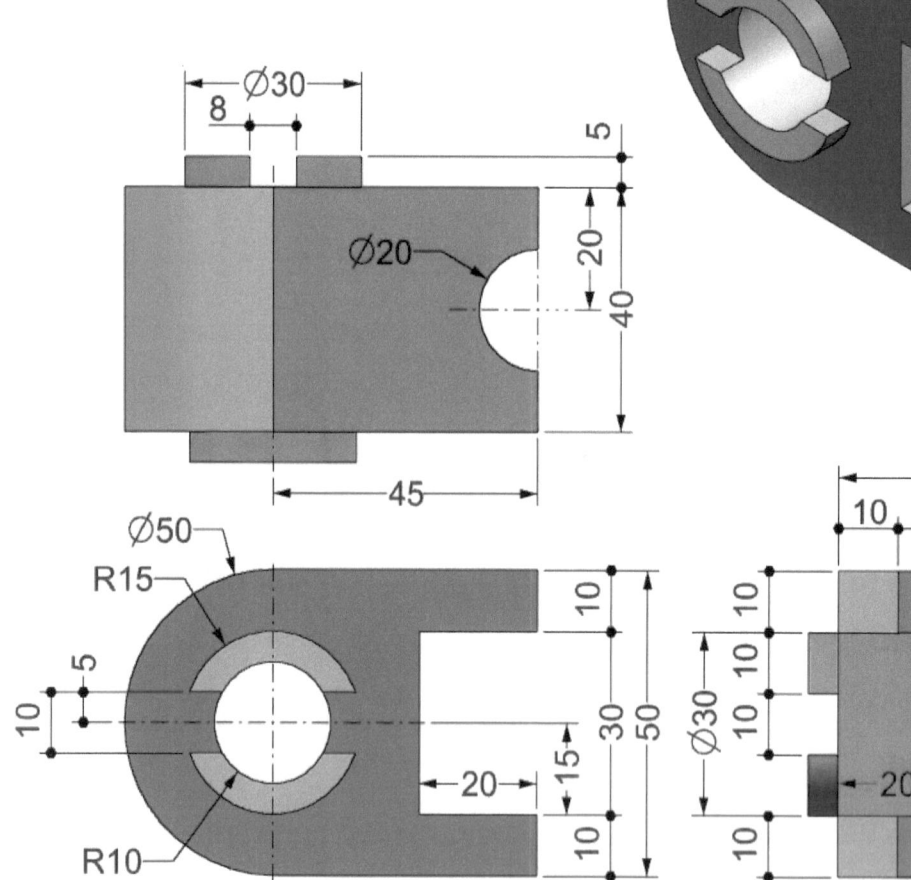

EXERCISE-189

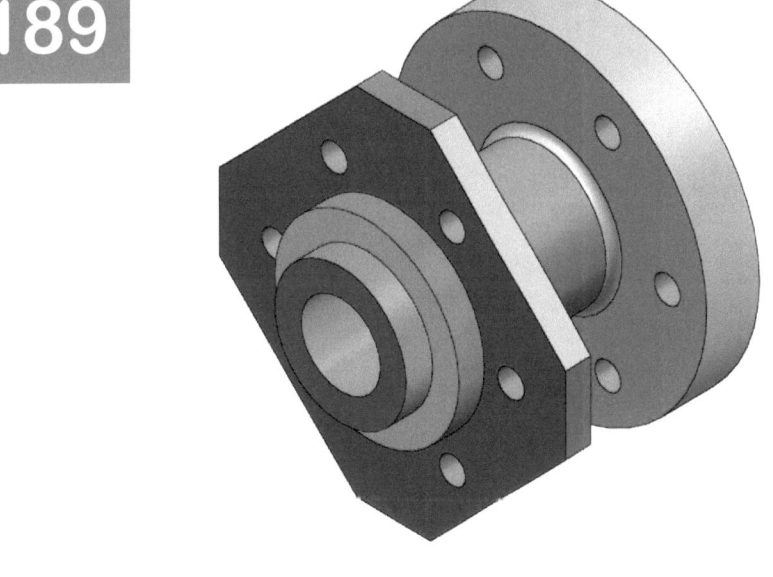
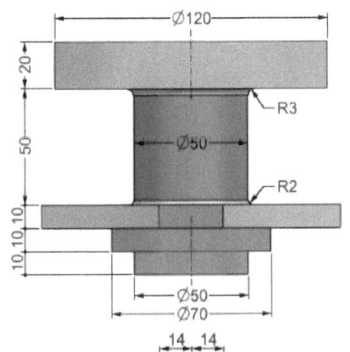
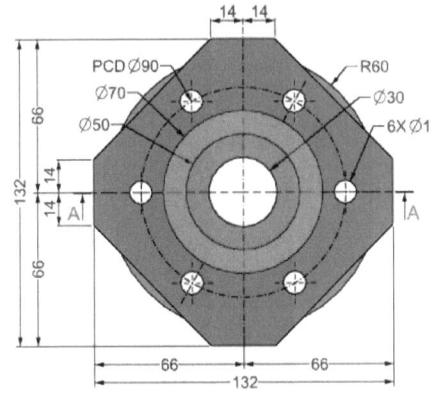
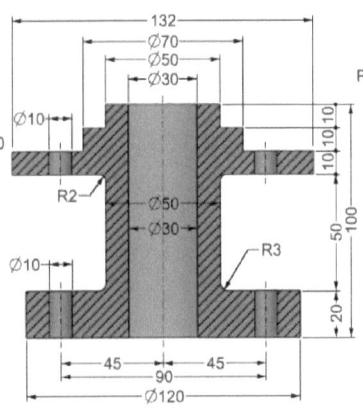
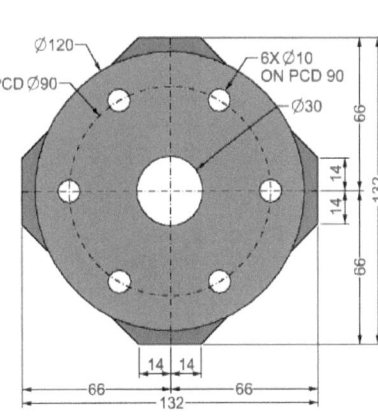

SECTION A-A

EXERCISE-190

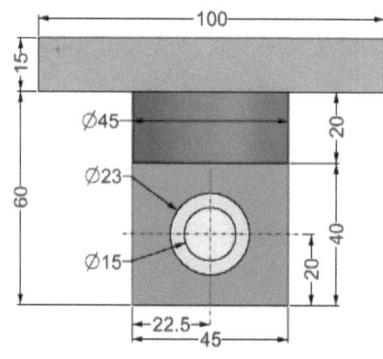

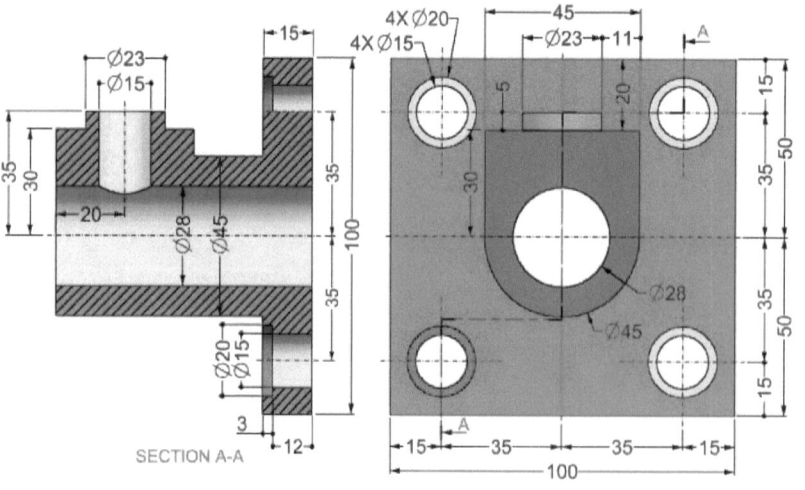

SECTION A-A

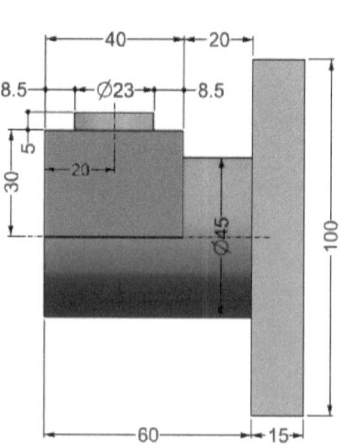

EXERCISE-191

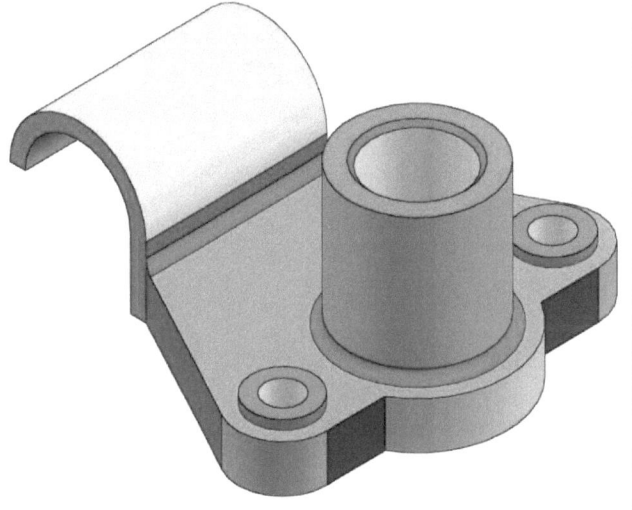

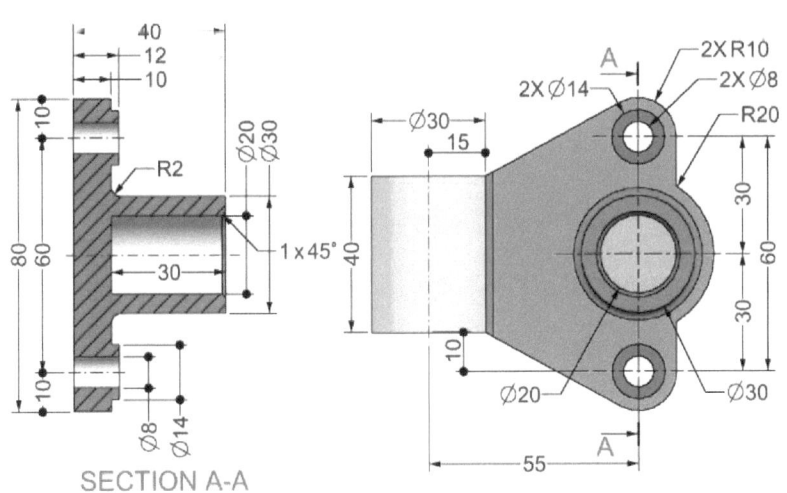

SECTION A-A

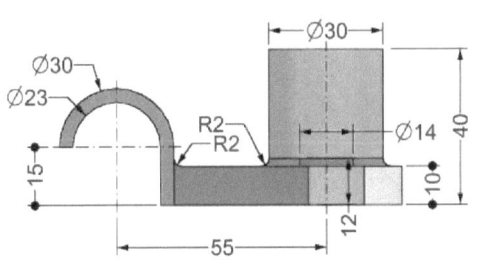
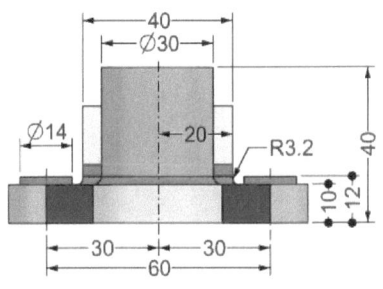

EXERCISE-192

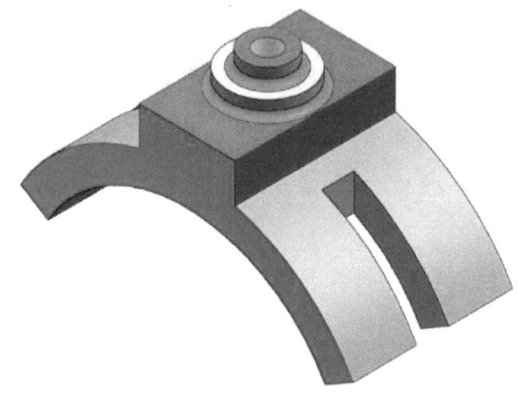

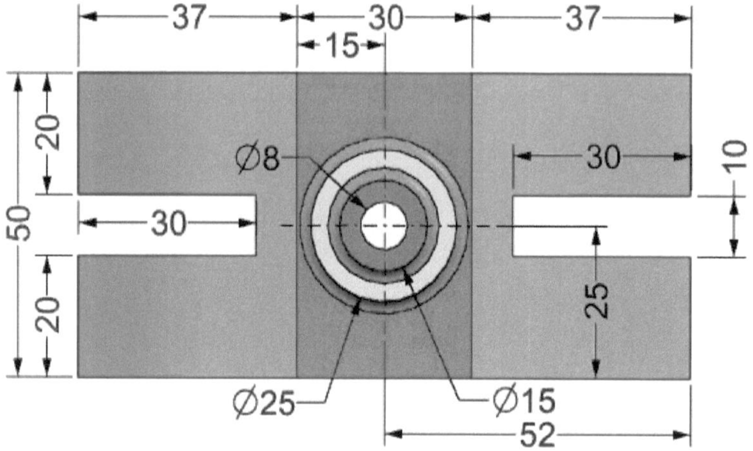

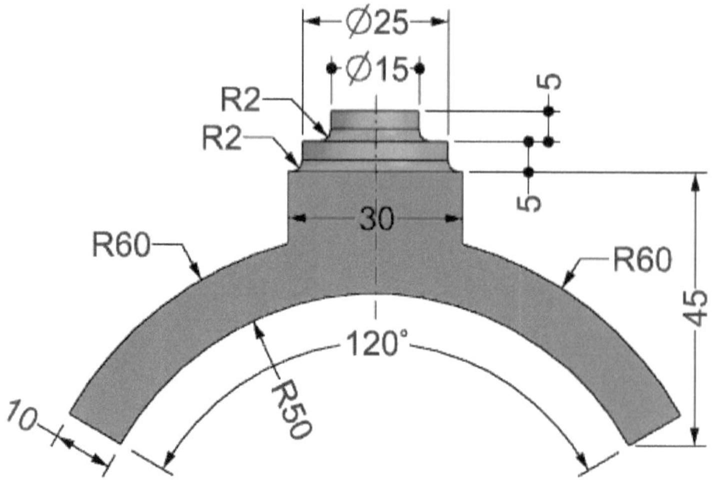

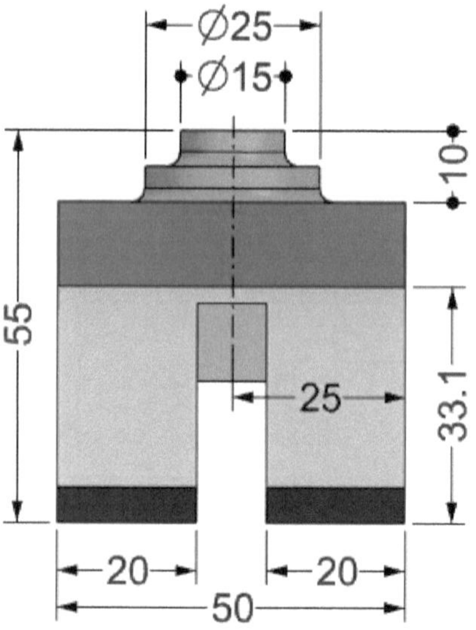

EXERCISE-193

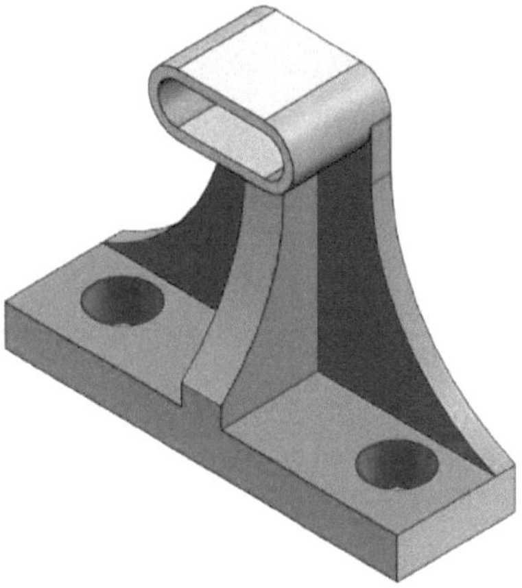

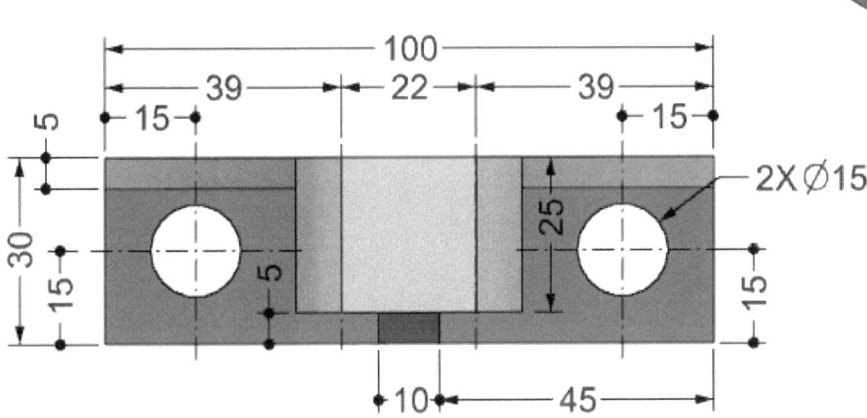

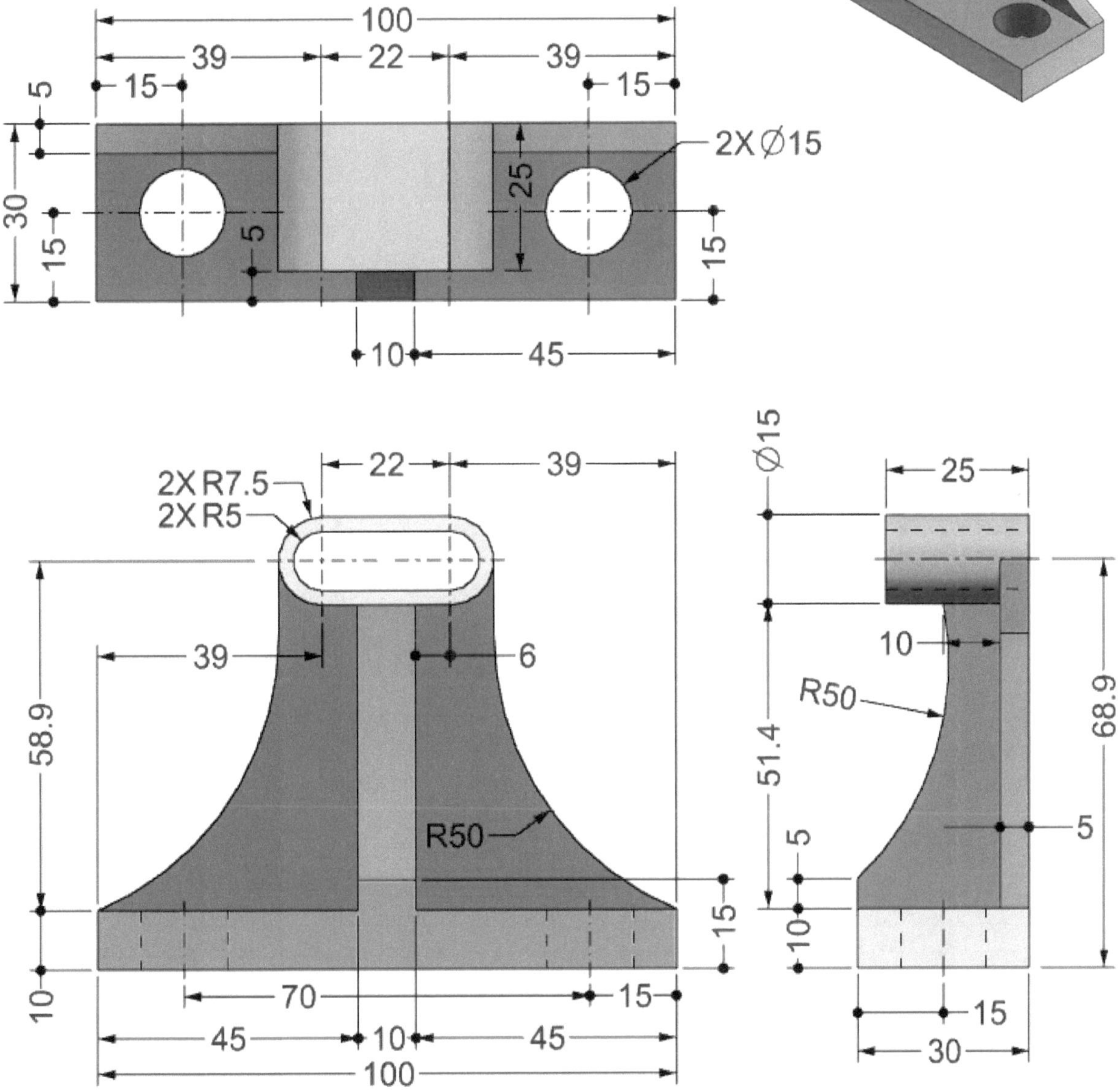

EXERCISE-194

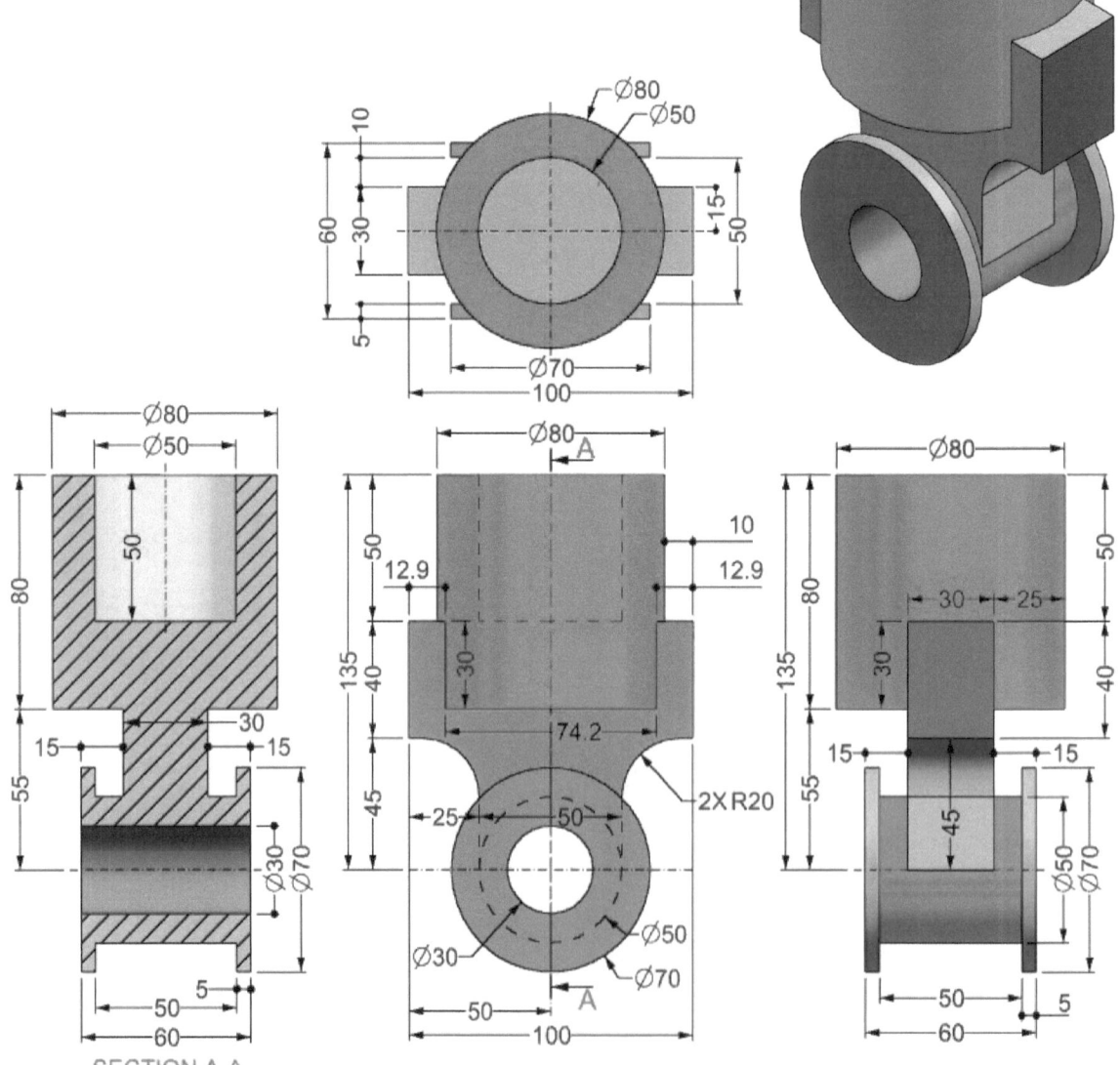

EXERCISE-195

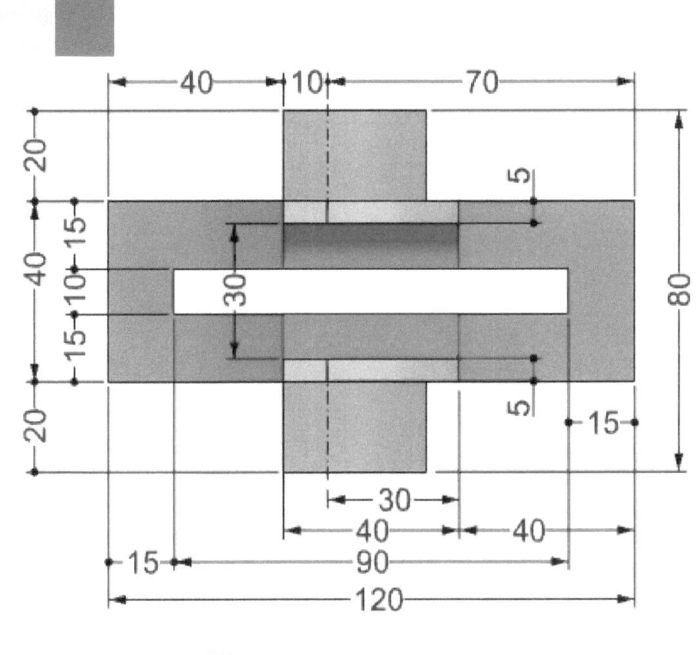
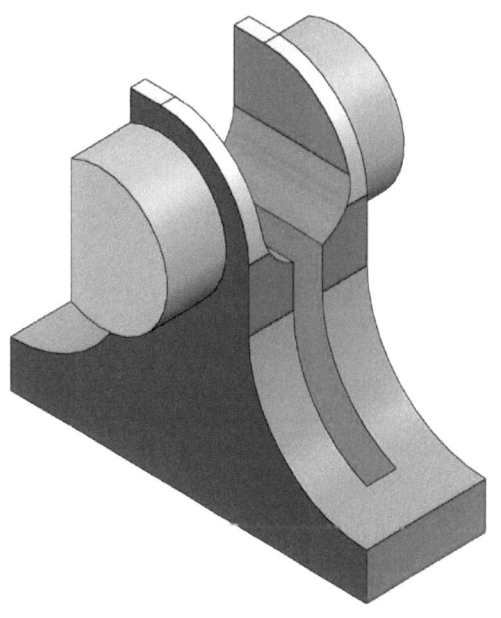
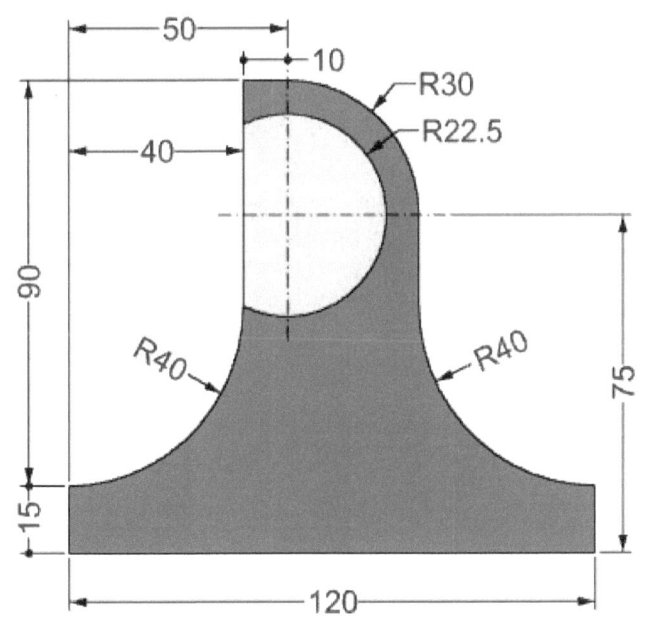
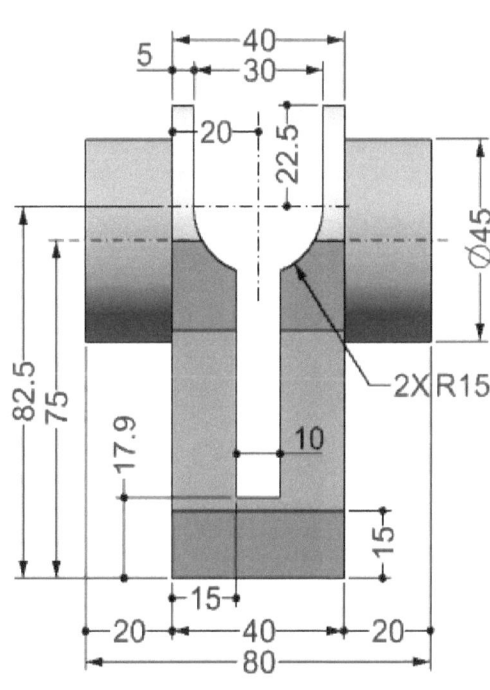

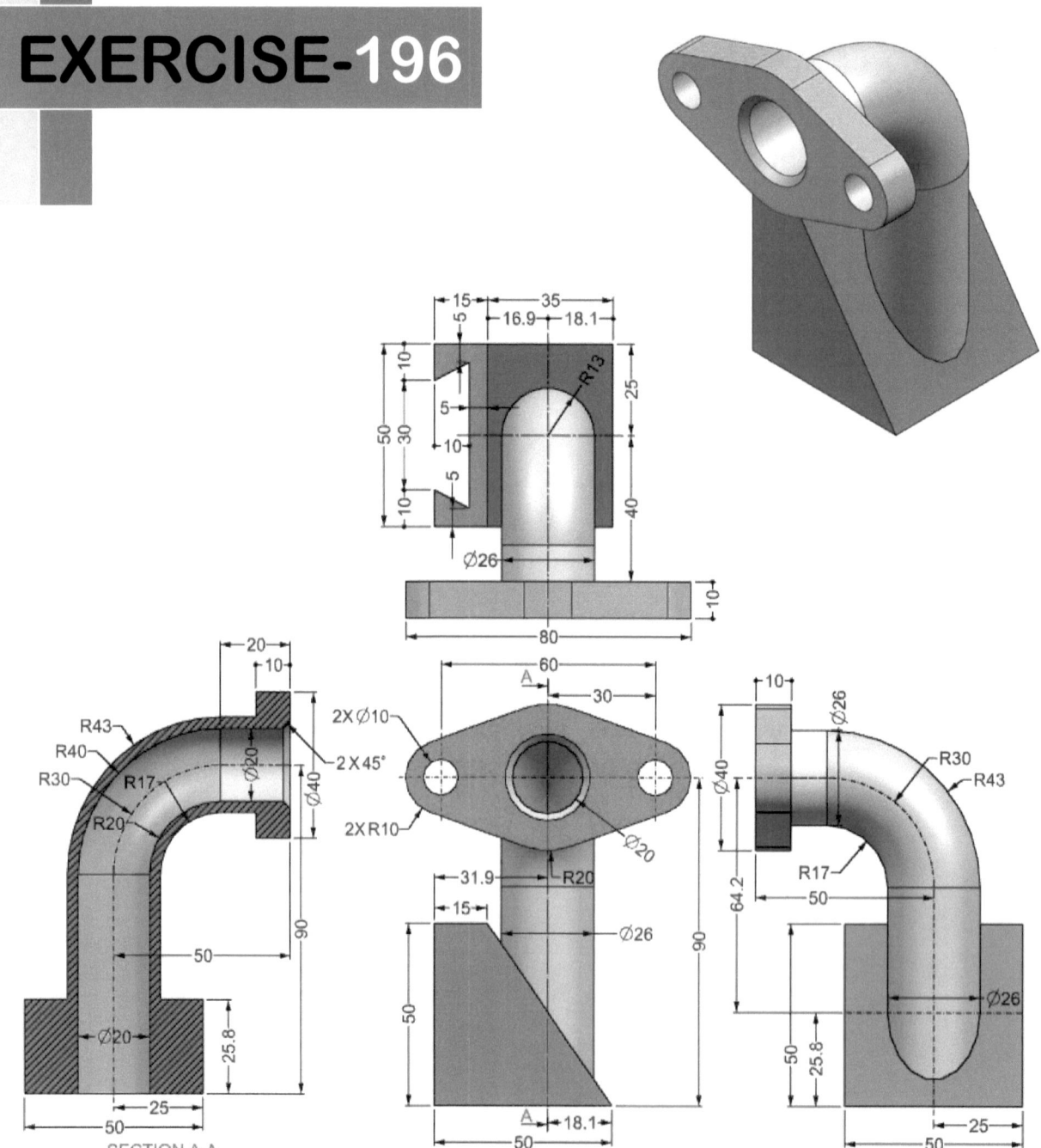

EXERCISE-197

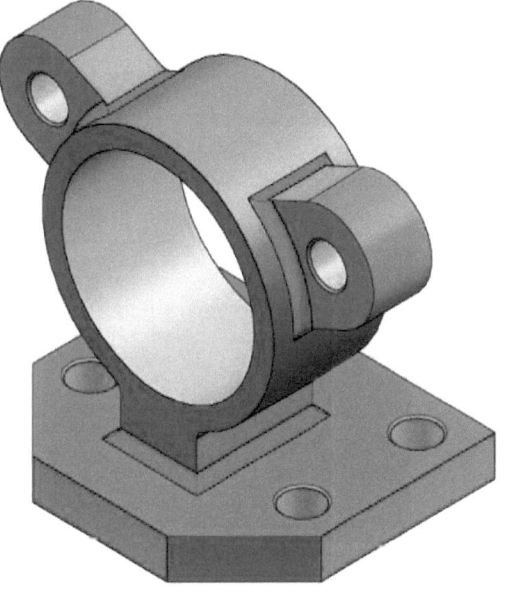

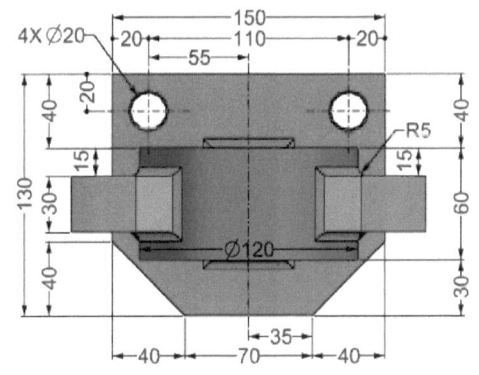

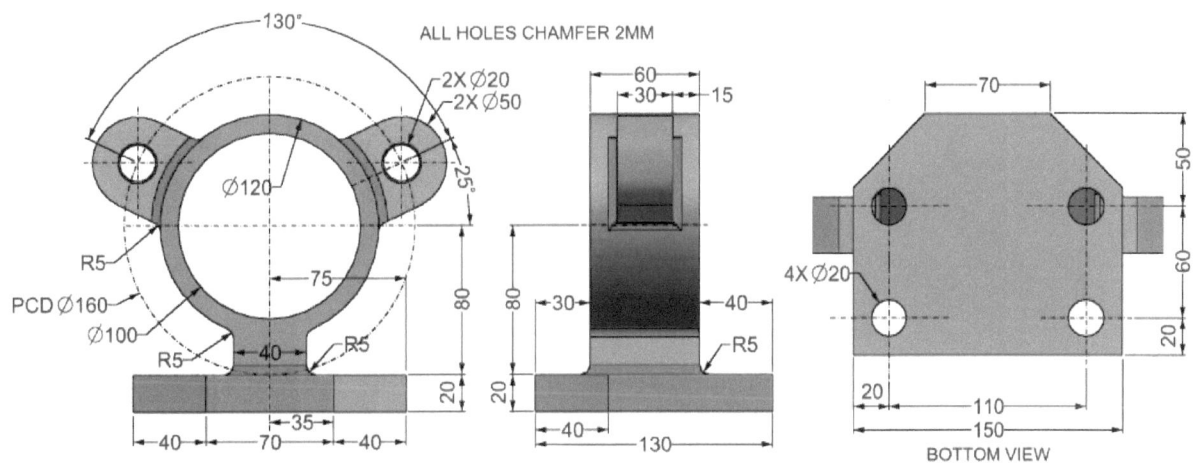

ALL HOLES CHAMFER 2MM

BOTTOM VIEW

EXERCISE-198

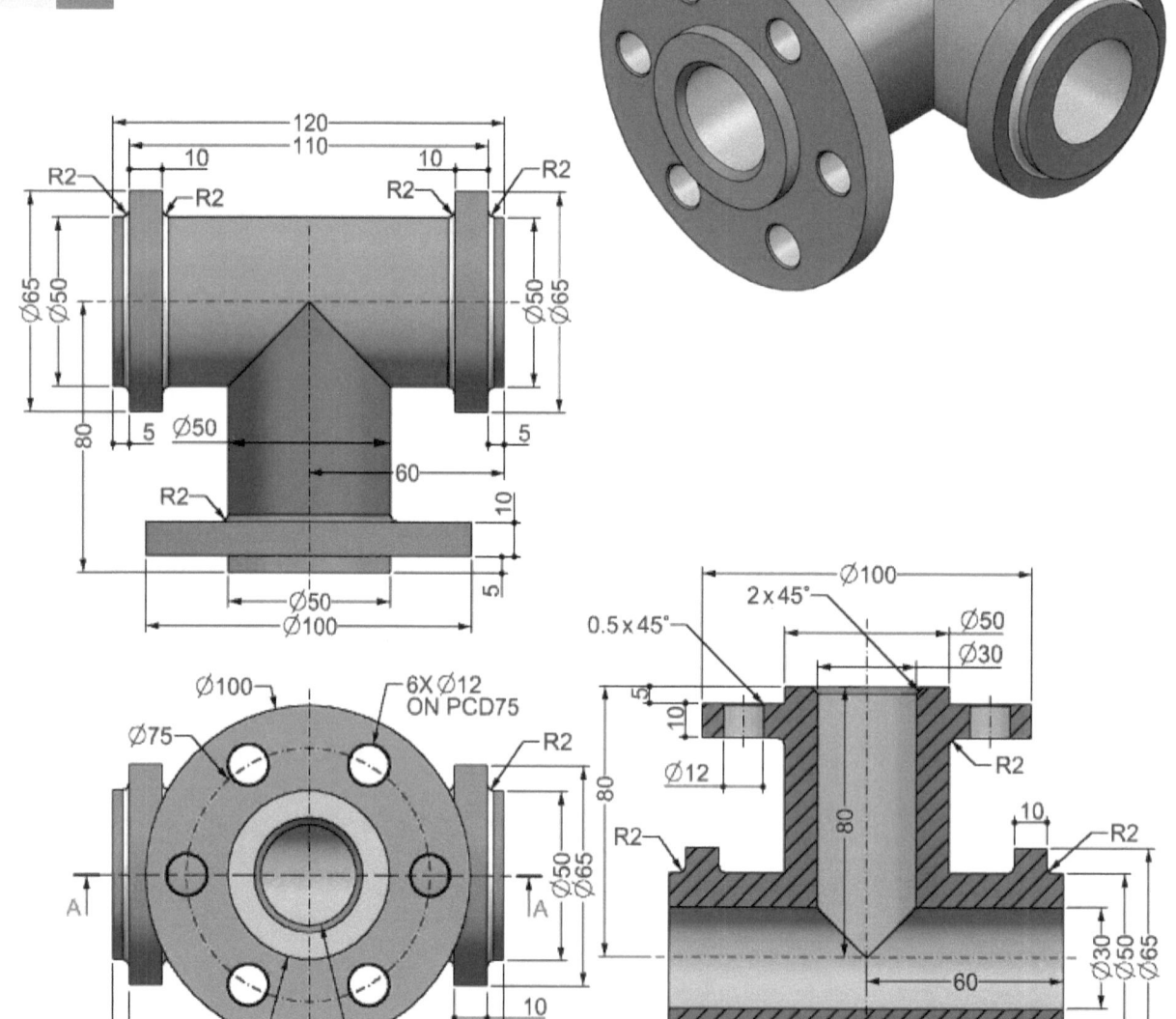

EXERCISE-199

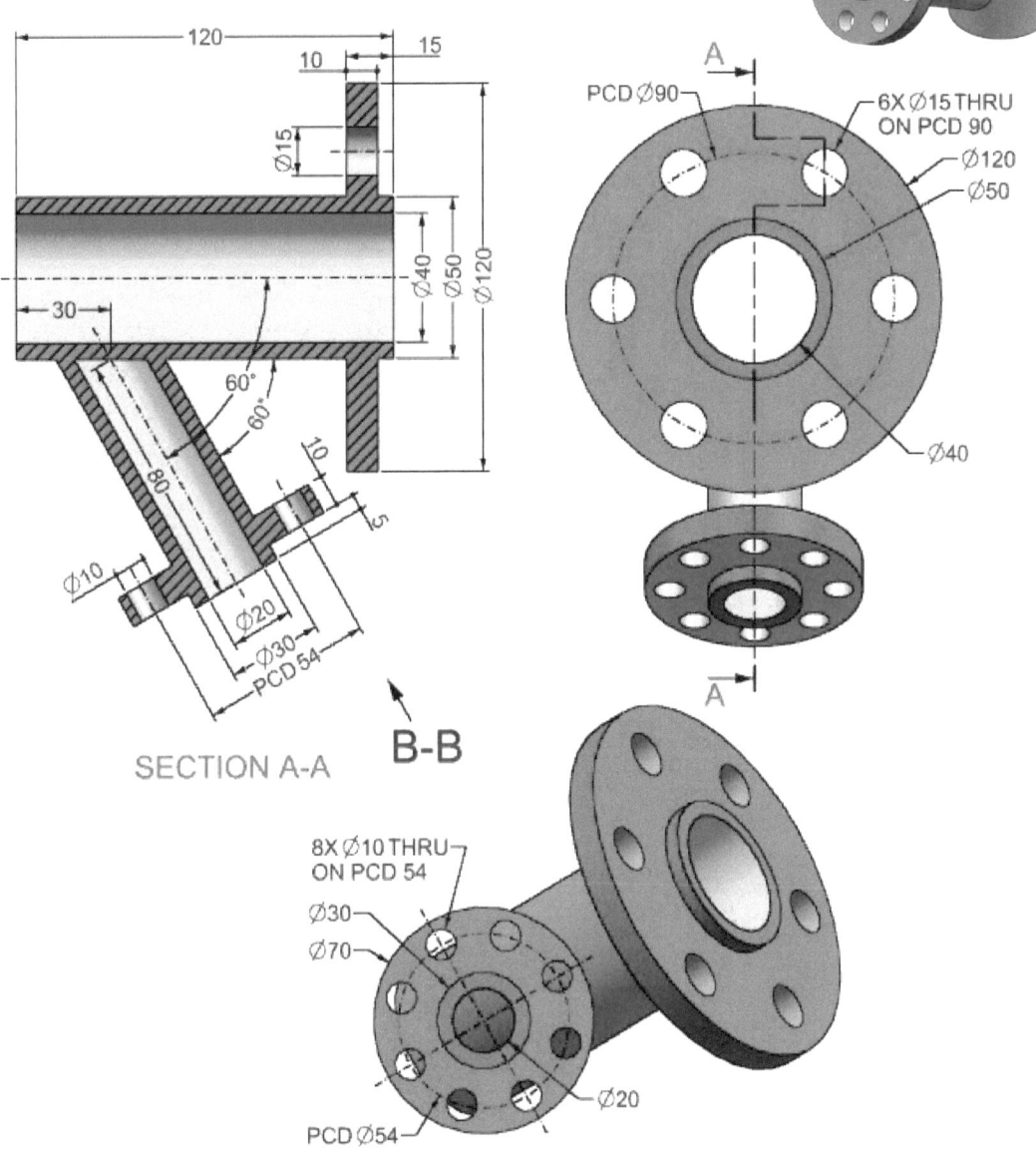

SECTION A-A

VIEW B-B

EXERCISE-200

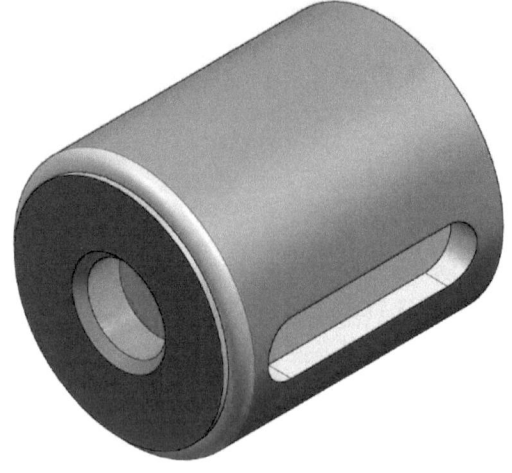

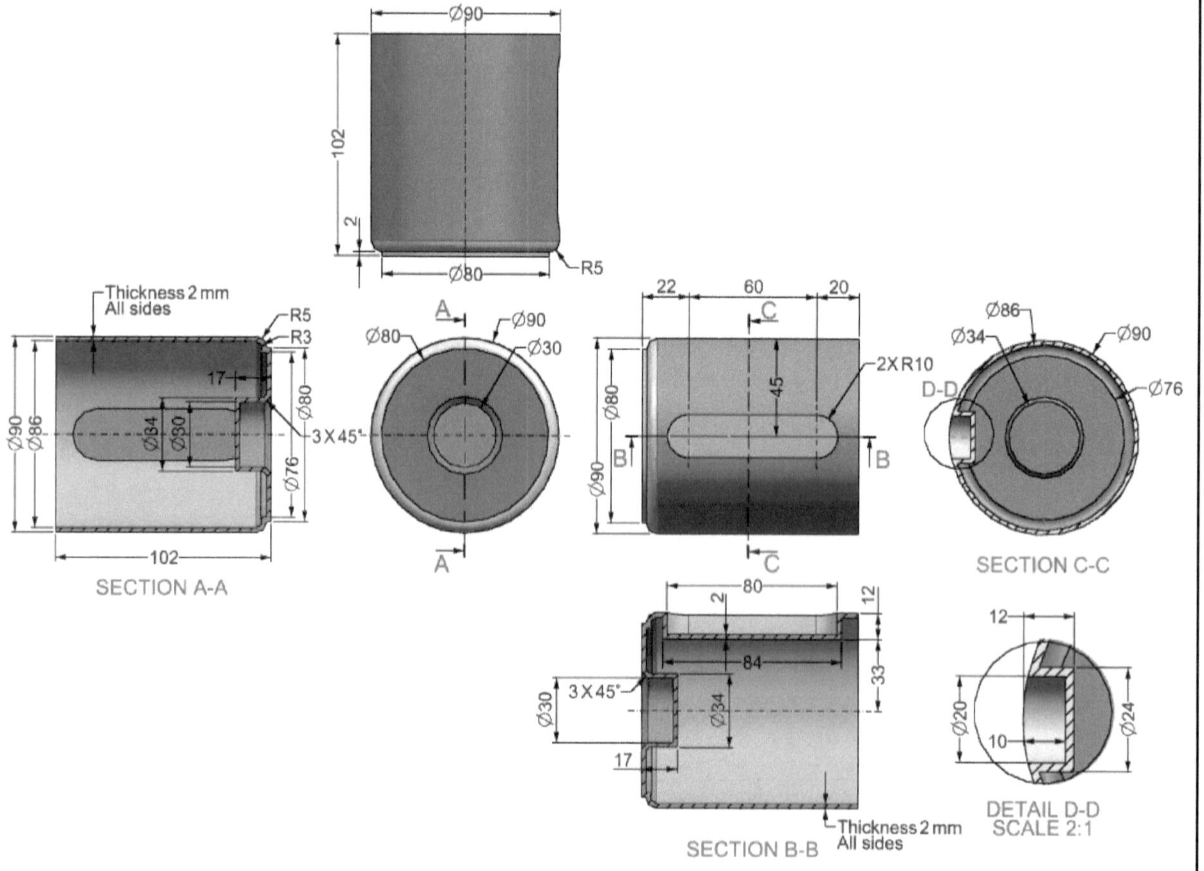

Other useful books by Sachidanand Jha

1. 150 CAD Exercises
2. AutoCAD Exercises
3. CAD Exercises
4. 50+ SolidWorks Exercises
5. SolidWorks 200 Exercises
6. Autodesk Inventor Exercises
7. Catia Exercises
8. Siemens NX Exercises

©Copyright 2019 CADin360, ALL Rights Reserved